HOLY WAR

HOLY WAR

WILHELM DIETL

Translated by Martha Humphreys

MACMILLAN PUBLISHING COMPANY
New York

Macmillan Publishing Company
866 Third Avenue, New York, N.Y. 10022
Collier Macmillan Canada, Inc.

Library of Congress Cataloging in Publication Data

Dietl, Wilhelm.
Holy war.

Translation of: Heiliger Krieg für Allah.
Includes index.
1. Islam and politics—Near East. 2. Near East—
Politics and government—1945-   . 3. Islam—20th
century. I. Title.
DS63.1.D5313   1984   956'.04   84-20124
ISBN 0-02-531530-7

Contents

[v]

Acknowledgments

IMMENSE THANKS to my patient friends whom I tortured for many months with a sole topic—this book.

I am glad that the inaccessible experts Mohammed Hassanein Heikal in Cairo and Prof. Dr. Anis Ahmad in Islamabad spent much time with me. My colleagues Dr. Peter Scholl-Latour of Paris and Dr. Saad Eddin Ibrahim, professor of sociology at Cairo American University, provided me with important material. If I noticed factual omissions, I could turn to Dr. Karl Binswanger in Munich; Prof. Dr. Werner Ende at the University of Hamburg; Fathi Osman, editor-in-chief of *Arabia* in London; and my kind British colleague Valerie Yorke at the International Institute for Strategic Studies. My Munich colleague Wolfgang Mueller also provided advice.

I also want to mention the supportive relationship to Dr. Alexander Kudascheff of the *Deutsche Welle* in Cologne (editor for the Near East). Gisela and Otto Mann, who live in Beirut, opened doors for me. Magda Saleh was of great assistance to me in Cairo whenever there were language problems. Angelika Schwarz-bauer-Respall of Munich provided support in the form of quick translations.

I mention Dr. Rolf Cyriax, the editor of this book in its German edition, last only because he usually had the last word. Had he not persevered at this manuscript with such exactitude, even to the point of what seemed to me sadism, the outcome would certainly have been less gratifying.

Author's Note

Some time ago I sat glued in front of the television set and viewed the events on the screen with nostalgia. Entertainment in the best sense of the word glimmered in my living room. It was a vivid portrayal in the year 1962. Heavily armed camel riders galloped from the left; from the right, equally well armed, came Turks—and they did each other in. In the film everything was hot and sandy. The setting for this celluloid drama was the deserted Arab peninsula. Only occasionally was there a glimpse of those gardens of paradise, Cairo and Damascus. Sitting before me, in the exotic environment on the TV screen, were Emir Faisal and the legendary Englishman for whom the wide-screen opus was named. "Do you know," asked Emir Faisal thoughtfully, "do you know that Cordoba already had two miles of lighting for its streets when London was still a village?" "Yes," replied Lawrence of Arabia, "you were powerful—and it is time to become powerful again."

This statement excited me. I was certain that neither the author of *The Seven Pillars of Wisdom* (first published in 1926), Thomas Edward Lawrence, nor Peter O'Toole, who portrayed him with such icy blue eyes, knew how relevant this assertion was to become. Once characterized by the haughty Europeans as Musselmen and Mohammedans, the Muslims are now well on the way to new strength. The Islamic world of the late 1970s and early '80s is a growing giant. The resurgence of a religion that programs both the social and political path of the individual has begun.

Already that was clear to me when I saw the famous popular spectacle, for I had been working on this book for months. I was in Egypt the day Anwar el-Sadat died. For quite some time I had been in contact with the Islamic underground. One Afghan religious fighter, a *mujahed* en route to an armed attack in Herat, frankly told me: "We love to kill Russians and to be killed." Those are situations that make an impression.

It is that kamikaze mentality that makes all those fighting in the name of Allah so strong. From the outset they are ready to die; many even take their coffins with them into battle. With the Koran and a weapon in their hands, they are willing to march into doomed encounters. There is altogether an inflation in "martyrs." On the front lines of this unfortunate war on the Gulf, even Iranian children, by the thousands, have lost their lives in the defensive fire of the Iraqi troops. Each carried only a large key and a heavy wooden club. Their *mullahs*, the priests of Islam, had allegedly told them that if they died, they could open the door to paradise with the key. The Islamic heaven is pictured as a splendid oasis, a fairytale country with dates and figs, beautiful female servants, and handsome boys—pleasures to make life in the hereafter the highest goal on earth.

Islam is also a shaping force in this life, but its leaders believe it can survive only if it has its own firmly established state. For this reason, the Islamic republic of the Imam Khomeini came into being in painful anguish. From the shooting of the generals faithful to the Shah and the killing of former Prime Minister Amir Abba Howeida up to the execution of Sadegh Ghotbzadeh, a Khomeini follower of the first hour, everything occurred in the name of the one God. The humiliation of the greatest superpower by the occupation of their Tehran embassy was a sign that fit into the scheme of things. Placards of Khomeini now hang everywhere, even from the fire hydrants at the Mehrabad Airport in Tehran. Moreover, the entire region feels threatened by his incendiary appeal. The fate of many rulers in the Islamic world is at stake; these days anyone who opposes Islam has only limited chances of survival.

The *ayatollah's* return was the opening shot. Aroused fundamentalists took over the Grand Mosque in Mecca, the most important religious shrine of Islam, and waged holy war against those they considered nonbelievers. Sadat was assassinated. Other politicians survived only because they barricaded themselves in their citadels and resorted to stern measures at any sign of opposition. When the ruling Alawites in the Syrian town of Hama put down a public uprising in February 1982, a greater number of people died than in all the wars against Israel, the arch-enemy of the Arabs. Since that time, only with difficulty has the Syrian graveyard peace concealed a powder keg ready to explode.

Such countries as Syria now spend more than half their budget for defense, mostly for defense against domestic unrest. The entire region is under the sway of poverty and misery, ruled by corruption, chaos, and dictatorship. Human life has but little value. Many governments make a case for their own nuclear armament. Holy war for Allah will continue to dominate the headlines in the future. From this point of view, this book might better be a looseleaf collection, open to supplements at any time. In its present form, however, it can point up background information and overlapping connections and clarify the breathtaking energy of a long-humiliated religion and its 723 million adherents en route to self-discovery.

New York, October 1984

Foreword

EVERYONE WHO READS newspapers and listens to news reports has heard of Yasser Arafat, the leader of the Palestinian Liberation Organization; Anwar el-Sadat, the assassinated president of Egypt; and Sadat's successor, Hosni Mubarak. But hardly anyone knows the name of the head of the powerful Muslim Brotherhood. Little has been said about what Sadat's assassins wanted to achieve. Who in general is behind the orthodox underground fighters of the Near and Middle East? And who tomorrow may have the say in the unsettled, rebelling Islamic world? These are the questions addressed by this book. Here are some of the leading representatives of Islam you will meet:

• *Golbuddin Hekmatyar* leads the Hizb-e Islami, the strictly fundamentalist-oriented freedom fighter organization of Afghanistan, allegedly consisting of 110,000 *mudjahideen*. He organizes and commands attack squads against the Soviet Army and their Afghan friends in the remote Hindu Kush as well as in Kabul. Like many of those I spoke to, the bearded religious fighter with the gentle voice is a member of the worldwide network of the Muslim Brotherhood. I sat with him and other leaders of the far-flung Afghan resistance.

• *Salem Azzam,* once the ambassador of the Saudis in London, has since detached himself from the official position of the nations in the Middle East. As general secretary of the Islamic Council for Europe, he now represents those in favor of the resurgence of

Islam. He explained to me in his London office: "I believe that there are many rulers in the Islamic world who are not true Muslims. Something has to happen, since none of us wants this situation. The masses of the Muslim world are not content with it, and they will show the governments their true power."

• *Dr. Sadegh Tabatabai,* the son of the famous Ayatollah Khomeini from the holy city of Ghom, studied and was awarded his degree in Germany. From the beginning he has been one of the key figures in the Iranian revolution. Along with his uncle, Imam Musa Sadr, Sadegh Ghotbzadeh, and Mustafa Chamran, Tabatabai performed important functions within the Khomeini International. After the revolution, he rose to some of the highest positions in Iran. I met him several times in Tehran as well as in Germany.

• In 1928, in Egypt, *Hassan al-Banna* founded the most important secret organization of Islam, the Muslim Brotherhood. Within just a few years, it attracted millions of followers. In Egypt, the Muslim Brotherhood became a state within a state. In terms of secret power, Imam Hassan al-Banna was on a par with the king. At all times the Muslim Brotherhood has wanted to create an Islamic state based on the Koran and the tradition of the Prophet Mohammed. Hassan al-Banna confided to one of his closest associates, with whom I spoke in Cairo: "We need three generations for our plans—one to listen, one to fight, and one to win." Hassan al-Banna did not survive the first; he was shot on an open street on February 12, 1949, by the secret police. Full details about his life and his powerful secret organization are given in Chapters 3 and 4.

• *Sayed Qutb* was the head ideologist for the Muslim Brotherhood in Egypt; indeed, for the entire organization. He was forced to spend the years from 1954 to 1964 in labor camps and prisons of the Nasser regime. Pardoned for a few months, he was arrested again in 1965 and executed on August 29, 1966. His writings are now found throughout the Islamic world and constitute an important theoretical basis for the militant resurgence of Islam. The new, radical movements in particular are frequently based on Sayed Qutb's ideas.

• *Dr. Ali Shariati,* the lay ideologist of the Iranian revolution, represented a kind of Islamic socialism. Among his followers were (and still are) millions of students, the rebellious intellectuals of Iran, as well as many *mullahs* and *ayatollahs*. For a long time Dr. Ali Shariati lived in Paris, where he helped to organize the resistance against the Shah. In the early 1970s, he returned to Tehran to fight against the despots on the scene. After giving more than 100 lectures, he was jailed for two years, but escaped abroad in 1976. On June 18 of that year, he was murdered in London by agents of SAVAK, the Shah's notorious secret service. This book describes in detail for the first time how Shariati was killed.

• *Hassan al-Hudaibi*, a judge, came to head the Egyptian Muslim Brotherhood in 1951. Although he was a conciliatory, diplomatic leader, he shared the fate of all members of the Muslim Brotherhood in decisive positions: his freedom was soon curtailed. After the unsuccessful assassination attempt on Nasser in 1954, al-Hudaibi was imprisoned along with many of his co-workers. He died in prison. Recently, in 1982, *General Mohammed Nagib*, Nasser's antagonist in 1954, disclosed that the assassination attempt was a put-up job by the secret service to provide Nasser with a pretext for destroying the Muslim Brotherhood. I spoke with the elderly Nagib about these background details.

• *Omar el-Telmisani*, born in 1904 and formerly a lawyer, is the present Supreme Guide of the Muslim Brotherhood. The resolute Egyptian received me, the first Western author to be granted an audience, twice in Cairo and once outside the country. In our meetings he spoke comprehensively about the history of his movement and about the situation in the Arabic world. Omar el-Telmisani underlined the claim of the still-banned Muslim Brotherhood to worldwide propagation of Islam: "We are spreading our opinion in Germany, France, England, America, Spain, Belgium, and Holland. In the process we are doing missionary work within Christianity. . . . That is completely normal." During the last weeks of his life, Sadat even had such a powerful Muslim leader as Omar el-Telmisani thrown into prison, which was a factor in Sadat's assassination on October 6, 1981.

• *Zeinab al-Ghazali* is the female counterpart of Omar el-Telmisani. According to her own assertion, she heads two million women of the Islamic world. Her organization—the Muslim Sisterhood—is structured like the Muslim Brotherhood and directed in the same conspiratorial manner. In two long discussions in Egypt and outside the country, she informed me about her organization. In her words: "Members of the Muslim Sisterhood are the heart of the Islamic movement!"

• *Qazi Hussain Ahmad* is general secretary of the Jamaat-e Islami Party, the Pakistani counterpart of the Muslim Brotherhood. From Lahore he directs the fundamentalist organization, which is still officially forbidden by the military government. During a discussion lasting several hours, in the Pakistani border city of Peshawar, he assured me: "We have chosen this country to provide the world with an example for the Islamic conduct of life. We will create a theocracy in Pakistan."

• I could not of course interview *Khaled el-Islambuli*, the murderer of President Anwar el-Sadat, because he was held by the investigating authorities. Nonetheless, I was able to find out a lot about his position within the Islamic underground movement from his lawyer *Abdel Halim Ramadan*. Questions about the motives behind the shooting of Sadat are answered in Chapter 5.

• *Dr. Ali Greisha*, a lawyer famous throughout the Arab world, is also an important leader of the Muslim Brotherhood. This scholar, who has residences in Medina and Cairo, travels on worldwide missions for the movement, without losing his frame of reference. He was able to tell me much about the situation in Egypt.

• *Mohammed Hassanein Heikal*, formerly Egyptian minister of information and a close confidant of Gamal Abdel Nasser as well as chief editor of the influential newspaper *Al Ahram*, is the star among the publicists of the Middle East. During the Sadat era he was among the opposition, and he does not yet wish to commit himself with regard to Mubarak. I met him in Cairo.

• *Sheikh Gad al-Haq Ali Gad al-Haq* is the leader of the highest authority on the faith of Sunni Islam. As head of the thousand-year-old al-Azhar University in Cairo and of the Azhar Mosque, he is, so to speak, the pope of Islam. His word is law for the traditionalists among the faithful. Sheikh Azhar granted me his first interview with a Western author since taking office.

• *Sheikh Said Belal* heads the Islamic fundamentalists on the West Bank, the hotly contested area annexed by Israel. He lives in Nablus and has always represented a course of action that differs strongly from the nationalist, secular PLO. Because Said Belal demands a purely Islamic state of Palestine, conflict with both the PLO and the Israelis is pre-programmed.

• *Sheikh Ikrima Said Sabri*, the highest Islamic preacher of the West Bank and director of Friday prayer in the Al-Aksa Mosque of Jerusalem, received me in his closely guarded office in the Muslim section of the holy city. In the discussion he openly threatened a radicalization of the religious war for Palestine if the Israelis do not make concessions to the Muslims. His model Islamic state is by no means limited to the West Bank; it would include the entire present state of Israel.

• *Ahmed Iskander Ahmed*, former minister of Information in Damascus, was one of the few Middle East politicians to enter into a discussion about the Islamic underground. This subject is taboo in the Islamic world; it is nearly always avoided or dismissed as unimportant. An increasing number of governments, however, are fighting for survival, not least of all the Syrian.

• *Rabab Sadr Charafeddine* is the courageous and influential sister of the Lebanese Shiite leader, *Musa Sadr*, who vanished mysteriously in Libya. Together with the heads of the increasingly self-confident Lebanese Shiites, she now directs business matters on behalf of her brother.

• *Ahmed Ben Bella* is a living myth, a father figure from the era of the anti-colonialist liberation struggles. The former president of Algeria now heads the International Islamic Commission for Human Rights and also belongs to the Muslim Brotherhood. I met him in Paris.

• *Hassan al-Turabi* was a longtime minister of justice and attorney general in the Sudan and is now security adviser to the president. A lawyer trained in London and Paris and receptive to Western influences, he leads the Muslim Brotherhood in his country and is a member of the International Committee, the highest authority in the movement. Hassan al-Turabi is gambling for time in the Sudan at present, hoping by doing so to achieve the goal of an Islamic state without the use of force. We spoke together in Khartoum.

• *Sadeq al-Mahdi* is the grandson of the legendary Sudanese Muslim leader *Mohammed Ahmed*, known as the Mahdi (redeemer). A keen intellectual, he carries on the tradition of his family and continues (with little success) to fight for power in the Sudan. He is backed by millions of members of the Ansar sect, which is one more reason for the head of state, Jaafar Mohammed al-Numeiri, who is fighting for political survival, to tolerate the grandson of the Mahdi (or, let's say, to jail him only infrequently). I met Sadeq al-Mahdi in Paris.

• *Dr. Tigani Abu Guideiri,* a U.S.-trained official in the new Islamic hierarchy who is familiar with life in both cultures, conducts systematic missionary work in Africa. With headquarters in Khartoum, his organization uses both the religion of the forefathers and the technology of the modern era, and petrodollars flow particularly freely for his cause. He explained his work to me in Khartoum.

1

Islam—Consecration to God

ISLAM IS THE LAST REVELATION in the series of monotheistic religions of the world. It recognizes only unconditional devotion to the will of Allah, who is regarded as the absolute ruler. The word "Islam" means "consecration to God," or "peace in God." Islam is commitment to the one and only heavenly God, the creator and master; the unapproachable, unfathomable, and omnipotent. God's word is contained in the Koran, whose 114 sections, or *suras*, are known by heart by many of the faithful. The longest *sura* consists of 286 verses; the shortest has three. During Mohammed's lifetime they were written on palm leaves, leather, or cloth and were communicated to him by God while he was in a visionary state. The Koran is written in the most perfect high Arabic. In addition to the Koran, there is the *sunna*, an orthodox codex of Islamic behavior dating back to Mohammed.

The entire belief is based on "five pillars":

1. *Profession of faith:* "I bear witness that there is no God except Allah and that Mohammed is the emissary of Allah."

2. *Prayer:* each Muslim must pray five times daily—in the morning, at noon, in the afternoon, in the evening, and at the onset of night. He must first ritually wash himself, turn toward Mecca, and throw himself on the ground before Allah.

3. *Fasting:* Muslims must fast for thirty days, from sunrise to sunset, during the month of Ramadan.

4. *Zakat, or contribution of alms:* a Muslim is obliged to contribute an annual tithe in the amount of two to ten percent of his income for religious and social purposes.

5. *Pilgrimage to Mecca:* at least once in his lifetime the believer should journey to the holy city.

The Islamic doctrine of duties and law covers all areas of life. Muslims are forbidden by the Koran to consume pork or blood, to eat dead animals that were not slaughtered (apart from animals of the sea), to drink alcohol or similar intoxicating substances, to gamble or engage in usurious practices. In recent years banks have been established in most Islamic countries, where they operate without collecting interest; they must make their profit in alternative ways (for example, through profit sharing). Most Eastern traders take it for granted that there are many possibilities in the economic sector for circumventing Islamic law.

The German Orientalist Dr. Udo Steinbach defines the Islamic concept of ownership as follows:

Islam in principle promotes private ownership. To this extent it is characterized by a basic attitude that is capitalistic. On the other hand, the right to ownership is restricted by a series of qualifications. The starting point of many theoreticians is that the actual owner of all things can only be God; only through work is it possible to acquire a share of the ownership. The creation of property is therefore related to a catalog of moral demands. Thus, ultimately, Islamic theoreticians view the "Islamic economic system" as something unlike either capitalism or socialism. It is distinguished from the one by the strong limitation against capital, as well as its connection to the general well-being, and from the other by the extent to which individual human striving toward profit is recognized, as well as its rejection of the class nature of society.

The Islamic law (*sharia*) recognizes divorce, but the marital contract does not recognize joint ownership of property. Muslims have the right to be married simultaneously to four women, although the Koran regards this with mistrust: "You can marry one, two, three, or four women if you are just to them, but you will not be just." The husband has the one-sided advantage of being permitted to apply for divorce.

Islam provides answers to all social problems, to questions of education, even to issues of military defense. On the other hand, the punishments set forth in the *sharia* and practiced in many Islamic countries are archaic. In Saudi Arabia and Pakistan, adulterers who are found out are stoned, and thieves are punished by amputation of one hand. Fornication is subject to whipping. To heighten the deterrent effect, punishment for these sins is usually administered before a large audience.

Under the title "Islam: A Plan for Life," it is stated in the basic declaration of the London-based Islamic Council for Europe:

The creation of justice on earth is one of the basic goals for which Allah sent his prophets and provided their guidance (Koran, 57:25). All human creatures have a right to everything that Allah made available, and for this reason Allah's gifts are to be distributed equally to all. The poor and needy have the right to share in the wealth of the rich (Koran, 51:19). . . . Only the orders of God confer legitimacy on governments, lawmakers, and institutions; legitimate power and authority can only be derived from the agreement with the order, as it is set forth in the Koran and the *sunna* of the Prophet Mohammed (peace be with Him).

Islam challenged the faithful to strive actively for knowledge, to acquire it, and to educate themselves further, and it approves the intuitive, rational, and empirical methods used in doing so. It promises all human beings the right to an honorable life, to freedom of the worship of God, to expression of opinion, of movement, and of thought as well as the guaranteed right to retain legitimately acquired wealth.

Every governmental system is Islamic as long as it maintains the obligatory principles set forth in the Koran and the *sunna*. . . . There are no mediators between Allah and the individual. Allah's guidance is available to all in the form of his book, the Koran. In utter clarity it provides the ideals, values, and principles that the human being needs in order to base his individual and communal life on truth and justice. This guidance of Allah corresponds to the demands of the changing era and makes possible development within this framework.

At this point the question may be asked: How is it possible in a deeply religious country to arrive at the concept of an Islamic republic? Islamic rulers, after all, are absolutely authoritarian and totalitarian, officially responsible only to Allah. The Western idea of a republic, therefore, must seem alien to both the Sunni caliphate and the Shiite imamate. But that is part of the inconsistency and lack of "logic" frequently found in the East.

An attempt to get out of this dilemma was made by the enlightened Muslim and well-known heretic Bassam Tibi, a Syrian who teaches international politics at the University of Goettingen, West Germany. In his book *The Crisis of Modern Islam*, he supports a secularization of faith. Only in this manner can the Islamic-oriented world accept industrialization, humanization, and true democracy. Only in this manner is the individual secured against state and religion and able to develop freely under the conditions of the modern era. The scholar states: "Industrialization is surely the only way. The dominant emphasis on a cultural return to the traditional values, as manifested in the goals of resurgence of Islam, is capable socially and psychologically of relevant effects, but certainly can make no contribution toward overcoming underdevelopment and the attendant worldwide social inequality." But Bassam Tibi is not permitted to express such thoughts in his own country. He would immediately be accused of intentional destruction of the faith. Moreover, the resurgence of Islam has for some time created its own norms and means for translating its ideals into deeds. To comprehend this fact, it is first necessary to know the history of Islam—its development into a world force, and its deep plunge into cultural and political meaninglessness.

2

In the Name of Allah, the Merciful

I have learned a lesson from the history of the Muslims. In critical moments of their history, it was Islam that saved the Muslims, and not the reverse.

—MOHAMMED IQBAL

IN 570 A.D. only a few barbarians lived in distant Arabia, a stretch of land approximately one-third the size of Europe. The majority of the population eked out a meager existence, living primitively and worshipping idols and plants, nature and fire. Some splinter groups of Christians and Jews had settled along the outskirts of the peninsula, where they founded small, unimportant settlements.

Mecca already existed at that time, a small oasis along the north-south trade route where was situated the Kaaba, a kind of temple built around a sacred black stone. According to legend, the stone was a meteor discovered by the ancestral Abraham during his wanderings in the desert. Originally it is said to have been white, but in the course of time it turned pitch black because of the sins of numerous believers who beseeched it to forgive their sins. Certainly even in pre-Islamic times, Mecca was an important pilgrimage destination for the tribes of Arabia. A kind of code of honor had come into being around Mecca, which fostered peace and harmony during pilgrimages. The code was respected by the tribe of Quiraish, the one responsible for preserving the site.

Mohammed, son of Abdullah and Amina Bint Wahb, was born into this setting. His parents died when he was five years old, and he was reared by an uncle. Mohammed worked as a shepherd. At age twenty, Mohammed became a camel driver employed by a wealthy businessman's widow named Chadidsha. At age twenty-five, he married Chadidsha, who was fifteen years older than he, and by whom he had six children. Through his business skill he increased the family's wealth. Often he withdrew into solitude to meditate, and in this became a precursor of the later mystical Sufi orders. Mohammed was forty years of age when, on one of his lonely sojourns on Mount Hira, he received the revelation of God, the holy book of Islam with its 114 *suras*, 6,236 verses, and 78,000 words. First, Mohammed convinced his family of Allah's inspiration, which, among other things, demanded the worship of only one higher being. (This stipulation was highly suspect to the people of Mecca, for a monotheistic religion might jeopardize their flourishing pilgrimage business, which involved a vast number of deities.)

In the beginning, the oldest members of the tribe of Quiraish listened. Mohammed proclaimed a complete social program, encompassing all life situations. He preached against avarice and stinginess, praised the virtues of a nomadic society, and demanded solidarity among the faithful. The Prophet must have been an impressive man. Tradition describes him as of medium size, with a bushy beard and a strong feeling for women. In verse 224 of the second *sura* of the Koran, the joyful Mohammed even proclaims: "The wives are your field; go to your fields however and whenever you wish, but first consecrate your soul to Allah [through prayer, alms, or good deeds]." Mohammed lived in a modest house and allegedly made free use of perfume, giving off a pleasant fragrance at all times. From the storytellers in the bazaars between Marrakesh and Lahore, one can learn countless similar details about the person of God's emissary.

The fact is that over the years Mohammed found life in Mecca more and more arduous, since he was attacked from all sides. So, in the year 622, when his life was threatened, Mohammed fled with a few close friends to Jathrib, now called Medina, 217 miles away. This event, the *hijira*, is considered by Muslims to be the founding date of the Islamic faith and starts the Islamic calculation of time. In Medina the new faith gained ground quickly, and the first Islamic state came into being, a model for many propagandists of the current Islamic renaissance. After some time Mohammed and his growing crowd of followers even made war against the antagonistic Quiraish, and in 630 A.D. Mohammed, with an armed force of 10,000 men, conquered the city that had once treated him so demeaningly. The new ruler of Mecca had by this time become a highly respected political and religious personage.

The triumphant march of Islam began. The tribes of the Arab peninsula rapidly accepted Mohammed's message, and Christians and Jews were tolerated. In the year 632 A.D. the Prophet died a natural death. The lack of a direct male successor immediately became a cause of contention. Later, Shiite Muslims would assert that Mohammed chose his son-in-law and cousin Ali to become the caliph ("caliph" means successor of the Prophet in the secular sense). Mohammed's first follower, Abu Bakr, who was also the father of Mohammed's second wife, Aisha, was victorious, however, and he was followed first by Omar, and then by Othman, one of Mohammed's sons-in-law. Ali, who was married to Mohammed's daughter Fatima, finally became the fourth caliph; his followers called themselves Shiat Ali (party of Ali) and split off from the Sunnis as a rebellious group.

Professor Fazlur Rahman writes in the respected *Cambridge History of Islam:* "It is impossible to speak of the Shia group as a protest movement until the Shiites had developed their own theology and their independent system. The protest was essentially of a social and political kind and was directed against pressure exerted by more powerful Arabs, particularly during the era of the Omayads. The Shiite rule soon ended its protest and reform phase and became a sect with the doctrine of the infallible imam." Whereas the Sunnis (those who are oriented toward the model, or *sunna* of the Prophet) recognized the caliphs as their rulers, the Shiites accepted only Ali, followed by a series of imams, who never ruled but were mostly persecuted by the caliphs. This series extends to the twelfth imam, believed to be the Mahdi (messiah), who in the year 873 A.D. vanished without a trace in a cellar while only a boy. According to the legend that has grown about him, he is merely hiding; some day he will return and lead Islam to victory. Orientalists of the younger generation—for example, Dr. Karl Binswanger of Munich—incline toward the version that the vanished twelfth imam fell victim to a sexual offense.

The split between the Sunnis (approximately ninety percent of the Muslims) and the Shiites is comparable to the split of the Christian church during the Reformation and the disagreement between Catholics and Protestants in Northern Ireland. To this date nothing has changed in the situation. On the contrary, the war between Iran, which is Shiite, and Iraq, which is Sunni, has intensified the polarization, driving the two sides further apart. Even before the war, the half-hearted efforts of an institute called Dar al Taqrib bayn al Madhahib al Islamiyya (House for the Reconciliation of Islam), which was set up in Cairo and financed by Iran, were in vain. The Academy for Islamic Research, part of the famous al-Azhar University of Cairo, has also been unsuccessful in healing the rift.

But back to the successors of Mohammed. The first four caliphs, who ruled between 632 A.D. and 661 A.D., started the Islamic campaigns of conquest of the Arab Peninsula. During the next ninety years, under the Omayads, the faith spread like a brushfire. United under the banner of the Prophet, the Arabs overran the entire Middle East. Although their dispute about the succession was still in full sway, they stuck together against the infidels. In 720 A.D. the rule of the Koran extended from the Spanish Atlantic coast to the Himalayas. Then, after bloody fights for power, the Omayads were replaced by the Abbasids. The caliphate moved from Damascus to Baghdad, and for 500 years the Islamic world was ruled from there. At this time contention developed between a Fatamid countercaliphate in Cairo, which was Shiite, and the Omayad countercaliphate in Cordoba, which was Sunni. The Spanish caliphate was later conquered by two enemy Berber tribes. Only in 1492 did the Europeans end the *reconquista* of the Iberian peninsula.

Starting with the early sixteenth century, there has been only one caliph, who resides in what is now Istanbul. At that time the Islamic realm became Ottoman, although the strength of Islam, like the extent of the area it dominated, was already shrinking. The Ottoman era was one of decadence. For the first time, non-Muslims were also oppressed, and even Ottomans were not spared. The Ottomans made certain that Islam, whose culture had rescued the Greek classics from oblivion and whose medicine, algebra, nautical skills, astronomy, and architecture had been a positive influence on Europe, acquired a bad reputation, one that has stubbornly persisted in the West up to the present. Since that time the Saracens have been regarded unfavorably, and the half-moon has come to be perceived as a symbol of the devil. Hamdy Mahmoud Azzam, a former consul at the Egyptian embassy in Bonn and Vienna and the knowledgeable author of a popular work on Islam, attempts to temper the historical assessment: "The reports of massacres and brutality in the conduct of war by Islam in many areas of Europe are as little typical of the Muslims as massacres and brutality are of Christians during the crusades into many Islamic areas. . . . What is involved in all these instances is the pursuit of the goals of power politics by means of military attacks in Islamic or Christian countries."

When America and the sea route to India were discovered, the Middle East slowly lost its importance. The Muslim world suffered severe economic losses and a spiritual petrification as well. Students in the Orient merely continued to study verses from the Koran; they learned nothing about Darwin or Copernicus, Newton or Karl Marx. Then the Westerners began to invade the Muslim empire and, starting with Napoleon's Egyptian expedition in 1798, they snatched it up. One colony after another came into being. France's influence came to dominate the Magreb, as well as what is now Syria and Lebanon. The British made their presence felt in Egypt, in the Sudan and Iraq, in Palestine and Transjordania, as well as on the gulf coast of the Arab peninsula, either as a pure colonial power or through mandate and protectorate treaties. Some time later the Italians appeared in North and East Africa. Then, at a later date, the interests of power politics were expanded mainly by economic goals, and the Americans entered the scene in the Middle East. The German Orientalist August Dillman offered a funeral oration for the Islamic world in 1876: "Surrounded on all sides by European culture and compelled to be consumers of European culture, they consume a poison that devours their innermost being." The sudden shift touched not only the national pride of the Arabs but their religious souls as well. The colonial masters accepted no religion that was also politically active. A part of the intellectual elite languished in apathy. Only reformers such as al-Afghani and Mohammed Abduh were successful in countering this development and interpreting Islam in accord with the times.

Dr. Ali Shariati, the Iranian sociologist and writer, offers in his works a diagnosis of the sickness of his faith: "A creature was made which first was alienated from its religion, culture, history, and its background, and then came to disdain all that." The Europeans (primarily the British and the French) were successful in separating the people of the Third World from their own history and in feeding them their own exported values. Old traditions and cultures crumbled; the peoples of the Third World first began to protect themselves against so-called progress only when it was altogether too late. Shariati laments that in his writing:

In the past the non-European countries were real and genuine. If you had visited these countries 200 years ago, they would not have had contemporary Western civilization, but each of them would have had its own genuine and sound civilization. They were unique: their desires, their way of doing things, their thoughts, their recreations, their tastes, their extravagances, their forms of worship and their good and bad behavior, their actions, their beauties, their philosophy, their religion—all those things were theirs. Everything they had, even though it was meager, was their own. They were not sick—they were poor, but poverty is something different from disease.

A new kind of statesman appeared at the end of the last century. Islam, it was concluded, had taken a wrong turn and no longer corresponded to relevant demands; it must therefore be given a new shape. The Turkish leader Mustafa Kemal, called Ataturk, was the spokesman for this impulse. Starting in 1924, he dispensed with the Islamic legacy. From that time on, there was no longer a sultan or a caliph. "All the power of the state emanates from the people," reads the first paragraph of the new Turkish constitution. That was the first step toward a secular republic. In 1928 the Turkish state, considering itself part of Europe, officially professed its laicism and eliminated Islam as the state religion. This radical step was a reason for the founding of the Muslim Brotherhood under Hassan al-Banna.

Ataturk did away with all external signs of religion, even the traditional fez. In a famous address to parliament he stated: "Can a civilized nation permit that the masses of the people be led around by the nose by a horde of *sheikhs, dedes, sayeds, jelebis, babas,* and *emirs,* and that the people entrust their fate and life to seers, fortune-tellers, magicians, and amulet venders? . . . In order to destroy once and for all the spirit of Islamic despotism

. . . we should like to prove that our people adhere neither to fanatic nor reactionary ideas."

Dr. Udo Steinbach, director of the prestigious German Orient Institute in Hamburg, describes the teachings of Ataturk:

In the course of time, Ataturk reduced his plan to six principles, which, as Kemalism, have had an effect up to the present:
—Nationalism: establishment of a Turkish national state.
—Secularism: separation of state and religion. This meant Turkey's withdrawal from the Islamic community and abandonment of the task posed by the idea of an Islamic realm, an idea the country had championed for centuries.
—Republicanism: founding of a republican state. This goal involved countering the reintroduction of domination by a sultan or caliph.
—Populism: equality of citizens without consideration of race, language, or faith.
—Budgeting: the leading role of the state in the economic development of the country.
—Reformism: This is an abbreviation of the demand for an enduring process of reshaping state and society.

Just how strong the traditional forces still were became evident following Ataturk's death in 1938. Immediately, a resurgence of Islam began, and many of Mustafa Kemal's anti-Islamic measures were rescinded. Religious instruction was again offered in the schools, training centers for preachers were created, and between 1950 and 1960 more mosques were built than schools. Under the majority party system, the resurgence of Islam became a campaign issue, since it accorded with the will of the people. During the 1970s, a fundamentalistic, political Islam was also revived. Together with the nationalist and radical extremists of the right, the National Order Party—the Turkish branch of the Muslim Brotherhood, founded in 1973 by Necmettin Erbakan—gained ground. Since the military takeover of September 12, 1980, however, their activities have been forbidden. Nonetheless, the new strengthening of Islam in Turkey, "the sick man on the Bosphorus," cannot be overlooked. Recently Turkey has become increasingly economically oriented toward the Arab world. Only the army, which is oriented toward Kemalism, currently impedes the further advance of Islamic forces.

For, in principle, the resurgence of Islam can no longer be stopped anywhere. The countermovement to colonialism and to Western and Eastern influence as such is expanding from the

Philippines to Morocco; it has representatives in Los Angeles as well as in Bonn and Samarkand. The Muslims no longer wish to be considered the losers; they do not see themselves as lacking freedom or diligence in cultural matters, or as immature in their rituals. "In the name of Allah, the Compassionate," they are striving for new self-confidence and for a united Islamic empire. It is merely that they have not yet found the joint tactics—that there is a split between Shiites and Sunnis, between states and leaders. As the Orientalist Detlev Khalid describes it:

The resurgence of Islam is not necessarily to be understood merely as a religious wave and certainly not as an era of faith that has arrived for the purpose of replacing an era of lack of faith. It is far more the expression of self-discovery in a large part of the Third World. In addition to religious elements, it also has numerous political, economic, national, and cultural components. . . . In the long run, the resurgence of Islam is certainly not a retreat into the Middle Ages, but it surely signals the end of Eurocentrism in the majority of the Third World.

3

The Main Theoreticians

THE ATTEMPT TO RESTORE to Islam its old strength is a phenomenon of the most recent past. The resurgence of Islam has gripped the peoples and underground movements of the Near and Middle East since the end of the colonial era and the waning of Arab nationalism. Yet, throughout history, voices have repeatedly cried out in the wilderness, demanding reform in Islam. They never wanted an accommodation to Western conditions or to changed conditions of the time; on the contrary, they appealed for a return to the roots of the faith, to the original Islam. For this goal, any means was (and is) acceptable, from verbal persuasion to the use of weapons in waging holy war.

The earliest of all Islamic revivalists was Ibn Taimiya, a Syrian about whom relatively little is known. He came from the strictly conservative Sunni corner of the country, and already in the thirteenth century—only 600 years after the death of the Prophet Mohammed—initiated a program to purge the faith of every form of degeneracy. The era of the great caliphs was past—the last of their kind, the Abbasid Al Mustasim Billahi, was murdered in 1258 in the attack on Baghdad by the Mongolians under Ghenghis Khan's grandson, Hulagu. The golden age of the Arab realm belonged to the past, and the Middle Eastern civilization has still not recovered from the blow.

During the lifetime of Ibn Taimiya, domination over the Arab peoples shifted to the Ottoman Empire, founded in Asia Minor in 1288. The thoughtful Syrian observed, however, that this new situation was merely a servile imitation of the era under the Prophet's successors. His biting criticism repeatedly brought him into conflict with the secular authorities. As would be true of subsequent critics, Taimiya was subject to mockery and disdain; for years he was imprisoned because he threatened to become a danger to those in power. Ibn Taimiya died in 1328 in the citadel of Damascus.

In his most famous work, *Politics in Islamic Law*, Ibn Taimiya wrote in his unique terse style: "Everything that is earthly has birth and death. Islam shows the way to the faithful up to the time of death, and afterwards shows the way to eternal life. Revolutionary commitment, or *jihad*, is the formula for eternal life. For this reason, scholars are in agreement that anyone who forbids Muslims the *jihad* deserves death." Here Taimiya did not mean *jihad* in the sense of war; rather, it represented the quest for a curative experience.

Ibn Taimiya's doctrine of a strong, uncompromising faith influenced another great thinker—Mohammed Ibn Abdul Wahhab—who became of decisive importance, particularly for present-day Saudi Arabia. The historian Henri Laoust characterized him as the founder of a "legitimately institutionalized theocracy"—the Community of Muslim Unitarians (Muwahhidun).

Mohammed Ibn Abdul Wahhab was born in 1703 in the Najd in the village of Ujaina (which no longer exists). His father, a member of the Bedouin tribe of Sinan, was a theologian who specialized in Islamic law. As a twelve-year-old, Wahhab is reputed to have known the 114 *suras* of the Koran by heart. He studied Islamic theology in Medina and traveled throughout the Islamic world. He is said to have spent four years in Basra as the tutor of a judge and five years in Baghdad. Abdul Wahhab's biography also reports that he studied philosophy and Islamic mysticism in Isfahan.

Following his return from Persia, Abdul Wahhab spent ten months in seclusion. When he began to disseminate his ideas publicly, however, he was banished from Ujaina. He moved to Dariya, where his doctrine was accepted by the secular ruler Mohammed Ibn Saud. Together they were successful in expanding Saud's sphere of power and in founding the first kingdom of the Saudis, with Dariya as the capital. Beginning in 1747, the Bedouin state in Eastern Arabia, which included several oases, conducted an almost thirty-year war with the sheikh of Riad. Every tribe in the vicinity of Dariya was forced by the Wahhabis to recognize the new theocracy. In their puritanical stance, they drew on the tradition of Medina, the first Islamic state in history. The worship of saints, mysticism, the cult of the tombs and sacred trees, all were a thorn in the side of Abdul Wahhab. He attributed the decline of the Ottoman Empire and the weakness of the entire Islamic world to a turning away from the pure faith. The Bedouins followed him with enthusiasm. Increasingly, Abdul Wahhab—who based his authority on the Sunni legal tradition of Ahmad Ibn Hanbal, also a rebel of the faith (he died in 855 A.D.) —became the idol of the tribes that had lived as nomads since the era of Mohammed.

In 1766 he and Ibn Saud's son, Abdul-Aziz, sent a delegation to the holy city of Mecca, where the scholars received them with all honors. The theologians from Mecca demonstrated the compatibility of Abdul Wahhab's doctrine with that of Ibn Hanbal and subsequently accepted it. In 1773 the warriors of the new theocratic state conquered Riad and thus came to dominate the entire Najd, which comprises a large part of present-day Saudi Arabia. Abdul Wahhab died in the year 1787. His doctrine is contained in the *Book of Unity* (of Allah), which mainly delineates the demands of the Wahhabis for a simple life; it forbids even the smoking of tobacco and expresses aversion to any form of veneration of the saints.

Sheikh Mohammed Ibn Abdul Wahhab was once asked about the meaning of the Muslim basic prayer form: "There is no God but Allah." He responded:

Know that this confession is the unique distinction between unbelief and Islam. It is the admission of the fear of God and of the strongest support; it is that admission which Abraham made into an enduring affirmation among his successors in order that they turn back. By that is not meant its utterance with the tongue without recognizing its meaning . . . rather, what is meant is its utterance, by which one recognizes and loves it with one's heart, and also loves those who utter it, and hates its enemies and anything that opposes it.

Know that this confession contains a negation along with a reaffir-
mation: the negation of the characteristic of God in creatures who are
not Allah, even with Mohammed and Gabriel, not to mention other
saints and pious persons. If you have understood that, think about his
divinity which is reserved for Allah Himself and of which He denied
Mohammed and Gabriel and all others even as much as a cucumber
seed. Know that it is the divinity which the simple people these days
call secret and power, for the meaning of the word "God" is a powerful
being who has a secret; hence people mention the fakirs and the
sheikhs, and the simple people also designate the Sayeds in this
manner. . . .

This has its origins in the fact that people believe Allah conferred a
special rank on chosen creatures and would wish that people take their
refuge to them, and would ask them to appeal for help and make them
intermediaries between Allah and themselves. But those now claimed
by the polytheists to be their intermediaries are the same ones which
the earlier polytheists called their gods. . . . The confession, "There is
no God but Allah," excludes such intermediaries.

When you have thoroughly reflected on that and know that the infidels profess that Allah is the only God, and that He in fact is the only
one that is effective and that receives and guides, and nonetheless
praise Jesus, the angels, and the saints in order that they bring them
one degree closer to Allah and intercede with Him, and if you know
that the Christians in particular are among the infidels, many of whom
pray to Allah day and night, live ascetically in this world, donate alms
from their wealth by retreating into a cell from the people, and despite
all this are lacking in faith and will enter hell eternally, because they
believe in Jesus or in some other saint to whom they appeal or to whom
they sacrifice and for whom they make vows: then it is clear to you how
Islam, to which your Prophet summoned you, is constituted; and it is
clear to you that many people are far removed from it; and the meaning
of the word of the Prophet is clear to you: Islam started elsewhere and
will again become alien the way it started.

"Allah is Allah!" My brothers, adhere firmly to the basis of your
religion. Your beginning and end, your basis and your center is the
affirmation: There is no God but Allah . . . Allah is Allah! Adhere firmly
to that in order that you meet your Lord without withholding anything
from Him. Allah, let us die as Muslims, and bring us to the pious!

This new religious concept—of not merely interpreting but ap-
plying the Koran and the tradition of the prophets (hadith) in daily
life and rejecting all innovations—as well as Abdul Wahhab's
alliance with the powerful, permitted the religious fighters to
expand their domination over the entire Arab peninsula. Within

three generations they had conquered Mecca and Medina, received involuntary written confirmation there from the *ulemas*, the religious authorities, of their "unbelief," and "purged" the centers of Islam of the "excesses" of conventional Islam. In 1802 they seized and plundered Karbala and Najaf, holy cities of the Shiites in Iraq. Only after 1811 did the Ottomans fight back, in the course of two campaigns that reached as far as Dariya. Muhammad Ali of Egypt and his son Ibrahim, vassals of the Sultan of Istanbul, slaughtered the religious zealots. They commanded that the Wahhabi palaces of clay, stone pillars, and palm timber be destroyed. Even the stone fortifications of Dariya could not stand up to the Egyptians' assault. The oasis fortress fell in the year 1818, and the ruler, Abdullah Ibn Saud, was brought to Istanbul, put on display, and finally beheaded, along with his subordinates. None of this, however, destroyed the teachings of Abdul Wahhab. The survivors of the House of Saud took refuge in Kuwait; at the beginning of the twentieth century, they initiated a new conquest of the Arab peninsula and later founded Saudi Arabia. Abdul-Aziz Ibn Saud was the one who would achieve new validity for Wahhabism. Even today the doctrine of the early fundamentalist is the state religion in the realm of the Saudis.

The influence of Wahhabism, however, extends much farther. It was a factor in the creation of the Mahdi movement in the Sudan, and the Sanussiyya in Libya, and it even influenced such reform theologians as Mohammed Abduh of Egypt. Wahhabism has impressed the progressives in a rigid Islamic world with its consistent rejection of everything new, especially Western influences, as well as its opposition to all variations of Islam that differ from the pure doctrine of the Prophet.

The Triumphant March of the Mahdi

At the end of the nineteenth century, a Sudanese by the name of Mohammed Ahmed aligned himself with the teachings of Abdul Wahhab. Ahmad's homeland had been subjected to a severe test of strength, for it was at the center of the battle by the British and French for colonial ascendancy in Africa. The Egyptian khedive, Ismail Pasha, was responsible to the British for this area along the Upper Nile, and he literally drained the wealth from the Sudan. The people became impoverished and withdrew into the mountains of West Sudan, where they continued to suffer from severe hunger. Even General Charles Gordon, who was appointed governor general in 1877 and was notorious for his gruesome suppression of the Taiping uprising in China, could not stop the decline in agriculture and trade, although he gradually replaced the old Egyptian officials with British ones. For a while the people were pacified.

The climate, however, remained favorable for a large-scale revolt against the hated colonial masters. The Sudanese looked with great admiration to Ahmad Urabi, the Egyptian who caused the British much trouble (but was later devastatingly defeated). A comparable revolutionary figure was lacking in the Sudan— until 1881 when, after experiencing visions during Ramadan, Mohammed Ahmed had himself proclaimed the Mahdi, or redeemer. According to Islamic belief, the Mahdi restores the true faith and appears at the Islamic turn of the century. In his heretical speeches about the need for justice and the expulsion of all foreigners, Ahmed won over the tribal leaders and nomads, the traders and large estate owners. Inspired by Abdul Wahhab and his moral precepts, a fanatic religious movement was swiftly organized. The leader of this movement was Mohammed Ahmed.

Ahmed is believed to have been born in 1844 on the island of Lahab in the province of Dongola. He came from a poor family of boat builders, allegedly dating from the time of Mohammed. At times he lived in Omdurman, which is now merged with Khartoum; at others, on the island of Aba in the Nile, where there was a settlement of Islamic beggar monks who traveled throughout the country as wandering dervishes. For seven years the ascetic Mohammed Ahmed intensively studied the Koran and the *sunna,* and he passed on his knowledge in an easily comprehensible form to the frustrated people. He appealed for an Islam aware of its pure doctrine and demanded the elimination of foreign domination. Like Abdul Wahhab, he attributed the crisis in faith to destructive influences from without. Ahmed traveled throughout the country and aroused the people to disobedience against the colonial rulers. In 1870 he married and settled on the island of Aba; many of his followers gathered around him there.

The administration had gotten wind of Ahmed's influence, but by the time they tried to nab the troublemaker, he had moved to the West Sudan. In the mountains he was protected by numerous uprooted people who had fled the tax collectors. When Mohammed Ahmed had gathered together a sufficient number of brave followers, he returned to the island of Aba and urged armed battle. One Egyptian military unit sent to capture him was annihilated.

In December 1881 the Mahdi and an army of tribal fighters first conquered the troops of the Egyptian-Sudanese governor of Fashoda and then a 6,000-man Egyptian corps led by Yusuf as-Shalaki. They did this armed only with swords, sticks, and spears.

The victory gave the rebels a strong feeling of self-confidence. Many of the faithful were reminded of the victory of Islam at the time of the Prophet. Mohammed Ahmed's followers, the Ansar (helpers), systematically organized the resistance. Their leaders proclaimed holy war, or *jihad*, against all nonbelievers, by which he meant primarily the tormentors from Egypt and Great Britain.

In the year 1883, the trading center of El Obeid fell into the hands of the rebels. War gripped the whole country. The British had to act, since their interests in the region were at stake, so in the spring of 1883 a fresh army of 12,000 men, under the command of General William Hicks, started their march. While Hicks advanced in the western part of the country, General Valentine Baker attacked the east with 2,000 men. The Muslim rebels defeated both armies and were in control of almost the entire Sudan when the governors of Darfur and Bahr el-Gasal capitulated one after the other. The old government continued to exist in Khartoum, moving its troops back into the capital. In November 1884 the siege began. Two and a half months later Khartoum, too, had to concede. General Gordon lost his life in the process. Although a new army, under General Garnet J. Wolseley, hastened to the scene, it could no longer stop the tidal wave of Islamic warriors. Five months after the fall of Khartoum, the Mahdi died in Omdurman of typhus. Abdallahi Ibn-Muhammad became his successor. With difficulty, he maintained the theocracy for thirteen years, before he was defeated in 1898 by a well-equipped army under General Horatio H. Kitchener.

Radical Islam versus Colonialism

During the first decades of the last century, what is now Libya was suitable only for agriculture and cattle-raising. This region was not the scene of political machinations, although Tripolitania, Cyrenaica, and Fezzan were part of the Ottoman Empire. Starting in 1843, however, this area became the scene of the most successful attempt by the Sanussiyya (part of the Muslim Brotherhood) to return to the fundamentals of Islam and build its own theocracy.

Mohammed al-Sanussi, born in 1787 in the village of Wasita, in western Algeria, came from a deeply religious family that traced its lineage directly back to the Prophet Mohammed. He studied for fourteen years in Fez and for a short time at the most important educational center of Islam, al-Azhar in Cairo. In 1824 in Mecca, Sanussi met the famous scholar Ahmad Ibn Idris al-Fasi, one of the founders of the Sufi order. He is considered the model for numerous conspiratorial Islamic organizations, the so-called Tariqas.

Sanussi constantly rubbed the conservatives the wrong way with his ideas of reform, so in 1840 he had to leave Mecca. He and his followers moved in the direction of Algeria, but they were not permitted to enter the country, which at the time was occupied by the French. Sanussi's role as an Islamic agitator was already known there. Nor could he return to Egypt, for the traditional-minded *ulemas* balked at the idea. Thus, in 1843, Sanussi and his followers settled in Cyrenaica in the vicinity of Benghazi. There the Sanussiyya started their missionary activity, which was directed mainly toward the rural population of North Africa. They offered not only the old faith, formulated in an easily comprehensible manner, but also social services and travelers' lodgings, and they assisted in reconciling disputes and in agriculture. The helpful followers of Sanussi were always at work in the centers they established, the so-called Zawiyas. These settlements were supported by agriculture and formed the basis for the communal nature of the order.

From 1847 to 1854, Sanussi again lived in Mecca, where he wrote altogether forty works about the Islamic revival and his own doctrine. In the world center of the Muslims, he zealously attracted support for his order and simultaneously warned of the dangers of colonialism. Early on, Sanussi recognized that the advance by the European invaders had by no means ended. After his death in 1859, his two sons, Mohammed al-Mahdi and Mohammed as-Sharif, continued his missionary activity, and the Sanussiyya extended their influence from Egypt to present-day Chad, southern Algeria, and Tunisia. But in the late nineteenth century, military clashes with the advancing French increased, mostly ending in defeat for the pious members of the organization.

In 1911 the Italians set foot on North African soil with the intent of occupying the area now known as Libya. The Turks had just withdrawn, so the Sanussiyya defended themselves alone, and bitterly, against the new opponents. The fighting ended in 1917, without consequence. The followers of the Sanussiyya nationalist Emir Idris were undefeatable outside the cities.

Emir Idris was already in exile in Cairo when the second war for the Bedouin theocracy started in 1922. At the helm of the Sanussiyya was the legendary hero of freedom, Omar al-Mukhtar, who is often mentioned by the present head of Libya, Muammar al-Qaddafi. The well-equipped Italian troops and their Abyssinian allies fought for a decade against the Sanussiyya before they were able to bring the Bedouins fighting in the name of Allah to their knees. Omar al-Mukhtar was executed on September 16, 1931. Fascist Italy was able to destroy the Sanussiyya as a community, but not the idea that motivated them. After World War II, in which a Sanussi liberation army also participated, the Sanussi ideology led to the founding of the nation of Libya. The United Nations assisted in creating the federated Sanussi kingdom of Emir Idris, who had, in the meantime, returned from Egypt.

In Algeria the so-called Qadiriyya fought against the French, who had been ruling the country since 1830. Like the names of other organizations, the name of this radical Islamic, anti-colonial movement derives from its leader: Abd el-Qadir. These fundamentalists managed for a short period of time to create a state. In 1847, however, the colonial rulers overcame the resistance of the Muslim forces, and it took a long time for the movement to recover from this defeat. In 1954 fighting among the successors of Abd el-Qadir spread to become a national uprising. The revolution was victorious, resulting in the founding of the Republic of Algeria in 1962.

An International Agitator

One of the greatest thinkers produced by Islam in more recent times was Jamal ad-Din al-Afghani, born in 1838. The reformer from Iran, or possibly Afghanistan, was one of the driving forces

of pan-Islamism—that is, of the resistance movement against colonialism and imperialism. He also wanted to make Islam again a
vital, active community, in which a theocracy could take hold. As
a revolutionary hero, al-Afghani should not be underrated. All
nationalistic protests against the influence of the Europeans at
the turn of the century, including the revolts in Persia starting in
1905, are attributed to him.

According to one biographical account, as a young man, al-
Afghani served an Afghan prince. When the British banished the
ruler, the days of his friend and subject were also numbered.
Jamal ad-Din al-Afghani first went to Egypt in 1869, where he
remained for forty days. He then traveled on to Istanbul, but was
expelled from the country when he became associated with the
highest Sunni spiritual leader, Hassan Effendi. Riad Pasha, the
top Egyptian minister at the time, invited him to Cairo and, with
the hope of keeping forceful intellectuals for Egypt, paid him a
salary of 10,000 piasters per month. Al-Afghani's lectures on the
outskirts of the highest institution of the Islami world, al-Azhar,
attracted a large, enthusiastic audience.

For the young Egyptian generation, he was a thinker stirred by
fury, wanting to drive the colonial powers out from the entire
Arab world as quickly as possible and to achieve unity and new
military strength. Again, though, in 1879 the power of al-Afghan-
i's words caused him to be declared an undesirable person in
Egypt. His attacks against the existing norms and orders had
become too vehement for the people he was attacking. He wrote,
for instance: "If all these scientific innovations, or whatever the
civilization of the Western world might be good for, were bal-
anced off against the wars and sufferings they cause, it would be
shown incontrovertibly that they offer too little and that the wars
and sufferings are too great. Such progress, a civilization and
science of this fashionable kind, is unabashed ignorance, sheer
barbarity, and utter chaff. Under these circumstances, the human
being holds a position beneath that of the animal."

When the discontent with the British began to increase in
Egypt, al-Afghani of course became involved in a conspiracy. He
was active in the preparation of the Urabi revolt of 1882 against
the viceroy of Egypt, and for this reason, too, his days in Cairo
were numbered. From 1879 to 1883, he lived in India and wrote
aggressive polemics to call attention to the situation of the Muslim world: "Misery, misfortune, and weakness oppress all classes

and levels of Muslims." He also engaged in an elaborate scholarly dispute with the reformer Sayyed Ahmad Khan, whose teachings were disseminated in his own school. Al-Afghani's attack against his competitor was entitled "Against the Materialists."

In 1883 al-Afghani traveled via London to Paris, where he met his best student, Mohammed Abduh, who had been forced to emigrate from Egypt because of his association with al-Afghani. Together, in Paris, they published the Arabic-language journal *Firm Tie.* Jamal ad-Din al-Afghani stressed in all his writings that the ideal state was to be realized only through Islam. Each Muslim, he proclaimed with certainty, should keep his eyes and ears wide open in order to detect the signs that proclaimed the coming of the wise revivalist who would reform the spirit and soul of the Muslims, put a stop to their degeneration, and reeducate them. He demanded the reunification of the Shiites and Sunnis in a common front against Europe, which in his view was possessed by the devil. His student Rashid Rida once accurately called him a "theologian who overcame politics." The fact that he had set up his tent in a homeland of the colonialists did not trouble al-Afghani. He hated England, the colonial power for Egypt, and continued his agitation against it while living in Paris.

The journal of Abduh and al-Afghani was reportedly published with the assistance of the French secret service (to embarrass the British). Outwardly, though, a secret Muslim organization bore the responsibility. But the restless al-Afghani did not stay very long in Paris. He traveled to London and later to Petersburg, where he is said to have counseled the czar in plans for a conquest of India and Afghanistan (and of course an expulsion of the British). Eventually he was expelled from Tehran, which was in turmoil. One reason was that one of his students, Mirza Riza Kirmani, had in 1896 murdered Shah Nasir ad-Din. The revolt of the Persians, also called "the first revolution," naturally was also directed against the domination of their territory by the great powers, particularly against the British. Jamal ad-Din al-Afghani, the great Islamic revolutionary, was to live only for a short while —as the guest and prisoner of the Sultan of Istanbul. He died in 1897.

Al-Afghani's writings have survived him, and they are just as relevant today as they were in his own time, particularly as they apply to the material and cultural domination by the Western powers in the Islamic world. In 1884 al-Afghani wrote about fate and predestination:

As for the assertion that the Muslims are in a state of decline and backwardness, the cause of this situation is certainly not to be sought in this belief [in destiny and fate] and also not in any of the other tenets of Islam. The situation of decline and faith is much more like that of a thing to its opposite; it compares most to that of heat to ice or of cold to fire. Certainly it happened to the Muslims that after their awakening they became dizzy from triumph and intoxicated from victory and honor. While they were in this situation, they were surprised by two heavy blows; one came from the East: it was the attack by the Mongolians, led by Ghenghis Khan and his successors; the other came from the West: it consisted in the campaign by the Europeans, all of whom together invaded the Muslim countries. In a state of confusion, such a blow affects the reason and causes astonishment and passivity in keeping with the natural order of things.

Afterwards various governments took over various states, and their commanders derived their support from foreign hireling peoples. Their interests were administered by people who did not know how to lead. Their rulers and commanders became seeds of corruption for the character and morals of the Muslims and the cause of their distress and their lament. Weakness overcame their hearts, and the perception of many was restricted to partial questions that did not extend beyond joys and pleasures. Each of them seized the other by the nape of the neck and tried to inflict harm and saddle the other with evil from all sides, and not even for a real reason or a strong motive. . . .

But I say—and I speak the truth—that this nation [the Islamic] will not die as long as this honorable belief [in fate] will maintain its influence on our hearts, as long as its lines shine forth from its thought and as long as its truths are disseminated among its scholars and elites. For all sicknesses of the soul and all complaints to which they are exposed are dependably averted by the strength of the true doctrine. Then things will again return to what they were in the beginning, and the Muslims will follow the teachers of wisdom and concentrate on saving their countries, and on keeping in a state of fright nations which desire the subjugation of the Muslims and will keep them from their borders.

Egypt's Islamic Reformer

Mohammed Abduh was al-Afghani's most important follower. Precisely because of their shared experiences, he became one of the most famous Muslim teachers of the modern era and the father of the Egyptian line in Islamic modernism. Mohammed

Abduh, born in 1849 to a peasant family in Lower Egypt, learned the Koran by heart at an early age. In 1862 he attended the religious school in Tanta and, starting in 1866, studied at al-Azhar, the citadel of faith in Cairo. In 1872 he met al-Afghani, who brought him back to reality from mysticism and strongly influenced him from the outset. While the impatient al-Afghani urged immediate action on behalf of the pure Islam, the theologian Abduh first wanted to liberate Islam from medieval ballast and only then propagate anew the sources of the faith. Yet for Abduh, too, conflict with the *ulemas* (the priests of Islam)—who wished to maintain a long-established tradition—became unavoidable.

The reformer rediscovered medieval philosophy, particularly the works of the greatest Islamic theologian, al-Ghassali (1058–1111). After his separation from al-Afghani, Abduh went from Paris to Beirut. There he began to write his basic theological work on the unity of God *(Risalat at-Tauhid)*. Four years later, in 1889, the British rulers of Egypt permitted him to return to the Nile: he was supposed to reform al-Azhar University. This task claimed the remaining life of the man who became a judge and later Grand Mufti (in other words, religious leader) of Egypt. In this role he was given a seat in the legislative assembly of his country. Under the direction of his student and friend, Rashid Rida, the monthly magazine *The Lighthouse (Al Manar)* began publication in 1897 as the mouthpiece of Mohammed Abduh's school of thought. During his later years Abduh was so energetic on behalf of his fatherland that he can be considered one of the founders of modern Egypt. Mohammed Abduh died in 1905.

Here is a quotation from his work *Concerning Religions:*

To judge from religion's comprehension of the well-being of the community and even of the individual, religions came into being when people were in a state comparable to the childhood of the infant. . . . For that reason, religions provided them with strict commands and stern prohibitions, demanded their obedience, and hence drove them to the limits of the possible. . . . Religions displayed miracles to them which dazzled their eyes and made an impression on their senses, and prescribed to them a worship service that fitted their condition. Thereafter time passed, and under the magic of events and of the experience of misfortune the soul [of man] felt feelings which were finer and penetrated more deeply into consciousness than sensory impressions, but which in general did not exceed what the heart of the woman feels or what accompanies the desires of young boys.

Then there appeared a religion which spoke to the feelings, addressed the inclination of seeking to win love, and spoke to the strivings of the heart. Hence it gave people ascetic rules which were intended to turn them away from this world and toward the realm of the beyond . . . and it introduced customs in the religious service that fitted their condition. Thereafter several centuries passed when the human will became too weak to bear them, and people found no possibility of remaining within the limits established by the religion and of following its teachings. . . . Finally the age of human society permitted the human being to reach his maturity, and past events had prepared him for his maturity. Then Islam appeared, which spoke to the reason, summoned the help of understanding and insight, and united them with the feelings and the senses in order to lead the human being to his fortune in this world and in the beyond.

Al-Afghani founded the first fundamentalist school, which was called Salafiyya. Mohammed Abduh was responsible for initiating all of its programs, and Mohammed Rashid Rida, the third in the group of great Islamic reformers, functioned as its spokesman. Born in 1865 in Syria and religiously reared, Rida was an ardent admirer of Al-Afghani and Abduh, and he accompanied the latter whenever possible. For thirty-seven years he published the magazine *The Lighthouse*, as well as the collected works of his great exemplars. As a journalist, he was a committed participant in the development of the Muslim world, and his word carried weight.

Rashid Rida preferred to address himself to the problem of why Islamic society was so backward. He concluded that a solution to all existing questions could not be forthcoming from an Islamic country under foreign domination; it could not come from an unperturbed sanctuary of learning (al-Azhar), and it certainly could not come from the West. Somewhere in the middle he established the idea of his Islamic Progressive Party. Rida believed that this party could reactivate Islam, which was in a desolate state, without changing its moral basis. He remained true to the vision. In one of his enlightened perspectives on the future, he stated: "The civilized nations of the West will have much trouble with their civilization and their political decadence, and must seek a way out, which can only be found in Islam. Not the Islam of the theologians and jurists, but the Islam of the Koran and of the *sunna*."

At the end of his life, Rashid Rida still maintained close contacts with the increasingly agitated Muslim youth and with the Muslim Brotherhood (which was founded seven years before his death). He placed all his hopes in these new, dynamic movements. Rashid Rida died in 1935.

A Faith "Manly, Ardent, Pugnacious"

The next important spokesman in the history of the Islamic renaissance can hardly be characterized more accurately than in Hermann Hesse's words: "Sir Mohammed Iqbal belongs to three realms of the spirit, three realms of the spirit are the sources of his powerful work: the world of India, the world of Islam, and the world of Western thinking. . . . Iqbal is a pious man, a man consecrated to God, but his is not a childlike faith; he is utterly manly, ardent, pugnacious. And his battle is not only a struggle for God, but is also a struggle for the world. . . . His dream is of a mankind united in the name and service of Allah."

On November 9, 1877, the man was born who, next to Mohammed Ali Jinnah, the secular Muslim politician, is considered the spiritual father of contemporary Pakistan. He is also revered as a poet and humanist in Afghanistan and Iran. A member of a deeply religious family, Iqbal grew up in the Punjab town of Sialkot. From 1895 to 1905, he studied in Lahore, which at that time still belonged to the western part of the British vice-royalty of India; afterwards he studied for three years at Cambridge. In England Iqbal graduated in law, and he was awarded the degree of doctor of philosophy in Munich. Those were important years for Mohammed Iqbal, years of encounter with the people of modern Europe and with their spiritual spokespeople. He was later to include these impressions in his works. He also never concealed his admiration for the experiments of the West in the field of the natural sciences.

Back in India, Iqbal served as professor of philosophy and English literature in Lahore, but he soon gave up both of these positions in order to devote himself to poetry. Since that activity was traditionally a nonpaying occupation, however, Iqbal continued to work as a lawyer. The Indian Muslims, oppressed by a threefold Hindu majority, drew new hope from Iqbal's poems, which promoted solidarity. Iqbal was also the first person to indicate the model of a future Muslim state beyond the reach of Hindu domination. This he did in his famous Pakistan address of

December 29, 1930, at the annual meeting of the Indian Muslim League in Allahabad. Speaking from the soul of all Muslims of the Indian subcontinent, he announced:

I have learned a lesson from the history of the Muslims. In critical moments of their history, it was Islam that saved the Muslims, and not the reverse. If you fix your glance at Islam today and seek your inspiration from the eternally stimulating ideas embodied in it, you will again collect your scattered strengths, regain your lost integrity, and thereby save yourselves from total destruction. One of the most profound verses of the holy Koran teaches us that the birth and rebirth of all of mankind compares with the birth and rebirth of a single individual. Why cannot you, who as a people can surely claim to be the first practical embodiment of this sublime conception of mankind, live and be active and own your being just like a single individual? I should not like to lead anyone astray by saying that things in India are not the way they look. But the importance of these words will dawn on you when you have achieved a truly collective ego, as is stated in the Koran: "Control yourselves. No one who errs can hurt you, provided you are well guided."

Repeatedly the poet and sometime politician (from 1924 to 1927, he was a member of the legislative body of Punjab) pled for an Islamic solution. In Iqbal's understanding, the Koran was supposed to bring people together and make them brothers. For this reason he was unable to endorse nationalism, which was popular at the time. "Nationalism makes impossible the human task of Islam," he wrote. At the same time, however, he sought to reawaken the community of Muslims in his homeland and, together with Mohammed Ali Jinnah, lead them into independence. He was not, however, permitted to achieve that.

In 1933 Iqbal was elected vice-president of the Muslim Conference in Jerusalem. Early in 1934, at the invitation of his friend King Nadir Shah, he visited Kabul to participate in developing a cultural and educational program for the Afghans. Iqbal died on April 21, 1938. Among the founding documents of modern Pakistan are his letters, which he wrote to Jinnah from his deathbed. In these letters he showed that the idea of a monolithic Indian nation would lead to civil war if the Muslims were not promised independence. The only possible solution was their own state. It is an irony of history that Iqbal's early and pessimistic statements were later realized in Pakistan: "Nations are born in the hearts of poets; they flourish and die in the hands of politicians."

During the last months of his life, the sensitive and moderate Iqbal was deeply disquieted by the atrocities of his era, atrocities also perpetrated against the Hindus by his own followers. This feeling is evident in Iqbal's last official speech, his New Year's address of 1938, which was full of dire predictions:

The thinkers of the world are horribly mute. Is this really supposed to be the end of all that progress, the end of that development of civilization—that people destroy one another in mutual hatred and make man's stay on earth impossible? That is what people are asking. Think about it: Man can only have his position on this earth by honoring mankind, and the world will remain a battlefield of vicious animals as long as and until the educational forces of the whole world are not directed toward inoculating man with respect for man.

Today Mohammed Iqbal's mausoleum at the Badshahi Mosque of Lahore is still a pilgrimage site for the great thinker's faithful followers. For the Muslim world, Iqbal's importance as the forerunner of the resurgence of Islam remains uncontested, especially the ideas expressed in his major work, *Reconstruction of Religious Thinking* (written in 1930). Here is an excerpt:

Completely overshadowed by the events of his intellectual activities, modern man has ceased to live soulfully—in other words, from within. In the realm of thought, he lives in open conflict with himself, and in the realm of economic and political life he lives in open conflict with others. He finds himself incapable of controlling his careless egoism and his infinite appetite for gold, which slowly kill off in him all higher striving and bring him nothing but boredom with life. . . . The state of things in the Orient is not better. The technique of medieval mysticism, by means of which religious life in its higher manifestations developed in both the West and the Orient, is now effectively gone awry. And in the Muslim East it has perhaps suffered still greater ruin than anywhere else.

Far removed from reintegrating the strengths of the average person's inner life and of preparing him for participation in the march of history, it taught him an erroneous renunciation of the world, and did not let him be completely content with his ignorance and his spiritual slavery. No wonder, therefore, the modern Muslims in Turkey, in Egypt, and in Persia are led to seek fresh sources of energy through the creation of new ties of loyalty such as patriotism and nationalism, which Nietzsche described as "sickness and unreason." . . .

The modern world needs biological renewal. And solely and only religion, which in its higher manifestations is neither dogmas, priesthood, nor ritual, can prepare modern man ethically for the burden of the great responsibility which progress in the modern natural sciences necessarily brings, and can restore to him that support of faith which enables him to achieve a personality here in this world and to preserve it in the hereafter. Only by rising to a new vision of his source and his future, his origin and destination, can man ultimately triumph over a society driven by inhuman competition, and win against a civilization which, as a result of its inner confict about religious and political values, has lost its spiritual unity.

"The Supreme Guide"

In the Middle East the most important apologist for the resurgence of Islam and the early, pure faith has been Hassan al-Banna. Of all the thinkers within the Islamic movement, he pursued his course in the most logical manner, and he was able to create a base for his ideas, which even today are an important factor in everyday politics between Sudan and Iraq, Turkey and Yemen. Hassan al-Banna founded the most powerful and best-organized secret organization in the Islamic world—the Muslim Brotherhood, an authority for millions of people all over the world.

Hassan al-Banna was born in 1906 in al-Mahmudiyya, ninety three miles north of Cairo. Like Mohammed Abduh, he came from the province of al-Buhayra. He grew up under the influence of a father who, although a watchmaker, also served as a prayer leader and teacher at the mosque. Sheikh Ahmad Abd el-Rahman al-Banna al-Saati had been trained at al-Azhar University during Abduh's tenure there. The strict study of traditional Islamic sciences had a great impact on the father, and in the course of time became a decisive factor for the son.

Even as a very young child, Hassan al-Banna received an intensive education based on the Koran and the tradition of the prophets. He entered school at age eight, and at age twelve founded an organization called the Society for Moral Behavior. That did not yet satisfy Hassan al-Banna, so he founded another group, the Society for Impeding the Forbidden. He and his schoolmates occupied themselves primarily with discovering infractions of the principles of Islam and attacking the perpetrators with anonymous threatening letters.

At age fourteen, al-Banna was attracted to Sufism, the Islamic version of mysticism. He liked the Order of the Hasafiyya and its mystic group, so the Hasafiyya Society for Welfare quickly came into being. Hassan el-Banna became secretary of the organization, whose goal was to strengthen the faith within the small village of al-Mahmudiyya. Many of the friends he made in this group later worked within the Muslim Brotherhood. Hassan al-Banna himself was swept up by the tide of Egyptian nationalism in 1919, when the revolution against British domination began. He took to the streets, and his participation in demonstrations had an effect on his later anti-colonialist thinking.

Hassan al-Banna wanted to become a teacher. He attended the nearby teacher-training school and, in 1923, moved on to study at Dar al-Ulum, a more advanced teacher-training institute in Cairo. Even during these years of apprenticeship, al-Banna preached in mosques, propagating his mixture of traditional and mystical Islam. He lived in Cairo, seeing everything through the eyes of a religious village-dweller, and he was horrified by what he saw in the capital city. When the parliamentary system was introduced into Egypt, for instance, there were vehement quarrels between the political parties. Hassan al-Banna was disgusted. Increasingly, it turned out, the parties represented only the interests of the large estate owners and the wealthy people in the cities. The poor people got nothing. The somewhat progressive Wafd Party was repeatedly kept from influence by King Farouq and his clique. Al-Banna was also outraged by events in Turkey, where Mustafa Kemal—Ataturk—strictly separated religion and politics. The young teacher felt that the Muslim world was helplessly exposed to the Western powers. As Hassan al-Banna later confided to friends: "Only God knows how many nights we discussed the situation of our country, analyzed the infirmity, and considered possible remedies. We were so upset that we started to weep."

Hassan al-Banna believed that al-Azhar University would not follow his idea of reform. For this reason, the profoundly religious Egyptian gathered an increasing number of like-minded people together and sent them out into the countryside to promote the resurgence of Islam. His first disciples proclaimed that the time for redress was at hand—the decadence of the society must be eliminated, and the people must return to their roots.

In 1927 al-Banna completed his training and accepted his first position as a teacher of Arabic in Ismailia, in the Suez Canal Zone. He kept this position until 1946. In his new residence, Hassan al-

Banna also maintained contacts with the various groups of discontented youth who sought their salvation in Islam. He assisted
them in founding the Young Muslim Society.

On March 23, 1928, the time had come for his own organization. Together with six other leaders, he founded the Muslim
Brotherhood, an organization that was to go down in history.
During the first years, the organization's members concerned
themselves primarily with spreading their message and establishing branches, from Port Said to Suez. Al-Banna used the teachings of Arabic and Islamic sciences for propagating the cause, for
praying, and for distributing pamphlets. In 1933 he was transferred to Cairo, at which point the movement began to spread
through all of Egypt. Members of the Muslim Brotherhood found
doors open to them everywhere, for the frustrated lower classes,
as well as numerous intellectuals, had been waiting for an alternative to the established government.

Hassan al-Banna and his associates soon became a thorn in the
side of the regime, particularly after 1936, when they began actively to support the Palestinian cause. The Muslim Brotherhood
organized its own schools and social institutions, and by doing
so gained the trust of the masses. Al-Banna, who stood tall with
his beard and fez, soon became the ideal of many Egyptians. Two
million people—ten percent of the population—soon professed
membership in the Muslim Brotherhood. The Supreme Guide (al-
Banna's new title) supported a defensive battle against colonialism and control by foreign capital; he also championed the reunification of the Islamic world into a strong empire. The longing for
the first Islamic state of the Prophet Mohammed was revived.

The emerging pan-Islamism helped the Brotherhood to imple-
ment its ideas in Egypt. The network of cells and clans in Cairo
was already perfectly organized before the government could act
against it. Members of the Muslim Brotherhood were also, by this
time, in Beirut and Geneva. In 1940 they increased their demands
in Egypt for political independence. At the same time, though,
they met with the parties condemned by them, and once Hassan
al-Banna even visited King Farouq. As he left the palace, he commented: "A generous meeting with a generous king." The imam,
who had become the equal of the king, displayed caution. He did
not want to fight prematurely for leadership in the state. As noted
earlier, he told a close co-worker: "We need three generations for
our plans—one to listen, one to fight, and one to win." His gen-

eration listened, and while they listened, they built the Muslim Brotherhood, a system which has been compared with the Mafia, the Assassin Order of the Persians, and even, in terms of organizational structure, with the Jesuits.

After the war, the political system of Egypt found itself in a crisis. Since it had proved impossible to get rid of the British through negotiations, small guerrilla groups began to attack the installations in the Suez Canal Zone. Prime Minister Nukrashi recognized the emerging danger from the Muslim Brotherhood. During the 1948 war against the Israelis, in which units of the Muslim Brotherhood participated, he had their facilities closed and made a large number of arrests. When demonstrations ensued, the regime responded with brutal force. One day, as he entered the Minstry of the Interior, the prime minister was shot by the student Abd al-Majid Ahmad Hassan, a member of the Muslim Brotherhood since 1944. Six weeks later, on February 12, 1949, a murderer's bullet hit the leader of the Muslim Brotherhood, Hassan al-Banna, as the charismatic imam was leaving the headquarters of the Young Muslims in Cairo. Al-Banna was just getting into a taxi when, suddenly, Colonel Abdel Megid and police officer Mohammed Hassein appeared. They shot at him and fled in a car driven by Mohammed Mahfuz (the automobile allegedly belonged to the acting minister of the interior). Hassan al-Banna died in a nearby hospital. True to his words, the time for fighting had come: "Every innovation not based on religion deviates from the correct route; it must be opposed with all means, it must be eliminated with all means."

Among the many theoretical writings of Hassan al-Banna, most of which deal with the desperate situation of Islam, one work stands apart—the *Confession of Faith of Members of the Muslim Brotherhood:*

1. I believe that all things hark back to God; that our master Mohammed, may he be blessed by God, is the last prophet and was sent to all people; that the Koran is God's book; that Islam portrays a general law for the order of this world and of the beyond. I vow to memorize a part of the noble Koran, to adhere to the edifying *sunna* [the Prophet's tradition], and to study the life of the prophet and of his noble companions.

2. I believe that virtue, uprightness, and knowledge are the foundations of Islam. I commit myself to be upright, to fulfill the precepts of ritual, to avoid forbidden actions, to be virtuous and of good morals, to

give up bad habits, to adhere as precisely as possible to the Islamic rites of faith, to prefer love and affection over strife and lawsuits, to be proud of the customs and the language of Islam, to spread knowledge and useful information among the people.

3. I believe that a Muslim should work and earn money, that every person in need and suffering has a right to the money he earns; I vow to work and to save for the future, to contribute alms and to spend a part of my income for good works, to encourage all useful industrial projects, to give preference to the products of my country and of members of my faith. I vow not to practice usury, regardless of the business, and not to devote myself to matters that exceed my capacity.

4. I believe that the Muslim is responsible for his family, that his duties include preserving their health, their faith, and their good morals. I vow in this sense to do everything possible to impart the Islamic teaching to members of my family; not to send my children to any school that does not teach the morals and faith of the Muslims; to avoid all newspapers, publications, books, organizations, groups, and clubs that oppose the teachings of Islam.

5. I believe that a Muslim has the duty of enlivening the fame of Islam by promoting the renaissance of the peoples and restoring Islamic legislation. I believe that the flag of Islam should rule mankind, and that it is the duty of every Muslim to instruct the world in the rules of Islam. I vow to fight all my life in order to fulfill this mission, and to sacrifice to it everything I own.

6. I believe that Muslims constitute a single and united great nation that is united by Islam, and that Islam commands its sons to show kindness to all. I vow to do everything I can to strengthen the brotherhood of all Muslims and to overcome their indifference as well as to reconcile the differences that exist among their groups and brotherhoods.

7. I believe that the secret of the backwardness of the Muslims must be explained by their distance from their religion, that the basis of a reform must consist in returning to the teachings and judgments of Islam. This is possible if the Muslims are in this sense active, and the teachings of the Muslim Brotherhood are directed toward this end. I vow to adhere to these basic tenets, to remain loyal toward each person who is active on their behalf and to be a soldier and, if necessary, to die in their service.

A New Chief Ideologist

Following the death of Hassan al-Banna, Sayed Qutb became recognized as the chief ideologist of the Muslim Brotherhood.

Born in 1906 in Assiut in Upper Egypt, he too graduated from the teacher-training institute of Dar al-Ulum. He taught Arabic language and literature, worked as a school inspector in the Ministry of Culture, and also gave lectures about the Koran at his former school. In 1948 Sayed Qutb was sent by the Egyptian government to pursue his studies in the United States. He attended several universities on both the East and West coasts and also traveled through a large part of the country during his free time. Qutb returned to the Nile by way of England, Switzerland, and Italy. He was outraged, he said, at the "godless materialism in the spiritual, social, and economic life of the people" of the West. More than ever, he was convinced that only Islam could offer a genuine future.

This conviction prompted him to join the Muslim Brotherhood, which had by this time been banned by King Farouq. Qutb soon advanced to become a member of the executive committee and director of propaganda. In 1953 he represented the Muslim Brotherhood of Egypt in Syria and Jordan, and in 1954 took over the editorship of *Ikhwan al-Muslimun*, the publication of the Muslim Brotherhood. When Sayed Qutb criticized in its pages the treaty with Great Britain concerning the withdrawal of troops, Colonel Gamal Abdel Nasser banned the newspaper. Following an unsuccessful assassination attempt on Nasser in October 1954, an unprecedented wave of arrests was initiated against members of the Muslim Brotherhood. Sayed Qutb did not escape the secret police, and he was gruesomely tortured in prison. His sole response to his tormentors was the Koran: "Allah is great, and praise and glory are due only to Him!"

On July 13, 1955, Sayed Qutb was sentenced to fifteen years in a labor camp. Barely one year later, an emissary of Nasser arrived to offer Qutb his freedom if he would ask for mercy. His answer was entered into the history of the Muslim Brotherhood: "I am surprised that the oppressed are asked by their oppressor whether they want to ask for mercy and forgiveness. By God, if a few words of apology could save me from death on the gallows, I would not utter them. I want to come before my Lord in a state of mind of being content with myself and He with me."

Sayed Qutb spent the years up to the middle of 1964 in various prisons of the Nasser regime. Three years after his sentencing, his situation improved—more and more his relatives were permitted to visit him, and he was able to study religious writings, even to write himself. His most important work during these years was a three-part commentary on the Koran. In 1964 Qutb was pardoned during the visit of the Iraqi head of state, Abdul Salem Aref. But his freedom did not last long. By 1965, Qutb, his brother Mohammed, and his sisters Hamida and Amina were again behind bars, accused of having preached the violent over-throw of the regime. Nasser had just returned from a state visit to Moscow, where he had announced a new plot by the Muslim Brotherhood against him. Twenty thousand members of the Muslim Brotherhood were immediately arrested. The machinery of the state got a lot of practice in doing that.

Starting in 1966, ongoing show trials were conducted against members of the Muslim Brotherhood. When too many eyewit-ness accounts of torture in the prisons reached the public, how-ever, the courts continued to function only behind closed doors. Sayed Qutb was condemned to death and was executed on Mon-day morning, August 29, 1966. From the entire Muslim world, there was a hail of protest against Gamal Abdel Nasser.

In the course of his life, Sayed Qutb wrote twenty books and numerous other works. He formulated the ideology of the Mus-lim Brotherhood and disseminated its theses. In his writing, Qutb repeatedly denied the possibility of creating anything really new. For this radical opponent of modernity, the sought-after golden era lay in the past. He spoke constantly of the bankruptcy of the Western world. Here he castigated even Mohammed Abduh and Mohammed Iqbal as liberal apostates of the true faith. Although Qutb's position was at first a simple appeal for social justice, he developed into a radical agitator. In his main work, *This Faith, Islam,* he reaches the following conclusions:

People as a whole are now further removed from God than ever before. The gloomy clouds that have settled over the true nature of man are larger and more dense than ever before. The former uncertainty about God derived from the general ignorance, simplicity, and primitivity; the present ignorance has its origin in learnedness, in the diversity of real life, and in man's superficiality and frivolity. Mankind is suffering from hypocrisy, duplicity, and meanness. All these bad characteristics are barriers along the route *to which God wants to lead man,* and obstacles to efforts toward an upright obedience to the religion of God. . . . But how can they prepare and arm themselves? All that they can arm themselves with are: respect for God, awareness of the actual presence of God, direct cooperation with God, and complete trust in His explicit promise:

"We took vengeance on the guilty, and rightly succored the true believers." (Koran 30:48)

The Sparks Spread to Syria

The Muslim Brotherhood produced two thinkers who, based on their area of activity, should be credited to Syria: Mustafa al-Sibai and his successor, Said Hawwa.

Mustafa al-Sibai was born in 1915 in Homs, north of Damascus. His father, Husni al-Sibai, was a well-known preacher and himself provided his son with a thorough training in Islam. His instruction fell on fertile soil; at an early age, Mustafa al-Sibai began to represent his father in the mosque. He completed his schooling at age fifteen and became intensely preoccupied for several years with the basic principles of Islam. One of his teachers was the Mufti Tahir al-Atasi, whose fame spread far beyond Homs. By this time al-Atasi had already been imprisoned twice, in both instances for protests against the French occupation.

In 1933 Mustafa al-Sibai began his studies at the Sharia department of al-Azhar University. Two years later he landed in jail for taking to the streets in opposition to the British colonial domination. The Syrian lived in Cairo among people who shared his views, all the while intensifying his fundamentalist training. By 1940 he had come to the point of founding his own secret society, whose members agitated against the British. The consequence: six months in jail. Al-Sibai returned home in 1941, after being imprisoned in Sarfad, in what was then Palestine. He did not, however, intend to sit idly by and watch further developments. Two conferences already held in Homs in 1937 and a meeting in Damascus in 1938 were to lead to the founding of the Syrian Muslim Brotherhood. Once back home, Mustafa al-Sibai immediately plunged into organizational work and was promptly arrested by the French mandate authorities. An additional two years in jail guaranteed his underground activity.

Only in mid-1943 was al-Sibai released in Lebanon. The precise circumstances of his internment are difficult to come by. Allegedly, the Muslim leader was mistreated for a long period of time and, as a result, contracted an incurable disease that repeatedly interfered with his official tasks and frequently required hospitalization.

Scarcely was al-Sibai again free when a conference was held in

Homs; the decision was to create a paramilitary organization. Thus, in 1946, the Society of the Muslim Brotherhood of Syria finally came into being. Mustafa al-Sibai was elected its leader, but from the beginning he was subordinate to the Supreme Guide, Hassan al-Banna. Within ten months, the Muslim Brotherhood had built up a complete organizational structure. Mustafa al-Sibai announced the organization's motto: "An *ummah* [people] of God who want to free themselves will neither be deterred by oppression nor frightened by calumny." The Muslim Brotherhood of Syria also held a strictly rejecting attitude toward Western influences and trends.

Mustafa al-Sibai always expressed himself clearly; he was able to articulate current events without any trace of the ambiguity of Islamic writings. In an article concerning foreign businesses and their quest for oil concessions, he wrote:

They are the direct reason for foreign intervention into the domestic matters of the country and are the great obstacle toward the realization of independence and dignity. On the one hand, the concessions are the legacy from the era of the Turks; on the other hand, the concessions were granted under the veiled assertion that it would be economically good for the country and the people. But history has shown that such firms constitute the beginning of colonialism.

Following his release from prison, Mustafa al-Sibai taught Arabic and religion in Homs, and later in Damascus, but most of his time was spent in the leadership activities of the Muslim Brotherhood. In 1948 members of the Muslim Brotherhood fought with their own contingent in the first Middle East war against the Israelis. But, even with the personal intervention of Mustafa al-Sibai and Hassan al-Banna, they were unable to avoid defeat. After March 1949, three colonels, one after the other, staged coups in Syria. There was also a short-lived assembly, which drew up a constitution providing for a parliament. Mustafa al-Sibai was an elected representative of the people to both bodies of the parliament.

In 1949 al-Sibai completed his doctorate in jurisprudence and Islamic legal history, and in 1951 he married into one of the most prestigious families of Damascus. His wedding was commemorated by good wishes from the prime minister. Throughout, the fundamentalist led his radical Islamic organization, even during the years it was banned. When the ban was lifted in 1954, his group partially took over functions for the Egyptian Muslim Brotherhood, many of whose members had been arrested. As a consequence, in the summer of 1957, Mustafa al-Sibai was promoted to head of the executive committee of the entire organization. The leadership of the Syrian Muslim Brotherhood passed, for a brief period of time, to Issam al-Attar, who lived in exile in Aachen, West Germany.

Even after Mustafa al-Sibai became partially disabled, his zeal for work was unflagging. He continued to perform important functions at the University of Damascus, where he lectured on the socialism of Islam. (This is the subject of his most important book, which demonstrates that the good ideas of socialism are also anchored in Islam.) He published newspapers, traveled in Western countries as long as he was physically able, and spoke at many conferences. Mustafa al-Sibai died on October 3, 1964, after a long illness.

A newspaper article from the year 1948 serves as an affirmation of faith by the fundamentalist al-Sibai. There he states:

We want to establish a society in which there is neither injustice nor poverty nor theft. We want to establish a state in which there is no egoism, despotism, and suppression. We want to build a fatherland in which there is no imperialism, no anarchy, and no ignorance. We want to create a people with strong nerves and with the manliness of heroes. We want an *Ummah* that finds death agreeable and that shakes mountains. We want to liberate Palestine from the Zionists, the British, the Americans, the Russians, and all the nations of this earth. We want to achieve faith in our hearts, morality in our souls, knowledge in our tears, light in our eyes, and the electricity of death in our nerves.

Very little is known about the life of Said Hawwa, the only theoretician of the Muslim Brotherhood who is still alive. The plump man, in his mid-forties, is a member of the triumvirate of the leadership of the Islamic revolution, which is to say that he fights the Assad regime in Damascus while living underground. His writings have been disseminated throughout the Islamic world, especially in Syria, along the Gulf, and in Turkey (in translation). Said Hawwa is a hunted man—today he may be in Jordan, tomorrow in Kuwait, the day after in Rome. If one meets him in his hideout or at some spot determined by the Muslim Brotherhood, he is willing to engage in open discussion and begs no question, no matter how disagreeable.

In his most important work, *Fifty Years of Muslim Brotherhood*, Said Hawwa notes that a member of his secret service should not laugh excessively. But he himself is a person who enjoys conviviality; he chuckles, amused by many topics of conversation. Asked how he sees his role as chief ideologist, he has his answer ready: "I myself do not consider myself such, but wherever our members assume roles, we try to fulfill them." Occasionally, however, the bearded Said Hawwa lets one see that he is proud of his title. In his view, his person is not so essential. What he considers important is "to change the face of the entire region within the next twenty years"—that is, to carry out a revolution in the sense intended by the Muslim Brotherhood and to set up a powerful Islamic state.

The following is from an unpublished discussion held in 1981 between Said Hawwa and Dr. Karl Binswanger, the German Orientalist:

"You have written numerous books that are more ideological than political."

"We wrote them at the request of members of the Muslim Brotherhood. In general, we always try to offer our members the basic features of the Islamic interpretation. And simultaneously we try to provide political training for a world that is very complicated, so the policy in general conveys the art of dealing with the possible."

"You would like to do away with national states within the Islamic world. You would like to restore a unified Islamic realm. What should that look like?"

"We would like one state within the entire Islamic world, and any nation that wants to can also have sovereignty within the whole state. We would have nothing against it if the Kurds or the Baluchis or other peoples had their own status. Each of these nations can have its own constitution, its own legislature, its own executive."

"What should the state association look like?"

"There is already something similar—in fact, the United States. The federal states all have their own laws, but that does not contradict the fact that there is one law to which they all adhere. Just what the future *dar al-Islam*, the house of Islam, will look like, we alone do not wish to determine. That is something the Islamic governments themselves should decide."

"In doing this, are you also striving for a reestablishment of the caliphate?"
"The caliphate is the goal of every Muslim. In the way we strive for it, our caliphate should take the errors of the past into consideration, doing away with the failures and what has harmed us. We would like the caliphate to be the symbol for constant consultations and the symbol of law and justice. Our legal steps in this direction will be very precise, so that we can avoid the errors that brought us to our historical situation."

Maududi, the Father of Islamism

The most important Islamic thinker of Asia was Abul Ala Maududi. There is hardly anyone else with whom the Orientalists so strongly associate the concept of Islamism, the transformation of the faith into a political direction. Radical Islamism, which is not far removed from fascistic tendencies, was created in the explosive climate of Pakistan, and it is still practiced today by Abul Ala Maududi's fundamentalist party, Jamaat-e Islami. Following his death in 1979, the extremely camera-shy, slight man, with his white beard, black-rimmed glasses, black fur cap, and white Pakistani dress, became more myth than ever. In the eyes of his followers, he has become a redeemer figure, whose teachings are capable of bringing to the Indian subcontinent and to all concerned the only true Islamic future.

Abul Ala Maududi was always silent when asked about the details of his life. Born in 1903, he came from an average family from the southern part of Central India. Many of his forefathers were members of the mystical Sufi orders, but he himself seems never to have had any such connections. The deeply religious autodidact managed to earn a living as a journalist from 1918 until 1941, when he founded the Jamaat-e Islami. With this instrument of power, he hoped to obtain greater respect for the Islamic faith in an antagonistic environment of Hindus, to fight against the British colonial domination, and to carve out an Islamic state from the Indian motherland. These goals were later to be realized by Mohammed Ali Jinnah and his Muslim League.

As early as 1937, Maududi was asked to participate in the Mus-

lim League by the poet Mohammed Iqbal, but he preferred to
become director of the Islamic Institute of Research in Lahore. For
two years he also served as director of the School for Islamic
Theology in Lahore. With his strictly conservative viewpoint, he
became uncomfortably conspicuous after the founding of the
state of Pakistan. Indeed, because of his fundamentalist attitude,
the Pakistani government put him in jail in 1948, and again in
1952. Maududi was considered the instigator of the student unrest in West Pakistan, even though he and his students continually denied such accusations. In this regard, their position stood
in contrast to that of other Islamic movements, which were always proud of the attacks that provided them with their revolutionary identity.

Starting in 1935, the uncharismatic Maududi systematically organized his party machine, Jamaat-e Islami (Islamic Society). First
he founded a newspaper, and close contacts were set up with
Hassan al-Banna's Muslim Brotherhood. Both organizations still
consider themselves branches of the same movement. At times
the Muslim Brotherhood even recognized Maududi as the legal
successor to its ideologists al-Banna and Sayed Qutb. Maududi,
however, was always skeptical about the founding of the state of
Pakistan; he believed that such a strategy should have an Islamic
but not a nationalistic aspect. Nationalism he condemned
altogether: "Egoism in individual life is nationalism in the
context of social life. A nationalist is usually narrow-minded and
stingy."

From the beginning, Abul Ala Maududi's books and brochures
(eighty in all) exerted an influence on the Pakistani masses; they
thus became a factor in the politics in the poor developing country. His party was alternately forbidden and permitted, according
to which government was on top. Repeatedly, Maududi sat in jail
—a fact, however, that merely increased his popularity. Since the
Jamaat-e Islami was always well financed, with Saudi money, it
was able to build a powerful propaganda machine, disseminating
Maududi's works throughout the Islamic world. Even in Turkey
his thoughts fell on fertile ground. And intellectuals like Sayed
Qutb derived inspiration from the amir, or leader, which later
found expression in their own works.

In particular, Maududi's definitions of the correct Islamic state
became a base for many of the fundamentalist movements. As
the opponent of Western democracy explained his ideas:

The difference between Islamic democracy and Western democracy is, of course, the following: while the latter is based on the conception of the sovereignty of the people, the former is based on the principle of the caliphate [leadership] by the people. In Western democracy, the people are sovereign; in Islam, sovereignty rests with God, and the people are his caliphs or subjects. In the West the people themselves make the law; in Islam the people must follow and obey the laws that God communicated through his prophets. In one system the government carries out the will of the people; in the other the government and people together must translate God's intentions into deeds. In short, Western democracy is a kind of absolute authority that exerts its power freely and in an uncontrolled manner, whereas Islamic democracy is subject to the divine law and exerts its authority in harmony with the commands of God and within the framework established by God.

The relationship of Jammat-e Islami to the Pakistani state was always troubled, for the state was viewed as not Islamic enough. The Islam Party in fact played a decisive role in the fall of President Ayub Khan in 1969. Although after the religious General Zia ul-Haq seized power in July 1977, the Jamaat-e Islami was officially banned, since that time it has again been permitted to work freely under another name and to exert its influences on schools, universities, as well as the army. It constitutes an important support for the concept of the Pakistani military dictatorship—combining, so to speak, both the civil and the religious elements. Abul Ala Maududi, however, did not live to see this further development; he died of heart failure in September 1979 while visiting a son living in America in Buffalo, New York.

Nevertheless, Maududi lives on in his followers' strivings toward the realization of the "kingdom of God." In his words:

A better designation for the Islamic political order would be "the kingdom of God," which in the West is usually called "theocracy." But the Islamic theocracy is something entirely different from the theocracy with which Europe had bitter experiences, in which a class of priests that sharply differentiates itself from the rest of the population exerts unlimited domination, and in the name of God attains validity for laws they themselves made. In this manner, the priesthood in effect imposes on the people its own deity and equality with God. Such a system of government is more satanic than divine. In contrast, the theocracy of Islam is not dominated by a particular class, but by the entire Muslim community, including the simple people. The entire Muslim population guides the state in accordance with the book of God and with the example of His Prophet's manner of conduct.

The Bourgeois Revolutionary from Iran

An unusual figure in the resurgence of Islam was Dr. Ali Shariati, the Iranian who created enthusiasm for his brand of Islamic socialism even among radical youth who were Western in both training and feeling. His devotees ranged from inflexibly reactionary fundamentalists (Imam Khomeini did not withhold approval) to urban guerrillas such as the Mujahideen-e Khalq that now battles the regime in Tehran. The present leadership of Jamaat-e Islami has also been profoundly influenced by Ali Shariati. Some of his followers regard the established Islamic parties and organizations as "agents of the imperialists and bourgeoisie." Nor do the socialists and communists of the Muslim countries escape the criticism of the intellectual from northeastern Iran.

Ali Shariati was born on November 31, 1934, in the village of Masinan, on the outskirts of a desolate salt desert in the province of Khorasan. He studied Persian literature in Mashhad. Later he went to Paris, where he received a doctorate in sociology and Islamic history at the Sorbonne. In his homeland, Shariati had at an early age already encountered the explosive tension of the Shah era, not least in the Islamic center of revolution run by his father, Professor Mohammed Taqi Shariati. He developed a sensitivity to the problems of underdeveloped countries and the conflict between the Third World and colonial powers. From this background it was logical that, as a student, he participated in Dr. Mohammed Mossadegh's movement for nationalization of the petroleum industry. After the ousting of Mossadegh in 1953, Shariati joined the National Resistance Movement. Together with his father and fourteen other activists, he was arrested in 1957 and spent six months in prison.

The Shah's notorious secret service, SAVAK, thereafter followed every step of the potential troublemaker. Shariati was denied a visa after he was recommended for study in Paris on the basis of his excellent accomplishments. Only in 1960 was it finally issued. In France Ali Shariati participated in Iranian student organizations and also supported the Algerian liberation movement, which at that time preoccupied the thinking of leftist youth. At the same time he founded an Iranian liberation movement. The first congress of the Iranian National Front for Europe, which similarly came into being with his assistance, took place in Wiesbaden. The activist Shariati was deeply impressed by the freedom fighters Houari Boumedienne and Ahmed Ben Bella; by the leading exponent of anti-colonialism, Frantz Fanon; by Jean-Paul Sartre and Jean Cocteau. All these influences are reflected in his later works.

In May 1965 Ali Shariati returned to Iran. Immediately upon reentry he was arrested, separated from his family, and taken to Tehran. There was, however, no evidence against him, so the authorities had to release him. After a long period of unemployment, Shariati obtained a post as a mere village teacher in Ferdows, in the vicinity of Mashhad. This job gave him the time to write and to cultivate contacts with the opposition. In his works he cites class conflict as the basis for change and offers a dialectical interpretation of religion, which reflects the conditions of the times. Although he describes the alienation of man's self resulting from capitalist society, Shariati never wanted to admit that, in this, he drew on Karl Marx.

From 1970 to 1973, Shariati was considered the most important speaker in the Tehran discussion forum Hosseynieh Ershad. A tribute by the Union of Islamic Student Organizations in Europe makes the following statement about this period: "Dr. Shariati showed the alternative character of Islam in comparison to the other ideologies in the battle against colonialism, imperialism, and oppressive domination. He made it possible for new blood to flow in the veins of the people. The people recognized the indigenous Islamic value system once again and were freed of confusion and helplessness. In this manner, the people returned to Islam as the doctrine of freedom and justice." Shariati's importance shows that the Iranian revolution was fostered not only by the old *mullahs* and *ayatollahs*, but also by agitated youth who to some extent were influenced by other models.

As many as 5,000 listeners attended the public lectures given by Shariati. His writings were distributed in the hundreds of thousands, although arrest and torture were the penalty for owning them. Often, the modest, quiet Shariati spoke all day and then held discussions late into the night. After he had given more than 100 lectures, SAVAK tried to arrest him, but Shariati escaped; he gave himself up to the police only after they had seized his father as a hostage. For two years he was gruesomely tortured in the Komiteh Prison. After his release he was not permitted to indulge in any teaching activities or to maintain any conspiratorial contacts. The secret police followed his every move. Nonetheless, he managed to flee abroad on May 16, 1976. At 3:00 A.M. Ali Shariati flew to Brussels, and from there to Paris. In France he met battle companions who two weeks previously had resolved to found a Shariati foundation, for which the Lebanese Shiite leader Musa Sadr had promised financing.

Ali Shariati flew on to London, where he wanted to wait for his wife and two daughters before continuing their trip to join his eighteen-year-old son in the United States. His family's arrival was scheduled for June 18. On that Saturday morning Ali Shariati, properly dressed as usual in a suit and tie, visited a department store in downtown London. There he was wounded by a SAVAK agent using a device with a high success rate—a small needle, 0.3 millimeters wide and 1.5 millimeters long, which can be fired from a distance up to 189 feet by a weapon (a CIA invention) the size of a package of cigarettes. The needle had been tipped in cobra poison. The shot is registered merely as an itch. (The same weapon was used to kill Khomeini's son Mustafa in 1977, a step that significantly heightened the revolutionary fervor.)

An hour after leaving the department store, Ali Shariati complained of headache and dizziness. During the afternoon he learned that his thirteen- and fifteen-year-old daughters had cleared the visa officials in Tehran, but that his wife had been recognized and detained. He went to Heathrow Airport to meet his children, and they subsequently talked for three hours. Then Shariati went to bed, but he never awakened: embolism of the brain. Following his death the battle for his corpse began. The Iranian Embassy in London laid claim to it, but so did his friends from the underground. Finally a telex from his grown son Eshan arrived, empowering a London attorney to claim the body.

The Iraqi government, which considered the presence of the Ayatollah Khomeini extremely disagreeable, refused burial in the Tragi Shiite pilgrimage village of Najaf, so, with the assistance of Imam Musa Sadr, Damascus was chosen. There, in the presence of many revolutionaries who later became famous, Ali Shariati was buried beside Zeinab, the granddaughter of the Prophet. After a forty-day period of mourning, a large demonstration was held in honor of Shariati in a Beirut mosque. The main speaker was Musa Sadr. Representatives of twenty liberation movements, including the PLO leader Yasser Arafat, paid their respects to the deceased.

In one of his programmatic writings, Ali Shariati states:

What should we do now? We must restore the continuity of the culture. We must try to know ourselves in order to find out what we should vote on. We must constructively, creatively, and dynamically shape all historical factors, which have now deteriorated to superstition and to numbing thoughts, and all religious and mystical factors and that literature which has the effect of a sedative and which causes the inertia and decline of our society. . . .

In contrast to the history of the Africans, the Westerners have unfortunately never denied our history. . . . We have looked at our history and been repelled by it. We fled from this image that was drawn by us and took refuge in European culture, history, religion, philosophy, and art. Our escape consists in destroying this image and of drawing the image of reality in our thoughts, of exploring and developing our great cultural sources, of consciously demonstrating capability and responsibility toward our society—but not in the manner in which the West has done that for us, which is to be abhorred. Just as in the economy we transform raw materials into energy, build up large industrial and production centers, and unleash movements, we must act in a similar manner in thinking, in spiritual activity, in the formation of our personality and cultural independence.

4

Within the Movements

The Muslim Brotherhood in Egypt

THE EMBLEM is as green as Mohammed's coat. Most of the space is occupied by two crossed swords, which have remained the symbol of power even in the era of the universal weapon, the Kalashnikov. "Be prepared for anything," counsel the words beneath the swords. Above this is a red book, the book of books, the Koran. "Oh, truly this is a merciful book," it is stated on the title page. Only Islamic fundamentalists—in this instance, the Muslim Brotherhood—could choose such a combination as weapons.

The Muslim Brotherhood operates in strict secrecy. Although several attempts have been made to write the history of the Muslim Brotherhood, each has proved only partially successful. Historians ran into obstacles because their investigations were not always well received, and authors from the ranks of the Muslim Brotherhood became hesitant. A non-Muslim has difficulty getting a look into the organization, and in the Muslim world the very attempt to do so is considered taboo.

The Society of the Muslim Brothers (Al-Ikhwan al-Muslimun) is the most powerful secret religious organization. Its influence is felt in places where its name is scarcely known. Its members have created a strict organization in Indonesia; they are fighting in Afghanistan, distributing religious writings in the southern Soviet provinces, and they have proclaimed holy war in Syria. In Yemen they are trying to realize their model of the Islamic state. They publish magazines in the United States and direct Islamic centers throughout the Western world. The members of the Muslim Brotherhood are everywhere, connected with one another by an elaborate network of secret contacts.

The Muslim Brotherhood was founded with very clear goals: elimination of all Western influences in the Islamic world, opposition to the relaxation of Islamic traditions and customs, return to the pure teaching of the Prophet, and creation of an Islamic theocracy on earth. For the pious membership, this includes primarily the restoration of the caliphate, eliminated by Ataturk, as the highest political and religious authority, as well as more extensive social reforms.

Al-Murshid al-Amm (roughly the equivalent of general director) Hassan al-Banna emphatically stated: "If we turn away from Islam, we will gain nothing and will lose our soul. On the other hand, if we adhere firmly to it, grouping ourselves around it, if we let ourselves be led by it, then without doubt we will save our soul, and it is very well possible that by means of our union we will gain the respect of the Occidentals."

At the beginning, the faithful from all classes—students, peasants, craftspeople, small businesspeople, bureaucrats—followed Imam al-Banna. They met in nearby mosques, prayed together for Islamic goals, and deplored the sins of the world. After long discussions, and with clear instruction from the leadership, they decided to found a fighting alliance. The majority of the *fellahs*, created by the ruling elite (still a monarchy) and the British colonialists, were quickly won over to the idea, and influential supporters guaranteed economic power. There were no critical arguments concerning the faith and the position of the individual.

During the first twenty years of its existence, the Egyptian branch of the organization permeated all realms of public life and much of business life. It became a factor to be reckoned with by both the king as well as any political party. For a long time, though, members of the Muslim Brotherhood were more preoccupied with the British colonial masters than with their own countrymen. Those tensions emerged only later.

Typical of the agitation of this era was a prayer written by the charismatic Hassan al-Banna for his fellow members:

Great God, Lord of both worlds, protector of those who fear themselves, humiliator of those who imagine themselves great, destroyer of the powerful: hear our prayer and heed our call. Give us back our freedom and independence. Great God, the British, those tyrants, have occupied our country and spread corruption. Great God, free us from their malice, thwart their attacks, destroy their unity, punish with severe measures them and those who help them to victory, or those who support them, or those who humiliate themselves before them, or those who like them, for they all deserve severe punishment. Great God, bring your ruin quickly over them, spread plague among them, debase their state, drive their domination out of your country, and do not let them rule over even a single person among your believers.

In 1941 the British could no longer stand idly by, listening to this agitation: they put Hassan al-Banna into prison for several months. Scarcely had he been released than the Brotherhood started to build up its so-called secret apparatus, a paramilitary organization. Its members had already attracted the enthusiasm of the faithful by offering spiritual support during hard times, literacy campaigns (by teachers during vacations), cost-free medical care once a month by doctors from the Muslim Brotherhood, and practical courses of instruction. With the "special section" (the name within the Brotherhood), they closed a previous gap; the route to power became simpler. Members of the Muslim Brotherhood justified the creation of a fighting troop by the disputes about Palestine: it was the duty of all Muslims to fight for their own country against outside dangers. The highest leader of the Muslim Brotherhood at present, Omar el-Telmisani, provides the following explanation: "After we again had to experience how the Islamic governments hesitated to act on behalf of Palestine, we started to build up a secret organization." In terms of its conception, then, it was not directed against the Egyptian government.

While the training of the first paramilitary unit was still in progress, the secret organization split off and started to lead its own existence, occasionally even opposing Hassan al-Banna and his faction. Members of the Muslim Brotherhood were compelled to realize how easily power corrupts. The military leader, Abd el-Rahman el-Sanadi, entered into competition with al-Banna. Omar el-Telmisani looks back: "This phenomenon—that people in certain positions suddenly exploit their power— is not restricted to the Muslim Brotherhood, but el-Sanadi let himself be led astray by the devil." In any case, Hassan al-Banna expressed his displeasure—initially in a roundabout way, in two articles in which he condemned the commando attacks.

Why was it all-important for the Muslim Brotherhood to have its own instrument of power? According to Omar el-Telmisani, "This instrument was for the purpose of earnestly training the youth. I admit that some errors were made, although most of the cases dealt with in court were slanders." The climax of the conflict with the leadership was reached when el-Sanadi insisted on a separate vow of allegiance from his supporters, a clear affront to Hassan al-Banna. Traditionally, all members of the Muslim Brotherhood had to state to the imam: "I swear with the great God that I work in this group—honestly toward God (praise be to the Sublime One), obediently to its leader, in good and in bad times, whether I want to or not, with the exception of committing a sin, because God's emissary (praise be with him) said: 'No obedience to anyone who is not obedient to God.'" El-Sanadi now demanded a special oath, which was to be taken on a revolver in a darkened room.

In a sensational interview published in 1982 in the Egyptian magazine *Mussawar*, Omar el-Telmisani provided this explanation for the situation at that time:

Often it happens that the increasing power of a member of a group is not recognized until this person already constitutes a danger for the entire group. . . . The machinery was originally built up for the purpose of battling the foreign presence, but it was then used negatively and diverted from the proper course. If the government would have believed us—would have believed that we had only made mistakes and, instead of arresting us and torturing us in prison, would have negotiated with us—then the situation now would be a completely different one.

It is not surprising, however, that the Egyptian government felt itself threatened by an organization that was constantly becoming stronger and more aggressive. Sooner or later it would have to react, but in the mid-1940s a truce still prevailed. Members of the Muslim Brotherhood were permitted to enter additional fields of business and open new schools. In 1946 the organization was even permitted to publish a daily newspaper, *Al-Ikhwan al-Muslimun*, in addition to its magazine *Al Dawa* ("The Call").

Now the strengthened Muslim Brotherhood faced the first test of strength—a dispute with the popular, nationalistic Wafd Party. There was bitter contention and fighting in and around the universities. About the same time, on November 29, 1947, the United Nations decided, in opposition to the votes of the Arabs, on the partition of Palestine into a Jewish and an Arab state. The avenue toward the founding of Israel had been cleared. The increased danger of military conflict caused Hassan al-Banna to order the mobilization of his own units. Army officers were among the volunteers who promptly streamed in from all directions. On April 25, 1948, the first volunteer battalion moved toward El Arish.

The British mandate ended at midnight on May 14. The following morning the armies of Egypt, Transjordania, Iraq, Syria, Lebanon, and contingents of troops from Saudi Arabia attacked. They were strengthened on all fronts by members of the Muslim Brotherhood, who, during the war, stood out mainly because of their fanatic fighting spirit. With the aid of the religious fighters *(mujahideen)*, the Egyptians came within twenty-five miles of Tel Aviv. The Arabs, however, encountered stronger resistance than they had expected and, after months of fighting, were repelled. The cessation of hostilities between Egypt and Israel, on January 7, 1949, signaled the end of the first war of the Middle East.

By this time members of the Muslim Brotherhood were no longer among the contingent, for, on December 8, 1948, the Egyptian government had banned their organization and begun to arrest a large number of its leading members. The government considered the move an act of self-protection, since it had gotten wind of a planned attack against the state by the Muslim Brotherhood—as revenge for the military defeat, now apparent. Prime Minister Mahmud Fahmi al-Nukrashi Pasha, who had to answer for the death of members of the Muslim Brotherhood, was shot on December 28 by a twenty-three-year-old member of the organization. The High Council of al-Azhar University condemned the murder as anti-Islamic. Negotiations by the Muslim Brotherhood with the new prime minister, Abd al-Hadi, concerning the release of the imprisoned members failed. The dispute spread all over Egypt. On February 12, 1949, Hassan al-Banna was shot on the open street by civilian policemen. The Muslim Brotherhood continues to maintain that his life could have been saved. But, on instructions from King Farouq, the Kasr-el-Aini Hospital in Cairo refused to treat him and let him bleed to death.

The Muslim Brotherhood continued to function underground. Only with the end of martial law two years later, on May 1, 1951, was the ban on the organization lifted. In October the new leader was announced, the twenty-five-year-old judge, Hassan al-Hudaibi. From the outset he distanced himself from the secret service division of his own organization: "There can be nothing secret in the service of God. There is no secret in our message and no religious terror. Why should we use a weapon when we have a tongue? Why do we need a hand grenade as long as the cries of the persecuted are louder than dynamite explosions?" Al-Hudaibi was an entirely different type of person from Hassan al-Banna. But when an issue concerned the goals of the Muslim Brotherhood, he acted just as uncompromisingly.

The guerrilla war against the British troops in the Canal Zone came to a climax on the so-called Black Sunday, February 25, 1952. The center of Cairo was in flames, and the government placed the blame on the Muslim Brotherhood. The government fell. For months the leadership of the Egyptian state changed repeatedly. Finally the armed forces seized power in a bloodless coup during the night of July 23. King Farouq was forced to abdicate and leave the country. A group called the Free Officers, led by the thirty-four-year-old Gamal Abdel Nasser, headed the coup, and their executive command formed the "leadership council of the revolution" following the seizure of power. Nasser remained the actual strong man after General Mohammed Nagib had become prime minister. In the ensuing power struggle, the Muslim Brotherhood sided with the official head of government and lost.

Several of the leading Free Officers, particularly Abdel Moneim Abdel Rauf, were members of the Muslim Brotherhood. The movement also maintained close contact with an old acquain-

tance of Hassan al-Banna, Captain Anwar el-Sadat. The young
Sadat had long been sympathetic to the Muslim leader. In his
biography, *In Search of Identity*, Sadat described a speech by al-
Banna that he had heard in 1940 while still a young lieutenant:

His choice of topic was excellent, his comprehension and his interpretation of the religion thorough, and the manner of his speech expres-
sive. From all standpoints, in fact, he was the best qualified to be a
religious leader. In addition, he was a genuine Egyptian: humorous,
respectable, and patient. . . . This man spoke of secular matters and
also spoke about the hereafter. For a religious preacher, his style was
extremely unusual. My admiration for him was boundless. . . . I was
very impressed by his splendid organization of the Muslim Brotherhood
and also by the respect, even the extraordinary veneration, accorded
this highest leader. Members of the organization treated him almost like
a saint. They almost even kneeled before me, and were on the verge of
kissing the floor I walked on, merely because he had invited me to visit
him in his office.

During Anwar el-Sadat's years of arrest in the famous Cell 54,
the Muslim Brotherhood helped his family by paying the rent
and contributing money for their support—ten pounds per
month. Sadat was filled with gratitude, but at the same time
careful: "Without doubt, the Muslim Brotherhood was a power
that one could not offend with impunity." Toward the end of his
life, he seems to have suppressed this early insight.

The Muslim Brotherhood refused to participate in the new Republican administration, but they exploited it thoroughly in order
to gain more liberties than any other political group in the country. Their state within the state became increasingly powerful,
and by 1954 seemed to constitute a danger for Nasser, as no
administration could long assert itself beside the Muslim Brotherhood. Thus, in January 1954, the cabinet again ordered that the
Brotherhood be dissolved.

Many members of the Muslim Brotherhood—among them al-
Hudaibi, who a short while previously had ousted el-Sanadi from
power—were jailed in August, but they were again released during the climax of the test of strength between Nasser and Nagib.
The armed clashes and demonstrations increased, particularly
after the signing of the British-Egyptian treaty covering troop
withdrawal. On October 26, 1954, seven days after the historic
event, the charismatic Gamal Abdel Nasser spoke before 10,000
workers in Alexandria. Suddenly Mahmud Abdel Latif, a mem-

ber of the Muslim Brotherhood from Embamba near Cairo, fired nine shots at Nasser, without wounding him. Nasser considered this attack a provocation calling for complete destruction of the Muslim Brotherhood. Through drastic measures, including rigorous punishments and constant monitoring, the secret police managed to force the Muslim Brotherhood to its knees for the next sixteen years. When there were rumblings of renewed opposition in 1965, Nasser suspected a coup in the making and again eliminated the leadership of the Muslim Brotherhood. Until his death in 1970, he had no further problems with the radical Islamic movement.

Characteristically, in the relationship between al-Azhar University, which purports to be the highest authority of Islamic faith, and the Muslim Brotherhood, whose members consider themselves the only true believers, conflicts have been initiated by both sides. In response to the murder of Nukrashi Pasha and the attack on Nasser, and again in 1965, the *ulemas* of al-Azhar published a *fatwa* (a religious interpretation of the law). In 1965 the Grand Sheikh of al-Azhar condemned the Muslim Brotherhood in these words: "Terrorist groups have managed to distort Islamic teaching and to provide false interpretations to a group of beginners. A religious orientation cannot be inoculated by force or terror. . . . God knows what responsibility Egypt and its leaders are now carrying on their shoulders. He is leading them and is protecting them against betrayers and enemies."

The "betrayers and enemies" were not silent. Their condemnation of the Azharis sounded still more agitated: "So O head of the government, O men of the true Azhar, O members of the organizations and parties, O patriots of this country—O to all of you who are its children, I address these words: Return to Islam, use the opportunity, become Muslims again!"

Hassan al-Hudaibi was condemned to death during the lengthy trial against the Brotherhood which followed the attempted assassination of Nasser. Later, however, he was pardoned and sentenced to compulsory labor for life. Still, for six members of the Muslim Brotherhood, including the perpetrators, the sentence was death. Al-Hudaibi's cell neighbor, Mustafa Amin, reported in his memoirs how provocatively friendly the head of the Brotherhood was toward his torturers. When they rebuked or beat him, he merely smiled. Once al-Hudaibi is reputed to have told his people: "You are the stronger. I do not blame the persecuted when they scream in pain. I do not blame those who have been stabbed when their blood spots my clothing. I do not ask you for mercy, but I ask you to take the matter before God, the Avenger, the Irresistible One. God's punishments are more severe than all those you could inflict against your tormentors."

The background of the turbulence on October 26, 1954, was long unknown. Only with the publication of the memoirs of General Mohammed Nagib, the first president of Egypt, was some light shed on the matter. In the chapter "Between Abdel Nasser and Sadat," Nagib states:

With sound mind and clear reason I intend to disclose for the first time one of the greatest and most secret concerns of the July Revolution of 1952, and I swear to tell the truth and nothing but the truth. The alleged plot to kill Abdel Nasser in 1954 in Alexandria was invented and lied about from the beginning to the end. The attack was hatched by a CID [secret service] officer who was rewarded with an attractive governmental post for his successful plan. That only can I confirm, since the details of the plot were related to me by one of my agents before they were carried out.

Mohammed Nagib further confirmed this version in an interview with the Arabic-language magazine *Al Shark al Awsat*, which is published in London. When I interviewed Nagib in Cairo, he repeated his statements to me in a somewhat more cautious form: "At that time the Muslim Brotherhood did not have a particularly good reputation. They did not support my suggestion to subvert the army. I do not believe that they subsequently wanted to shoot Nasser. Everything points to the secret service."

The ideas of the Brotherhood—"The realm of God is our fatherland, the Koran our constitution, the Prophet our leader, holy war our route"—could not be stamped out. With the change of leadership in Cairo, the ill-treated members of the Muslim Brotherhood gradually returned to freedom. All had been tortured, many executed. Omar el-Telmisani recalls his seventeen years in prison: "In the year 1954 I was hung up like a slaughtered cow. They put me on a chair, bound and tied me to the ceiling, and then removed the chair, so I hung in the air like a slaughtered animal at the butcher's. The young people who experienced such torture were simply unable to imagine that such deeds could be conceived and carried out by believers."

The new president, Anwar el-Sadat, opened the prison gates.

By May 15, 1971, the Muslim Brotherhood had again become a force when the pro-Soviet wing of the Arab Socialist Unity Party under Ali Sabri lost its influence. Vice-President Ali Sabri and his group constituted the biggest danger for Sadat. Following the expulsion of the powerful rival, the so-called corrective revolution, Egypt's liberalizaton process—the great turning away from the despot Gamal Abdel Nasser—got under way. The Muslim Brotherhood won back the sympathy of the Egyptian masses, not the least because of the humiliating defeat in the Six-Day War against Israel in 1967. The Muslim Brotherhood was ready with the argument that the humiliation was God's punishment for the nationalistic government's rejection of the true Islam.

Anwar el-Sadat never lifted the ban against the Brotherhood; he merely tolerated it. This tolerance and the worldwide resurgence of Islam encouraged the Muslim Brotherhood once again to build up its far-flung organizational structure in the country of its origin. In accordance with tradition, the oldest authority, Omar el-Telmisani, took over the leadership in 1976. In 1978, through Sadat's generosity, the publication *Al Dawa* was again distributed. Chief editor Omar el-Telmisani fashioned this publication into a militant paper opposing governmental policy, particularly the peace accords of Camp David. Surprisingly enough, the aggressive tone of *Al Dawa* was not questioned. The paper of the illegal Muslim Brotherhood continued to appear regularly up to within a few weeks of Sadat's death.

During the peace negotiations with Israel, the Muslim Brotherhood issued the following statement:

The Palestine problem must be taken out of the narrow regional framework and again placed on the broad Islamic horizon. A suitable place must be created for an aware Islamic education within the shadow of the liberties which Islam defends, and the *ummah* [people of God] must be prepared to rise up and throw themselves into the decisive battle whenever the suitable opportunity presents itself. If this route should be arduous and long, it is nonetheless the route which God—He is sublime—chose for us; it is elevation to his work and strengthening for the *ummah.* For the Muslim there is no redemption in the choice of a different route from this. . . . The soil of Palestine in its entirety is usurped Islamic soil. For this reason, the *jihad* is obligatory and is in fact an individual obligation for the Muslims in order once again to regain everything that was occupied in 1967 and previously."

An Appointment with the Supreme Guide

Omar el-Telmisani had me picked up punctually at the appointed time at my Cairo hotel by a chauffeur in a van. Beside me sat a gentle older man wearing a prayer cap, who introduced himself as Secretary Gamal Fawzy. He prepared me for the appointment with the highest leader of the Muslim Brotherhood. It was to be his first meeting with a Western journalist.

Omar el-Telmisani lives in El Zaher, one of the poor sections of Cairo. His apartment is dark. A room with a bay window serves as his work space; another room is used for meetings. (I am unable to see the other spaces.) In his workroom, which is lit by a lamp containing four neon bulbs, we sit on couches opposite each other. The plaster is crumbling from the walls. A small Luxor television stands on a small table; in front of it are five packages of medication. Omar el-Telmisani is fighting age.

A gray telephone on a small table is within reach in front of the Amir. Tea is served, and with it sugar from a green plastic container and sweets marketed under the name "Rosina." El-Telmisani has the most important books, including of course the Koran, beside him, at his fingertips. Wearing a hooded *galabia* and a wool sweater and socks underneath, my host could be an elderly pensioner living on a meager allowance (which is actually how he presents himself). Immediately after the brief but polite greeting, he assures me, "I am not an important man, just an ordinary person."

His expression looks otherwise. Omar el-Telmisani is a tall man with snow-white hair and a white beard on his chin and cheeks; he calls to mind historical associations. This is how the "old man from the mountain" of Marco Polo's time must have been— proud, inflexible, self-aware, energetic, a leader. Omar el-Telmisani does not answer every question; some he decisively rejects without much explanation. The telephone rings repeatedly; long-distance calls come through. The overriding impression is of a manager with power, and in fact his Muslim adherents number in the millions. His appearance is simple and modest—just the way he understands his faith.

Omar el-Telmisani, born in 1904, comes from an extremely pious Cairo family. Since his grandfather was a convinced fundamentalist, Omar el-Telmisani had heard of Ibn Taimiya and Ibn Abdul Wahhab by age ten. He learned the Koran by heart at an early age. While studying law, he was the model student when it came to Islamic law. In his own words: "Although after graduation I could have accepted a position as state prosecutor or worked in the court, I preferred a job as a lawyer, since by nature I trust only my morality and faith."

In 1933 el-Temisani met members of the Muslim Brotherhood for the first time, including Imam al-Banna. He was so impressed by al-Banna that he decided to become a member of the conspiratorial organization. During the general hunt for members of the Muslim Brotherhood in 1954, he was arrested and incarcerated for seventeen years in various camps and prisons. He comments:

I always worked in the group and shared everything with other members—their joys and sorrows as well as their mistakes and their good deeds—and I stuck by each one of them. In 1965, a difficult year, several people asked me: "You are a man of peace, what compels you to remain in this group, which in many respects is condemned?" I answered: "I joined this group in order to work for God (the Sublime One be praised). Apart from that, I have no other goal. But if a group, as a result of its deeds—regardless of whether they are wrong or right— finds itself in a crisis that affects all its members, I find it immoral for a person to withdraw from the group in situations of danger."

Omar el-Telmisani was a member of the old leadership from 1933 to 1954. When he was released from prison in 1971, he received a pension—sixty pounds a month, he repeatedly stressed. "I have no wealth," he insisted, "nothing but time, and that I use for the cause." Is the high Muslim leader married? I wondered. In his words: "I am the first person to respect a woman; I was the happiest husband in the world. I lived for fifty-three years with my wife (God be merciful to her), and we never had any basic differences. She was very mild when I was cross, very patient and generous, and she made me happy, even during the time of arrest. She was the model of the good wife."

At this point we turned to my underlying questions.

"What does the Muslim Brotherhood want?"
"We have again reminded all Muslims on earth of Allah's command. We continually prove that our faith includes not only prayer, sacrifice, pilgrimage, and fasting, but business and politics as well. We have a just system, and with that we show that all people are equal, whether the ruled or the rulers, Muslim or non-Muslim. In the true Islamic idea there is no suppression, no

misuse of the other, just peace everywhere. Contrary to what our enemies maintain, Hassan al-Banna's idea was not violent. We are the enemies of no one, not even of the Jews. We want only to live our Islam."

"How do you see the phenomenon of the resurgence of Islam?"
"The resurgence of Islam was not initiated by the Muslim Brotherhood. It is a completely natural thing. What in the past was lost to us in terms of good thoughts is now being retrieved. The result is in God's hands. We will pray that all people wake up and find the true faith. Only that can bring peace to the whole world."

"Many people in the Western world fear that a danger emanates from the Muslim Brotherhood."
"At the most, what exists is a dangerous environment for Islam. We do not topple governments; we commit no assassinations. We have no plans to murder. It is not our goal to take over governments. We want merely to live in a country whose government is truly Islamic and in which Islamic laws shape the reality, for our faith constitutes the highest fortune in life."

"Is there already an Islamic state of the kind you want for yourself?"
"Not yet. We consider all Islamic countries as brother states—without differences."

"Do you want to do missionary work with your faith? Is the export of Islam and its ideals important to you?"
"Everywhere in the world, without a doubt. We are spreading our ideas in Germany, France, England, America, Spain, Belgium, and Holland. In the process we are doing missionary work within Christianity, but we are also doing missionary work within Islam. That is completely normal."

The Muslim Brotherhood makes no claim to being a political party, but it does claim to be an Islamic union. That changes nothing in the organizational structure, which is strictly secret. The various levels of the organization mostly know nothing of each other; only chosen persons maintain connections, which in all important matters occur exclusively by courier. The smallest unit of the Brotherhood is the *usra* (family). It comprises the members of a district who meet weekly for readings from the Koran, training, and discussion. Two families constitute a squadron, several squadrons a branch, and several branches the regions of the country. Together, the leaders of the countries make up the so-called International Committee.

Because of the uncertain situation in the Middle East, this highest, top-secret organ of the Brotherhood often changes its membership for security reasons. Its leaders in various countries are constantly in danger of being imprisoned because of their activities. The representatives of Sudan (Hassan al-Turabi) and Turkey (Necmettin Erbakan) are particularly at risk. Omar el-Telmisani was even interned again for several months during 1981 in the notorious Tura Prison in Cairo.

The Egyptian is the supreme commander of the International Committee since he is recognized by almost all the lesser leaders and also comes from the movement's country of origin. The International Committee meets whenever there is a reason, and then preferably in the West. Once it met in Germany. In 1979 news of a meeting in London leaked out; the leftist Beirut paper *As Safir* reported that the leaders of the Brotherhood from Egypt, Syria, the Sudan, Jordan, Pakistan, and Afghanistan had gathered in London. The Saudi Arabian head of secret service, Adham, was also present at the meeting, since Saudia Arabia is one of the most important contributors to the organization.

The leadership of the Brotherhood disputes the allegation that dissension within the International Committee followed Khomeini's assumption of power in Iran. Several well-informed members confirm this report, however. Many members of the Muslim Brotherhood admire the Khomeini revolution and have provided him with assistance. The older generation of the Brotherhood, however, remains true to their own line and opposes the Khomeini revolution. As one of their spokesmen, whom I met in Cairo, expressed their position: "Our Koran states that one is not permitted to end one crime by committing another. Therefore we cannot blindly follow the Iranian model." The entire region is carefully observing what is happening in Iran. In the present situation in the Arab world, open support would be disastrous, unleashing a new wave of persecution against the Muslim Brotherhood. Support for Khomeini, for instance, would lose the last bit of sympathy for the Muslim Brotherhood by such moderate regimes as that in Jordan. Moreover, el-Telmisani notes, Tehran maintains friendly relations with Damascus, and between Assad and the Brotherhood there is now a state of war.

How does one become a member of this secret organization? Any believing Muslim can apply. After a period as an "aspirant," during which the applicant acquires extensive knowledge of the faith, he is permitted to move up to the status of "member brother." If he proves himself for a long time, he is considered ready to be a "genuine Muslim," to pledge himself completely to the Brotherhood and to be taken into the group of the "activists." He must provide detailed information about his life, as well as a passport photo, for a kind of personal record sheet; he must also draw up a personal plan for memorizing the Koran and forty of the Prophet's sayings, and participate in training at both summer and winter camps.

It is only the activist who commits himself to the special doctrine of the Muslim Brotherhood who gets to know its precise structure. The *zakat* paid by the activist to the organization is an alms tax stipulated by the Koran, which is no longer collected by any Islamic state except Pakistan. The Muslim Brotherhood uses this money for social services, and when necessary pays support money. Any activist who has proved himself in some particular way is permitted to become a *mujahed* (fighter for the faith). Membership in the military wing of the movement, however, is not open to everyone; it carries special obligations and requires strict religious duties. The *mujahed* makes contributions to the International Committee and to a "treasury for the propagation of Islam." He must will a part of his wealth to the Brotherhood.

The Muslim Brotherhood is by no means alone in its activities —there is also a Muslim Sisterhood, which was founded in 1933 in Ismailia by Hassan al-Banna as the Institute for the Mothers of the Faithful. Before it was possible officially to form the Muslim Sisterhood, however, opposition by members of the Muslim Brotherhood had to be overcome. By 1944 that was possible, and by 1948 there were 5,000 women members. The Sisterhood concerned itself primarily with the families of prisoners, but its members were also taken into custody in large numbers whenever the Egyptian government made a roundup of the Brotherhood. When I met the chairperson of the Sisterhood, Zeinab al-Ghazali al-Gebeily, in Cairo, she reported an active membership of 200 groups, or two million women in the entire Islamic world. The figure has been rising, reflecting the growth of the new Islamic consciousness.

The childless Zeinab al-Ghazali is a resolute woman, who

speaks with a clear, deep voice, stressing each word. I asked her about the basic position of the Muslim Sisterhood.

"The members of the Muslim Sisterhood are the heart of the Islamic movement," she replied. "Together with the Muslim Brotherhood, we should like to teach people the correct Islamic position. Then the women can continue the instruction by themselves in their families and in the entire society."

"How far do the Islamic women want to go in their activity for the faith?" I inquired. "Are you also permitted to participate in *jihad?*"

"In every respect," she affirmed. "Since the time of the prophets, the women have fought in the medical sector as well as in the realm of nutrition. If it were necessary now, we would also fight with weapons beside the men."

In some countries that is already happening. But compared with all other Islamic movements, the Muslim Brotherhood is at present peaceful and moderate (other than in Syria). In striving toward the resurgence of Islam, no movement has had to invest more. That creates mistrust and utmost caution. Many men holding high positions in the Brotherhood now occupy key positions in the Islamic world. They head ministries and universities, run large economic enterprises, and counsel heads of state. Under these circumstances, they can patiently await the day that will permit the realization of their model society. The Muslim Brotherhood has become a synonym for a far more extensive development in the Arab world. Economic difficulties and demographic-political problems may increase, but the refuge in faith remains an alternative. Time is on the side of the Muslim Brotherhood.

The Violent Underground Groups

The numerous small and medium-sized fundamentalist fighting units constitute a danger, for it is impossible to estimate their numbers. In Egypt alone, thirty were allegedly discovered since Sadat's death. The one called Takfir wal Hejra (proclaimed unbelievers who have emigrated) is an extremely radical group. The name itself was actually given by the police, who didn't know what to call this group (the extremists simply called themselves "Islamic group"). In time, however, the extremists came to like this name and retained it.

Takfir wal Hejra came into being, as did almost all new Islamic movements, following the defeat in the six-day war with Israel in 1967. In the early '70s, the radicals found it easy to form groups, as President Anwar el-Sadat had his hands full coping with the Nasserist opposition and he did not concern himself with the Islamic home front. Takfir wal Hejra was unmasked on June 1, 1975, when the daily *Al Ahram* reported its existence. It turned out that Takfir wal Hejra was founded by a twenty-eight-year-old agricultural engineer and former member of the Muslim Brotherhood, Shukri Ahmed Mustafa.

This group, outwardly completely secret, quickly became known for its inflexibility. Its members controlled each other to the utmost. The fanatics of Takfir wal Hejra regarded their amir, Mustafa, as Allah's representative on earth and were unconditionally devoted to him. Takfir wal Hejra was and is so ultra-radical that it even considers prayer in the mosque to be wicked; without exception, it rejects Egyptian society as corrupt, Westernized, immoral, and sinful. Members of its sects must first sever all personal ties and withdraw into the desert; they are allowed to marry only among themselves. In the desert and in their cave retreats—usually in Upper and Central Egypt in the vicinity of Minia and Assiut—they are permitted only to pray. They are also required to complete a grueling military training program. Only after this interlude do the members, who wear long *galabias* and bushy beards, return to society for the purpose of reforming it— by force if necessary.

By the early 1970s, members of Takfir wal Hejra held positions in ministries, universities, and the Egyptian army, even in the Muchabarat Harbeya, the military secret service. Eleven members of the Takfir wal Hejra were first arrested in May 1975, with others arrested in 1976 and in January 1977. During the night of July 2, 1977, one of the group's squads abducted the former minister of religion, Sheikh Mohammed Hussein al-Dhahabi, who was a liberal theologian, member of the Azhar establishment, and author of numerous books attacking religious fanaticism. The abduction occurred in Heluan, south of Cairo, and the ransom demanded included a fee of 200,000 Egyptian pounds and the liberation of sixty militant prisoners.

The authorities refused the demands, and Takfir wal Hejra subsequently sent back the corpse of the former minister. A systematic hunt for the religious terrorists began. The sect bombed a movie house and music school that was headed by a brother-in-law of Sadat. On July 8, 1977, the police seized Shukri Ahmed Mustafa and fifteen of his followers; the next day they arrested Mustafa's representative, Anwar Mamun Sakr. August 23 marked the start of the trial conducted by a military tribunal against 465 of the 620 imprisoned members of Takfir wal Hejra.

Then there was another incident. The accused seized their guards. By the time the police freed their colleagues, six uniformed men and ten prisoners had been wounded. The sentence was handed down on November 20, 1977: the five ringleaders, among them Mustafa, were condemned to death and were executed on March 19, 1978. Their deaths were incomprehensible to ordinary members. An additional 198 members, including 22 women, were given long-term sentences.

During the investigations it was disclosed that the Takfir wal Hejra had received support from Egyptians who had emigrated to the Gulf states to Jordan and North Yemen. Its substantial arsenal of modern automatic weapons (500 guns and many explosives) had been supplied by officers and soldiers of the Egyptian army, who were also members. Abdel Halim Ramadan, who later defended the assassin of Sadat, Khaled Islambuli, represented Shukri Ahmed Mustafa during the big terrorist trial of 1977. At the time Professor Ali Greisha, a member of the Muslim Brotherhood, was a judge of the highest court, and he had close contacts with his colleagues concerned with the Takfir wal Hejra case. He presented me with the following thesis:

I am of the opinion that the government itself instigated the abduction of the minister of religion in order to find a pretext for crushing the Islamic movement in Egypt. There are three proofs of this: one of the accused admitted in court that he had been sent by the secret service to Takfir as a spy. Second, the government *could* have given in to the demands of the kidnappers before the murder of the abducted minister. Why did the government set the inmates free for a short period of time and then arrest them again? In addition, behind the hunt for our members of the Muslim Brotherhood was none other than Prime Minister Mamdud Salem, who had been head of the secret service for a long time and particularly enjoyed torturing political prisoners.

In November 1979, the guerrilla fighters of Takfir wal Hejra participated in the international commando unit that occupied the Grand Mosque of Mecca. Takfir wal Hejra also proved to be

responsible for the unrest in Assiut in Upper Egypt three days
after Sadat's death. Only after great losses on both sides and the
massive use of parachute troops was this last revolt put down.
And, even so, the radical group is still present in Egypt: according
to unconfirmed reports, 4,000 men are armed.

The leaders of Takfir wal Hejra and other extremist groups
have been influenced by the writings of Hassan al-Banna, Sayed
Qutb, Abul Ala Maududi, and Ali Shariati. In addition, they
maintain contacts with the forbidden Muslim Brotherhood. What
does Omar el-Telmisani say to that?

Shukri Mustafa was an inmate with us in the Tura Prison. During the
entire time I neither saw him nor spoke with him. I do not know him at
all. When several members of the Muslim Brotherhood informed me in
prison that the idea of declaring people to be unbelievers (takfir) had
arisen, I spoke with brother Hassan al-Hudaibi, who was also with us.
He later stated in his book that he forbids any person to declare another
to be a nonbeliever. The idea for Takfir came from a group of young
people who were tortured very brutally while incarcerated and who
later rejected the peaceful direction of the Muslim Brotherhood.

I then asked el-Telmisani about Sayed Qutb and his book *Milestones*, which is the basic guide of the militant fundamentalists.
Omar el-Telmisani answered:

If one reads *Milestones* by Sayed Qutb, one recognizes that he reacted
very strongly to the events in Egypt at that time [in the year 1976].
Perhaps some young people have concluded that the brutal treatment
they received from the government justifies a reaction of force on their
part. . . . How often have I said that the government should give us an
opportunity to speak with the youth in order to teach them to understand? . . . When they were sitting in prison, we sent them lawyers.
But these, too, they declared nonbelievers.

Things were no different with a secret organization that called
itself the Organization for Islamic Liberation (al-Fanniyya al-As-
kariyya). This group, led by a former member of the Muslim
Brotherhood, Dr. Saleh Siriyya, also came to the fore as a result
of the business slump of the early '70s. On April 18, 1974, a squad
of Islamic Liberation members attacked the military academy in
the elegant Cairo suburb of Heliopolis. The goal was to first take
control of the weapons depot and to then move on to the Arab
Socialist Union (ASU), where the top leadership of the country
was listening to a speech by Anwar el-Sadat. On this occasion the

Egyptian elite were to be killed. The terrorists, however, did not get beyond the military academy. As the newspaper *Al Ahram* reported two days later, during a violent gun fight, eleven people (unofficially thirty) died and seventy-two were wounded. The guerrilla troop was defeated. Siriyya and another leader of the group were executed; thirty others were given long-term sentences. This attack came as a big surprise at the time, as the October War against Israel, in which Egypt was generally victorious, had taken place only a few months earlier and Sadat was still riding a wave of popularity.

The security forces became nervous. On June 20, 1974, they uncovered a new movement, the Islamic Liberation Party. Its history is very difficult to trace. Apparently, it was founded in Jordan during the '50s under the name Hizb el-Tahrir el-Islam by a former member of the Muslim Brotherhood, Sheikh Taghiud Din Nabhani, a judge from Haifa. For many years it was active in Israel, Jordan, Lebanon, and Iraq. A high-ranking sheikh told me in Nablus: "Nabhani had his headquarters in Kalkelia, twenty-eight miles north of Nablus. The Tahrir people carried out attacks on Israeli installations. They considered themselves to be absolutely the elite of the Islamic movements and did not want to become an organization of the masses. They accepted only a few new people and firmly believed that the masses would support them after their final victory. In 1967 Tahrir ceased all activities in West Jordan and withdrew to Jordan." In Libya, too, they went into hiding. In Egypt countless numbers of Tahrir members were taken into custody and after a period of time were set free. Amir Nabhani died in 1978.

Things went similarly for the loosely organized, relatively peaceful group called Jamiyat Islamiya, headed by Dr. Hilmi al-Gazzar, a member of the Muslim Brotherhood. Membership in this group was spurred in 1971 by cooperation between Sadat and Qaddafi. This organization, however, never stood out for any particular violence, and it restricted its activities to Egyptian universities.

It was a different matter entirely with a unit by the name of Jund Allah (Soldiers of God). According to a report in the Egyptian magazine *October* (issued on August 28, 1977), 104 of its members, including its founder Eido Osman, were arrested. Two days later *Al Ahram* reported the arrest of eighty people in the fighting organization Jihad (Holy War) in Alexandria. Neither of

the mass arrests was accompanied by heavy gunfire. In both instances the police were well informed and had the upper hand.
The investigative authorities announced that both groups had
planned attacks on police stations and more extensive incidents
against the state. Large quantities of weapons and explosives
were seized from both groups.

The name of Jihad popped up again in 1980. In mid-January
the Egyptian government announced the arrest of seventy members. The chief public prosecutor, Salah el-Rashidi, spoke of a
"fanatic terrorist group." The militant fundamentalists had already been imprisoned in October 1979. For security reasons,
however, the incident was kept secret. According to the descrip-
tion given by the chief public prosecutor, the organization was
financed from abroad and was armed with weapons, explosives,
and technical equipment. Writings had also been seized in which
Jihad called upon the population to revolt against the "un-Islamic
government." Handbills and brochures demanded the return to
fundamentalist Islamic traditions. One of the members who was
arrested admitted having been assigned to make contact with
Palestinian groups by leaders of his organization. The intent was
to organize the military training of the secret cadre.

The Jihad group made the headlines once again on October 6,
1981, when a commando squad under Khaled Islambuli shot
President Anwar el-Sadat. Following arduous investigations during the summer of 1982, it became known in Cairo that the Jihad
group was part of the large family enterprise of the Muslim Brotherhood. When I asked, this was conceded by the Muslim Brotherhood. In the meantime, in a unanimous statement, the Jihad
group "condemned to death" Sadat's successor Mubarak. In September 1982 the three most important leaders of the Jihad group
in Egypt were tracked down and arrested.

An analysis made by Sayid Yassin, director of the Cairo Center
for Strategic Studies, showed numerous parallels between the
organizational structure of most of the new Islamic fighting
groups and the Muslim Brotherhood of the '40s. To him, it seems
that the feared secret organization is coming to life again, more
militant and more dangerous than ever.

The Cairo professor of sociology, Saad Eddin Ibrahim, a middle-aged intellectual who thinks in practical terms, has made the
only large-scale study to date on the rise of Islamic militancy.
During the Sadat era he was able to speak with thirty-four im-

prisoned terrorists. Ranging in age between seventeen and twenty-six, they were all gripped by the militant Islamic idea. Two-thirds of them came from rural districts and were sons of government employees. Ibrahim found that the interviewees were not at all despairing, nor did they seem uprooted. On the contrary, they were clearly motivated and well trained—particularly the students among them. The feeling of solidarity, the warmth provided by the organization, and firm faith drove them forward.

During the years of its suppression in Egypt the Muslim Brotherhood continued to build its branches, under the leadership of Mustafa al-Sibai in Syria, Hassan al-Turabi in the Sudan, Mohammed Abdurrahman Khalifa (also the spokesman of the International Committee) in Jordan, and Said Ramadam (of the Islamic center in Geneva) in Western countries. In other words, they did not have to start again at the beginning. During the 1960s in Iran they promoted the military organization called Fedayane Islam (something like: Kamikaze of Islam) under Navvab Safavi. Their existence proves that the Sunni and Shiites are capable of forgetting all differences when it comes to the defense of the true faith. When the Iranian revolution came closer, the Fedayane Islame slipped into oblivion.

In Kuwait, which is considered extremely pious, a group oriented toward strict fundamentalism, the Salafiyin, took hold, in addition to the already strong Muslim Brotherhood. Salafiyin means those who are adherents to the Islam of the forefathers; its members demand that a caliph elected by the faithful should again rule instead of the sheikhs and kings. In Kuwait the Salafiyin mainly oppose Westernization, corruption, and the neglect of the laws of the Koran. The government has already secretly given in to them by imposing stronger punishments for infractions of the ban on alcohol, ordering more religious broadcasts on radio and television, and announcing the introduction of an exclusively Islamic law. The al-Sabah ruling family knows where the real dangers lie and how quickly the extremists could create serious trouble—regardless of whether the attack comes from Khomeini's Liberation Front for the Gulf, from the very recent Lebanese-Iranian Shiite Jihad Movement, or from the Sunni opposition.

The Pakistani Muslim Brotherhood

Whenever the Muslim Brotherhood and its closely related group got into difficulties, they could depend on finding refuge in Pakistan. The Jamaat-e Islami, an organization quite similar to the Muslim Brotherhood, has been at work there since August 1940. (It has only seemingly been banned since the coup by the Islamic military dictator Zia ul-Haq.) Of all the parties in the country, the Jamaat-e Islami is the best organized, the group most capable of sustaining any test of strength from non-Islamic forces. Its connections to the Indian and Afghan branches are extremely close. Indeed, the Jamaat-e Islami was originally established in India, and has merely changed location since the founding of the state of Pakistan.

In contrast to the Muslim Brotherhood, the Jamaat-e Islami has never maintained a violent secret organization. Whenever violence broke out—for instance, against the Hindus or during the war of secession against East Pakistan—there was a sufficient number of fanatic participants to attack in the name of Allah. The party, however, has never made a particularly good showing in elections. Of the 488 nominated candidates, only eight were elected by the people in 1970. The fundamentalists of Abul Ala Maududi consoled themselves with the thought that with only 2,500 active participants, they had received 2.5 million votes. The Pakistanis have never liked the Jamaat-e Islami, but they have always respected it. Ultimately, it has always been a factor in the power setup, since its members hold positions in schools, universities, the army, and large business enterprises. The military uprising against the secular Islamic ruler Zulfikar Ali Bhutto merely worked in their favor.

A Pakistani writer who, out of fear of revenge, preferred to remain anonymous, told me of his experiences:

The Jamaat-e Islami would receive forty percent of the votes in a free election and the Bhutto party the rest. Nonetheless, the Islamic forces would sooner or later be the victors, because they would not rest until they were in control of power within the state. Broadly scattered sympathy among the poor, as well as among the future intellectual leaders at the universities, works in their favor. They are strictly organized and offer something for the dreariness of leisure in our country. The run-of-the-mill cultural offering is thin—there are few movie houses and clubs, few youth organizations. The Jamaat-e Islami has everything. It exerts strong pressure on all who do not immediately accept what they offer. The organization uses this situation as an opportunity to provide religion. My children tell me about it almost every day. The most important consideration is that Jamaat-e Islami is a factor of the future, since at present this party constitutes an alternative to the washed-out ideologies of the others.

On the tracks of the banned Jamaat-e Islami, which is extremely active in Lahore Mansurah headquarters, I repeatedly encountered new names for their subdivisions. In Peshawar, the border city on the Khyber Pass, the group is now called Idara Ahyaul Uloom, or Institute for the Renaissance of Knowledge—a flowery name that would not deter the secret police if they wished to undertake anything against the fundamentalists. Closely connected is the Institute for Regional Studies, which is housed in a villa. This is the site from which the war in Afghanistan is portrayed in words and in writing from the Islamic point of view. (Religious writings of all kinds are translated into Russian and taken on remote mountain byways through Afghanistan into the Asiatic provinces of the Red Kingdom.)

At the Jamaat-e Islami in Peshawar, I met the local representative, Dr. Murad Ali Shah. In a non-stop outpouring, he explained to me that the Germans unjustly felt themselves guilty for the death of the Jews. After all, it was war. Moreover, the West was noticeably deteriorating and was coming under the all-consuming Israeli influence. Israel and the Soviet Union would make common cause, he asserted, and would very soon confront the rest of the world with a big surprise.

Qazi Hussain Ahmad, the supreme secretary general of Jamaat-e Islami, came more to the point. He was wearing a white Pashtoon suit and a *karakul* cap when he received me. The squat man's full beard was gray-white, and behind his black-rimmed glasses his alert, friendly eyes moved animatedly back and forth.

By the summer of 1982, he explained, Jamaat-e Islami had 4,500 full members and a million sympathizers and supporters. Its basis is the message of the omnipotent God in its pure form, as propagated by his Prophet Mohammed. "We preach this message and would like everyone to order their lives in accordance with it," he told me. "That is the message of the Jamaat-e Islami of Pakistan. And we have chosen this country in order to provide an example to the world." The Jamaat-e Islami also works toward the pure Islamic state, Qazi Hussain Ahmad added. After we were presented with a bowl piled full of fruit, plus tea and cake, he continued, "In my opinion, communism and capitalism have much in common. Both are materialistically oriented. In our world we want to create a spiritually elevated civilization. With the others, this is an entirely different matter. The secretary general was unable to name an already-existing, genuinely Islamic state. He does not think of Pakistan in that context, although "General Zia ul-Haq is striving for it." That at least is something. I asked him further questions:

"What should the Jamaat-e Islami state look like?"
"It should provide peace, brotherhood, and spiritual life. That we will show in practice when we achieve power."

"How will things look in actual practice? Will there also be a parliament?"
"Yes, of course. A parliament is planned, because we believe in democracy for all those areas not covered by the guidance of the Koran and *sunna.*"

"What does the Jamaat-e Islami want to change?"
"We are striving for moral changes. We want the men at the helm to provide the simple people with a good example. We want to eliminate corruption, both moral and financial."

Like the Muslim Brotherhood, the Jamaat-e Islami also has a strong tie to Europe—in the form of the Islamic Foundation, which is housed in an elegant villa in Leicester in England. The Islamic Foundation was established in 1973 by the present chief ideologist of the Jamaat-e Islami, Professor Kurshid Ahmad, for the purpose of spreading the faith in the West and providing assistance to fundamentalists. But Khurshid Ahmad, for a brief period minister of economics under Zia ul-Haq and at present the most important Islamic expert in the economic sector, has again left his academic research institute, since the entire Muslim world needs him. He continues, however, to direct the Institute for Political Studies in Islamabad, a mouthpiece of a reawakened Islamic that is closely allied with Jamaat-e Islami.

During a visit with his successor in Leicester, Khurram Murad, I asked about the organizational structure under Pakistani martial law. "Jamaat-e Islami exists at home, but simply under another name," he replied. "However," he continued, "we have our branches in various states, but all with different names. That can be in the U.S.A. and Canada or here in England. There are groups working informally all over the Middle East." He did not confirm that the Islamic Foundation cooperates closely with the international branch of the Muslim Brotherhood.

During my discussions with leading representatives of the Jamaat-e Islami, no explanation was ever given for the fact that the party actually consists of two flanks that disagree ideologically. On the one side stands Khurshid Ahmad, who represents the Karachi faction, which originated in India and which would like to provide Pakistan with a system of parties. The leader of the party headquarters in Lahore, Muhammad Tufail, follows the position of Abul Ala Maududi and his admirer General Zia ul-Haq, who is Tufail's nephew. According to their thinking, there should be only one party, the party of Allah. Officially Muhammad Tufail has a dual existence. Since the ban on Jamaat-e Islami, he is no longer permitted to call himself "amir," so he is now "Founding Member of the Council of Mosques." This is a subcommittee of the League of the Islamic World in Saudi Arabia, which is the financial backer of Jamaat-e Islami.

Pakistan's fundamentalists must repeatedly learn new concepts in order to be able to function in their offices with dignity. As stated by Abul Ala Maududi, who in cases of doubt also approves force: "But man is so constituted that there are two aspects to his life, there are two separated realms of his activity. There is the sphere in which he feels himself completely dominated by the divine law. . . . But there is another area of his activity, for he is equipped with reason and intellect: he has the capacity to think and to form an opinion, to will and not to will, to accept and to reject."

Guerrillas of Islam in the Far East

The Masjumi Party, founded in November 1934, is striving for a theocracy in Indonesia, the most populous Islamic country in the world. Masjumi, which stands for Consultative Council of Indonesian Muslims, draws its membership from the Muhammadiya movement. Muhammad Natsir, the most important Islamic reformer in the region, became prime minister after the war of liberation against the Dutch in 1950; he prefers to concentrate his attention on the educational sector. In the 1950s, the Masjumi Party received twenty percent of the vote, making it the strongest party, closely followed by the more conservative Muslim party, called Nahdatul Ulema. Neither party succeeded in creating a unified Islamic state, because President Ahmed Sukarno, who in 1945 had led the country to independence, knew how to stop them. What Sukarno had in mind was more a one-man democracy.

In 1958 the repressed Islamists of Sumatra tried to topple the unpopular head of state in a hasty coup. That failed. Masjumi was banned by Sukarno, and Muhammad Natsir was jailed. After the fall of Sukarno, the Islamic party was again permitted to exist under the new designation of Parmusi. In 1971 the religious parties were required to blend into the United Development Party, and received only 30 percent of the vote. The fundamentalists had failed in Indonesia. That could only occur because Masjumi —in contrast to the Muslim Brotherhood (to which it is related), and to some extent in contrast to the Jamaat-e Islami—had always functioned as a registered, legal party; it had no secret apparatus and no provisions for underground work. Nonetheless, time has worked in favor of the Islamic forces of Indonesia. Although the number of overt followers has diminished as a result of military pressure, the popular ideology of Islam cannot be suppressed. Its representatives know that the days of the corrupt and inefficient generals and colonels are numbered.

In this way, their position is more favorable than that of their brothers at the eastern end of the Islamic world, the Philippines. There a violent underground war led by the Muslim Moro National Liberation Front (MNLF) has been raging against the dictatorship of President Ferdinand Marcos since 1969. Allegedly the battles have already taken a toll of 60,000. The Moro National Liberation Front is fighting for the autonomy of the southern islands; it is supported by Libya's Qadaffi, by Malaysia, Saudi Arabia, and Indonesia. Should the Moros, mostly led by their chief ideologist Nur Musuari, a former student official and instructor of political science at the University of Manila, gain the upper hand, then they, too, want to establish a theocracy based on the Prophet's example.

The crop sowed by Hassan al-Banna, Sayed Qutb, Ruhollah Mussavi Khomeini, and all the other revolutionaries of the faith is growing. The Tehran daily newspaper *Kayhan* wrote in one of its lead articles in August 1982:

Today the battle against all our enemies is a necessity for our existence and survival. Islam is in danger. For this reason, Sunnis and Shiites should join together to fight against their enemies. The enemy has mobilized against Islam, not only against Sunnis and Shiites. Even if we—incorrectly—assume that the Sunnis were not revolutionary and only rarely rebelled against the ruling regime, they should nonetheless start with a far-flung Islamic movement.

Islam against the rest of the world?

5

The Death of the Pharaoh

OCTOBER 6, 1981, began like all holidays in Cairo. Egyptians who could afford it were already in their weekend houses in Alexandria or in the Nile delta. On this particular morning traffic flowed somewhat more smoothly than usual, but by no means more quietly. A blue sky and, for Egypt, mild temperatures were conducive to family outings. People were looking forward to the Muslim celebration of Bayram two days ahead.

As every child there knows, October 6 is a national holiday in Egypt. Starting early in the morning, radio and television continuously explain that the country on the Nile is celebrating its regained national honor. The Yom Kippur War against Israel began on October 6, 1973. At 1:00 P.M. on that date Egyptian units from the Sinai and Syrian troops met on the Golan Heights for the attack. By evening the Egyptians had conquered twenty-five of the thirty-two armed positions of the Bar-Lev line on the eastern side of the Suez Canal. It was the biggest day in President Anwar el-Sadat's life. His triumph restored self-confidence to the Egyptian nation—"and also the trust of the world," he said. The eighth anniversary of this triumph was to be the day of Sadat's death.

On this day Mohammed Anwar el-Sadat, spoiled by success and at the time inclining toward injustice and an erroneous assessment of the domestic political situation, felt himself "under the protection of the people." The people, however, viewed him with increasing mistrust. In a moderately good mood, he ate breakfast around 9:00 A.M. at his villa in the Dokki section of Cairo, which offered a view of the Nile flowing sluggishly past. This morning he was wearing, as he did for all military occasions, the blue uniform of the field marshal, with its green sash covered with gold stars and an Egyptian heraldic eagle. All his military insignia were displayed on the left, the "Star of Sinai" on his collar. An escort secured the route to the Ministry of Defense, where his host, Lieutenant General Abdel Halim Abu Ghazala, and a number of army commanders awaited him. Sadat's appointment with the top brass was for 10:30 A.M.

By this time, a twenty-four-year-old artillery lieutenant, Khaled Ahmed el-Islambuli, had already been on his feet for seven hours. Since sunrise he had prayed twice to Allah and begged for divine assistance in his bold plan: "Allah, I am doing it in Your name. I will punish him for his impiety." The thin, well-trained Islambuli was in the company of friends—the book dealer Abdul Hamid Abdussalam Ali, the engineer Ata Tayal Hamida, and the noncommissioned reserve officer Hussain Abbas Mohammed. All wore the olive-green combat uniform of the Egyptian army.

The quartet did not speak much. The men, ranging in age from twenty to thirty, communicated with glances—there was not much more to say. Each of them knew what he had to do. Thousands of soldiers and officers of the army and navy were gathering in the Medinet Nasr section of the city. One after another the vehicles closed ranks in an order determined by protocol to form a vast column. Everyone was waiting for the beginning of the big parade of troops. Nervous military and secret police once more explored the terrain and eyed the chatting groups of soldiers. For three days every weapon, every truck, every tank had been checked by the security division. It was absolutely forbidden to bring along live ammunition. For four weeks the parade had been rehearsed. Dozens of times the units (including Islambuli's) had had to pace off the dusty street between the sleepy town of Medinet Nasr and Abbasia, where they were to end up, and repeatedly they had passed by the pompous honorary reviewing stand. Nothing suggested that anything would be different this time.

No one within the enormous administrative apparatus was concerned when Lieutenant Khaled Islambuli reported the breakdown of his Soviet Zil-151 truck equipped with a North Korean 130-millimeter cannon. He sent it back early in the morning, and it was left to him to see about a prompt replacement. Everyone, except the driver of the truck, was in the know about the planned deed, and they were prepared by a week of training. Ammunition and hand grenades had been in their possession since 4:30 A.M. The equipment had been concealed in a house in the Benha Street near the Pyramids.

In keeping with tradition, Sadat and the officers went to the grave of Gamal Abdel Nasser and said a prayer. There Sadat switched to an open black Cadillac, which was protected by eight bodyguards. He mentioned to Vice-President Hosni Mubarak that he would prefer not to have to review the parade. Mubarak advised him to go home and relax, but Sadat referred to his duty to participate in the celebration of the nation's great day. Immediately afterward, though, he would fly to his native village of Mit Abu el Kum and visit the grave of his brother, who had been killed on October 6, 1973. He then wanted to commemorate the sacrifice with his family. He was looking forward to seeing his grandson Sherif.

Opposite the free-standing reviewing stand and within view of the concrete houses of Nasser City stands the triangular war monument, which is where Sadat's entourage stopped. The president placed a wreath on the grave of the unknown soldier before entering the reviewing stand, which was already full. Anwar el-Sadat shook hands with the honorary guests and moved toward the middle of the first row, just behind the balustrade.

The area in which Sadat sat formed a kind of four-cornered protrusion from the large reviewing stand. In this section, which was accessible only to personally invited guests of the president, there were approximately 100 people. They sat on green, thickly upholstered chairs with high arm rests. The floor was covered with expensive red-green carpets.

At 11:00 A.M. Anwar el-Sadat took his place in his stone loge. Its front showed a relief with a motif from the Balkan War from the previous century, with the Egyptian army under Muhammad

Ali and Ibrahim Pasha. Behind and beside Sadat sat the most important figures in Egyptian political life, as well as foreign guests of the state and diplomats from all over the world. Beside Sadat were Sheikh Mohammed Bisar, the leader of thirty-four million Egyptian Sunni Muslims; Presidential Assistant Said Marai; Minister of Defense Abu Ghazala; Vice-President Hosni Mubarak; Sultan Qabus Said from Oman; and Egypt's former prime minister, Mandonh Salem.

More than an hour passed before Khaled Islambuli and his accomplices started out on the route to the sealed-off parade street. The Egyptians had long ceased feeling close to their president. With few exceptions, they simply watched this festivity on television. They looked at a large video image of their *rais*, or leader, and saw how reverentially he listened to the introductory *sura* from the Koran. This parade was to occur in the name of Allah. Sadat nodded with strong approval when the minister of defense, in his opening remarks, explained that "history judges people through their deeds." Then Sadat leaned back to follow the two-hour proceedings. He repeatedly conversed with Mubarak and Ghazala. Sadat proudly pointed out where old Soviet weapons had been replaced by newly arrived American models.

The show proceeded with much sound and fanfare. Cannons shot off small parachutes that bore Egyptian flags and portraits of Sadat back to earth. With chains rattling, highly polished M-60 tanks from the U.S. rolled past by threes. The Hagganah border troop, wearing turbans, rode by on their camels. Sadat greeted them in military fashion, then again leaned back in his chair, drew on his pipe, and finally took off his cap as the sun's noontime rays became increasingly hot. The air force demonstrated a parachute maneuver and showed the newest helicopters. A formation of six Mirage fighters thundered so low above the onlookers that many put their hands over their ears. Through his binoculars Sadat got a close view of the flying feats of these supersonic craft. Their trail of smoke painted the Egyptian national colors—red, blue, orange, green, and grey—in the sky. The parade was coming to an end. Hardly anyone was focusing on the vehicles with the Korean cannons, Hauzer D-30s which passed the reviewing stand in threes. The sight of the Mirage-5Es flying in formation was much more exciting.

Suddenly one of the trucks stopped briefly in front of the honorary reviewing stand, moved on, and stopped again. The few who noticed the truck at this time thought it was only engine trouble. In fact, mechanical failure is nothing unusual in the Egyptian army—a motorcycle and another army vehicle had had to remain behind during the first part of the approach to the parade site. Anwar el-Sadat mopped the sweat from his brow and continued his conversation with Hosni Mubarak about the next big parade, to be held on the return of the Israeli-occupied Sinai on April 25 of the next year.

Then he noticed that several soldiers had leaped from the stationary transport vehicle. He did not know that, in defiance of strict orders against stopping in front of the reviewing stand, they had forced the driver at gunpoint to stop or that they themselves had pulled the hand brake. He did not know they were carrying live hand grenades, that their Kalashnikov automatics were loaded with genuine ammunition. It was 12:59 P.M.

Sadat stood up to greet the soldiers. Then Khaled Islambuli threw a hand grenade into the crowd. The explosive charge landed at Abu Ghazala's feet. It did not go off. The minister recognized the danger, but was for a moment paralyzed. Then the second grenade hit Major General Abdrab Nabi Hafez, the chief of general staff of the army, in the face. This hand grenade, too, proved to be a dud. Islambuli reached back into the truck and pulled out an automatic weapon of German make. Shouting, "May Egypt live, attack!" he ran toward the reviewing stand, approximately ninety feet away, emptying his ammunition as he ran. The television camera was swiveling in the sky when the cameraman leaped from the tower.

For a moment the onlookers thought that what was happening was simply an additional part of the parade. Then they noticed how serious the situation was. Several of the honorary guests were wallowing in their own blood. Then a hand grenade exploded along the long side of the reviewing stand. The splinters hit Sadat and his immediate neighbors. Abu Ghazala and Sadat's personal assistant threw the president to the ground, but it was already too late. The attackers stood directly in front of the low balustrade of the reviewing stand and shot at Sadat's group. Sobhi Abdel Hakim, president of the Council of Elders, later said: "I was extremely surprised when I found myself face to face with the president on the ground. His entire face was soaked with blood."

The minister of defense shouted at Khaled Islambuli that he

should stop at once. Extremely agitated, the latter answered: "I want nothing from you or Mubarak; I want only this dog!" With a quick motion, he pointed to Sadat. At this moment Khaled Islambuli stood on the same level as the leaders. Everywhere people were screaming and running for their lives. They stumbled over toppled chairs, and over the dead and wounded, too. Abdul Hamid Abdussalam Ali stood to the left of the loge, Ata Tayal Hamida to the right. They shot simultaneously in Sadat's direction.

The sixty-two-year-old recipient of the Nobel Peace Prize was hit by five bullets. Two lodged in the left part of the chest, one in the throat, one in the left knee, and one in the right hip. Blood flowed from his wounds and mouth. Two bodyguards, his adjutant, and his personal photographer, Mohammed Rashwan, also suffered mortal wounds. Sadat's private secretary, his press spokesman, and his brother-in-law Sayed Marai survived, even though they were riddled with bullets.

The bodyguards, who had been trained by American security experts, failed completely. Instead of running forward, they had run toward the back of the reviewing stand, from which point they shot back only after thirty seconds had passed. By that time, after an onslaught of merely ninety-six seconds, it was already too late. By the time the attackers were hit, they had already achieved their goal. In this exchange of fire, numerous civilians also seemed to have been wounded. Islambuli's defense counsel, Abdel Halim Ramadan, reported an interesting aspect: "Sadat was also wounded by a bullet that hit him from behind to the right. How could that happen? How could it occur when the attackers were standing either directly in front of him or slightly to the side? When I requested of the court that I be given the uniform as a piece of evidence, they imprisoned me for a time."

People in Cairo had even heard of an investigation by weapons experts, allegedly providing proof that the lethal shots did not come from the assassins' weapons. Sadat's personal photographer, Mohammed Rashwan, was allegedly killed by a .38 revolver, a weapon used by the presidential guard. No confirmation of this can be obtained from official government circles.

Fuad Ataby, a young government official, told me several hours after the attack: "Perhaps a minute passed before President Sadat's bodyguards fired back, but by that time it was already too late. We knew that something dreadful had happened and that it would never again be as it was before." Egypt's army and police are to be blamed for the fact that the soldiers entered the vicinity of the reviewing stand under cover. According to eyewitness reports, the first counterattack came from bodyguards of foreign diplomats. The spell broke when Islambuli's group fell to the ground. Then the minister of defense intervened: "I commanded everyone to remain silent and told the military police to take care of all the rest."

In the meantime Hosni Mubarak, who was only slightly wounded, had Sadat brought by a helicopter of the Gazelle type to the Maadi Hospital a little over nine miles away, where one year previously the Shah of Iran had died of cancer. Mubarak followed in a Volvo from the president's fleet. Sadat's wife Jehan, who had observed everything from where she sat in the upper part of the reviewing stand, was taken in a second helicopter to the Maadi Military Hospital.

When the president's helicopter landed, the severely wounded man was already in a coma. His pulse could hardly be detected; his eyes no longer showed any reflexes; and blood was still flowing from his mouth. Several teams of doctors tried to save him, but the shock had been too great. Despite artificial respirators, heart massage, and immediate treatment of the wounds, the doctors had to give up after eighty minutes. The heart no longer showed any response; measurement of the brain waves yielded a value of zero. A doctor announced the death with the Islamic phrase, "Only God is eternal." In a television address that same evening, Mubarak explained, "Allah arranged that Sadat should die on a day that he liked—among his soldiers, among the heroes and the people who proudly celebrated with him the day the Arab nation regained its dignity."

Four days later Sadat was buried at the grave of the unknown soldier, where he had laid a garland of flowers before the parade. In gold letters on the black piece of marble in front of the tomb is a saying from the Koran: "Do not believe that those who die for God's cause are dead. They are standing at the side of the Omnipotent One." Below it in the same print is an epitaph that Sadat himself wanted on his grave: "Mohammed Anwar el-Sadat, the hero of war and of peace; he died for his principles and values."

Both statements apply to his murderers, who have meanwhile been executed. They, too, acted in the firm conviction of receiving a place in paradise as a result of doing that favor for Allah—in other words, as *shahid*, or martyrs for the Islamic cause.

The reaction to Sadat's death was typical of the situation in the Arab Islamic world. While the West mourned for a friend and partner, salvos of joy were fired off in the streets of Beirut and Damascus. In Libya, Qaddafi was ecstatic, and only the crowned heads of state remained cloaked in affected silence.

Sadat's secular and spiritual enemies agreed on the judgment that Allah's just wrath had finally hit the Egyptian pharaoh. For instance, when Abu Ijad, Yasser Arafat's representative in the militant Palestinian organization Al Fatah, spoke before a crowd drunk with joy at the Arab University in Beirut, he exclaimed: "The execution of Sadat symbolizes the end of despair that the imperialists tried to plant in our hearts. It symbolizes the elimination of all forms of treachery imparted to our region, and all kinds of shame and disgrace that Sadat brought to our Arab nation, particularly to the Egyptian people."

In Cairo during the week after Sadat's death, I asked a leader of the Muslim Brotherhood who had gone underground, "Who is responsible for the murder of Sadat? Was it the Muslim Brotherhood?" His answer:

You will be astonished when I tell you that Sadat himself committed suicide. He is responsible for the attack. Sadat himself was a murderer of our members. The families of his victims left the revenge to Allah's justice. As a consequence, Sadat's provocations constantly became more audacious. He trampled on all his ideals and opened the prisons to more than 1,500 representatives of the Egyptian elite, particularly young men and scholars. He withdrew licenses from newspapers and nationalized 4,000 mosques. He terrorized and repressed the people with his special security unit. In addition, there are his errors in foreign policy. Violent reactions were to be expected.

The Muslim Brotherhood always denied any participation in the assassination of Sadat, but it did concede that the perpetrators came from related groups. I inquired about the cross-connections:

As for what concerns the "Islamic coalitions" that came into being in recent years in Egypt, I should like to say that we have respect for them, and have respect for them for many reasons. They came into being when all the members of the Muslim Brotherhood were in prison. Nonetheless, they have the same principles. In an era, too, when wild impulses and excesses were tolerated, they adhered to the morality and precepts of Islam. They adopted principles for which others were grue-somely tortured. That is true courage. If some of them incline toward force, that is to be cured by dialogue and not by repression, prison, and torture.

But as was evident in the nervous days following the assassination, the police and secret service inclined toward the old, proven methods. They arrested everyone who was already known to them or who had not shaved off his beard (a mark of the fundamentalists) quickly enough. The prisons filled up, and the chief public prosecutor's investigations of a national plot began. Only a fragment of the 754 pages of the strongly worded indictment against the murderers of Sadat was later made public.

On October 6 and immediately afterwards, it was stated that the attackers were part of the radical Islamic underground group Takfir wal Hejra.

The connection to Takfir wal Hejra was very easy to establish, since most of the group's members live in the town of Minia in Central Egypt, in Assiut, or in the extremely remote surrounding countryside of Upper Egypt. Riots broke out there two days after Sadat's death. On the holiday celebrating Courban Bayram, a group of heavily armed Islamic fundamentalists, under the command of Assem Abdul Maged, attempted to storm the headquarters of the police and the state secret service in the city of Assiut, 248 miles south of Cairo. At 6:00 A.M. on October 8, they traveled in two cars through the capital of Upper Egypt, a city of 250,000 inhabitants, to the main police station and wildly fired automatic weapons. Several policemen were killed. When the protectors of order fired back, the fighting started in earnest. Four days later I was able to determine that there was hardly a spot in the police building that had not been hit.

The street battles increased in intensity and lasted three days. The government in distant Cairo was able to gain the upper hand in the "Wild South" only when it dispatched several parachute units to the scene. The last members of the radical Muslim groups were taken into custody when the funeral procession for Anwar el-Sadat moved along the parade street. At least 300 people are said to have been killed.

For days there was extreme nervousness and an atmosphere of civil war in Assiut. The airport and the university were closed. The photographer George Delanoff and I, disguised as tourists passing through, were the first German journalists in Assiut. We arrived after an arduous nine-hour taxi ride. Approximately every six miles along the way, we passed a control post manned by the police or the military. The closer we came to Assiut, the more thoroughly we were frisked. Barrels and blockades at the entrance to the city, as well as to all streets, ensured that traffic moved slowly, in only one lane, as it passed by parachute troops, who watched mistrustfully. We rode through Assiut in 105-degree heat. There was not a square yard of public street that was not within shooting range of cocked AK-47 automatic rifles. The sentries behind the sandbags trained their weapons on us until we were out of sight. In such a situation, any spontaneous movement can be the last. Under martial law almost nothing is permitted.

Nonetheless, business continued as usual in the center of town. Dark-skinned Nubian-Sudanese types predominated. The fury, the hatred in the faces of the local inhabitants was clear whenever a military patrol marched past, checking in all directions. The fact that the fundamentalists put all their eggs into one basket was proved that week, and not only in Assiut. In Cairo and Alexandria, too, they attacked police stations, but were beaten back considerably more quickly than in Assiut.

The residence of Minister of the Interior Nabawa Ismail, in the Cairo suburb of Mohandissen, was attacked with automatic weapons, security officials being killed in the process. The perpetrators fled undetected. The next encounter with the extremists took place immediately afterward at the Pyramids, where five sought-after leaders of the fundamentalists of Assiut encountered the police. In the exchange of fire in Gizeh, involving automatic pistols and hand grenades, the police were ultimately able to overpower all five of those sought. Among them were two members of the wealthy Zomor family of Cairo. A police record shows that this group wanted to exploit the murder of the president in order to "disturb order and security in Egypt, to spread unrest among the population, and to acquire weapons for additional attacks in other provinces."

Was the Islamic revolution to spread to Egypt in imitation of the Iranian model? More precise details were not available at that time, and even today the situation is difficult to explain. Within the country, word leaked out that the Sadat murderers belonged to a tight network of revolutionaries. Their goal was to establish a regime based on the rules of the Koran and of the *sunna*. Cassettes were reportedly seized which had been prepared for use in a radio broadcast following the coup. The sound engineer had already been selected. There was also allegedly a complete list of ministers. Officially more than 700 persons were arrested in connection with this plot. Unofficially, however, word had it that 1,500 were imprisoned.

Minister of Defense Abu Ghazala provided the first information about the four Sadat assassins. A week after the attack, he announced that Khaled Islambuli and his accomplices had regained consciousness in the intensive care unit of the hospital and that at the hearings they had provided "clear details about everything having to do with the assassination." Abu Ghazala predicted swift legal proceedings by a military court and the official execution of the assassins. Proceedings of the kind mentioned by Abu Ghazala are detrimental to the Egyptian legal system. Said Abu Ghazala: "I will personally see to it that el-Islambuli is publicly hanged and that he is left to swing for a whole week."

At the same time all means were used to keep the army free from any suspicion of conspiracy. Abu Ghazala proved that only one of the attackers came from the ranks of the army. "A brother of this man, Mohammed Ahmed Shukry el-Islambuli, was arrested on September 2. Khaled Islambuli himself was in the army only a few years." Abu Ghazala added that the brother was considered a member of the Takfir wal Hejra group. The civilian state security service had allegedly informed the Ministry of Defense some time ago of Khaled Islambuli's religious inclinations. The military secret service subsequently observed him, but found no proof of infidelity. "He conducted himself well, was never absent, and was known for his loyalty and discipline," said the minister. The three co-conspirators had also been in the army, but had either been dismissed or had left.

In the meantime large-scale cleanup operations were started in the armed forces (the favorite instrument of the leadership of the Egyptian state), because it was known to be a potential source of great danger. Two hundred army officers were transferred to civilian posts. Unofficial sources even mention 800 officers. When the new president, Hosni Mubarak, was asked why, he answered: "They had religious ties. Abu Ghazala spoke with them. They then requested a civilian assignment outside the army in order to keep the army pure." Three-fourths of Sadat's bodyguards and security officials were arrested and interrogated intensively. Reluctantly, the Egyptian government shifted from its earlier version that every bodyguard had done his duty. It was confirmed that not a single armed guard was in front of the reviewing stand in which Sadat had been sitting. Moreover, the bodyguards had left the reviewing stand shortly before the attack.

Abbud Hassan el-Zomor's name came to be mentioned. The former secret service officer was nabbed on October 13 during the gunfight at the Pyramids. He had been in contact with the four Sadat assassins and was himself the leader of a radical Muslim group. He had already planned the murder of Sadat several times —once by means of an attack on Sadat's villa in the Nile delta, another time by an attack on Sadat's car using explosive gas bottles.

In an interview published by the newspaper *Al Ahram*, President Hosni Mubarak stated that the orthodox Muslims had planned a revolution in three phases, based on the model provided by Ayatollah Khomeini. Mubarak stated that documents had been found, according to which the plotters wanted to spread their ideas by means of religious institutions and mosques. In this way, they would attract followers who would then be provided with weapons. After the proclamation of a theocratic system in Egypt, the plan was to murder the leadership class within the state, to occupy the Ministry of Defense, and take control of the mass media.

In terms of the faith, the perpetrators had been made secure. A blind *mufti* by the name of Dr. Omar Ahmed Mohammed Abdel Rahman had given them dispensation in advance. He interpreted the Islamic law in the sense of the group. Accordingly, the members of the Cairo leadership were considered atheists and heretics (*kafara*). The blind chief ideologist also permitted the fanatics to steal in order to finance their deed and, after completion of the mission, to enjoy themselves as they pleased with the wives of leading members of government.

Large sums of money in Egyptian and American currency were found in the *mufti*'s possession. Among the cache of weapons were also the blueprints of important governmental buildings and military installations, secret codes, writings of Khomeini, and a book by Mao Tse-tung about the theory of guerrilla war. It became known that, in the event of a coup, the terrorist group wanted to found two councils—one to guide governmental matters and the other, a religious commission based on the model of Iran.

To counter the radical Islamic virus, Hosni Mubarak met with the faculty of the 1,000-year-old Azhar University, the highest institution for instruction in the faith. Mubarak demanded that the teachers of religion familiarize the young people with the correct interpretation of Islam. Cairo newspapers quoted him on October 21 as stating: "Your task is to cleanse Egypt of fanatics and to protect the youth from religious confusion."

Weeks later, Mubarak's criminal prosecutor energetically took a hand in the cleanup. In the second half of November, the military prosecution presented parts of the indictment, which listed twenty-four defendants. The list of names was subdivided. The four actual perpetrators were accused of the intention to murder, of conspiracy, illegal possession of weapons, and various other offenses. Number five was the engineer Mohammed Abdel Salam Farag Attia, who was labeled the instigator and a misguided religious fanatic.

The other nineteen included students from Cairo, Assiut, and Zagazig (in the Nile delta), as well as a doctor, a teacher, a truck driver, and a house painter. Precise details about their roles within the plot were never revealed. In the published passages of the indictment, there was a lot of talk about a murder plot, an attack on the leader and the leadership, a sinful lack of faith, and spilled blood, but the Egyptian authorities remained silent about the background of the deed. In the few reports in the mass media there was no perceptible red thread between the defendants and the deed. Only one thing was clear: the indictment demanded the death of the fundamentalists.

Under the chairmanship of Major General Samir Mohammed Fadel, the highest military court opened the first session of the three-month-long trial. The setting was in the middle of Cairo-Heliopolis, in a barren room of a walled-off military barracks, called Jebel Ahmar after the rust-red sand dunes of the surroundings. During the proceedings the twenty-four defendants sat in four room-high steel cages. With the exception of the uniformed former secret service colonel, Abbud el-Zomor, the mostly bearded men wore floor-length white *galabias*, the traditional garment of the Bedouins and Islamic fundamentalists.

On the day of the opening, they laughed and joked before the cameras of the world press covering the event. They waved small copies of the Koran and quoted *suras*. Good-humoredly they talked with their thirty-five lawyers and chatted with intimates. Only the wives wept. When the state prosecutor mentioned the accusation of secret meetings and conspiratorial activities, they screamed: "That is not true. Allah is our counsel." In addition, they stated that they had been tortured during detention pending investigation.

In public there was no longer any discussion of the fact that the defendants in the Sadat murder trial were members of Takfir wal Hejra. They were generally referred to as *irhabiyun*, or terrorists. Only later did it leak out that most of them belonged to the less popular organization Jihad (Holy War). According to a statement by the Egyptian chief public prosecutor, Salah el-Rashidi, as long ago as October 1979, seventy activists of the radical Jihad group had been arrested. At that time, as after the assassination of Sadat, large quantities of weapons, ammunition, and equipment were found. Writings confiscated at that time had called on the population to oppose the Sadat administration, which was called un-Islamic, and had demanded a return to fundamentalist Islamic traditions.

The boundaries between the Jihad organization and Takfir wal Hejra seem to be vague, however, since they share a common goal. Mohammed Hassanein Heikal, the best-informed journalist in the Near East, states: "Seven to nine political groups competed to eliminate him [Sadat], so at some time one of them had to meet with success. Unfortunately his days were numbered. The fact that it happened on October 6, of all days, I consider to be irony."

The military trial against the twenty-four fundamentalists took place in complete secrecy. Khaled Islambuli's defense lawyer, Abdel Halim Ramadan, was arrested when he spoke with a London journalist and was subsequently quoted. He was released again only on a bail of $500. All participants in the trial were obligated to remain silent about the details, and all documents stayed in the court. For this reason, reporting about the trial resumed only when the sentence was pronounced.

The following details, however, were passed on illegally. As their basic explanation, both Abbud Hassan el-Zomor and Khaled Islambuli stated: "We killed a pharaoh. And that is right!" Islambuli reported that the planning and execution of the deed took precisely one week, which was also the length of time he knew of his participation in the parade. He was always solely concerned with Sadat and no one else: "We aimed our hand grenades—we did not simply throw them into the crowd. We merely wanted to intimidate the people in order to be able to lay claim to our freedom to kill this dog."

Who gave the assignment? According to Islambuli, "I had a vision and saw the Prophet Mohammed—God protect him and his family—and he gave me a sword and told me to kill Mohammed Anwar el-Sadat, for he is against God. He does not govern according to the rules of Islam." Islambuli stuck by this defense.

During the proceedings Khaled Islambuli once displayed two photos of Sadat's wife Jehan. In one of them she was dancing with Ezer Weizman, the former Israeli minister of defense; in the other, she was dancing hip to hip with a popular singer. In great excitement, Islambuli asked the judges: "Do you want to know why I killed him? Then you get this as proof. Here is the ruler of a Muslim country! You say that the constitution provides the Koran and the *sharia* as the law of our country. Look here, so you can know why I killed him."

As a result of torture, the defendant Mohammed Ali Salamuni could not move his jawbones. The defendant Abdel Salam Farag Attia accused the court: "I was tortured, but why did they arrest my father, a sixty-seven-year-old man? And why did they threaten to rape our wives?" A bullet in the shoulder of Tarik el-Zomor, the nephew of the former secret service officer, had still not been removed six weeks after his arrest.

The family of Khaled Islambuli identified with his deed. They are upper-middle-class Egyptians. Islambuli's father and uncle are lawyers; another uncle is a judge in the supreme court. All the male family members were in jail because of Islamic agitation. His mother, Umm Islambuli, and his sisters offered visitors sweets and fruit juices; they celebrated Khaled's martyrdom with them. As early as December 1981, Khaled Islambuli wrote to his mother in his last will: "Be just to me; I have not been involved in any criminality. I did it for Allah. I defended Islam. I was not concerned with position and prestige. If I have caused you any trouble, forgive me."

In court the defendants repeatedly mentioned that the most important political reason for their deed was Sadat's signing of the Camp David peace accords and "his lone decision to capitulate to the enemy." Khaled Islambuli explained: "I by no means committed a base crime. I am proud of what I accomplished with my own hands. You must recognize who is criminal and who is innocent. Now, it is enough for me to know my ending. I will be in the garden of eternity with the honorable messengers of Allah and the angels. In addition, I must only be patient, because I know that everyone on earth is mortal. All will expire except Allah."

One piece of information I obtained from a leading member of the Egyptian Muslim Brotherhood was never discussed in the trial: two additional commandos would have been ready to carry out the deed once and for all if Khaled Islambuli and his accomplices had failed in the attack on Sadat. Not until February 1984 was this information officially confirmed, when the Egyptian minister of the interior released a new report on the case.

The defense of Khaled Islambuli was built on the basic thesis that the Koran permits the killing of a tyrant and violent ruler. The military court countered that argument with a *fatwa*, a decision by the highest authority on matters of faith, which was issued by Sheikh Azhar Gad al-Haq. He stated that Islam provides for no such action, that there was no basis for appeal to the Koran. For more than 1,300 years, in accordance with high Islam, it has been accepted that the authority of God is established, and a ruler can be held responsible only by him. In the classical legal commentary by Abu Yusuf, it is stated: "Do not slander the regents, for they act well, so grant them God's reward and have patience. If they act badly, sin burdens them, and you are obliged to be patient. They are the scourge with which God punishes if He wishes to punish; do not oppose disaster with fury and outrage, but receive it with humility."

In Cairo I met Islambuli's defense counsel, Abdel Halim Ramadan, who was protected by the secret police. The legal expert, a prominent figure in Egyptian history, was one of the leading persons in the historic Wafd Party in King Farouq's time. Forbidden immediately after the revolution of 1952, the Wafd Party was again legalized under Sadat. In protest against the restrictions against it, it then dissolved itself.

Afterwards Ramadan made a name for himself as a political lawyer and legal representative of the imprisoned Muslim fundamentalists. In the 1970s he had defended members of Takfir wal Hejra, including the organization's founder, Shukri Ahmed Mustafa, who was hanged in 1977. Abdel Halim Ramadan is an

Egyptian of the old school—a strict believer, yet worldly and widely traveled. At the beginning of our discussion he referred to his independence, mentioning that he belongs to no fundamentalist organization and serves only justice.

"Where did Sadat's assassins get their ammunition, and how did they manage to bring this forbidden equipment to the parade?" I asked him. Abdel Halim Ramadan answered in the tone of a preacher: "It happened in the name of Allah. How should I know His ways? He saw to it that they were able to perform their duty."

Questioned about the right of the four men to do this deed, Ramadan replied: "When people are constantly offended in their dignity and are attacked, when they see how they as believers are disdained, then they must react. Sadat removed all ties to his people; he closed all windows and doors. He was no longer one of us, but was our enemy—until these heroes arrived. Their deed was a defense of the values of this tradition-bound society."

The court concluded the main proceedings on March 3, 1982. On March 6 the death penalty was given to the four main perpetrators and the engineer Farag, who had obtained the weapons and provided the ideological justification. Five additional defendants, including the two Zomors, were sentenced to life imprisonment. Twelve received prison sentences of five to fifteen years. The blind *mufti*, Rahman, and the other teacher of religion, Salamuni, were freed. Announcement of the sentences took place in chaotic circumstances. The picture offered to the press and to the families was the same as that from the opening of the trial: the defendants, mostly bearded, clad in white *galabias* and wearing prayer caps, were hanging on the bars of the cages, as if in a zoo, or standing apathetically in the corner. Attached to the bars were cut-up bedsheets and T-shirts with religious messages ("We are the army of God"), as well as hangmen's ropes made of brown and white shawls.

Three days before the defenders had been suspended. The reason: they had entered pleas for only ten defendants and had therefore protested against the early sentencing date. Moreover, as later became known, up to this point only eleven of the twenty-four cases had been dealt with in court. The biweekly Islamic publication *Crescent International*, which is published in Canada, stated: "The secret service had reported to the authorities that a longer trial would increase the popularity of the defendants among the masses, and that it could possibly lead to a revolt if they were then condemned to death."

Some time earlier the lawyers had already lodged a protest, when the court rejected the testimony of witnesses and denied evidence they had demanded. It is a fact that the Cairo military court placed no particular value on the statements of witnesses for the defense.

The uproar started when the spectators streamed into the hall to hear the sentencing. All screamed at one time: "Allah is greater," "Only Allah is our judge," "Death to the Jews; death to the Americans." In a penetrating voice, Islambuli shouted: "The blood of Muslims must not be spilled for Jews and Americans." Sayed el-Salamuni, a professor of religion, provided an explanation in English for the journalists: "Oh, friends, you know what freedom is, you have freedom. We are no terrorists, we are no murderers; we are pious Moslems. Tell that to the whole world. During the last years, Sadat made himself into a king, into the worst king in the history of Egypt, into the worst pharaoh. . . .Sadat condemned himself by his behavior and his actions. . . . Our blood for our religion, Islam, Islam."

The defendants started singing songs, to which they themselves and Hassan al-Banna had provided texts: "We stood on the path of Allah, and we tried to hold up his flag. Our dreams were not for the cause of just any party. We are sacrificing ourselves for our faith. Let Islam regain its brilliance. For that we will sacrifice our blood." Chants in unison followed: "Our state is Islamic, Islamic. Not Jewish, not Zionist. We are neither of the Eastern nor of the Western bloc, we are one hundred percent Islamic."

One of the defendants confided to a journalist: "These military sentences are a guillotine that was prepared without legal basis. How strange that for this trial they rejected both civil law and Islamic law [*sharia*]." Murder threats against Menachem Begin were shouted. Led by Khaled Islambuli and Abdul Hamid Abdussalam Ali, the fundamentalists started a new song: "Oh, you Jews, Jerusalem will return, Islam will return in its full brilliance, and if that does not happen, blood will flow. We stood on the path of Allah and tried to hold up His flag. Allah is greater, and all reverence is for Allah, and the Koran is our constitution."

Carl E. Buchalla, Middle East correspondent for the *Süddeutsche Zeitung*, captured the mood precisely: "The quick but by no

means surprising judgment of the military court has not closed
the books on the assassination of Sadat. Rather, it has created a
climate in which legends of martyrs come into being."

Protests hailed from the entire Islamic world. In Beirut the
Committee for the Defense of el-Islambuli and His comrades was
founded. The Islamic Council for Europe in London stated that
Sadat's assassins had had no chance for a fair trial, since they
were not tried by a civil court. The International Islamic Commission for Human Rights under the chairmanship of the former
president of Algeria, Ahmed Ben Bella, appealed in one of four
statements to Hosni Mubarak: "In the name of our most sacred
values and our traditional generosity, show greater composure
and greater justice."

The World Organization of the Muslim Brotherhood also raised
its voice. In a long statement it demanded the abolition of martial
law, the freeing of political prisoners, and the reopening of the
trial before a civil court. It called for an investigation into the use
of torture and brainwashing of the defendants and demanded
that a non-Egyptian defense be permitted to appear in court. It
pleaded that the five heroes be saved and their motives be taken
into consideration in any judgment of the deed.

That of course did not occur. President Hosni Mubarak approved the sentences of the highest military court, clearing the
way for their implementation. Kadiya Hamid, the mother of
Khaled Islambuli, appealed to the Muslim world to stop the execution. Once again she clearly stated:

Khaled and his comrades killed Sadat only because he said, "Islam is a
comprehensive lifestyle, but I repeat that there can be no religion in
politics and no politics in religion." He equated his words with those of
Allah, and tried to realize his theory by contradicting Allah's commands. . . . My son Khaled acted in the name of millions of Muslims,
who are now obligated to intervene in order to save his life. . . . As the
holy Prophet said, "Anyone who does not concern himself with every
Muslim issue cannot be one of them."

From all parts of the Arab world, contributions—large sums of
money—were sent to the Islambuli family. But not even with
money could the sentence ratified by President Mubarak be rescinded.

Shortly before dawn on April 15, 1982, in strict secrecy, Khaled
Islambuli was executed by a firing squad on the grounds of the

Jebel Ahmar barracks. When they fetched him in his cell, he spat into the faces of an officer and representative of the chief public prosecutor. He thrashed about wildly and would not let himself be manacled. "I am Khaled Islambuli," he shouted excitedly, "and I will not let myself be forced to anything. I myself am capable of walking to be executed as a martyr. May Allah stand by me." When he stood before the firing squad, he refused to put on the obligatory blindfold. Instead, he said a last prayer and fixed the soldiers with a rigid glance as they took aim at him. Reserve officer Hussein Abbas Mohammed was also executed by the firing squad. The other three men condemned to death died on the gallows at the same time in Bab al Khalq Prison.

6

Egypt at the Crossroads

For the Temple of despair has powerful columns; who is capable of tearing
them down?
—Nasser, *Philosophy of Revolution*

SCARCELY WAS THE CORPSE of Anwar el-Sadat in the mausoleum
than Egypt again resumed its daily routine. After a forty-day
period of mourning, all the banners and posters put up by the
rais, the "popular leader" of the people, vanished. The Egyptian
people were incapable of mourning the man who always considered himself their father, who always believed that he knew
the feelings of the forty-three million people on the Nile. Khaled
el-Islambuli's shots had burst the bubble; only now did the world
notice how much Anwar el-Sadat had adopted and even greatly
intensified the dictatorial characteristics of his predecessor,
Gamal Abdel Nasser.

The signs of the slipping popularity of the politician of peace
had been visible for years. While Sadat's star rose ever higher
outside of Egypt, within the country it sank to a nadir for years
before his death. The beginning of the end of the Sadat era was
the year 1977, even before the triumphant success at Camp
David. The best-informed publicist of the Arab world, Mo-

hammed Hassanein Heikal, Nasser's friend and minister of information, who even served as a counselor to Sadat for several years, considered "what happened in Egypt since 1977 a tragedy." Heikal continued: "At that time it became clear that a profound discontent had gripped the country. You can suppress such a thing by the army, policy, martial law, and curfew for a while, but violence was simply in the air, and things took their course."

In 1977 the aura of the great commander of the Seven-Day War had faded, and Sadat was experiencing the first difficulties arising from the militant Islamic opposition. The disputes with Nasserists persisted. Several years before, Sadat had expelled the Russians and opened his country to the West. *Infitah* was the magic formula of switching allegiances. Mistrustful investors hesitated; only the tourists came in ever greater numbers to "the country where man first glimpsed the dawn of time" (as Sadat wrote in his memoirs).

Sadat ran up against the limits of power in the so-called food riots of January 19, 1977. Following bloody brawls by workers and students in Cairo and Alexandria, resulting in ten deaths, he had to contend with the effects of significant price increases that had been decided on by the government. Wherever demonstrations occurred, the police opened fire. In the two largest cities of the country, curfews were imposed and the schools and universities closed. The Egyptian people did not understand why they should pay 100 percent more for food while the spoiled civil service received salary increases. "Sadat, you are making millions, and we are starving!" shouted the discontented crowd in front of the Abdin Palace in Cairo.

Even at that time the extent of the rift within contemporary Egypt was clear. In few countries of the Third World are the social differences as striking as in the poorhouse of Arabia. An extremely small, immensely wealthy upper class, which can afford everything, is typified by such people as Contractor Osman Ahmed Osman, a father-in-law to a daughter of Sadat; by the dealer in everything, Abu el-Enem of Port Said; by the king of the textile industry, Hamdi; as well as by the Sadat family, whose wealth derives from many profitable sources. In the social pyramid there is a thin layer of the middle class, but it is one that lacks both front and back. A government salary ranges from 50 to 100 Egyptian pounds per month, which corresponds to the purchasing power of $385 to $765. Most Egyptians vegetate at the fringe of existence, with 1 pound per day, or just under $8. Day in, day out, they eat mainly the national dish, *ful*, which is made of beans. Food is subsidized, but the majority cannot afford any meat. Many products such as soap, rice, and sugar are constantly in short supply and can be obtained only with food cards. Sixty percent of the food supply is still imported.

Inflation increases annually by thirty percent. The cities are growing rapidly in an uncontrolled manner, and there is a short-age of 80,000 dwellings in the entire country. The increase in the birthrate is three percent. No program of birth control has thus far been successful.

When Sadat signed the Camp David Treaty and decided in November 1977 to travel to Jerusalem, he characterized his ac-tions not as peace with Israel, the arch-enemy of the Arabs, but as peace plain and simple. The sobering-up process was initially slow in coming. The vitally important support of the wealthy Arab nations was immediately withheld, and most of the govern-ments of the region broke off diplomatic relations with Sadat. Only Numeiri in the Sudan and Sultan Qabus of Oman, both of whom were similarly menaced, supported the Egyptians. Sadat sought help from the Americans, who promptly jumped in with money and know-how.

Believing the solution to its problems was to be found in the West, Egypt isolated itself from the Arab world. Not much time elapsed before people noted parallels between Sadat and the Shah of Iran, and began referring to "Shah Sadat." Columnist Tahar Ben Jellou recognized the essence of the problems in his assessment of Sadat in the French magazine *Jeune Afrique:* "I see this murder as a revenge, not as the revenge of an individual or a group, but as the revenge of an attitude: the attitude of a world whose soul Sadat had attempted to steal. The ruler went too far when he no longer recognized the roots."

Heikal was always capable of analyzing the situation clearly, but in the general ecstasy about peace his comments were not fully comprehended. In an interview with the German news mag-azine *Der Spiegel* (volume 10, 1982), he explained:

Sadat's domination had led to political violence. Seven to nine political groups ultimately competed to remove him, so at some time one of them had to meet with success. . . . His greatest mistake was that he lost contact with reality, and in fact lost it totally. He felt himself chosen to play the role of a prince of peace, and he played it with such devotion that he constantly removed himself further from reality. I once advised him no longer to use a helicopter, and said: "Mr. President, if you sit in a helicopter, you get only a helicopter view of the economic and social problems. One then sees only the Nile Valley and romantic villages, and even the desert looks attractive."

Secretly, the Muslim Brotherhood had again gathered strength. After Camp David it systematically began to oppose everything non-Islamic. Omar el-Telmisani railed in his mouthpiece *Al Dawa* against "excesses" in the nightclubs, against "immoral" films in movie houses and on television, and against the general corruption that was incompatible with the Koran. He resolutely announced: "The ideologies of the West must be opposed. They are the forerunners of corruption, the silk curtain concealing the greed of the avaricious and the dreams of the power-hungry." Sadat wanted personally to exclude the only opposition worthy of mention. In 1979 he met twice with Sheikh el-Telmisani. Nothing constructive emerged from the discussions, however, since both lived in their separate worlds and conducted only monologues. Some time after the meeting Sadat explained that Omar el-Telmisani was one of the reasons for the domestic tensions. The signal for the duel had been given.

Active disputes between Muslim fundamentalists and the rest of the country started during the first five days of January 1980. Strictly religious students beat up their fellow students at a dance party. Bombs exploded in Alexandria in two Coptic churches. In Minia and Assiut fighting broke out between radical Muslims and Copts. The Copts are Egyptians who are orthodox Christians. Like the orthodox Christians of Ethiopia and Armenia and the Syrian Jacobites, the Copts are Monophysites; they subscribe to the doctrine declared heretical by the Council of Chalcedon in 451 A.D. The special proselytizing efforts that came with the new wave of Islam brought latent tensions to the fore.

At the Friday prayer service, members of the Muslim Brotherhood preached against Anwar el-Sadat's "godless society." In 1980 and 1981, in clear Arabic, comprehensible even to uneducated Egyptians, the blind Sheikh Abdel Hamid Kishkh, an extremely charismatic Islamic loner, even appealed, in the Ain-El-Hiyyat Mosque in Cairo, for revolt. The star preacher argued against the presence of foreigners, against coeducation, and against the moral duplicity of the oil sheikhs. People traveled

great distances to hear his compelling speeches, and the fundamentalists disseminated their new idol's statements on tape
cassettes.

Unrest started during the first six months of 1981. In late June
fighting occurred between Copts and Muslims in the poor section
of Cairo, El Zawia el Hamraa. What began as a harmless dispute
ended with seventeen dead and more than a hundred wounded.
Sadat declared that both sides were to blame for the incidents.
While the fighting was still in progress, the mutual hatred was
fomented from the Coptic chancels and Islamic mosques. The
representatives of eight million Christians announced that 300
members of their faith had been killed by Muslims and that ten
churches had been burned down. In the mosques the sheikhs
announced the death of 400 Muslims. Sadat used the opportunity
to get rid of his critics, and in a first wave of arrests had 1,536
people put behind bars, including politicians of the opposition
and disconcerting journalists such as Mohammed Heikal. Many
others were forcibly transferred elsewhere.

The "hero of peace and of war" (according to an obituary in
Cairo)—who in the last months of his life behaved in an uncontrolled manner, prone to outbreaks of fury and nervously fidgety
—had 40,000 private mosques nationalized. From that moment
on, the Friday prayers were subject to censorship and the preachers had to be licensed. Not even Nasser at the peak of his power
had dared that. *Al Dawa* refused to be intimidated by the move.
In its last leading article before it was banned, the journal of the
Muslim Brotherhood stated: "God, Lord of Heaven and of earth,
abundantly provided people with freedom, and no creature has
the right to tailor it according to his mood. . . . A country that
governs without law is a country of tyranny. . . . A regime pre-
tends that under its rule freedom prevails, that the basic law is
respected, and the laws have domination, but the reality looks
entirely different." The passage that followed became reality on
October 6, 1981: "Injustice is dreadful. The person who uses it is
a tyrant. Anyone, however, who frees an oppressed person from
tyranny is rewarded for it by God under the sole condition that
he considers his action only according to pleasing God and acts
from love of justice." At this point Omar el-Telmisani was incarcerated in the Tura Prison—and, along with him, almost the entire leadership of the movement. Sadat's death could only be a
question of weeks.

In the opinion of the Islamic opposition, the new pharaoh (in the Arabic world, a synonym for oppressor) closed his eyes to reality and refused to recognize that the tense situation in his country was the result of his own policy. He lived in his ivory tower and underrated the strength of the Muslim groups. He alone, or so Sadat believed, represented the feelings of the Egyptian people. The leader from the Nile misjudged the radical "Islamic societies" to be merely terrorists of conviction. He considered the style of the Prophet's beard and the ankle-length white *galabias,* as well as the complete veiling among the women, mummery. Sadat remarked that veiled women looked like "wandering tents with peepholes." In his last interview he stated: "During times of decline religious zealots have regularly emerged in the Islamic world. Here in Egypt I am in contact with a group of American and European hippies, young people who rebel against the accepted values. This partial rejection is expressed in the West by going barefoot and even completely naked. In contrast, young people here simply take an overdose of religion." At the end of his life Sadat regretted the mildness and liberality he had shown to members of the Muslim Brotherhood: "If at that time [in 1971, when they were freed] I had known what I know today, I would have left them in the camps. They in fact exploited the liberalization measures and the unaccustomed democratic freedoms that were introduced after the successful October War of 1973. They felt themselves secure, but unfortunately they made bad use of this freedom."

The flexible meaning of the Egyptian concept of freedom is reflected in Islambuli's reference in court to the "freedom" available to him to get a tyrant out of the way. In the three weeks before the deed, Sadat expelled important Soviet diplomats as well as Western correspondents whom he found disconcerting. He banned new political parties and their newspapers yet simultaneously spoke of his country as an "island of security, of human rights, and of democracy." The confusion was complete. Something had to happen. Mohammed Heikal was in prison when he heard of the dramatic event of October 6. The Muslim extremists, so he said, would have known of the matter in advance: "Borne by the wind, their prayers reach us, saying as much as 'God's enemy is now in heaven!' "

Sadat, himself a believer, was shot by Islamic zealots, and the Muslim Brotherhood immediately sent his successor a warning:

If things continue in this manner, then expect more counterforce. Natural law states that for each action there is a reaction of the same strength. Those who now use torture and force should know that an entire people cannot be tortured and that the thinkers cannot be made mute through torture. They should know that for them, too, there is an end, so they should learn from history before it is too late. But if they do not permit force and terror and give Islamic and other thinkers freedom of action, release the prisoners, and ask forgiveness of them, that, then, is the road to stability, peace, and security in the nation, and that is what we want: "And if they incline toward peace, then incline toward and trust Allah."

But at the outset Hosni Mubarak's administration knew only revenge. Kemal al-Sananiry, as the most prominent opponent and the representative of Omar el-Telmisani, had to believe that. For three decades the bearded Sananiry had been the leader of the southern section of Cairo; for twenty years of that time, he had been in prison. Now he was jailed again, together with thousands holding similar views—and each day the number increased. In late October 1981—the exact day can no longer be determined—Kemal al-Sananiry died from the effects of torture. In a hasty explanation, the notorious Minister of Interior Mustafa Abu Basha spoke of suicide. But that seems unlikely for a pious Muslim, because in Islam suicides have no right to a place in heaven. In Egyptian government circles it was rumored that Sananiry had close connections to the murder squad Jihad and had known of the preparations for the assassination. That information, it was said, could under no circumstances be squeezed out of him.

Only after a long harangue was the body of the member of the Muslim Brotherhood handed over to his family. The government watched to make certain that Kemal al-Sananiry was secretly buried. His wife Amina, the daughter of Sayed Qutb, was able to see him once more; she later described the traces of torture on the face of her dead husband. In a long, dramatic poem, she took leave of him:

Oh, my beloved husband, the martyr! I can no longer wait into the late hours. I can no longer look forward to the arrival of the train that fulfills my hopes. I can no longer expect your return, the greeting, and the conversation. I can no longer listen for your light steps and then turn on the light for you. I can no longer leap up when you, despite fatigue, smilingly enter the house. Are you with the Almighty in paradise, in greatest mercy? Are you along with all the others, in the presence of justice, in security and protection? If so, then *Marhaba* [hello] to death, to the martyr's death. I will meet you there. For me it will be the end of suffering. Yes, I shall meet you. That is a promise accompanied by fidelity.

Within months the new president, Hosni Mubarak—a career officer, worldly, Western—released most of the victims of the greatest purge in the history of modern Egypt. On December 28, 1981, the seventy-eight-year-old Omar el-Telmisani, whose arrest was probably the last trigger for the assassination of Sadat, was permitted to return to freedom. The murderers of Sadat were executed in 1982, shortly before the return of the Sinai to Egypt on April 26.

Members of the Muslim Brotherhood are said to have found out that Israel had tried to intervene in Hosni Mubarak's long decision-making process about reducing the sentence to life imprisonment, pointing out that in this instance the president would take a position against Camp David and protect the opponents of the agreement. In a long article that was kept secret, Khaled el-Islambuli confided indirectly to members of the Muslim Brotherhood shortly before his execution: "All who fight for the cause of Allah should meet under the roof of the parent organization."

The most important fundamentalist organization once offered an official assessment of the Mubarak regime. In el-Telmisani's words: "He started well by freeing prisoners, and he invited them for discussions with him. We pray to Allah that he continues along this route." But since then radio and television have come under stronger control to reflect the regime's viewpoint. Fear of spies from the state security services causes everyone to keep silent as soon as the talk turns to the question of Egypt's internal crisis.

A new kind of wind is also blowing at Cairo University. The center of learning is occupied by the police, a special detail designated "university guards." Discussions are forbidden, as is the expression of a critical attitude toward the government. Only after many appeals was I permitted to enter the university, and then I was guarded by several security people and was not permitted to speak freely with any of the students. On two occasions when I started a discussion in English with them, the guards immediately intervened, stating categorically that the persons queried did not understand the language.

Finally five selected interviewees were presented to me. Their spokesman, a chemistry student named Mohammed Hishan el-Behiry, age twenty-four, stated with overriding conviction: "The Egyptians are united behind their President Mubarak. The few deviants are insane persons who are stirred up by outsiders. We students are glad that we no longer need be afraid of bad influences since the new university regulations. The guards protect us from such people."

I voiced my doubts: "You are protected, but a guard cannot be placed beside every Egyptian. The stability of your country continues to be jeopardized."

"You see that completely wrong," the spokesman countered. "Egypt is the most stable country in the world, more stable in fact than the USA or Germany."

"Who says so?"

"That is the opinion of the entire country."

"Is that also the opinion of your fellow students?"

As if in response to a command, the others nodded in assent. Following this interview, the five students were permitted to proclaim their conviction once more in front of the cameras of Egyptian television. Grinning students who gathered around the scene and characterized the programmed question-and-answer game as a caricature were pushed away by the police.

Inside the country there was increasing discontent with a government that displayed weakness in decision making, could not deal with corruption, and was itself guilty of economic mismanagement and misuse of its public offices. Almost nothing changed under the new president, for he was not in control of the entrenched bureaucracy that was impeding progress. The technocrat Hosni Mubarak, born in 1929, who had been Sadat's deputy for six years, admitted that the seeming economic miracle accomplished by his predecessor had for years taken place only in the statistics. The true figures show that Egypt is near bankruptcy and that at every turn the state has been ruined by bad management. It is an ideal breeding ground for the discontented. Egypt's fourth president has distanced himself in many ways from the most recent past: "Perhaps I will do some things different from Anwar el-Sadat. My principle will be: wait, analyze, act. . . . We are all Egyptians with body and soul; there is no difference between Muslims and Christians. We are all part of the same caravan."

The country's discontent started after the Israeli campaign in Lebanon, when Mubarak, in his own interest, distanced himself from the peace partners in Jerusalem and, in response to pressure by enraged Egyptians, withdrew. Anyway, below the line, the peace with Israel had scarcely brought any tangible advantages to Egypt. For the weak Mubarak, it was politically inopportune to visit Jerusalem. In late 1982 the angry voice of the people already spoke of rule by a trinity of *"abus"* in Egypt: Abu Bashea (the minister of the interior), Abu Ghazala (the powerful minister of defense), and Mubarak "Abu Shaha" (meaning someone who defecates in his pants).

Mubarak's half-heartedness and the steadily deteriorating situation under martial law brought the Muslim Brotherhood an undreamed-of number of new members following Sadat's death. Cairo, which is bursting with masses of starving, aggressive people, is an ever more fertile breeding ground for the fundamentalists who are still observing Mubarak's activities with silent mistrust. The chaotic developments in Arabia's most populous state—which has a sixty percent illiteracy rate and is held together only by a pampered army that is faithful to the party line —cause many Western observers, whose attitude toward the Muslim Brotherhood is by no means favorable, to feel anxious about the future. For the trigger is already cocked in the "beating heart of the Arab nation" (as a radio announcement put it during the Nasser era). What the French intellectual Guy Sitbon predicted has come to pass: "The people, exhausted by modernity, have inhaled to rest and to return to the lukewarm lap of tradition."

Nothing, not even reconciliation with the other Arab states, which themselves are pressed, can help Hosni Mubarak combat this phenomenon. The unrest and frustration of the Egyptian masses have already progressed so far that an accommodation by the state to Islamic law—something that has been considered and repeatedly postponed—would at best merely slow the development for the short term. The showdown for Mubarak is within view. He can then again haul out the explanation he gave to the cabinet one day after Sadat's death and can admonish the people to stand firm in the manner earlier favored by the Shah of Iran: "Oh, great people of Egypt, peoples of the Arab nation, the sufferings of history have accustomed us to the departure of great heroes who with their battles determined the great annals and the course of history. We, too, have learned to endure the death pains of our wounds with patience, consecration, and trust in God's will, and have learned to continue the march with tenacity and resolve."

Egypt—*Misr Umm el-Bilad*, the mother of all countries (according to an old song)—is standing at the crossroads.

7

Al-Azhar: The Heart of Islam

ONLY ONE STREET—one always blocked by stinking, honking lines of cars—separates Khan al-Khalili, the bazaar, from a paradisiacal oasis. Behind the high, gray-brown walls of the old al-Azhar Mosque, one of Cairo's most important sights, another completely different world opens up. There young people are sitting and talking. Others are meditating, leaning against one of the eighty-three columns of the interior court. The faithful are praying alone or in groups, withdrawn into themselves in the mosque's fully carpeted interior space.

Greek and Roman, Persian and Byzantine stylistic elements are present in the impressive mosque. The center of the sanctuary is a simple niche called Al Mehrab, showing the direction of Mecca. The thick walls, the three minarets, and the interior space crowned by two cupolas date from the tenth century. At that time the decision was made to erect the spiritual center of the Islamic faith in Cairo rather than in Mecca because of the hot climate there. Ever since then, al-Azhar has been known as "the flourishing," the Vatican of Islam.

Al-Azhar is considered by the Sunnis to be the highest authority for faith and doctrine, but the Shiites are also not entirely
excluded from the pronouncements of the scholars along the
Nile. Old ties from the days of the Shiite Fatimid Dynasty still
exist, but there are also contacts from recent history. Only Imam
Khomeini constitutes an exception. The deliberations of the
Egyptian guardians of the faith do not fit into Khomeini's scheme
of things. He equates the Azhar with the hated Cairo government, and therefore regards as insufferable this supra-confes-
sional Islamic world center. Khomeini prefers to place trust in his
own centers of teaching and faith in the holy city of Ghom.

That changes nothing about Azhar's thousand-year-old function and task dating from the era of Caliph El Muizz. The caliph
had made his former Sicilian slave Gohar into a commander, and
in 969 A.D. had him conquer the fertile country along the Nile.
The new capital, Cairo, was founded. The caliph moved into two
palaces that had been hastily constructed for him between the
city gates. Three mosques were also built in record time, one of
which was the Azhar. Caliph El Agig, the successor of Muizz,
determined in 988 A.D. that it should be the university of Islam
for scholars of religion, law, and the Arabic language.

In the course of subsequent centuries, the large mosque was
repeatedly rebuilt or enlarged. In the massive earthquake of 1303,
it suffered significant damage and had to be partially rebuilt.
Today this most important academy of the Muslim world has,
among other things, a famous library with 80,000 volumes, 20,000
of which are valuable handwritten works.

The strictly orthodox authority on faith unites all fields of instruction with Islam. Following reforms in 1936, 1954, and 1961,
in the present structure, the faculties are divided into three
groups: the scientific (theoretical) faculty, which includes the theological department; the legal department, with its subdivisions
for higher Arabic and Islamic studies; and the department for
Arabic language, which comprises as well the school for business
and management. Engineers, doctors, and agronomists are
trained in the second group. A separate small university constitutes the division for women. It is subdivided into branches for
Arabic and Islamic studies, psychology and sociology, foreign
languages, business, and medicine.

All the faculties are strictly tailored to Islam, for Azhar does not
consider its sole task to be the promotion of worldly expertise.

Graduates from this religious institution, which is clearly distinguished from Cairo University and Ain-Shams University, are supposed to receive basic religious knowledge. Many of the students who have come to study here are from African countries south of the equator, and they are trained to be propagators for the Islamic mission.

This prestigious center of culture of the Islamic world had 11,000 students in 1945. By 1950 the number had doubled, and by the end of the 1960s, the rector referred proudly to a student body of 30,000. One-fourth came from foreign countries—from Indonesia and India, from Senegal and the Comoro Islands, from the emirates along the Persian Gulf as well as from urban centers of North America (Black Muslims). Starting at ages twelve to fifteen, the students are entrusted to approximately 1,800 teachers. Anyone striving for the highest spiritual offices leaves Azhar only seventeen to twenty-two years later.

Contributions and philanthropic foundations cover most of the expense of faculty salaries. The rector (Sheikh el-Islam) and his five associates, who comprise the institution's highest body, determine the use of the funds. Those students not housed in the extensive complex of the mosque live in one of the thirty-three-story halls (*riwaks*) that from time immemorial have housed students who are unable to pay. Among the basic subjects for all students are dogma, law, interpretation of the Koran, instruction in tradition, logic, prosody, and rhetoric. A prerequisite for studying at al-Azhar is that the applicant be able to recite the Koran by heart.

The Grand Sheikh of al-Azhar University is also the head of the other Egyptian schools of religion in Alexandria, Tanta, Zagazig, Damiette, Assiut, Shibin el-Kom, and Kena. In all of them, seven degrees are awarded, the highest being the title of master (*ostad*). Azharis, the graduates of this elite school, have achieved influential positions everywhere in the Islamic world, serving as *ulemas* (Muslim scholars), *muderris* (professors), or *kadis* (judges).

For a thousand years the uniform for the rector and the professors has been the same—a dark blue *galabia* and white turban. Their appearance corresponds to the immutability of the "true and unique teaching" they represent. Up to the present, Azhar University was always able to parry attacks against orthodox values. Only two revolutionaries of the faith, the Persian Jamal ad-Din al-Afghani and his student Mohammed Abduh, were able to escape the network of al-Azhar. They are the fathers of Islamic modernism in the nineteenth century. The Egyptian Mohammed Abduh characterized the state of Islam at the end of the last century as decadent. He believed that a renaissance of the former high civilization could be achieved by a melding of the ancient faith with the achievements of the modern Western world. Mohammed Abduh's ideas of reform were first realized under the Grand Sheikh Mahmud Saltut (who died in 1963).

Azhar University was always a factor in the battle against British colonial domination. It changed its position of rousing the people to protest, however, following the takeover by the Free Officers, in the Egyptian revolution of 1952, accommodating then to the machinery of the state. Since that time, Azhar has restricted its role to that of being a traditional religious and political institution. In this it stands in contrast to the Muslim Brotherhood, which very soon initiated its opposition to Gamal Abdel Nasser. A split developed between the conservative clergy of Azhar and the still more conservative secret organization that was striving for power. The secret organization has nonetheless managed to place its own representatives in important places in Azhar. The Muslim Brotherhood equates Azhar with the government, an assessment dating from the era when Nasser consistently used the university for his goals. Following the English-Egyptian treaty of 1954, as well as during the Suez crisis, the charismatic leader gave speeches at Azhar, which in normal times would have been regarded as an intrusion into the supreme authority of the *ulemas*. In the early '60s, Nasser subordinated the university to his state party. Only during the Sadat era was this strong tie loosened somewhat.

The Muslim Brotherhood continues to be of the opinion that al-Azhar, the leading voice of the Islamic world, has failed in its role of communicating a living and dynamic Islam. It has also decidedly failed to oppose all the temptations posed by foreign ideas and values. From many statements by leaders of the Muslim Brotherhood, the conviction emerges that Azhar University has permitted Egypt to lapse into backwardness and impotence in the areas of religion, morals, politics, law, business, and culture.

One of the spokesmen of the Muslim Brotherhood, Sheikh Mohammed el-Ghazali, accused the administrators of Azhar of having fallen asleep, taking along with them the entire Muslim community. Hassan al-Banna, the founder and first leader of the Muslim Brotherhood, criticized Azhar for producing religiously educated graduates but failing to provide spiritual models. During the era of King Farouq, as well as in later years, the Muslim Brotherhood repeatedly accused the *ulemas* of Azhar of letting themselves be corrupted by the government, of succumbing to the pleasures of life in the shadow of power, and of forgetting the defense of Islam. Ghazali complained in his florid manner: "I know sheikhs of Azhar who live in Islam like the worms of bilharzia in the blood of the impoverished peasants." The members of the Muslim Brotherhood coined a phrase for those *ulemas* known for their cooperation with whatever government was in power; they called them "hired *ulemas*," a severe offense for Sunni clergymen. In the opinion of the radical organization, accepting money from the rulers dishonored them and their religion as well. During the early '6os, the Muslim Brotherhood finally founded its own university in the city of Medina in Saudi Arabia.

In recent Egyptian history, then, there has been an ongoing spiritual battle between the modernists, the traditionalists, and the super-conservatives. The reformist ideas for law and training have been repeatedly discussed, with intensity. Not even at the leadership level, consisting of approximately thirty people and dominated by the council of the grand *ulemas*, has there been total agreement. Still, the highest authority on Islamic doctrine stopped once and for all new interpretations and upheavals within the faith.

Even now the orthodox sheikhs of almost all Islamic countries heed the statements and directives of the rectors, and pass on these *fatwas* to their adherents. The official Azhar policy is set either in response to a specific occasion (such as the trial for the murder of Sadat) or at conferences of the Islamic Research Academy, which is part of Azhar. The leading theologians of almost all Islamic states meet periodically at Azhar and subsequently publish their perceptions in a tone that is imperious, militant, and uncompromising. They are guided by a statement by the Prophet Mohammed, which is printed above one of the gates to Azhar: "Truly, actions are judged according to their intentions, and everyone is rewarded on the basis of his intentions."

Nearly all proclamations by Azhar are disseminated with a very clear intention. For example, within the framework of a conference held after losing the Six-Day War against Israel, the Grand Imam and Rector of Azhar University made the following announcement:

It is unthinkable that Allah would permit the infidels to win against the believers. Therefore the defeat which we suffered is merely a sign of Allah's concern about our well-being, for we definitely have the sole correct feeling for religion, even though we lost the path of the pious. . . . We *ulemas* must also make clear to the Islamic peoples that the lingering spirit in Israel of past pilgrimages, which had been decisively eradicated by the heroic deeds, the bravery, and the heroic resistance of our forefathers, made contemporary Zionism into a spearhead that is hurled by the enemies of mankind and the protagonists of imperialism against the Muslims.

Other speakers were outraged by the defeat, especially by a people that had always kept the Arabs in a servile, subordinate condition. The Islamic people have always considered the Jews merely a cowardly people, and they were now in the process of acting contrary to God's plan and the course of history. Professor Abdul Sattar el-Sayyed, the *mufti* of Tartus in Syria, added that according to the Koran the Jews were enemies lacking in human feeling. Following the Camp David agreement of September 1978, the administration of Azhar judged otherwise.

In large letters on the old administration building of Azhar University is printed the greeting from one conference of *ulemas* to "one billion Muslims." Although this figure is still a daydream, by the year 2000 it should be true. The realization of this goal is one of the most urgent tasks of the Azharis. They are not permitted, however, to discuss the topic in a sanctified place with a nonbeliever. In fact, people at the university do everything possible to avoid disagreeable discussions with inquisitive visitors. Thus when I tried to hold a basic discussion about Islam and its renaissance with a group of students who had agreed to talk with me, it was stopped several times with transparent excuses. In the end the discussion never took place. The university administration finally let me know why: "Security reasons." Security for whom?

I was, however, accorded the honor of being permitted to speak for thirty minutes with the Grand Sheikh of Azhar, Imam Gad al-Haq Ali Gad al-Haq, former minister of religion under Anwar el-Sadat. This highest dignitary of Sunni Islam is on a level with the pope. He is also altogether as unapproachable as the pope. Only one extensive discussion with the Western press is known to have been held by his predecessor, Abdel Moneim al-Nimr.

Abdel Moneim al-Nimr was fundamentally different from Gad al-Haq, who has held the office since the spring of 1982. The highly respected doctor of theology and professor of Koranic law was a champion of a militant resurgence of Islam. He always believed that the rebirth of Islam would destroy the differences between Sunnis and Shiites and that a mutual effort was necessary to become free of the "thought patterns of the Western world." Moreover, al-Nimr was also sympathetic toward Khomeini. "What is the use of throwing off the domination of colonialism if its ideas and ideologies continue to exert spiritual slavery?" he asked. "This fact has become clear to us. Hence our awakening, hence the drive toward liberation from everything foreign which has crept into our thinking and living, hence the reflection on our own tradition, on our own history."

One of the assertions made by Sheikh Azhar al-Nimr in an interview with the Zurich *Weltwoche* was:

We are awakened anew, are returning to our original values, to the straight path and to everything offered by Islam from the outset. Foreign ideas from the West and the East attempted to divert us from our own legacy and made our lifestyle into a pale and servile imitation of alien ways. Even the reattainment of our political independence initially changed nothing in regard to that situation. Intellectual and spiritual life remained permeated by models that do not derive from Islam. And that is the starting point for the current resurgence of Islam: the attainment of our intellectual, spiritual, and legal independence. And not merely for the attainment of national independence. For me and for the Islamic clergy, spiritual independence is in fact still more important than political independence. Only the reattainment of independence in the spiritual area will overcome one of the worst consequences of the colonial era—the alienation of entire peoples from themselves and their cultures!

The present Grand Imam of Azhar University was born in a small Egyptian village named Batra. At an early age he made the decision in favor of a life devoted to religion. He left the *sharia* faculty of Azhar University in 1943, however. After a brief career within the Islamic judicial system and as a politician, he returned to the university as the highest dignitary of the Muslim world.

Imam Gad al-Haq received me in his study, located on the first floor of the rectory. Around him sat a group of advisors, and they remained for the ensuing discussion. The room, muted by thick walls and many carpets, is paneled with inlaid wood. Heavy wooden chairs with high backs and sturdy leather upholstery stand side by side, making the similarly richly decorated desk in one of the corners of the space seem almost lost. The few paintings on the wall show motifs from the Koran; these are interspersed with tapestries.

Imam Gad al-Haq, a resolute gentleman with a trim white beard and lively eyes behind dark sunglasses, was dressed in the traditional *galabia* and white turban. He came several feet forward toward me, greeting me with a strong handshake. We sat down in chairs facing each other. The "pope of Islam" emerged as a dignified personage with a capacity for intellectual empathy and forceful articulation. He answered my questions politely and briefly, with diplomacy and yet with clarity. Gad al-Haq mentioned no names when he spoke of Egypt's opponents, although he expressed himself with florid elaboration.

During the interview (which was conducted through an English interpreter), he remained serious, nodding briefly when he thought he had answered a question sufficiently. At the end, however, he laughed and, with a gesture, offered me the tea that a servant had brought in for us. He remained politely sitting beside me until I had packed up my papers. We stood up simultaneously, and after a brief farewell the Grand Sheikh returned to the work corner of the room, where a secretary was already holding out the telephone receiver for him.

Here is my interview with Sheikh Azhar Gad al-Haq:

"Imam al-Akbar, Egypt and most of the other Islamic countries have a much more Islamic image than was noted a decade ago. What is the spiritual motive, the force behind this?"

"The spirit you refer to comes primarily from al-Azhar itself, for we teach the people and preach about the true roots of Islam. But that is not something just of the present. We could say that it dates from a thousand years ago and that al-Azhar is a beacon for all Muslims all over the world, regardless of where they live. We here in al-Azhar receive many Islamic ambassadors and emissaries from countries all over the world. Our guests study both modern and Islamic sciences. That is what happens on the one hand.

On the other hand, al-Azhar sends its students and professors everywhere in the world to teach Muslims and to preach."

"The so-called resurgence of Islam has become a strong force in the Arab region, in the entire Islamic world, and in Europe too. How should we regard this phenomenon?"

"Concerning that, I must simply state that the Muslims in the whole world—like all human creatures, indeed like all living creatures—are experiencing a kind of fatigue. But there follows a new high, a renewal. Permit me to say that for an extended period of time the Muslims experienced fatigue and are now returning again to the accustomed form—to the correct understanding and to the correct approach to Islam. You may be reminded of Europe before the Renaissance. And as a German you know what Martin Luther and his Protestants did. That is something very natural and normal. We are reactivating everything. To express it briefly, you can say that Islam itself is not weak and never was; the Muslim world itself was merely somewhat ill."

"Should we regard the actual events in Iran as a renaissance of Islam? What is your position concerning the Islamic revolution of the Ayatollah Khomeini?"

"What is happening in Iran is a political event, a political activity, and that has nothing—but nothing at all—to do with Islam."

"In various states of the Islamic world, the jihad, *or holy war, was proclaimed against communism and all other enemies of the Islamic faith. This* jihad, *however, is also directed against a political movement known as 'Arab socialism.' What is the relationship today between Islam and 'Arab socialism'?"*

"First we must establish that Islam is a divine religion and cannot be brought into association with any political theory. We cannot, therefore, associate Islam with any political thesis, be it socialistic or capitalistic. Regardless of what people may invent, Islam is, as God the Almighty stated, exclusively the religion of God. Islam therefore constitutes for us divine religion. But, quite simply expressed, *jihad* means finding the true path, rejecting bad habits and bad traditions. This kind of *jihad*, familiar to people as martial dispute, can be accepted only under very special circumstances. The most important meaning of the concept of *jihad* is to reform oneself and one's own spirit by becoming clear about all matters of faith, by convincing oneself and providing others with a good example.

"It is good for the people if they are led toward finding the correct approach to the nature of the religion and distancing themselves from bad attitudes. Islam is the path. It provides discipline and order for those who have gone astray. It guides people in prayer in the one direction, the true direction which is the Kaaba in Mecca. Sometimes the prayer lasts a whole hour, and it brings with it the duty for all believers to pray together in groups and in mosques. It also lets the people come together once a week for Friday prayer. In addition, twice a year there are prayers for the high holidays and the big meeting during pilgrimage. That is all determined by the goal of assisting people in the comprehension of their religion and in the approach to their religion and of discussing all problems with them. That is, quite simply, *jihad* in Islam.

"Islam is rich enough, since it carries socialism within it. It is not at all necessary to pay attention to the inventors and propagators of socialism. Islam itself provides social justice and community. The *zakat* of Islam, a kind of tax, means nothing other than that the wealthy donate something in order to make life possible for the poor. That is demanded of us by the almighty God Himself."

"What is your attitude toward the actual events in Afghanistan and Syria, toward the so-called holy war against the Soviet-oriented governments in both of those Islamic states? Is it still possible there, in the sense in which you mean it, to separate politics and religion?"

"Without doubt the people of Afghanistan are fighting against the Russians because they occupied their country. That is clearly a war. There is a duty for all Muslims to take up arms against unlawful invaders. The people of Afghanistan quite simply must fight against the Russians and expel them from their country. And the faithful of the entire Islamic world have the duty to stand by the Afghans in their battle. That can occur in the form of money, in the form of weapons, or also by personal participation.

"As for the situation in Syria, I believe that there what is involved is a kind of uprising against the leadership of the country. We must adhere to the statement in the holy Koran, according to which two combatting groups of Muslims have to strive for a compromise. For this reason, there is a big difference between the one war in Afghanistan and the other war in Syria."

"You are well aware of the situation in both instances and thus know that a solution satisfactory to each side is nowhere in view. In both instances the Muslim Brotherhood is fighting against the existing systems. What is your attitude toward the Muslim Brotherhood?"

"Not in each instance is the Muslim Brotherhood fighting against the system. But it supports a certain Islamic system and works for it. I continue to be against the view of members of the Muslim Brotherhood that the path to an Islamic order is unconditionally connected with war, for Islam strictly forbids war and fighting among Muslims. If these people are striving for a genuine Islamic system, then they must also adhere to the doctrine. That is exclusively God's word. The basis of Islam is the call for reform by good will along a peaceful route."

"The assassins who killed President Anwar el-Sadat said they were doing so in the name of Allah. Was that also a wrong conception?"

"That is absolutely wrong. As I already mentioned, fighting between Muslims is forbidden by Islam. One principle of Islam is good counsel, which is provided by the religion. That applies both for the ruler and for the ruled. The path of force and of killing is forbidden to us. These people took the wrong path when they killed."

"What kind of future development do you anticipate in the Islamic world and in the Islamic religion?"

"I hope that the Muslims will again find their way to the true principles of Islam in accordance with the holy book, the Koran. They also should adhere completely to the *sunna*. The *sunna* are the good examples from the life of the Prophet Mohammed, God protect him and his family. In addition, Muslims must eliminate their differences of opinion. That we need for a fruitful life."

"Only one question concerning al-Azhar University. Everywhere there is discussion of the very successful expansion of training and of the great importance of Azhar for Islam. How do you view the role of this traditional institution for now and for the future?"

"From the beginning the main goal of Azhar has been to teach both modern sciences and Islamic knowledge. These days this task is attuned to the necessities of the modern world. We have kept up with the times and will continue to do so.

"Al-Azhar will remain the decisive authority of the Islamic faith. Our message has not changed for a thousand years. Only the manner in which we proclaim it is always adapted to the times and the circumstances."

"As a last question, do you have a message for the people in the Western world, an official message from the center of the Islamic world?"

"Yes, I have a message for the West. I should like to convey to you that Islam is a religion of humanity. And it does not distinguish between Muslims and non-Muslims."

8

Holy Country for Allah

AROUND 8:15 A.M. on Easter Sunday in 1982, the thirty-eight-year-old, bearded Allan Harry Goodman left his modest hotel in the Beit-Hakerem section of Jerusalem. He was wearing a green Israeli army uniform and carrying a black M-16 automatic rifle with six full rounds of ammunition, one of which was already in the weapon. The American immigrant, who had arrived from Baltimore, Maryland, in 1977, had for four weeks been on reserve military training, and it was for this reason that his luggage did not attract more attention. Only his strange farewell remark surprised the people working at the reception desk: "I probably will not be coming back very soon." Allan Harry Goodman, known as an Arab-hater, traveled by bus to the old part of Jerusalem. He resolutely walked in the direction of Tempelberg, "the temple mount," and at the Ghawanima gate in the vicinity of the Aksa Mosque, the third-largest shrine of Islam, he disregarded the ban against carrying firearms.

What happened at 8:50 A.M. was later characterized by Harry

Allan Goodman as a "political and patriotic act." The fanatic follower of the ultra-religious American-Israeli Rabbi Meir Kahane
and his Jewish Defense League, or Kach Party (meaning "us or
the Arabs"), shot his way to the Dome of the Rock, Jerusalem's
emblem, which is crowned by a golden cupola. This was an offense beyond compare, for, according to legend, it was at Mt.
Moriah that Abraham led his son Isaac to the place of sacrifice.
Here Solomon built his temple, the house of the Lord. The Muslims believe that one year before leaving for Medina, their
Prophet Mohammed came in a mysterious manner during the
night from the Kaaba in Mecca to Jerusalem (which the Muslims
call Al Kuds), in order to ascend into heaven with his horse Burak
and to receive there a revelation of Allah. "Praise be to him," it is
stated in the seventeenth *sura* of the Koran, "who made his servant go by night to the farther temple whose surroundings we
have blessed in order to show him our sign."

At this sacred place Goodman mowed down two Arab guards
and wounded approximately twenty other people. When he had
emptied his ammunition into the blue-tiled portal of the Omar
Mosque and its interior, he let himself be arrested by the Israeli
police. While that was taking place, he boastfully stated: "They
kill Jews every day. I had to do that." The police had their hands
full trying to protect Goodman from the infuriated crowd. He
would have been lynched if the pious Muslims had caught him.
While the protectors of order ran through a rear exit to safety
with Goodman, they fired into the air and exploded tear gas
among the quickly gathering crowd. A state of martial law prevailed. Not only was there unrest in Jerusalem, but in all parts of
the West Bank, which has been occupied by Israel since the 1967
war. These outbreaks resulted in three deaths and more than 100
wounded. Led before the magistrate, Goodman gave the victory
sign with his right hand and shouted: "Justice, justice for national
liberation."

Once again the Islamic shrine had become the target of an
attack from the ranks of ultra-rightest Jews. As early as 1969, an
Australian sheep-shearer by the name of Dennis Michael Rohan
had opened fire in the Aksa Mosque in order, in his words, "to
be able once again to establish the kingdom of God." Hardly
anywhere does the religious hatred between Muslims and non-
Muslims resound so brutally as in the holy city of Jerusalem. The
city's liberation from Zionism had always been the most impor-

tant goal of the protectors of all holy shrines, the kings of Saudi Arabia. In the streets of Tehran one million people demonstrated against Goodman's act. Imam Khomeini repeatedly stated that he would carry the war in the Gulf further in order to drive his enemy Saddam Hussein from Baghdad and to be able afterward to reconquer Al Kuds (Jerusalem) for the Muslims. In Khomeini's words: "The people should rise up in order that Israel, this cancerous growth, can be destroyed." A typical Iranian statement points out that "the fascistic and usurping regime of Palestine and of beloved Jerusalem reports every day of more death, which again tears open the wounds of the Muslim masses in the whole world, consequently challenging millions of Muslims' will to fight."

There are some 115,000 Muslims living in the city of sixty mosques, where, according to a hadith, a written tradition of words of the prophets, it is considered "an act of veneration," like thousands of acts of veneration elsewhere. Except that the city is the center of a very special trouble spot—the area west of the Jordan. The West Bank, Israel's booty from the war with Jordan, is the mother country of the Jews, including Judea and Samaria, which are mentioned in the Old Testament. It consists of a strip of desert and arid, hilly country in which olive groves and vineyards flourished 2,000 years ago. For the last 1,300 years the country belonged to the Arabs. The fact that the Jews were successful when they set out to get it back is something that cannot be forgiven by the Palestinians living in West Jordan. Still less can they forgive the Israelis for wanting to keep it.

The Israeli settlement policy along the border with Jordan is extremely offensive: since 1967, much more than 100 new villages and kibbutzim have been built, and 25,000 Israelis have emigrated there. The Jewish settlements in the occupied territory, with their chunks of concrete behind barbed wire and their extremely religious inhabitants who are armed to the teeth, seem like medieval fortresses. In order to ensure the continuation of the West Bank policy, Rabbi Mosche Levinger of the militant Gusch-Emunim ("Group of the Faithful") and Rabbi Meir Kahane —who is originally from Brooklyn, New York, and has at times been subject to legal prosecution, even in Israel—instigate their fanatic followers, most of whom are from the U.S.A., to an ongoing series of actions. The attacks are financed by American sympathizers.

But the opposition is no longer asleep. A new front line against Israel, one which is arrogant and self-confident, is emerging within the heavily guarded borders of the promised land. And this has not happened merely since the temporary defeat of the Palestinian Liberation Organization in Lebanon. Muslim fundamentalists have been arming themselves for years, and they have managed to build up a secret, smoothly functioning underground organization. The activities of the orthodox Muslims have always been determined by the Palestinians' fight for their own state and by the constant confrontation between the sons of David and the followers of Yasser Arafat or Georges Habbash. Each time the Israeli military forces on the West Bank have responded with measures of immense brutality against the activities of PLO sympathizers. The Bir Said University in Ramallah has repeatedly been closed by Israel's civilian governors. The mayors of the cities of El Bireh, Ramallah, and Nablus had to leave because they refused to cooperate with the representative of the powerful state. They were replaced by Israeli officers. Nightly curfew has become the rule on the West Bank.

The use of force and humiliation has created irreconcilable hatred; its outbreak is merely a question of time and weapons. In particular, the resurgence of Islam within the occupied territory is creating the conditions for such an outbreak. I asked Hassan Tabub, the general secretary of the Supreme Islamic Council of Jerusalem, about his attitude toward the resurgence of Islam on the West Bank. His answer: "We have observed that all ideas that come from the people provide no usable solution for the problems of this world. For this reason, in the meantime we let ourselves be more strongly guided by God, who is wise, who has power, and who knows precisely what benefits His creatures. Here we are under the worst occupation in the history of the world. Our life, our position, our property are threatened. The radical Jews want to drive us away from our holy shrines with threats and open force, because they believe they have a right to ownership." The Israeli claim to the territory derives from the location of the famous Wailing Wall. It reputedly was part of the Temple of Herod, which was destroyed by the Romans in 70 A.D., but which also supports the area of the Haram es-Sharif, the Aksa Mosque.

Asked whether the Muslim Brotherhood makes its influence felt, Tabub became visibly uneasy and changed the subject. I wanted to find out from him whether there have been Iranian-controlled forces on the West Bank since Khomeini seized power. Tabub looked up with a jolt and smiled politely: "That can certainly be said." His words had the effect of malicious delight. The fact is that Khomeini's book, *The Islamic Rule,* was permitted to pass Israeli censorship, and became the number-one best-seller in Jerusalem in 1980 to 1981. The fact, too, is that the Muslim youth, in particular, who have resumed the traditional dress and live with greater religious awareness, believe they have an idol in the Iranian revolutionary leader. During my visits to the bazaar, I frequently became involved in discussions with bearded fundamentalists, all of which led to the same statement: "Soon the redeemer Khomeini will come and make short work of the Israelis."—an illusion that stubbornly persists.

The cosmopolitan mayor of Bethlehem, Elias Freij, a free spirit among the Palestinians, recognized the signs of the time. He explained to me:

In 1979 the spirit of the Muslim renaissance started to spread everywhere. That is also one result of the incompetent Arab governments. Religious fanaticism is rapidly spreading in the entire Middle East. The people believe in religion as the cure-all. They believe that they will thereby improve their own situation and be able to break the selfish domination of the Arab families who want only to increase their own wealth. But if that is the issue, we need another 500 years.

Freij, a faithful Christian, observed that the influence of the Muslim Brotherhood is increasing ("it can no longer be ignored"); at the same time the majority of the population sides with Iran on the issue of the Gulf war. In Freij's words: "Teachers, sheikhs, students, and doctors are members of the Muslim Brotherhood. They are getting many members from the villages, where the illiteracy rate among the older population is high. I am afraid that it could lead to a dictatorship if they should win. But that we see in the unlimited domination of a single man in Iran. That we see as the model."

Even during the 1950s, when the territory still belonged to Jordan, there were three fundamentalist groups on the "Wild West Bank" (Freij's term). They disagreed with each other, and worked mainly against King Hussein, whom they hated the way the Iranian *ulemas* hated their shah. The groups then disappeared, even the liberation party, Hisb el-Tahrir, which had split

off from the Muslim Brotherhood. Things became quiet among
the orthodox, since the youth turned out to be receptive to the
Western consumer society of the Israelis and to the nationalistic
as well as the leftist theories of the Palestinian liberation movements. Sheikh Said Belal, the leader of the West Bank Fundamentalists, explained this development to me. In appearance he was
a typical Palestinian, with the white turban (*kefija*), a dark green
galabia, a checked gray jacket, and a callus the size of a raisin on
his forehead (a sign of frequent contact with the prayer rug). In
his words:

Up to 1967, we here in Nablus had only nine mosques. Then came the
loss of the war, and the people again returned to the faith of their
fathers. Great activities started, and since 1967 the young people have
again attended the houses of prayer and let everything else go. We have
had to build twenty-one new mosques. All the people have recognized
that the future can only be in Islam. They have noticed that the teaching
of Allah will solve their problems. In addition, there is the fact that
events in Iran have warmed the hearts of the people and given them
hope. We are always glad when the brothers achieve victories. That
feeds our hopes for the Islamic state of Palestine.

The influential Sheikh Said Belal, whom I visited in his house
on the northern outskirts of Nablus, long ago rejected cooperat-
ing with the PLO since, in his opinion, "it does not promote any
Islamic interests." Belal and his people have lured many sympathizers away from the PLO. Belal considers Arafat "a friend of
the Russians, our enemy in the faith." He would sooner bank on
the Americans. Asked how the fundamentalists plan to come to
power, Belal answered: "Since we cannot carry weapons here,
under the present circumstances the battle would be pure suicide
—it would be *intihar*, as we say. We also cannot convince the
Israeli leaders to become Muslims. Therefore we must wait for
our time. At the sign of the slightest opposition, the government
still has the power to send us to Damascus or Amman in order to
get all of our land. We are at its mercy, and for the time being are
waiting for a political solution."

Incidents occurred, however, evidently because many fundamentalists were incapable of biding their time. These actions were
never restricted to the West Bank, but included all occupied Arab
areas under Israeli domination. The commando squads of Hisb
el-Tahrir el-Islam were capable only of limited attacks, but they

shot and killed Israeli soldiers. In 1981 members of the Tahrir Party were arrested, including the young bearded members of an Islamic underground movement called Al-Jilal, which had formed in Galilee—in other words, in the Israeli motherland. Its members came from wealthy families sympathetic to the Iranian model. Large quantities of weapons and ammunition were found in Arab villages, and their owners were summoned to military courts. The members of Al-Jilal are reputed to belong to a still larger organization called "Family of the Holy War," which is in Umma al-Fahm, south of Nazareth, and is connected with the Muslim Brotherhood. In January 1981 alone, the Israelis arrested twenty *ulemas* for support of a radical secret organization. These champions of religion had modeled themselves on the example provided by the leader of the first religious uprisings against the Jews of Palestine, Sheikh Iss al-Din al-Qassam, who was killed in 1935 by the British, and by Al Haj Amin, who led the large-scale revolt of 1936.

On June 1, 1979, the imam of Gaza, Sheikh Hashem Khusandar, who had voiced support for the Egyptian-Israeli peace agreement, was murdered. In the battle for power between the PLO and the fundamentalists, another sheikh from Gaza was killed. At that time a storm of young people influenced by Islam attacked liquor stores and movie houses. On October 12, 1980, riots in Gaza between Palestinian Khomeini admirers and old-guard fundamentalists resulted in injuries to three people. Early in 1982 there was a fire in the library of the religious academy, Al Askar, in the largest Palestinian city. The incident was a PLO act of revenge against the rector, Sheikh Mohammed Awad, a member of the Muslim Brotherhood.

For a long time the Israelis were pleased with the rivalry between the religious people and the PLO, so they left the fundamentalists alone and only stopped the PLO. But this policy of toleration had limits, as is shown by measures taken by the state against the citadels of radical Muslims.

In addition to the Islamic University in Gaza, these citadels include the Polytechnic Institute in Hebron, which is the burial place of the ancestral Abraham and ranks fourth among the most important Islamic shrines, and Najah University in Nablus, thirty-seven miles north of Jerusalem. It is at Najah University, which was founded in 1918, that the discussion is furthest advanced. Rector Hikmat al-Masri, the head of the most important family of Nablus and a former spokesman of the Jordanian parliament, entered into an alliance with the fundamentalists against the most prominent PLO representative on the West Bank, Mayor Bassam Shakaa of Nablus. The Islamic students won a total of eleven seats in the elections allowing co-administration that were held early in 1982. Student spokesman Nasser al-Din al-Shaer told me: "We want to pass on clear knowledge about Islam to all fellow students. That was so often misunderstood, especially by Muslims. Then we should like to attempt to transform this theoretical concept into practice. We are in the process of reactivating the faith in that direction altogether." They have already proved that, in the powder keg of Bir Said. In the last elections the orthodox Muslims won forty-two percent of the seats, leaving a smaller share to the PLO forces than ever before. The Israelis no longer bother to differentiate, at times closing one university, at times another.

In May 1982 four *ulemas* were even arraigned before a military court of the West Bank. The investigating authorities accused them of anti-Israeli sermons during the Friday prayer and of calling for revolution against the occupiers.

The sensitivity of the occupiers is growing since a poll by *Time* magazine in April 1982 showed that the inhabitants of fifty-eight cities and villages of the West Bank are flirting with the idea of an Islamic state, although at that time the PLO was still in full possession of its power. I requested an interview with the highest Islamic preacher on the West Bank and the leader of the Friday prayer at the Aksa Mosque, Sheikh Ikrima Said Sabri. The religious leader is a member of the Committee for National Leadership, a former PLO supporter, and a nationalist from the Islamic establishment. Here is our discussion:

How will things continue on the occupied West Bank and in Jerusalem?"
"The best solution is for the Israelis to get out and to leave their territory to us, the traditional inhabitants. We should first peacefully convince them of that. If that does not help, then we could also seek other routes."

"Does that include the use of force?"
"Relations between two nations are always peaceful or belligerent, so it can involve only one of the two. Every reasonable person, however, prefers the peaceful route."

Wilhelm Dietl with Salem Azzam, the Secretary General of the
Islamic Council for Europe, an organization anathema to the
official governments of the Near East.

Dietl and one of the Imam Khomeini's closest advisers:
Dr. Sadegh Tabatabai, himself a son of a revered *ayatollah*.
(Photo © Jupp Darchinger, Bonn)

With the leaders of the Muslim Brotherhood and the Muslim
Sisterhood, respectively, Omar el-Telmisani and Zeinab
al-Ghazali al-Gebeily.

Qazi Hussain Ahmad, Secretary General of the Pakistani
Muslim Brotherhood, Jamaat-e Islami, and Dietl in the border
city of Peshawar.

The author with the "pope of Islam," Grand Sheikh Gad al-Haq
Ali Gad al-Haq, at Cairo's Azhar University.

Mohammed Ali Jinnah founded the Muslim state of Pakistan.

Dr. Ali Shariati, a bourgeois revolutionary from Iran.

Sheikh Omar el-Telmisani, the Supreme Guide of the
Muslim Brotherhood.

Imam Hassan al-Banna founded and developed the
Muslim Brotherhood.

Sayed Qutb, the head ideologist of the Muslim Brotherhood,
with many of his followers, likewise indicted, at his
trial in Cairo.

"But considering the superior strength of the Israelis, what if that should prove to be senseless?"

"Even then we will get our rights. As has already occurred, we are extending our hand to all Islamic movements and are including them."

"Would the Islamic state of Palestine that you are striving for remain restricted to the West Bank?"

"No, certainly not. It should also include the area of present-day Israel, which exists illegally—in other words, it should include everything that geographically belongs to Palestine."

"Do you get support for this model from your benefactor, Saudi Arabia?"

"For us, Saudi Arabia is the furthest removed from the ideals of Islam. We profoundly regret that the Saudis do not care for the Muslim community and that it uses the oil that is the general property of the Muslims exclusively for its own purposes. In a formal sense, Islam is the state religion in Saudi Arabia, but in a practical sense it is not."

Dr. Amin el-Khatib, the brother of the former mayor of Jerusalem who was expelled by the Israelis, is a thoughtful man who chairs the Union for Philanthropic Organizations. He is moderate and conciliatory, except when the free practice of religion is threatened. "For me, the fundamentalists are too extreme," he confided to me. "But the more the Aksa Mosque and the Islamic system [which he represents in the Supreme Council] is attacked, the more all Muslim forces draw together. In an emergency our people will use all means to defend the Aksa. For that we would also spill blood. For us Muslims, the Aksa Mosque is, according to the Koran, the first direction to which we must turn in prayer."

Dr. Amin el-Khatib is confident in regard to the future: "In the long term, if we are not permitted to live under our own rule, then the riots will increase. And if we lose the fourth battle, then the fifth and sixth will follow. This will shake up everything and will be accompanied by still more force and blood and suffering for us. But our lobby is also growing. The decisive test of strength is by no means very far away."

As if in confirmation, the Muslim Brotherhood has published a detailed plan for the liberation of the region. It states:

The Islamic Revolution holds the view that a radical solution of the Palestinian problem can be reached as follows:

1. By declaring the Palestinian problem to be a cause of Islam and by keeping all Islamic resources in readiness so they can be placed in its service.

2. By rejecting all resolutions that have been made on the matter by the United Nations and other institutions.

3. By clearly and tenaciously proclaiming our categorical refusal to accept entirely or partially the presence of the Zionist form of state.

4. By refusing to recognize the legality of any Jewish presence in Palestine to the extent that it can be proved that this presence consisted in the purpose of colonialization in preparation for the birth of the Zionist form of state.

5. By returning under the banner of the *jihad* to Jerusalem and into the country of Palestine and by admitting that Islam has the right to take up the battle for it after being excluded from it for the duration of a third of a century. For victory can be achieved only by Islam and by *jihad* for God's cause. The emissary of God (peace be with Him) stated: "The day of the last judgment will not come before the Muslims fight against the Jews."

6. By having the Islamic revolution state that its actual battle against the Zionists will take place and that the battle against the sectarian regime in Syria is nothing more than an advance skirmish for this decisive battle. The Syrian regime has been involved in order that it serve as a cover and keep the people in Syria in suspense, diverting them from their real battle against the Zionists. For this reason, the regime is pleased to get support from the East and from the West. The battle cry of our Islamic Revolution is: "Anyone who believes in God and in the Last Judgment should not hold the Fajr prayer [morning prayer] except in the territory of Jerusalem and in the vicinity of Jaffa, Haifa, and Hebron. That is truly the Islamic method in the solution of this problem, and that is precisely the measure by which the degree of patriotism of each individual, each party, or group can be understood.

Repeatedly I must remember what the Israeli journalist Dani Rubinstein of the daily *Davar* told me: "The radicals have only a few thousand followers, with their supporters perhaps ten thousand. But is it not the prevailing climate that matters? The number of followers is not always decisive. Motivation is what matters. And that will certainly make problems for us here in Israel."

On September 21, 1982, Khomeini sent this message to the Muslim world:

Oh, thou drops released from the ocean of the Koran and Islam, awaken and ally yourselves with this divine flood, let yourselves be radiated by the divine light in order that the greedy eye of the devourer of the world is disappointed by you and that an end be made of your exploitative and aggressive domination. In this way, you can achieve a worthy life, reflect on the true human values, and liberate yourselves from a mound of vandalizing Zionists who before your eyes trample under their boots the Muslims, who are deprived of their rights. Oh, God, show us, the stunned, the favor of awakening, and persuade the rulers in the Islamic countries to discover themselves in order that they may solve the questions of Muslims in accordance with Islamic principles and destroy the idols of selfishness and arrogance.

9

Death in Hamah

STANDING IN THE DEAD STREETS of Hamah, in front of ruins of houses and of rubble, one is overcome by a feeling of helplessness. It becomes clear that something incomprehensible has happened here: mass murder. Looking at the final, unchangeable result to reconstruct the fate of individuals is senseless. The only thing that still counts is the arithmetic of killing. The angry word "genocide" comes to mind; even the cynical Syrian government spokesman no longer calls it war. It was a three-week slaughter that the so-called civilized world politely ignored. In the name of Allah and of the Syrian President Hafiz el-Assad, the fourth largest city of the country was to a large extent destroyed. In the process, men, women, and children who protested in the name of the same Allah lost their lives.

Hamah, 124 miles north of Damascus, is one of the oldest cities of the Orient. It was described by the chroniclers as early as the second millennium before Christ. Around 1550 B.C. it was one of the centers of the Mitanni, an Indo-European people. Then came

[130]

the Aramaeans in 1100 B.C., followed by the Hittites, Assyrians, Seleucids, Romans, and Byzantines. The ancient city of Hamah was taken over by the Arabs in 700 B.C. and by the Mamelukes in the fourteenth century.

The city is famous worldwide for its enormous water wheels on the ancient Orontes River (Nahr el-Asi). In the official guide still distributed by the Ministry of Information in Damascus, it is stated: "Hamah enchants the guest with its picturesque ancient part of town. The former residence of the governor of the city, Assaad Pasha El-Azem (1742), was turned into a museum. Hamah is one of the large centers of the Syrian interior. It has particular importance as a market center for the nomads and in the production of silk wares. It is also the city with the best racehorses of Syria."

In a more recent history book, however, it should be stated: "Hamah is the city in which in February 1982 the horrible Middle Ages returned. In three weeks of heavy fighting between the population and the Syrian army, 24,000 civilians and 6,000 soldiers lost their lives. Approximately 10,000 inhabitants of Hamah were put into jails and internment camps in all parts of Syria. Most of them never returned. The regime of President Hafiz el-Assad in Damascus once again avoided being toppled."

What happened? The Muslim Brotherhood has existed in Syria for thirty years, since the revolutionary spark of the anti-colonialist movement of Imam Hassan al-Banna spread from Egypt. But only since 1976 has the extremely powerful organization become a household word. The Syrian Muslim Brotherhood raises the spearhead of opposition against Assad, who uses his whole family to sustain his rule by brute force. The Muslim Brotherhood in Syria is ninety percent Sunni; they are oppressed by the minority sect of the Alawites (eleven percent), a branch of the Shiites.

The long-suppressed rage against the Assad clan broke out for the first time on June 16, 1979. On that Saturday Islamic fundamentalists attacked with unaccustomed strength. Previously they had only a series of small bombings and attacks to their credit.

The setting was the artillery school of Aleppo, Syria's second-largest city, along the Turkish border. On this day Captain Ibrahim al-Yusuf, a member of the Muslim Brotherhood, was the officer in charge. He smuggled a number of religious fighters (*mujahideen*) through the security controls. He then summoned the cadets to an urgent meeting in the officer's mess. When they

were lined up in the hall, he commanded those sharing his opinions to open fire. Members of the Muslim Brotherhood used modern automatic rifles and threw hand grenades. In a few moments,
more than 200 young cadets were dead.

After the massacre at Aleppo a countrywide campaign was
started to get rid of the Muslim Brotherhood. It began with the
execution of fifteen members who had been captured. A decree
by the state security courts, on June 27, 1979, stated: "Imperialism
and Zionism have sent their agents into our country to perpetrate
crime, including murder and destruction, and to spread the seeds
of rebellion among the sons of our people. All this is occurring
under the mantle of religion which even distances itself from it."

Assad's Decree 49 claims that every member of the Muslim
Brotherhood must expect the death penalty. Moscow's most loyal
vassal in the Middle East has tightened his security measures
against the danger from within. In 1980 riots flared in all Syrian
cities. More political murder was carried out in Damascus than in
Italy during the days of the Red Brigades or in terror-ridden Turkey before the seizure of power by the military. In a demonstration in Aleppo, the police alone shot 300 people on the open
streets. Hamah, the center of the Sunnis, was repeatedly the
scene of bloody street slaughters. The outrage against the Assad
regime reached its high point when soldiers disrupted faithful
Muslims in the Friday prayers.

In the middle of May 1981 special units of the Syrian army ran
into armed groups of the Muslim Brotherhood approximately
thirty-one miles west of Hamah. In revenge, several units from
Assad's private army slipped into the city during the night of
May 23 and opened fire. The special units, supported by regular
troops, allegedly also used tanks and gave the command to shoot
at the Omar Ibn al-Chattab Mosque. A tank commander refused,
resulting in fighting between the army and the special units. Altogether, it is alleged, 165 civilians, thirty of Assad's guards,
twenty-eight soldiers, and approximately fifty secret service
agents lost their lives.

The *Washington Post* also reported a massacre of the civilian
population of Hamah, supposedly during the night of April 24,
1981. According to that account, Syrian soldiers stormed into
apartments at random and rounded up all the men. Shooting
could be heard until morning. The streets of Hamah were strewn
with corpses. A more recent incident occurred in December 1981,

when there was considerable shooting in connection with house searches.

The Muslim Brotherhood of Syria, led by Ali el-Bayanuni, Adnan Sadeddin, and Said Hawwa, was out for revenge. Using international connections, they prepared a large-scale revolt that in one blow would take over the entire country. The organizers of this coup had their weapons transported mainly through Iraq. Assistance also came from Jordan, where members of the Brotherhood could move about without interference. The West German branch of the Muslim Brotherhood of Syria had an important share in the preparation of the people's uprising of February 1982.

Despite that, something happened that no one had counted on: the efforts were subverted by a vengeful agent provocateur within the Muslim Brotherhood. Adnan Okla, a thirty-year-old engineer, was the military commander of the Muslim Brotherhood in Aleppo, and he was striving for command over the *mujahideen* in all of Syria. Eight years earlier he had wanted to achieve power by any means. As a result, he was excluded from the organization, but was later taken in again through the intercession of Adnan Saddedin. This same Adnan Okla took advantage of the fact that shortly before February 2, 1982, contacts between the supreme command of the Islamic Revolution and the bases in Hamah were interrupted; he traveled into the city and posed as coordinator for the impending countrywide uprising.

It was known that a vast attack was in the offing, since the leadership of the Muslim Brotherhood, in denial of its true strength, had prematurely issued statements to that effect. Adnan Okla announced in Hamah that when the "voice of revolution" in Baghdad broadcast a certain code word, then the hour would have come. On February 2, tension was at a height. Moreover, Assad's troops had again started one of their searches. They systematically combed through the entire city, house by house. In the process, several important bases blew up. The soldiers were engaged in skirmishes. The connection between the bases of the Muslim Brotherhood broke off. At this point Okla's code word sounded through the air. The drama took its course, at the end of which Adnan Okla was again suspended. For some time, he left the country and went underground in Paris.

This is how death came to Hamah. As a prelude, a military

patrol was ambushed the evening of February 2. During the ensuing night, heavily armed Islamic religious fighters in groups of five, cloaked in traditional *kefijas* (turbans) and with automatic pistols and cocked Kalashnikovs in hand, crept through the dark streets of Hamah. Around 5:00 A.M. they reached their battle zones. At the new apartment buildings in the north, housing officials faithful to the regime were surrounded; so were numerous other buildings in the city.

Simultaneously the *mujahideen* stormed the apartments of twenty-two members of the secret service and high officials of the ruling socialist Baath Party (which together are Assad's most important instruments for suppression of the opposition). Before the eyes of their wives and children, the representatives of the state were taken from their beds and killed. In the process, the sister of the Damascus minister of defense, Mustafa Tlass, is said to have died. She allegedly attempted to defend herself with a pistol that was lying on the nighttable. The loyal servants of the regime didn't have a chance. All telephone lines to the police and army had been cut. Street blockades assured that the site was left to the Muslim Brotherhood.

The next phase of the big attack was controlled by the Sunni imams. In enthusiastic appeals they summoned the population of Hamah to holy war against the godless Alawites. The revolts spread.

The official version of the Muslim Brotherhood concerning the outbreak of fighting around Hamah is somewhat different. In Kuwait the organization published the following explanation:

In the name of God, the Merciful, the Compassionate. Peace be with His messenger, the seal of the Prophet and the common leader of the *mujahideen*. The situation exploded at its most extreme the evening of February 2, 1982, after heavy firing on the city of Hamah by artillery and rockets. The bombardment was even heard in the city of Al-Rustan, twelve miles away, and many buildings were completely destroyed. Under the leadership of the *mujahideen* the people revolted as if they were one man. The people occupied all government buildings as well as the headquarters of the Baath Party, the headquarters of the police and the military, the main jail, the governor's palace, and the weapons depot. Weapons and ammunition were passed out to the brave citizens, who liberated the city within a radius of nine miles. A clean sweep was made of Hamah, and fifty spies and agents were executed. Our people took over the airport, thus keeping it from being used in opposition to them. The Forty-seventh Brigade that occupied our city joined the rebels.

According to the statement by the Muslim Brotherhood, the air force was ordered from Damascus to bomard the city and its population. Six pilots refused, however. In a discussion in Damascus I learned from members of the air force that the pilots in question had relatives in Hamah and therefore did not want to undertake anything against the city. They were arrested and executed at an air force base along the Iraq border.

People in the capital now slowly began to notice what was happening in Hamah. Troops moved forward from two sides— initially, two tank divisions and one unit with helicopters. They set up road blockades between Homs and Hamah as well as between Aleppo and Hamah. The Twenty-first Brigade from Al-Katifa got under way with its heavy tanks. "But our heroes," stated the Muslim Brotherhood, "blew up the bridges along the Al-Rustan dam, and access to the city from this point was impossible."

In the suburbs of Hamah fighting broke out on one side between the Forty-seventh Brigade and the *mujahideen,* and on the other side between the Twenty-first Brigade and Assad's special units under Ali Haydar. Every ten minutes military ambulances are said to have brought the wounded and dead from the government's side into Homs, twenty-eight miles away. Forces of the regime suffered severe losses, according to information provided by the *mujahideen.* There was talk of 3,000 dead and wounded just along the road to Homs.

Hafiz el-Assad recognized that this revolt in northern Syria was the greatest and most serious threat to his power to date, so he commanded that all government facilities in Damascus be made secure and that the revolts in Hamah be crushed—without delay and at any price. Professionals who more than once had proved themselves in suppressing Syrian centers of unrest were called in to assist in the campaign. Damascus also sent in the Third Tank Division. The people shut up in Hamah, however, were roused by their leaders by tales of revolt all over Syria. Reports of defeats and of severe riots in the capital caused them to fight even more bitterly. Anyone who even remotely came under suspicion of sympathy for the government lost his life during the first days of the uprising.

When Assad sensed that much of the army was unwilling to comply with the command to attack Hamah, he dispatched to the front, in ever greater numbers, forces under the command of his brother, Rifaat el-Assad, who is head of the Defense Brigades. This notorious blood-thirsty militia formed a large ring around Hamah, destroying water and power lines. After Hamah had been taken, it carried out acts of absolutely unparalleled brutality against the civilian population.

Two days later approximately 12,000 soldiers with 100 tanks were just outside of Hamah. A first attempt by parachute troopers to conquer the citadel failed. Both sides took up positions of all-round defense. The *mujahideen* blew up an another bridge and further impeded the advance of the soldiers. General strikes were proclaimed in other places—in Aleppo, for example. Isolated clashes between the rebels and government troops occurred in Damascus, Aleppo, and Latakia.

Sheikh Abul Nasr el-Bayununi, leader of the oppositional Islamic Front, appealed to all Syrians to fight against the Assad regime: "Everyone has to assume his share in the responsibility, because everyone knows that he is a soldier of Islam. No one can shrink from the fulfillment of his duties, for these days are critical. History will be an exacting witness, and Allah is all-knowing and all-seeing."

By issuing a new statement daily, the Syrian administration postponed the reopening of the international highway connecting Turkey with Jordan via Aleppo, Hamah, and Damascus. Ten days after the start of fighting, Hamah was to a large extent still blocked off. The shooting increased in intensity. Since there was no end to the fighting in sight, the Syrian authorities opened up an alternate route on Feburary 15, and international traffic could resume.

Government troops bombarded the city with 130-millimeter grenades, fired rockets from helicopters, and allegedly also used poisonous gas grenades. At the same time, for the sake of appearances, Foreign Minister Abdul Halim Khaddam invited foreign reporters to visit Hamah, calling Syria the most stable country in the entire region of the Middle East. Even two months later, however, no one had accepted his invitation.

On February 16, the number of besiegers had increased to 17,000. According to unconfirmed reports, Syrian called in 7,000 men from its Arab Deterrent Force from Lebanon and stationed them on this front. On February 17, Algeria's former president, Ahmed Ben Bella, in his capacity as chairman of the International Islamic Commission for Human Rights, wrote a letter to Hafiz el-Assad, in which he condemned "the increase in acts of blind force, randomly perpetrated by the security troops against the inhabitants of the city of Hamah in particular and against the Syrian population in general." Ben Bella spoke of "anti-democratic measures and absolute tyranny by the state." He deplored the use of force as a means of managing the Syrian crisis and demanded the immediate cessation of fighting and other unlawful attacks; he also demanded that all political prisoners be freed.

On February 18, a heavy barrage against Hamah continued around the clock. By the sixteenth day of fighting, no one except Ben Bella had intervened to deter Assad from the destruction of Hamah and the killing of the Syrian population. Syria's financial backers in Saudi Arabia, who were kept informed by their embassy in Damascus through news services and through personal contacts, remained quiet. Then the city fell, and the bloodiest internal dispute of an Arab country since the end of World War II came to a dramatic climax.

In Hamah I spoke with a businessman, one of the few survivors. "The last heavy fighting took place in the bazaar section in the old part of town," he told me. "After a number of soldiers had been killed while entering a narrow alley, they moved forward only in tanks, causing the walls of houses to collapse. Many people were buried beneath the rubble. Where this measure was to no avail, the houses, along with the people in them, were simply blown up."

The Muslim Brotherhood fought bitterly for every square foot of their citadel. They defended the mosques particularly vehemently. The sacred area of the Grand Mosque (Jami el-Kebir) was a complete shambles when I visited the destroyed city of Hamah. The mountains of rubble could in no way be recognized as a former house of God. All that remained of the centuries-old mosque was a tangle of broken stones and fragments of clay, and nothing was left of the ruins of an old Byzantine basilica in the vicinity of the mosque.

Another of the ninety-five completely destroyed mosques bore signs of heavy tank fire in the cupola. Seeing the fields of rubble and ruins of the former Kelaniye, Sambaiye, or Harmediye sections of the city immediately prompted me to compare them with

Berlin and Dresden in 1945. Despairing people were everywhere, poking around with sticks in their former dwellings. In many places corpses were thought to still lie under the rubble. Up to the end of the fighting, a Hamahwi told me, everyone who came into view was shot. The streets were covered with corpses. The regime in Damascus later sent bulldozers to push aside the debris and even out the mass graves.

It was hell for everyone who had to see and experience it. Assad's soldiers became vandals, burning and plundering anything that still remained. Any woman who crossed their path became a victim of the hordes gone wild. Two months later 300 survivors from Hamah petitioned for abortion. Rarely had there been so much brutality in the Islamic world.

"It was as if the fire had come down from heaven," one of the inhabitants told me, unable to find words to describe everything. "They made us poor. Our only wish is just to get something to eat and some quiet. None of us knows how things are supposed to continue." There was no family in Hamah that did not mourn the loss of at least one member. Mostly, entire families were killed. The fate of Hamah is an unparalleled example of things run amok.

Andreas Kohlschuetter, a German expert on the Middle East, was one of the few foreign visitors to the destroyed city of Hamah. He noted in *Die Zeit:*

Fear of death, inhuman mistrust, the feared paratroopers, and the terrorizing special units of the president's brother, Rifaat Assad, rule the hour. Every discussion reveals new images of the horror of the "War for Hamah," which broke out during the night from February 2 to February 3. All the men from one street of houses were commanded by the troops to distribute bread and were summarily executed. Approximately seventy men in front of the city hospital were gunned down on February 19. At the same site lie the horribly mutilated corpses of an eye doctor well-known in the city and an internist. A mother for a week was not permitted to remove the corpse of her son, who had been shot in the front of the door to her house. There was a mass execution of all inhabitants of an apartment house in the center of town. Nobody inquires about names or documents, about guilt or innocence.

Gradually, more and more details about the end of Hamah, a city known from the days of the Old Testament, leaked through into Damascus by means of whispers. A member of the air force told me that Soviet officers, experts in street fighting, were present at the scene. The numerous military advisors in Syria had to do something to protect the regime that was still their Middle Eastern ally. On Feburary 9, Syria's security service boss, Ali Douba, requested help from the chief Soviet advisor, General Jaschkin, and his deputy, General Afamasyer. The twelve Soviet officers used in Hamah allegedly went to Damascus on February 12, and flew away again on February 18. Three days later, three coffins containing the corpses of Soviet officers—two captains and one lieutenant—reportedly arrived at the capital's Al-Maza Airport and were taken with military honors onto an airplane. It was said that they were victims of a trap set by members of the Muslim Brotherhood.

From Islamic circles in London it became known that Pope John Paul II had interceded with President Assad—not for Hamah, but for the nearby town of Maharadeh, which is inhabited exclusively by Christians. The residents of this village had eagerly supported the rebelling Hamahwis. For this reason, Assad wanted to destroy Maharadeh, too. The warning from Rome came in time; it was heeded in Damascus.

What was the Assad regime's purpose in the bloodshed and ruthlessly severe revenge? I asked the minister of information, Ahmed Iskander Ahmed, a member of the advisory council of the Baath Party and one of the president's closest advisors. "Our society is not violent," he replied. "And our party, the one that heads this society, is not a party that exerts force for the sake of force. Only in past years has political murder increased in Syria as a means of combat. These attacks in Hamah reached the highpoint. I must tell you, however, that we did not start that way, for politically and morally we condemn killing. But ultimately we had to defend ourselves and our people, and for this reason we killed the criminals."

"Did the response have to occur in such a merciless manner?" I inquired. According to Minister Iskander: "Every state in this world has the right to protect itself against terrorists and murderers. In our case, we simply had to kill several hundred people. But these people themselves had already killed many citizens when we came to Hamah. We did not want to attack so hard. It was quite simply a result of the circumstances."

My next question was: "In your opinion, who is behind the events in Hamah?" He answered: "The Muslim Brotherhood is one of the tools that the United States uses against Syria. The

American imperialists provided them with armaments. The Zionists also played a certain role in it, too, and our enemies in
Jordan and in Iraq."

Immediately afterwards the opponents of the Syrian regime
closed ranks more tightly. On March 11, 1982, in Paris, they published a "Charter of the National Alliance for the Liberation of
Syria." In addition to the Muslim Brotherhood, members included the pro-Iraqi wing of the Baath Party, the Arab Socialists,
and various other splinter groups, but not the communists.
Sheikh Ali el-Bayanuni explained at a press conference in Paris
that the founding of the alliance had been simplified by the
bloody clashes in Hamah.

The alliance is particularly active in the U.S., where it has already organized student demonstrations, and in Europe, especially in Paris. The leaders declare themselves independent and
very optimistic in regard to toppling the Assad government. In a
confident tone of voice, they proclaim that neither support by a
superpower nor help from Europe is needed. All that is needed
is a little understanding.

With Allah's help, people in Syria will also conquer the "godless one." In a programmatic statement, the "Manifesto of the
Islamic Revolution" predicts:

Since it has responsibility for *jihad* [holy war], God's word is upheld,
and His law rules on earth in order that all mankind share in the
blessedness here on earth and in the beyond, and since it is confronted
with attacks of utmost severity by the enemies of God and of the people,
it is the wish of the present Islamic Revolution, which is confidently
familiar with the fact that the promise of God is fulfilled, to inform you
that the Islamic flood, which is now in the process of increasing, is
moving foward and will not stop—not before the complete victory
against all forces of evil, of darkness, and of ignorance is achieved with
the help of God.

If this occurs, people could discuss at length with Islamic scholars whether it is God's will to accept fatalistically the death of
30,000 people and the destruction of the city of Hamah. God
created Hamah along the Orontes—so it is stated in the records
of the ancients—during gray, primordial times, and upon His
return to earth will recognize it as the only city, because it has
not changed. Since February 1982, that will no longer be possible
for God. The ancient city of Hamah no longer exists.

10

Holy War Against the Lion

SYRIA IS IN A UNIQUE SITUATION; it resembles a citadel that is besieged from within and from without—which is precisely what makes Hafiz el-Assad's position appear difficult. No country of the Middle East is as isolated as this military dictatorship with an Islamic coating and loyalty to Moscow. Entirely surrounded by enemies, it has a pact with the widely unpopular country of Iran and with the superpower that has lost respect in the entire region since recent incidents in Afghanistan. Since the withdrawal of the PLO from West Beirut and Tripoli and since President Amin Gemayel's government is extremely weak, Syria can only provide Israeli presence as an explanation for saddling its small neighbors with its 30,000-man deterrent force. As a consequence, the arguments for massive financial assistance from Saudi Arabia have also become invalid. Syria would stand alone in another clash with Israel.

Syria is internally split and externally stronger than ever. After Hamah and after Lebanon, the opponent is more than ever to be sought in the National Alliance for the Liberation of Syria, whose greatest strength is the Muslim Brotherhood. After Mustafa al-Sibai gave up the leadership of the organization because of health considerations, Issam el-Attar advanced his position and in 1962 even campaigned openly for elections in Damascus. Within the Muslim Brotherhood, though, his leadership was hotly disputed, and he was replaced during the 1960s by a highly respected professor of religion, Abdel Fattah Abu Ghodda.

The sheikh's life was in danger, however, and he had to leave Syria in the early '60s. People knowledgeable about the Muslim Brotherhood believe that Sheikh Abu Ghodda, who is over seventy and now teaches within the security of Riad, does more than merely follow developments in Syria from a comfortable distance.

The movement of members of the Muslim Brotherhood is inseparable from the postwar confusion in Syria. Before Assad's assumption of power on November 16, 1970, one regime after the other ruled for brief periods of time. Policy was determined by the Baath Party, which is to say that it was strongly determined by Arab nationalism. The viewpoint of the Arab Socialist Baath Party is that residents of the Near East constitute a spiritual and cultural unity, a composite nation made up politically and economically of various countries. For almost four decades intellectuals and the military have been seeking an Arab route to noncommunist socialism, and for this reason oppose the resurgence of Islam.

"The Arabs constitute a nation that possesses an eternally enduring mission." That is how the founder of the Baath Party, Michel Aflak, formulated the slogan of his pan-Arab movement. He never managed, however, to spread the idea from Morocco to Iran. It remained restricted to Syria and Iraq and, despite ideological agreement between the two states, led to a quarrel that is still going on. After the withdrawal of the French, the Baath Party was set up in 1946 by Aflak, who is Christian, and Salah Ed-Din al-Bitar, who is Muslim. The two men knew each other from their student years in Paris (1929–1934). The greatest triumph of the Baath Party was the temporary union of Syria and Egypt in 1958. It did not last long, though, as the Syrians realized that Nasser was the superior partner; he laid claim to sole leadership. In 1963 the first Baath regime was established with coups in Baghdad and Damascus.

In 1964 Salah Ed-Din al-Bitar became prime minister and General Amin al-Hafez the head of state. Leftist radical forces toppled the moderate regime in 1966 and ushered in cooperation with the Soviet Union. Toward Israel they pursued a hard line and consequently made themselves partly responsible for the outbreak of the 1967 war. Defeat strengthened the position of Hafiz el-Assad, then head of the air force and minister of defense. His hour came in 1970. After his bloodless coup, he used the slogan "Corrective Movement" to introduce moderation in both domestic and foreign policy, accompanied by a liberal economic policy. When the ideals slowly gave way to a brutal dictatorship, Aflak and the leading representatives of his view went into exile in Baghdad.

The Islamic opposition did not fail to take note of this development. As early as 1963, the Baathists were condemned by Islamic fundamentalists in Kuwait. In the newspaper *Rai Al Aam* it was stated: "The main problem of the Arab nation is not in the economic area but at the level of morality and the spirit. What we need at this stage is a religious rebirth, since the materialists and the so-called national parties have provided proof of their bankruptcy. Without Islam there is no Arab rebirth." After Radio Damascus believed it had discovered signs of antiquated religious ideas in Nasser's "philosophy of revolution," the Egyptian *rais*, in a speech in Alexandria, accused the Baathists of being godless. As usual, the Sheikh of Azhar at that time supported the accusation, with a condemning *fatwa*.

The movement within Syria gained in militancy as early as 1964. In addition to the old, conservative Muslim Brotherhood of Mustafa al-Sibai, there was a young, angry generation, which demanded armed struggle against a regime it considered too worldly. Doctors, lawyers, and engineers supported this idea. One of them, an engineer from Hamah named Marwan Hadid, attracted public attention during the first religious riots in 1964 and again in 1973, after a long period in detention. On March 13, 1973, the Socialist People's Democracy proclaimed its first constitution, but it did not declare Islam the state religion. The outraged *ulema* called for resistance, and bloody street fighting ensued in the centers of the Sunnis, Hama and Homs. The military intervened. Among the numerous people arrested was the leading member of the Muslim Brotherhood, Marwan Hadid, who died in prison a year later under mysterious circumstances. Chief ideologist Said Hawwa escaped the state torturers in 1974 and vanished underground.

At that time an additional reproach was voiced against Assad —one that has not diminished in relevance. The Sunnis accused the president and his family of being members of Alawite or even Nusairite sects, which from the orthodox point of view are not recognized as Islamic. The Alawites make up seven to eleven percent of the Syrian population, while the Sunnis comprise seventy percent of the 9.5 million Syrian population.

The Alawites were founded in the year 872 A.D. Their first leader, Mohammed Ibn Nussair, incorporated Islamic, Christian, and heathen-gnostic elements into the faith. The French mandate authorities promised them their own state with Latakia as its center. For the sake of simplicity, they called them Alawites, taking the name from their ideal, the stepson of Mohammed, whose name was Ali. The four tribes of the Alawites still live in the vicinity of Latakia. The powerful people of the country—among them Assad's family—all belong to the Al-Matawirah tribe, which differs only in nuances from the religious community.

Since 1973 the Muslim Brotherhood has systematically prepared for the big exchange of blows with the "regime of the infidels." Mosques and universities became centers for conspiratorial gatherings and recruitment, and its membership increased. One site of weapons training for the most active among the *mujahideen* was the Palestinian camps in Lebanon. Today membership in the Muslim Brotherhood has spread throughout the whole country; to an increasing extent its members are even in the army, on which Assad continues to base his domination. The Syrian army constitutes a power within the state and also has an important say in the Baath Party.

"And arm yourselves against them with as much as you are able to muster in war power and steeds in order to deter the opponent" is the motto taken from the Koran (8:61) by the Muslim Brotherhood in its fight for the Islamic state. According to a lengthy declaration, their state should be democratically oriented. In the underground war between the Baathists and the fundamentalists, however, there have long been too many victims to be counted. Up to the time of the Hamah uprising, attacks by religious volunteers had become increasingly elaborate and efficient; the state had likewise steadily resorted to a larger caliber of weapon.

Assad wants to eliminate the Muslim Brotherhood. Since the issuance of Decree 49 in 1979, each of its members has had to expect the death penalty. In present-day Syria mass arrests and executions are such an everyday occurrence that only large bomb attacks and massacres awaken general interest. In previous years regularly as many as 100 were dead and wounded as a result of car and truck bombings in front of the elaborately protected public buildings or the dwellings of the leading Baathists in the capital. Attacks by the Muslim Brotherhood have noticeably decimated the ranks of Assad's leadership and his extended family since 1976. Occasionally, too, some of the estimated 10,000 Soviet advisors lose their lives.

Assad—the name means "the lion"—will tolerate nothing and, as the example of Hamah shows, he strikes back with utter brutality. In doing so, he always tries to save face, and dispatches in advance his brother and designated successor Rifaat, who is infamous in the Near East. As head of security in the country, General Rifaat el-Assad has under his command both the huge, far-flung secret service and the so-called special units (*Saria al-Difaa*). What is involved are security troops consisting of 20,000 excellently equipped young Alawites, who formerly made up the president's bodyguard and who today control the Syrian capital in the manner of a "bodyguard regime." They are unshaven, unkempt hooligans who would like best of all to turn the Near East into the Wild West. I have seen them move through Damascus in gangs, many not in uniform, dressed merely in jeans and cowboy boots. They always carry large-caliber pistols loosely in their waistbands and seem just to wait for provocation.

The fractious "guardians of order" adorn themselves with skull-and-crossbones emblems made of fabric and metal; annoy passersby, preferably veiled women; and altogether make people nervous. When shots resound in Damascus in the quiet of the night, it may well be that members of the special units are shooting each other. In Hamah and in similar purges, they let off steam by committing atrocities of a kind normally heard about only from battle sites far removed from civilization.

In Palmyra, too, Rifaat el-Assad's followers were involved. The excavation site is internationally famous for the astronomical measurements made by the Arabs during the first centuries of the Islamic era. Nationally, however, it has become famous more because of the prison there. Jordanian television carried a report by a twenty-year-old recruitment officer, Ibrahim Fayad, on what happened in Palmyra on June 26, 1980. Two brigades of the "de-

fense commandos" were ordered into the old royal city, and Fayad's troop was posted in front of the prison in groups of six to
twelve men. The prisoners, many of whom were people merely
picked up in raids, had to line up in the courtyard and in a hall.
Then Assad's warriors opened fire until there was no longer any
sign of life among the prisoners. Fayad reported: "We shot a total
of 550 men—members of the Muslim Brotherhood, homosexuals,
and criminals. Then Major Nassif thanked our brigade for valiant
service, and each of us was given 100 Syrian pounds as a reward." In a second massacre in Palmyra, 180 members of the
Muslim Brotherhood were mowed down from helicopters. The
Western press named the regime as the slaughterer of both
groups of prisoners, who attempted to escape.

On the Jordanian television broadcast, the Syrian also admitted
his participation in a murder plot against King Hussein's prime
minister, Madar Badran. The assassination, planned for 1981,
was not carried out, because the preparations were discovered in
sufficient time in Amman. According to a contemporary Jordanian saying, "There are three things that Allah did not explain to
people: the truth about themselves, the true nature of women,
and what the Syrian is carrying behind his shield."

Rifaat el-Assad is scarcely known in the West, but he is Syria's
long arm and has his agents planted in all the hotels and mosques
of the country. They create a climate of anxiety in Damascus.
They fight the opposition and ensure that their commander's
activities are not interfered with. From Latakia the president's
youngest brother allegedly directs the extended family's business
activities, which range from supermarkets to housing construction and the smuggling of weapons and hashish. For these purposes, Assad absolutely needs Lebanon. Together with the clan
of the former president of Lebanon, Sulaiman Frandshieh, whose
members live in the northern part of the country, the Assads
dominate both the Christian Maronite and the Alawite population, and from Zghorta and Latakia distribute everything that
brings in money quickly.

Rifaat el-Assad is reputed to have invested his millions in luxury apartments in Paris and Geneva. The accusation, voiced in
Kuwait, was quickly denied in Damascus, but it seems fairly certain that in 1979 Rifaat el-Assad wanted not only to do away with
Jordan's leader but with President Saddam Hussein of Iraq as
well. Since that time, relations between the two states have

cooled. With the approval of the two Husseins, the Muslim Brotherhood is permitted to spill their *mujahideen*, weapons, and explosives across the green border. In Jordan they are tolerated, even their office and recruitment emblem. At the University of Amman they are officially active, although they guard against injecting their political accents into Jordanian current events. After all, the religious brethren do not wish to strain the leader's generosity or create any difficulties for the tiny king and his brother, Crown Prince Hassan, who has become particularly fond of them. Besides, the routes through Jordan are indispensable to members of the Muslim Brotherhood.

Numerous instances are known of Rifaat el-Assad's having Western journalists in Beirut who are critical of the regime murdered, wounded, or simply threatened by telephone. He also dispatches killer squads from the ranks of the Muchabarat (secret service) to track down members of the Muslim Brotherhood in distant countries and either kill or abduct unpopular diplomats.

Terrorists of the Syrian state have already attacked in numerous European countries. According to unconfirmed reports, in its revenge Syria has used the radical Palestinian group Abu Nidal (in civilian terms, Sabri el-Bana, which was repudiated by Yasser Arafat) and the phantom Carlos. The French magazine *V.S.D.* reported that the high Syrian officer Mohammed el-Kholy met with Carlos and gave him $2 million for the liquidation of political opponents. The Turkish magazine *Yankee* reported a meeting between the Venezuelan and Rifaat el-Assad, which allegedly took place on February 26, 1981.

On October 1, 1981, at 12:15 P.M., thirty-one-year-old Mahmud Wadaa from Hamah was shot from behind. Wadaa, a member of the Muslim Brotherhood, had been studying mechanics in the Yugoslavian capital since 1973. On the day of his death, he had just returned from a final examination in mathematics.

On May 17, 1981, at 8:30 A.M., thirty-eight-year-old Banan al-Tantawy, the wife of Issam el-Attar, a member of the Syrian opposition and head of the Islamic center in Aachen, West Germany, was murdered in her apartment by five shots. The perpetrators, two of whom were described as baby-faced, allegedly obtained weapons and passports from the Syrian Embassy in Bonn. Two of their names are known: Fady Hammady and Abd el-Karim Ateyya.

On January 14, 1982, at 6:15 P.M., a bomb exploded in the

Islamic Center in Munich-Freimann, which is under the direction
of the Muslim Brotherhood. The entrance was damaged in the
process. At a press conference the director of the center, Dr. Ali
Greisha, accused the Syrian secret service of the deed.

Following a confidential tip, the police arrested three Syrians
on March 1, 1982, at the main train station of Stuttgart. Among
the people arrested was a certain Ali Hassan, who has lived in
West Germany since 1960, and a man by the name of Shirko al-
Lusi. Found in their hotel rooms in Homburg/Saar were two pistols, 2.4 kilograms of military explosives, detonators, electrical
fuses, detonating fuses, wristwatches altered to serve as ignition
lags, and several forged passports. The Syrians were under
heavy suspicion of being on the hunt for members of the Muslim
Brotherhood.

The suspected assassins were imprisoned in Stuttgart, and the
state criminal office started its investigation. On March 16, 1982,
a letter arrived at the German embassy in Beirut demanding the
freeing of the Syrians. The previously unknown Organization of
the Martyrs of Azbakieh stated in a letter:

One of our groups pursued the criminals involved in the Azbakieh
incident* to West Germany. While this group was trying to do its duty,
it was impeded by the German authorities and imprisoned, as if they
[the Germans] would carry out the will of the murderers. . . . We therefore demand that the West German authorities act immediately and free
our comrades within ten days. If not, to our regret, we see ourselves
compelled to resort to measures that will expose the German authorities
everywhere to a great danger. . . . Right down to the last man among
us, we will avenge the martyrs of Azbakieh and will do so without
approval of the Syrian government.

The threat was taken seriously: all German institutions in Lebanon remained closed for several days. In "dutiful consideration
of German interests" (according to the Stuttgart public prosecutor), the Syrians were dispatched to their homeland before the
deadline. Then, on March 27, a letter of gratitude from the black-
mailers was received by the German embassy in Beirut. The long
statement was introduced with explanations about the "crimes of
the Muslim Brotherhood in the whole world, in the entire Arab

---

* In Azbakieh, a section of Damascus, the headquarters of three Syrian secret service
agencies was blown up on November 29, 1981 by a bomb planted by the Muslim Brotherhood. Allegedly, 200 people were killed.

world, particularly in Egypt and Syria." The crimes were characterized as being against humanity and civilization. Then it was stated:

The authorities of the Federal Republic [of Germany] opposed our group and impeded them in carrying out their mission—one of our many pursuit groups which carries out its mission of revenge and persecution without permission of the German, Syrian, or any other authorities in the world. By expressing our gratitude, we demand that the German people track down the dens of the criminals of the Muslim Brotherhood that have spread over all parts of Germany and which have been designed to serve as bases of support for training and conspiracy.

I asked the Syrian minister of information, Ahmed Iskander Ahmed—he has since passed away—if he knew the whereabouts of the Stuttgart terrorist group. He said they had not arrived in Damascus, and that he did not know them. The real terrorists, he added, were still in Munich, and they had freedom of movement and institutions all over Germany.

Four days after the arrest of the Syrians, the office for aliens in Aachen and the apartment of an interpreter who assists many Arabs were searched. The officials of the fourteenth precinct of the Aachen police found questionable documents—Ali Hassan, for example, popped up under two other aliases. The Aachen public prosecutor told the general attorney of the federal supreme court: "On the basis of the entries in this document, it is evident that the director of the office issued a residence permit even though the legal guidelines did not permit the issuance." In 70 of the 235 documents, personally checked by the high official, who was reputed to have close connections with mysterious Syrians, serious shortcomings were immediately discovered.

Assad's long arm attacked at least twice in Paris. The former Syrian prime minister and co-founder of the Baath Party, Salah Ed-Din al-Bitar, had been living there for years as the publisher of a journal that repeatedly condemned the Assad regime. In his last article in July 1980 he wrote: "It is a lie that the weapons paid for by the Syrian people with their daily bread are used against Israel. The weapons are intended for the destruction of their own country. The Arab people of Syria must finally recognize this fact and no longer let themselves be deceived. The people must nourish their revolution up to the time of the toppling of the tyrant

and his accomplices." On July 21, Salah Ed-Din al-Bitar was murdered. The Muslim Brotherhood named, as persons behind the
deed, the Syrian military attaché Nadim Amran and Ahmed
Abud, a relative of the Damascus head of the military secret police, Ali Duba. Three days after the murder, President Assad
announced that the hunt for his opponents would be continued
unrelentingly inside the country and abroad.

The next opportunity came on April 22, 1982, in Paris. A car
bomb went off in front of 33 Rue Marbeuf, just a few steps away
from the Champs-Élysées. The vehicle was an Opel, which had
been rented in Ljubljana. A thirty-year-old French woman suffered severe injuries, and sixty-three people had to be taken to
the hospital. Once again the Syrian secret service had been after
opponents. The building at 33 Rue Marbeuf houses the editorial
offices of the critical journal *Al-Watan al-Arabi,* which is published
by a Lebanese Sunni, Walid Abu Zahr, who has a price on his
head in Damascus. On the previous day the magazine had published an interview with the political leader of the Muslim Brotherhood of Syria, Adnan Sadeddin. The bomb was the answer—
but it was not the first bomb for *Al-Watan al-Arabi.* Because of the
massacre in the middle of Paris, the Syrian cultural attaché, Mik-
hail Kassuha, and the military attaché, Major Hassan Ali, were
expelled from the country by the French government.

During an investigation of ten bomb attacks, the prosecutor
also established connections to Qaddafi and Carlos. He spoke of
the "payment of debts with which France has nothing to do."
Queried about the expelled diplomats, President François Mitter-
rand answered a visitor with an Arabic saying: "If you beat your
wife, you perhaps do not know why, but she does."

Rifaat's people were also at work in Spain. On November 21,
1981, the forty-year-old Nezar al-Sabbagh, an official of the Muslim Brotherhood and organizer of several Islamic centers in Spain,
was shot on an open street by an unknown assailant. Syria had
previously demanded his extradition, but had been turned down
by the Spanish administration with the comment that al-Sabbagh
had found political asylum. Among Spanish circles, word leaked
out that the Syrian embassy in Madrid knew the background
details of this bloody deed but denied it.

The attacks in Europe did not improve Assad's precarious hold
back home in Damascus. The bad economic situation, boundless
corruption, a high rate of unemployment, thirty percent inflation,

and the increasing costs of the involvement in Lebanon, with high material losses, made for difficulties during 1982. An attempted takeover by the army and air force in January 1982 failed. A tip from the circle of the conspirators enabled Assad at the last moment to stop an attack by MiG fighters on a meeting of the central committee of the Baath Party and on his own and his brother Rifaat's private residences. Subsequently 170 pilots and officers were executed in Al Nabak and Damascus.

Assad gives the impression of being upright and earnest; he is always impeccably dressed. This pragmatic professional soldier, who was born in 1930, has always wanted to achieve the greatness of Nasser. Rarely seen in public, he is politically isolated and increasingly withdrawn. Heavily guarded, he receives only an occasional visitor; anyway, he prefers written news and explanations. The lion has been affected by the holy war against him. Considered by Henry Kissinger to be the "most interesting man of the Near East," Assad must still fear for his power. For the Mulsim Brotherhood, dismissed by him as "a small band of criminals," grants the president increasingly fewer breathers. "The Muslim Brotherhood is nothing other than a party by this name," he has said. "I am Muslim, but not a member of the Muslim Brotherhood. . . . I will permit no one to speak solely in the name of Islam, especially not the Muslim Brotherhood." Yet only occasionally does he still adorn himself with Islam, since he has seen how rarely his people accept his intentions "in the name of Allah." The hate-filled Sunni majority has long ceased to listen to Assad's speeches, in which he tells of the "crimes of the Muslim Brotherhood against Islam and for the enemies of the Arabic nation."

They prefer to support the secret squads of the chairman of the Islamic Front, Sheikh Mohammed Abul Nasr el-Bayanuni, a thoroughly trained, wiry man who is six feet three inches tall. El-Bayanuni is a technocrat with power, yet he is not without charm. He rejects comparing Syria's situation with pre-revolutionary Iran, but admits having learned from the events in Iran, especially from their errors. Adnan Sadeddin, the political leader, is a hawk, impersonal and cold. After the failed uprising of Hamah, he merely stated that the Muslim Brotherhood would no longer store their weapons in one place. Moreover, he added, there would no longer be a limited revolt, but only one large-scale, final attack against Assad's family enterprise. Together with Said

Hawwa, the chief ideologist, and Ali el-Bayanuni, the high-ranking member of the Muslim Brotherhood, he wants to create a new Syria and enrich the world with an additional variant of Islamic polity. For the time being, however, they must recover from the Hamah debacle. The military sector is suffering not only from the powerful opposition of the Alawite regime but from its own ongoing split. According to inside information from the ranks of the Muslim Brotherhood, Sadeddin and Hawwa are preparing new, large-scale attacks, but for the present are building up valuable international connections. Members of the Muslim Brotherhood of Syria travel extensively, engaging in relevant dialogue and in attracting support.

But Adnan Okla, the dissident within the movement, has returned to Syria, and from all appearances wants to establish a new organization, The Fighting Vanguard (Talia al-Mukatila). Even now, Okla's fighters claim to carry out operations against Assad and his regime, which is undergoing an internal power struggle. An official of the Talia group stated: "Armed struggle is precisely our political idea. . . . We do not attack blindly. We are attacking the pillars of the regime." The Okla group refuses to join the National Alliance. According to its spokesmen, their ultimate ideal is to establish not a democratic but an Islamic state. Such a state would not provide for elections of secular representatives, but would rely solely on God's leadership. It is said that recently still another very militant, extremely conspiratorial brigade split off from the Muslim Brotherhood. Its headquarters are in Amman, but further details about it are not yet known.

As of the summer of 1984, Syria is in a tense political situation. Despite its successes in foreign policy, as an outsider of the Arab camp it must rely on support from the Soviet Union and even from the international outcast, Iran. President Hafiz el-Assad is very ill. He has problems with all of Syria's neighbors and would like to withdraw from the risky Lebanon adventure. Assad must be on his guard against friends and relatives as well as against the internal opposition. A bloody power struggle seems unavoidable after his retirement. By that time at the latest, the hour will have come for the fighters of the holy war.

11

An Imam Vanishes

IT IS A FRIDAY, the twenty-second day of Ramadan of the Muslim era, when the trip from which there is no return starts. A conspicuous trio meets on this date, August 25, 1978, at 5:45 P.M., precisely one hour before the departure of Libyan Arab Airlines from the Beirut airport. The Libyan chargé d'affaires in Lebanon, Mahmud Ben Kora, meets them and bids them farewell. The group, consisting of the dignified, six-foot-three Imam Musa Sadr, the head of the Lebanese Shiites, along with his counselor, Sheikh Mohammed Sheada Jacoub, and the journalist Abbas Badreddine are en route on an official mission—as the invited guests of Qaddafi's Socialist Arab Libyan Jamahiriya. The anniversary of the revolution is near.

The Boeing 727, flight number LN 255, lands at 8:40 P.M. in Tripoli, where the delegation of Lebanese Shiites is met by Dr. Ahmed Ishehati, head of the Office for Foreign Relations of the People's Congress. The guests will stay at the Hotel El Shat (Strand Hotel). There they wait a day, two days, then one more

night without being received by Colonel Muammar al-Qaddafi.
The Libyan media, normally eager to be in contact with all foreign
visitors of rank, also remains silent. On the third day Abbas Badreddine makes contact with the Lebanese chargé d'affaires, Nizar
Farhat.

His countryman is surprised about the visit, having been told
nothing about it in advance. Badreddine asks Farhat for help. He
needs a recommendation to the French embassy in order to obtain a visa to accompany the imam on the continuation of his trip
to Paris. The diplomat promises his support. He also invites the
group to dinner on August 30; the Lebanese accept.

Quite in contrast to his usual custom, during these days Imam
Sadr is shrouded in silence. He does not even once telephone his
family in Beirut or write a letter. At the reception in the embassy,
at which Lebanese journalists also participate, the high Shiite
clergyman seems preoccupied. He says, however, that his meeting with the leader of the Libyan revolution has already been
postponed twice, and that a new appointment has finally been
made definite—for 1:30 P.M. the following day. "This meeting
could become quite stormy," he adds.

Nizar Farhat takes Abbas Badreddine's passport to make the
application to his French colleagues. He also promises Musa Sadr
and his advisor Mohammed Jacoub to have their entry permits
for France checked. Musa Sadr meets the Lebanese engineer Ali
Nizar, who is flying to Paris the next day, at his hotel. He gives
him a message for his family, already in the French capital waiting for him.

On Wednesday, August 31, the Shiite delegation is seen leaving the hotel by the Lebanese Assad Mokaddam. It is 1:00 P.M. A
half-hour later Nizar Farhat comes looking for Badreddine. Not
finding him, Farhat leaves his passport at the reception desk.
Somewhat earlier, a visa for the imam and Jacoub was issued at
the Italian embassy. A Libyan representative had inquired about
it.

That same evening three men leave Libya. One of them is wearing a black *gandoura*, the dress of a Shiite imam, and the obligatory black turban. The takeoff of Alitalia flight AZ 881 is delayed
one hour. At 9:00 P.M. it takes off in Tripoli on a course headed
for Rome. The trio—three "important personages" who were
personally accompanied to the airport by a member of the People's Committee—sits in first class. Following a brief conversa-

tion with the head steward, the three, with their economy-class tickets, were permitted to move into first class. Three Italians had to leave the first-class section of the almost completely filled airplane.

At 9:12 P.M. the plane lands at the Fiumicino Airport. Thirty minutes later a certain Abbas Badreddine appears at the office of the border police and requests a residence permit for forty-eight hours. He wants to stay overnight in the Satellite Hotel in Ostia and continue on his way to Malta on September 1 with flight AZ 490. He shows his ticket to the officer and receives the requested visa without difficulty.

On the following morning, at 9:00 A.M., Leonardo Nicolosi is finishing work at the reception desk of the Holiday Inn. His last customers are several Middle Easterners requesting single rooms. When they learn that there are rooms available, they go away. Minutes later one of them—small in stature, wearing European dress, age thirty-five at the most—returns with an Islamic clergyman. The new arrival waits in the salon while his companion fills out the arrival form. Nicolosi is replaced by Pietro Colangelo at the reception desk. Since he does not like the looks of the customer, he demands payment of a week's stay in advance. The guest does not refuse. He fills out the arrival form in the names of Mohammed Chehada and Musa A. Sadar. He promptly pays $400 and is assigned rooms 701 and 702. The clergyman, approximately six feet tall, bearded, thirty to thirty-five years of age, proceeds to the elevator. His companion follows with three suitcases and a small black briefcase. All the luggage is placed in the clergyman's room. The man in European dress enters his room, but leaves it immediately and goes to find the imam. Ten minutes later they both leave the hotel. Both of them now wear European-style suits. No one has ever seen the two of them since.

The porter Giuseppe Durante remembered the guests better than anyone else. The "civilian" in fact gave him a 5,000-lira tip. Durante noted: "The one in the elevator was very respectful toward the clergyman. He behaved as if he were fearful—you could say it was like a soldier in the presence of his officer."

Two days later, on September 3, it was noticed in Beirut that Imam Sadr has vanished; he was supposed to be present the previous evening for the closing celebration of the period of fasting *(aid el-fitr)*. No one had had any news of him. Greatly concerned, the Shiite congregation appealed to the Libyan embassy in Beirut on September 6, but the people there were "unable to make contact with Tripoli." As a last resort, the Shiites asked the head of government, Selim el-Hoss, for help. On September 10, he officially made contact with Mahmud Ben Kora of Libya. The answer was received the next day: "The imam and his companions left Tripoli on August 31, in the direction of Rome, via Alitalia flight number AZ 881."

The great search begins. A man had vanished who secretly was one of the key figures in the resurgence of Islam during the '60s and '70s—a man with many connections and tasks, someone who knew how to awaken the enthusiasm of the masses. Although Imam Musa Sadr was at the center of the newly gained Shiite power, his name was familiar in the West only to a few people in the know.

His background was fairly obscure, as he came into the public eye only in 1960—in Lebanon. Previously he had always lived in Iran. He was born on March 15, 1928, in the holy city of Ghom. There, eighty-five miles south of Tehran, he grew up in a family from which many clergymen had come. He attended school there and then studied at the famous University of Ghom, whose department of theology is a must for every spiritual leader of the Shiites. After his first course of study, Musa Sadr joined the juristic faculty of the University of Tehran. From there he returned to the University of Ghom in 1956, as a theologian entitled to teach—in other words, as a *mujtahid*. In addition, he was publisher of the religious magazine *Maktab Islam*.

A man who was to change the world became his teacher: Musa Sadr became the favorite student of Ayatollah Ruhollah Khomeini. It was a time when the self-confidence of the Shiites began to increase. Three years later Khomeini called for resistance against Shah Reza Pahlevi with the cry: "Battle against the Opponents of Islam." A ten-point program demanded of the ruler, among other things, the discontinuance of land reform. The arrest of Khomeini, ten months of imprisonment, and the subsequent expulsion of the religious leader produced severe riots that shattered Iran.

The clergyman had long known, however, that it was necessary to create, outside of Iran, bases of support manned by absolutely trustworthy, popular religious leaders of solid character. The buildup of the Khomeini International began in 1966 by dispatching the Imam Musa Sadr.

The leaders of the Shiites in Ghom and Kerbela chose Lebanon for the stately, dynamic preacher. Lebanon had always been the point of intersection for every frontier-crossing conspiracy in the Near East. In addition, it was important to separate the chaff of the worn-out Shiite community in Lebanon. The Shiites were at that time an unimportant, powerless sect. In keeping with tradition, they lived in the extreme south and in the northern part of the country. With the exception of a few wealthy families, the Shiites were and are peasants, exploited agricultural workers: a rural proletariat, oppressed by Christian as well as Shiite owners of large estates, and receptive to ideologies.

Representatives of the wealthy families were regularly elected to the parliament of Beirut by the underlings. Under the national pact of 1943, which regulated the benefices of the individual religious congregations, the Shiites gained the right to the post of parliamentary spokesman. For decades the post was held by the elegant playboy Kamal el-Assaad, patriarch of the largest Shiite family of southern Lebanon. The Shiites, however, never benefited from Lebanon's becoming the main center in the Near East for banking and commerce. In the north the Shiites lived as wild tribes, at times cultivating hashish and waging war against the regular army of the state. The conflicts were terminated mostly by targeted air attacks. In the south they owned the territory bordering Israel, a regrettable position since the Israeli response to Palestinian attacks mainly hit Shiite civilians. Lebanon's army for a long time avoided the area, which was thus relatively unprotected and an ideal substitute battlefield for Palestine. If it became too much for the Shiites, they fled to the suburbs of Beirut, to the shacks of the slum section—a frustrated potential in quest of a charismatic leader.

The head of the Lebanese Shiites at that time, Sayid Abdel Hussein Sharafeddine, a relative of Musa Sadr, was not the right man to fulfill this need. He died in 1960, and his last will mentioned that Imam Sadr should succeed him. From occasional visits to Ghom, he knew and admired the aspiring Iranian, who impressed him as humane.

Musa Sadr, precisely thirty-two years of age, came to Tyre with a great zest for accomplishing things. He soon founded a "Movement of the Underprivileged," which demanded of the government protection for the southern regions, assistance for the refugees, and weapons for the defense of property. His efforts were not crowned by success, since the government was more concerned with the mundane life of Beirut and money transactions. The Movement of the Underprivileged became increasingly militant. Some 100,000 people participated in numerous demonstrations.

As the Shiites became more aware of their oppressive situation through Musa Sadr, they adopted leftist revolutionary slogans and began to ally themselves with the PLO guerrillas. The Communist Party sent cadres into the villages and preached resistance against Israel. They increased the split between the poor people of the south and the bourgeoisie of Beirut. In the civil war the Shiites logically sided with the Sunnis, the leftist Druse, and the Palestinians. The Amal militia, the tool founded by Musa Sadr, at that time mostly kept out of the fighting. Only after the victory of the Iranian revolution did the Amal fighters become a factor that could not be overlooked in Lebanon, and then primarily in the Shiite south against the PLO, which steadily became more arrogant.

Even in the times of greatest disturbance, Imam Sadr retained his perspective, maneuvering cleverly and diplomatically. His strength was in the role of social reformer; he founded social institutions, schools, a sports center, and hospitals. His sister Rabab, gentle but resolute, who with his wife and four children now administers his legacy, described him to me as follows: "Musa Sadr always had both feet on the ground. The simplest man could come to him and describe his problems. He helped by providing not only money but rights. That may sound strange to you, but in this country most people need spokesmen if they want to achieve anything. Many cannot afford a stay in the hospital; many cannot send their children to school or work their land."

Approval was always certain for him, for he attacked social injustice: "You are not the slaves of the lords of the country," he said. "Each of you is his own lord. You must defend yourselves if they do not treat you well." Imam Sadr—whose lineage was found, upon examination in Ghom, to extend back to the Prophet Mohammed—gradually became the most popular personage for the simple people in Lebanon. In 1969 he led the Shiites out of the Muslim congregation with Sunnis and Druse, and founded their own Shiite "Supreme Council." Initially he was elected as chairman for six years, and subsequently for an additional period, up to his sixty-fifth birthday.

The only person who withheld support from him was Kamal el-Assaad, whose sinecure was jeopardized by the unrest among the Shiites. Through his own Council of the South, Musa Sadr wielded an instrument that exerted pressure on the government and accelerated the development of the border territory. As a consequence, relatively quick help was forthcoming for the victims of Israeli attacks. Before Sadr, there had never been any such thing. The social committee of the Council of the South distributed the assistance as justly as possible.

I asked Rabab Sadr Charafeddine—whose main occupation was the administration of an orphanage with a school for domestic science and a nursing school (which was destroyed by the Israelis in June 1982)—how her brother financed his diverse social enterprises. Her reply:

When his management associates were officially recognized, he received state funds. But he was also a Shiite *mullah*, which means that he was permitted to accept money from the people. One of our religious duties is that we must contribute one-fifth of our income to the imam. He of course does not use this money for himself but for everyone. This tax, which is called *khums*, is a curious arrangement. My brother used very little for himself and lived spartanly.

Imam Musa Sadr wanted to achieve social progress for the masses by his kind of Islamic reawakening. In 1977 he stated in an interview: "In the Koran it is stated: 'Have you not seen who calls religion mendacious? It is the person who casts out orphans and does not contribute to the feeding of the poor.' A heretic is someone who denies the existence of God, but a heretic is also anyone who is not prepared to concern himself with the need of his fellow man." Musa Sadr even saw himself as an Islamic variation of the Latin American worker-priest: "Our contemporary world longs for social movements that are based on belief in God."

He considered social commitment and religion inseparable: "The communists believe that the state and material satisfaction suffice for the well-being of people. But that is not true, for if man no longer believes in God, his action is determined exclusively by considerations related only to himself. That stops progress and in the end leads to the disintegration of society."

In contrast to his Iranian counterparts, the imam was by no means a fanatic. He had his own explanation for the renaissance of Islam: "For a while many Muslim nations tried out socialist models, but these attempts resulted in as little visible success as in other attempts by Western countries. Among the elite there is an additional consideration—that they juxtapose their own Islamic cultural assets to the foreign ones. They reject the idea of having their countries become a servile imitation of Europe, America, or the Soviet Union."

Musa Sadr by no means rejected the possibility of promoting reconciliation among related religions, and he always zealously tried to maintain a close relationship to representatives of the Christian religion. Even before a dialogue between Muslims and Christians came into view, he met regularly with the leaders of the other faiths. Imam Sadr was the only Muslim to travel to Rome in 1958 to attend the inauguration of Pope John XXIII. He later invited the progressive Roncalli pope to Lebanon. Pope John XXIII did not accept the invitation, but in the early 1970s Cardinal Franz Koenig of Vienna did. The head of the Maronites, Yussef al-Khoury, arranged a meeting between the exalted visitor and Musa Sadr. Cardinal Koenig reportedly said: "I have heard about you, Imam. And I believe that we can divide the history of Lebanon into two periods—one period before Musa Sadr and one period with Musa Sadr." A spectacular photo shows the leader of the Shiites at the opening service of the Christian period of fasting in 1974. Musa Sadr sat directly under the cross. He never rejected an invitation by the Christians. He became the first imam in the history of Islam to preach in a Christian church—in fact, in St. Louis des Capucins. Friendship united him with the Greek Catholic Archbishop Gregoire Haddad.

A close co-worker of many years claimed: "We are the disciples of the Imam Musa Sadr, who has founded a new school of humanity. We are the renaissance of Islam." He told me the following story:

The imam and I were in Strasbourg in 1968. When the time for the noon prayer approached, we were far from our hotel but close to the cathedral. The imam suggested that we should say our prayer in this house of worship. After all, it is the same Allah who is revered. Despite my skepticism, he was not to be deterred from his intention. When he was kneeling on his coat and praying, a priest with an extremely surprised face asked what we were doing there. With great charisma and a divine smile, the imam then said: "Peace be with you, my brother and colleague. Are we not in the house of the Lord? Are we not both the creatures of God?" The priest was so overcome that he movingly took the imam's hand. I then told him that he was standing before one of the leaders of the Muslim world.

In 1975 when Musa Sadr was daily confronted with the horrors of the civil war that was just beginning, he made the following statement in an interview with Katrin Acra-Ammann of the Beirut magazine *Monday Morning:*

Our religion, Islam, believes along with other religions in the one God as the basis of all teachings. He is the creator of the universe and of mankind. We believe that the best way of serving God's cause is by respecting the person, regardless of his race or religion. Basically the teachings of our religion, the examples of the Prophet and of the religious leaders, are not merely an appeal for forgiveness but are also a desire for cooperation, sympathy, and brotherhood. In feeling and in practice.

Musa Sadr strove for a council of religious leaders of Lebanon, through which he wanted to ameliorate the explosive situation in the troubled country. "We regard such a plan as the beginning of a new chapter in the history of religions and of Lebanon," he explained. "That would be the first step toward regaining national unity." The imam, who was exceedingly impressive in both word and appearance, was in every respect a practical man. In puritanical Iran he would have been accused of heresy for a remark like this: "Christ said that man does not live by bread alone, and I must add that man cannot live by religious thoughts alone."

Sadr was a realist. During the "hot" phase of the first civil war, he managed to change sides and to support the Syrians, who in 1976 were entering the country in support of the Christians as the controlling force. With the assistance of his Shiites, in 1975 he stopped a massacre of the Christian inhabitants of the village of El Qaa near Baalbek on the Bekaa Plain. He announced that if the Maronite village were bombarded, he would be among the inhabitants. He went to the mosque in the Beirut suburb of Safa and began a ten-day hunger strike against the civil war. Subsequently the Christians called him "the conscience of Lebanon."

In demonstration of his conviction, Imam Musa Sadr once purchased the stall of a Christian trader who was being boycotted by fanatic Moslems. In 1970 he traveled to Berlin in response to an official invitation, even though the entire Arab World had broken off diplomatic relations with West Germany. At the same time he contacted Egypt's Gamal Abdel Nasser: "We lose more if we do not resume our relations with the Federal Republic of Germany, for Israel will then get all the money." A half-year later diplomatic contacts were renewed.

Whenever Musa Sadr spent time in Europe, he first contacted his numerous Christian friends. He discussed with them the critical situation in Lebanon and invited them to join in a common front against the infidels—in other words, the communists. He always maintained that contention for Lebanon must be a basis for Christian-Islamic brotherliness, a touchstone for the future. As early as the summer of 1966, he announced in the south: "Lebanon is the country chosen by God in order to create brotherhood between the divine creatures." In Musa Sadr's opinion, the person who went to the mosque every day was not religious, but rather the person who was actively committed to the realization of the social ideal.

He confided to his secretary: "When I see hungry and suffering people, then I see God's visage before me." He was particularly upset by the idea that peace in the world could be maintained only through fear of total destruction by superweapons. For him, the issue was always a kind of peace resulting from humanitarian considerations. Politically he considered himself a mediator between Europe and the Third World. According to his thesis, some day these people must join together. Europe would have to supply the know-how, the Third World the raw materials, for in the long run he considered both superpowers a threat to the rest of the world.

Musa Sadr tried to free people around him of anxiety. And he himself had no anxiety. For this reason, he rejected the idea of bodyguards, even in the dangerous city of Beirut. He always traveled alone or accompanied only by advisors, and in doing so led an extremely risky double life. Toward Khomeini, he had to fulfill obligations relating to his career and religion. In the mid-1970s the old man from Ghom, driven by hatred, was about to introduce the last phase of his Islamic revolution, to harvest fifteen years of careful preparation. Ultimately Musa Sadr found himself in a decisive position within the revolutionary leader's international network.

His cousin was the Iraqi Shiite leader Ayatollah Mohammed Bagher Sadr, whom President Saddam Hussein kept under house arrest for a long time before having him executed in June 1980.

This bloody deed, along with the expulsion of Khomeini from Iraq and the ensuing victory of the Iranian revolution, was one of the true causes for the war in the Gulf. Musa Sadr's nephew, Sadegh Tabatabai, later rose to a high position in Tehran. Before the revolution he had lived and studied in Bochum, West Germany. Acquaintances of the present Special Commissioner to the Highest National Defense Council, who were living in exile, purchased and sent weapons to Beirut. Nowhere was it easier to sell illicit weapons than in Beirut. At that time automatic rifles were forwarded from there, via Syria, in shipments of sealed foodstuffs. They were directed to a bazaar in Tehran and distributed from there. The contact person for these deliveries was Imam Musa Sadr, whose Iranian passport had been seized by the Shah in 1973.

Iranian underground strategists were, however, able to fly to Beirut without interference. There they discussed the transactions with the head of the strengthened Lebanese Shiites. In Bochum, West Germany, Musa Sadr often met his nephew Sadegh Tabatabai and another revolutionary of the first hour, Sadegh Ghotbzadeh—both of whom arrived from the other direction. The son of a successful wood merchant, Ghotbzadeh had also been dispatched by Khomeini early on. Ghotbzadeh, who was later to become Foreign Minister of the Islamic Republic, left his homeland at age twenty-four.

Sadegh Ghotbzadeh went to the United States, to Canada, and later to several European countries. As a professional student, he organized demonstrations everywhere against the Tehran despot. His anti-Shah activities at Georgetown University in Washington, D.C., led to his expulsion after the Shah had his passport cancelled. With Musa Sadr's assistance, he obtained a new passport—a Syrian passport—in 1960. He received training in conspiratorial activities and went to live in Paris starting in 1963. In 1964 Musa Sadr obtained a permanent residence permit for him for Beirut. Outwardly Sadegh Ghotbzadeh functioned as chief editor of the newspaper *Payame Mudjahed* (*The Fighter's Message*), but in reality his position was in name only.

In the opinion of Western new services, Ghotbzadeh also functioned as a money courier—from Libya and the PLO to Khomeini as well as to Iranian Khomeini supporters. Ghotbzadeh's travels to Libya brought him together with Colonel Qaddafi more than once. Intermittently he studied at the Sorbonne in Paris and completed his degree in the philosophy of history. Only once did he visit Khomeini during Khomeini's exile in Iraq; this he did with a team from the French newspaper *Le Monde*. But in the fall of 1978, when he was back in France, he joined in support of the *ayatollah* —for the last stage of the assumption of power in Tehran.

A stroke of fate in fact saved the lives of Sadegh Tabatabai and Sadegh Ghotbzadeh. There were scheduled to meet with Imam Musa Sadr in Tripoli on August 21, 1978. Traveling from Frankfurt, they were supposed to meet the Shiite leader at Colonel Qaddafi's. Their task would have been to see about two broadcasts via Radio Tripoli to Tehran, which had twice been promised by the Libyan revolutionary leader. Imam Sadr's departure was postponed, however. In consequence, Tabatabai and Ghotbzadeh ran out of time and cancelled their flight.

Another key figure in the Iranian revolution was Mustafa Ali Chamran, whom Imam Sadr also supported whenever possible. Chamran left Iran in 1957 to study in the United States, and to be available later to assist Khomeini. Chamran took his doctorate in physics at the University of California in Berkeley, returning to the Near East during the early '70s.

Musa Sadr obtained for him a position as director of the vocational school for Shiites and Palestinians in Tyre. Sadr's main support to Chamran, however, was in helping to build up the combat troop called Amal (hope). Chamran was the contact man to the PLO and to Imam Khomeini's Iranian guerrilla fighters, who received their training in PLO camps. After Chamran's return to Iran in February 1979, he was the most experienced person in building up Khomeini's own defense system and later became minister of defense. He was killed in the war between Iraq and Iran.

In the meantime, however, relations between the Shiites of Lebanon and the PLO were very strained. But the PLO tactic of settling among the civilian population and thus exposing them to death from Israeli attacks caused the Shiites, now more self-confident, to lose interest in martyrdom. This factor may have affected the relationship to Syria, which was also supportive of the Palestinians, even though they did not directly choose Syria as their base of operations.

This theory, however, was decisively rejected in all my discussions with high PLO officials. Mahmud Labadi, Yasser Arafat's advisor and spokesman, stated: "The only conflict was between the PLO and the Israeli colonizers. All other conflicts were created by Israel and its agents."

Nevertheless, it may well be that Musa Sadr posed problems for the Palestinians and the Syrians, because up to 1978 he steadily came closer to his goal of uniting the warring religious factions of Lebanon. Neither side had any use for a peaceful Lebanon, which would then have been more forceful nationally. For this reason, the imam's efforts toward peace must have been a thorn in the side of both armed foreign entities in Lebanon.

Thus it came about that Musa Sadr started out again on one of his tightrope walks—this time to the colonel in Tripoli. Both were united in their commitment to the Arab cause, but in a humanitarian sense Musa Sadr had not the slightest thing in common with Qaddafi.

There was great concern among political circles in Lebanon when there was still no sign of Imam Sadr by mid-September 1978. Ex-President Charles Helou tried in vain to telephone Colonel Qaddafi. All he learned was that the telephone number had been changed. Finally the head of government, Selim el-Hoss, reached his colleague Major Abdul Salam Jallud in Tripoli and was informed that the imam was displeased when he left Libya, and had therefore not informed the authorities of his travel plans. When Musa Sadr failed to show up, word immediately went out from Beirut news services that he had not used the colonel's present, $7 million, as intended by the donor. That was decisively contested by Sadr's family. Said Rabab Sadr Charafeddine: "My brother did not accept a penny from Qaddafi."

A delegation from Lebanon was unable to find out anything in Libya. Conjectures began to be voiced—perhaps the opponent of the Shah had been abducted by the Iranian secret service, SAVAK. The Kuwait daily newspaper *Al Watan* reported that the Shiite leader had traveled to Iran on a secret mission. From "well-informed circles," it became known that Imam Sadr had flown to Addis Ababa from Libya, and had traveled from there by ship to Iran.

A denial followed promptly, by a spokesman of the Iranian clergyman: "It is not known to us that the imam is in Iran. We are more inclined to assume that the reports concerning his having vanished are intended to confuse. We believe he is being detained by Qaddafi." This statement was followed by the announcement that Iranian representatives would fly to Libya.

Initially that was unnecessary, because Qaddafi traveled to Damascus on September 21, 1978, to a conference of the front opposing Israel. The Lebanese Shiites organized a mass demonstration in front of the building where the conference was taking place, and four high-ranking Shiite sheikhs met Qaddafi for a discussion. The unpredictable Libyan stated that his appointment with Musa Sadr had been scheduled for August 31 at 1:30 P.M., but that he had waited in vain. Following detailed inquiries, he had been advised that the Lebanese group had left Libya. Qaddafi had no answer to the question of where the three Shiites were on the afternoon of August 31. The Shiite group meeting with the colonel also found it strange that Imam Sadr had not apologized for failing to keep the appointment. In addition, it was odd that Musa Sadr and his companions could have left a country having such a tightly controlled security system as Libya does without being noticed.

Colonel Muammar el-Qaddafi became perceptibly more nervous, according to eyewitnesses: "I was told that he [Imam Sadr] comes from Iran. Is that not true?" He then added that he considered the accusations against Libya an attack against the honor of his country, the Arabs, Islam, and the sacred right of hospitality, and that Libya would use all means to uncover the truth.

The investigations begun by the Libyan authorities caused the passenger list of Alitalia flight 881 to vanish. Inquiries by the senior public prosecutor at the court of appeals of the city of Rome produced more concrete results. Statements by witnesses —several Alitalia employees, officials at the Fiumicino Airport, as well as hotel employees—revealed that the three travelers from Tripoli bore no resemblance to the vanished Shiites. The impersonators had traveled to Italy under aliases, using the real passports of missing persons. The travel documents were available, since they had remained at the Holiday Inn. The managing director, Sigfrid Huber, had put them in safe keeping, along with the luggage, when the phony Imam and his companion failed to return.

Examination of Musa Sadr's passport showed that his photo had been damaged and for a period of time removed. The stamp had also been tampered with. Imam Sadr's belongings were crumpled in several suitcases. His small, black briefcase also contained objects belonging to Abbas Badreddine, whose dark gray Samsonite suitcase was also at the Holiday Inn—despite the fact that he had allegedly moved to the Hotel Satellite in Ostia (he never arrived there).

Finally Imam Sadr's watch was found. It no longer worked; its crystal was broken, and its band was missing. It had stopped on day one at 1:14 A.M. The characteristics of the handwriting on the arrival form did not at all resemble Sadr's handwriting. Jacoub's signature was characterized by the graphologist as crude; it could not possibly be that of someone holding a doctorate. None of the writing tests stood up to a comparison with original documents. In addition, there were errors in the names.

In response to international pressure, the Libyan investigating authorities finally started their inquiries only on November 3, 1979; at their conclusion, they provided the Italian appeals court with evidence that to some extent was absurd. One witness promptly admitted that at the point in time under question he had been in Saudi Arabia. Others became entangled in contradictions or could not possibly have been on the plane bound for Rome, as they claimed, because police documents showed that they had never set foot on Italian soil.

The statement by the Mauretanian ambassador to Libya, Mohammed Mahmud Wadadi, is particularly mysterious. For the record, he stated that he had seen the imam and his two companions and immediately recognized the famous Shiite leader. He happened to be at the airport to meet his country's delegation to the national festivities. The fact is that the Mauretanians had flown to Libya the previous day, so the ambassador could not possibly have been at the airport.

In the meantime the Lebanese Shiites had asked the secretary general of the United Nations, Kurt Waldheim, for help. In April 1979, 100,000 women had gone to President Elias Sarkis' residence to remind the head of state of their imam and his companions. Shiite children sang: "Bring back our father," and Minister Salah Salman broke into tears. PLO chief Yasser Arafat is reputed to have started to cry in the presence of a Shiite delegation on behalf of the imam. Sadr's family held a ten-day sit-in with prayers.

After Khomeini came to power in Iran, an investigative committee headed by Sadr's nephew, Sadegh Tabatabai, was founded. In a personal meeting Khomeini assured the sister of the vanished imam: "Imam Sadr was like a son to me, like a real son." When Qaddafi spontaneously wanted to fly to Iran in February 1979 to congratulate Ayatollah Khomeini on his victory, he was turned down. The leading clergymen had previously spoken out in the residence of the oldest and most respected *ayatollah*, Al Odham Golbaigani, in favor of a religious punishment (*fatwa*) for Qaddafi. He did not give up, but instead sent his representative Jallud to Tehran, who conveyed the message that "Brother Colonel would have liked to come to share this historical moment with the Iranian brothers." Khomeini responded curtly: "Qaddafi is heartily welcome if he brings Imam Sadr with him in his plane." Sadegh Ghotbzadeh even lodged a complaint against Qaddafi in Italy.

The hot-blooded Libyan did not want to give up, however. He still wanted to honor the Iranians with a visit, so he purchased tickets for himself and 150 associates on Air France. In April 1979 the uninvited delegation flew to Tehran on the French plane. When news of Qaddafi's approach leaked out, the control tower refused permission for the plane to land at Mehrabad Airport. Behind the refusal was a political decision that had been made at the highest level, including the acting minister of interior, Sadegh Tabatabai.

Once again Prime Minister Jallud had to hasten to Tehran in the name of the insistent colonel. A second time he was not permitted to see Khomeini. When, later, two Libyan ministers were in Tehran for a meeting, Imam Khomeini demonstratively left the hall because of them. Offended, one of the two Libyans then asked, "Did the Prophet receive his guests in this manner?" Khomeini, who was immediately informed of the question, answered bitterly, "Did the Prophet treat his guests the way you treated Musa Sadr?"

Judge Domenico Nostro from Rome meanwhile closed the files, because he had established without a doubt that the missing persons never set foot in his country and thus could not have vanished in Italy. In the Arab world speculation about the fate of Imam Musa Sadr continued. Only the Egyptians, who during Sadat's era were at odds with Libya, anyway, openly expressed what many thought. The mass-circulation paper *Al Akhbar* carried the following reproach in a commentary of June 13, 1979: "No doubt Qaddafi is the perpetrator of this horrible crime. He should take the consequences of his guilt. Can there be greater cowardliness and treachery than to murder a guest?"

Ayatollah Khomeini summoned Rome's ambassador in Tehran, Guillio Tamagnini, to provide him with a report about the Italian investigations. What the ambassador told Khomeini contradicted Qaddafi's account. The Saudis, normally extremely well informed, also joined in the deliberations. Crown Prince Fahd informed a delegation of the Lebanese Council of the Shiites that it was very likely that a discussion had taken place between Imam Sadr and Colonel Qaddafi. The discussion, in which Sadr had requested support for his policy, was very stormy. Subsequently Qaddafi ordered the arrest of his visitors.

A Libyan source reported that Qaddafi had informed the Lebanese of their immediate expulsion. The three guests were then chauffeured to the airport and, after the completion of exit formalities, were accommodated in a waiting room off to the side. They were called for by a car to take them to the airplane. Shortly before reaching the Alitalia plane, the vehicle turned off in the direction of a military plane. Immediately afterwards, the plane took off for the base in Sebha. A Libyan officer, Commander Rohaibi, and two of his men had allegedly taken the seats of the Lebanese on the Alitalia plane.

Palestinian informants asserted that PLO chief Yasser Arafat, surprised by the international reaction, proposed to Colonel Qaddafi that he take custody of the three prisoners so as to free them and attribute the guilt to a fictitious Palestinian group, and thus clear up the whole incident. Disgusted, Qaddafi replied: "You have abandoned Libya."

Then the fight really started. On December 11, 1979, the PLO publication *Falestin al Thawra* (*Palestine, the Revolution*) stated: "Mr. Colonel [Qaddafi], do you want the files on Sadr opened and the contents of a report that was given to you by the leader of the Palestinian revolution made available to the public? The report contains fourteen proofs of the fact that the imam never left the republic but was kept in Libya. This fact, Mr. Colonel, you cannot overlook. Your direct responsibility in the abduction is proved." On January 8, 1980, the Libyan news agency JANA shot back, accusing the PLO of the murder of Sadr and his companions.

Some time later this report was recanted. But it gives pause that statements of this kind are published at all. In the Moroccan journal *El Moharrir*, however, it was said that "the Imam Sadr, Sheikh Jacoub, and Abbas Badreddine were executed by Lieutenant Frej Boughalia and four noncommissioned officers because of an erroneous interpretation of a command. The execution took place in a shooting gallery of the government of Jonzour, eighteen miles from Tripoli."

The Lebanese Shiites refuse to accept the death of their leader. Several times they have conducted countrywide strikes to call attention to his fate. Operating under the name "Sons of Imam Sadr," they have hijacked airplanes to attract attention worldwide. On the anniversary of the date Musa Sadr vanished, bombings were carried out in his name in Beirut, which anyhow had been destroyed. In conjunction with the bombings, the demand was made that the government search more thoroughly for the imam.

During my visit, Sadr's sister Rahab said in farewell: "We know definitely that he is still alive. And he will return to us." At least 100 girls, dressed in blue school uniforms and wearing white scarves on their heads, stood in front of the door. For a long time their song lingered in my ear: "Musa Sadr, you are our leader. You are our father. We are prepared to die for your cause. . . . Bring us back our father!"

12

Lebanon's Slow Death

He comes from the desert, which rejected him.
Took flight to the mountains, which rejected him.
Hurled himself into the sea, which rejected him.
No one recognized you,
No one understood you,
And you plunged into the blood.

—UNCI AS-SADR

THAT IS HOW the Lebanese poet, born in 1947, paraphrased his countrymen's three conceptions of their own identity. The desert is the birthplace of Islam; it is the rough Arab hinterland. The mountains are the grand ideals of the educated, better-situated Lebanese; they can be self-sufficiency and tolerance, the capacity for perseverance and pragmatism. Situated on the mountain, the Francophile Christian from the Middle East always directed his glance toward Europe. The sea symbolizes the distance from France, which is progressive, but it also symbolizes the spiritual roots of the Muslims. Everything together describes the endless identity crisis of the Lebanese—the fact that they were able to realize only fragments from each of their cultures and must go on living with their longings and ideals in the bloody, irrational, daily grind. Lebanon is not synonymous with great, humanistic Europe; nor is it synonymous with *dar al-Islam*, the house of Islam.

The population of Mount Liban was last counted in 1932. At that

[171]

time there were more Christians than Muslims, but that has basically changed. The Christian minority tried everything to codify the prevailing political conditions. In 1943 the political and social leaders sat down together and agreed on a national pact that regulated how public offices would be distributed according to a proportionate formula. The Christians were to have the presidency, the commander-in-chief of the armed forces, and fifty-one percent of the delegates. The Sunnis, the next strongest group, would provide the prime minister. The chair of the president of parliament would go to the Shiites. Offices were determined for all other minorities. In addition, the national pact established the special role of Lebanon as mediator between East and West.

Soon after World War II, things improved for the eastern corner of the Levant, because even during the most difficult times the Lebanese are masters at commerce. For this reason the Syrians always wanted to incorporate their small neighbor to round off a large, imaginary Syrian realm. Dozens of banks made Beirut the financial center for the entire Middle East. The city became a trade and amusement center. Tourists from Paris, Kuwait, and New York enjoyed themselves at the gaming tables and midnight shows in the worldly Casino de Liban or other nightclubs.

The experiment of peaceful coexistence between Christians and Muslims failed in 1958. The Muslims, inflamed by Nasser's nationalistic pan-Arabism, became increasingly self-confident. Following the union of Egypt and Syria and the revolution in Iraq, a civil war began in Lebanon, which President Camille Chamoun was able to stop only with the help of 10,000 American marines. With a slightly pro-Arab exchange rate, the Lebanese just managed to make ends meet up to 1975. In the meantime the head of the Palestinian liberation groups and their commando units, which were expelled by King Hussein from Jordan in 1970, had arrived in Lebanon. Yasser Arafat's PLO had begun to spread throughout the country and set up a counter-state. In the late '70s, the PLO, originally a dangerous terrorist organization, became a far-flung, business-oriented fighting group with accredited diplomats as representatives. Together with the approximately 275,000 Palestinians living in camps since 1948, they had sufficient manpower to realize their goals in Lebanon. The rights of a total of 400,000 refugees were set forth in the Cairo accords of 1969, but the treaty was scarcely worth the travel expenses of the negotiators.

Through the presence of the Palestinian Liberation Organization, which the antagonistic Israelis wanted to drive into the sea, the other leftist Muslim movements also gained impetus. The religious factor was one of the many reasons for the outbreak of the new civil war in April 1975. Another major factor was the social disadvantage of the Muslims and the quest for power by the Palestinians, who are extremely impressed with their importance. During the months before April 13, one word led to another, and provocations came in increasingly rapid succession. Only one small push was needed to make the house of cards collapse, and that was not long in coming. On April 13, 1975, an eight-man PLO fighter battalion showed up at the dedication of a church in Ain Rummaneh in East Beirut. The Fedayin shot into the crowd, killing four Christians. That same afternoon the Christians stopped a bus carrying twenty-seven Palestinians in the same section of town; not a single one was left alive.

Mutual slaughter began and lasted until June 1976. The Syrians then took advantage of the opportunity and occupied Lebanon, for the purpose of ending the butchery, they said. Since, at this point in time, the Christians were in an unfavorable position, they joined sides. The Syrians came off as "rescuers of the Maronites," but intermittently continued to side with the Palestinian National Council, its subsidiary organizations (like the PLO), and the left, depending on what suited their interests. In all instances the Syrians behaved as if there were no government at all in Lebanon—as the PLO always does and as the Israelis did in the summer of 1982.

Certainly Elias Sarkis' administration, which was elected in 1976 in the middle of contentious battle negotiations, did not have much say. Sarkis, a colorless technocrat, wanted to do right by everyone, and in the end, he was pleasing to everyone because he did not interfere in the mass murder. From 1975 to early 1982, 65,000 people died in Lebanon, a torn country, ruled by greed for power, delusions of courage, and obsession with weapons. The Israeli campaign of destruction against the PLO and the sixty-nine day siege of Beirut killed at least an additional 20,000. The number of wounded, homeless, orphaned, uprooted, and emotionally devastated Lebanese is not contained in any set of statistics.

The civil war was stopped only by the Israeli attempt to bomb the troublesome PLO back to the Stone Age. Instead of being an enduring success for the invaders, however, that resulted in the death of almost 600 soldiers and by no means brought peace to Lebanon.

After a year of relative quiet, produced by the Israelis and 5,800 multinational peacekeeping troops (MNF) of the United Nations, the civil war resumed again in early September of 1983 following the withdrawal of the Jewish occupation forces to the Awali River 21 miles south of Beirut. As expected, the Christian militia fought Druse tribesmen from the Shuf Mountains, members of an Islamic sect whose proclaimed doctrine is also that of the Progressive Socialist Party. The goal of the Druse was to topple the weak administration of President Amin Gemayel and establish a new proportionally representative government that would provide more rights to previously disadvantaged groups of the population. The Druse, curiously enough supported by Israel and Syria, fired grenades of as powerful a caliber as 124 millimeters from their artillery positions in the mountains into the outskirts of the capital and onto the operational area of the airport.

The advance of the Muslim militia and the government, whose power was in effect restricted to Beirut, was stopped only by the artillery of the American Task Force 61 and the Sixth Fleet operating in the Mediterranean, supported by the enormous battleship *New Jersey*. A deceptive cease-fire, the result of negotiations by Reagan's special emissary Robert MacFarlane and Prince Bandar bin Sultan bin Abdel Aziz of Saudi Arabia, went into effect in late September. Ultimately it was heeded by no one.

The peacekeeping troops, made up of Americans, French, English, and Italians, was the next target of the forces intent on the destabilization of Lebanon (and the entire region). Early in the morning of October 23, 1983, two Islamic fanatics drove trucks loaded with explosives into the headquarters of the American marines and French paratroopers. The cargo of the kamikaze trucks exploded, causing the collapse of the buildings. Dead in the rubble were 241 American and 58 French soldiers. *Newsweek* headlined the gruesome incident as "the most fatal hour for U.S. troops since Pearl Harbor."

A previously unknown organization, Islamic Holy War, claimed responsibility for the deed. Western secret service organizations quickly pinpointed it in the ancient city of Baalbek in the Bekaa Valley of East Lebanon, which is also headquarters for the radical Shiite splinter group Islamic Amal, headed by the former teacher Hussein Musavi and Sheikh Subhi Tufaili. At a press conference immediately afterwards, Musavi stated that his organization did not carry out the attacks against the peacekeeping troops, a fact that he regretted, since he considered the attacks heroic deeds.

An additional 60 persons died a few days later in the city of Tyros in Southern Lebanon when the headquarters of the Israeli military secret service was car-bombed. Once again the Jihad group claimed responsibility. The revenge started just a few hours later, when the Israeli force flew attacks against Syrian and Palestinian positions in central Lebanon. While the investigations against the Shiite terrorists were still in full sway, the *London Sunday Times* reported on actions intended by the U.S. The newspaper stated that "The revenge . . . will be a sharp, carefully prepared surgical operation with the goal of killing those people backing the suicidal attacks against the U.S. Marines and of avoiding the death of innocent civilians."

But that did not come about. Instead of the Americans, it was the French and the Israelis who fought back. In several air attacks, which were particularly concentrated on November 16 and 17, 1983, they destroyed housing, emplacements, and support bases of the Muslim combat organization Hizbollah (meaning "God's Party"), the Islamic Amal, and the Pasdaran ("Guards of the Revolution") that had been sent by Tehran into the Bekaa Plain. The fighting was by no means over, as it was precisely these bombardments that led to further radicalization within the Shiite commandos. Attacks against the American and French peacekeeping units persisted until the withdrawal of the troops in the spring of 1984.

During the months of November and December 1983, reports of fighting between the MNF units and Islamic guerillas were replaced in the headlines by news of other heavy engagements. North of Beirut in Tripoli, Lebanon's second largest city, the Syrians collaborated with Arafat's enemies within the Fatah, the strongest group in the PLO, in an attempt to destroy the guerilla boss who, along with his followers, had secretly returned to the scene. The Palestinian civil war began when the dissidents within the Fatah, under the leadership of Abu Musa and Abu Saleh, overran the Nahr el-Bared and Baddawi refugee camps situated north and east of Tripoli. At least 9,000 Palestinian civilians fled to Tripoli. The attackers encircled the harbor city and for weeks subjected it to massive attack. Sometimes as many as 30 grenades and missiles per minute landed in Tripoli—a gruesome slaughter among the refugees, the local civilian population, and Arafat's followers.

On several occasions I was in Tripoli during that period of time, and twice was able to speak with Yasser Arafat. On the day of the heaviest bombardment we sat together on a folding cot in the communications center of his headquarters. He was wearing olive green pants, a bright green shirt, a matching sweater with epaulets, a black-and-white scarf around his neck, and on his bald head the green military cap bearing the yellow eagle insignia of the PLO troops. A revolver swung freely from his right leg. Yasser Arafat had become noticeably thinner, but seemed to me more relaxed and in better condition than at the start of the murderous fighting around Tripoli.

During this period of time Arafat's views were for the first time in his political life clearly and undiplomatically formulated: "Since Syria and Libya failed in getting control of the PLO, they now want to liquidate us. But that is not their only goal. They want to disarm this courageous and self-confident city, because the national Islamic forces are so strong here. That is a crime against the Lebanese people and against our movement. Listen for yourself, listen. . . . ," he suddenly shouted in increasing excitement, pointing upward. The bombardment had started again. Missiles mounted on mobile launchers screechingly sought their targets. Grenades landed around us. At this same moment a heavy artillery shot destroyed the facade of a nearby apartment house between the seventh and ninth floors. Fortunately no one was hurt, as the people of the ancient section of town called Zahariyeh, like most of the mobile inhabitants of Tripoli, had already fled the city.

Arafat had expressed his connection with the Islamic fundamentalists of the city, which pointed to a completely new development. For the first time the PLO boss openly made a pact with a subsidiary of the Muslim Brotherhood, the Tauhid Islami (Islamic Unity) headed by the blustering Sheikh Said Shaaban. In North Lebanon it was an open secret that Tauhid Islami had accepted weapons and money from Arafat, confirming the existence of a mutual defense alliance. The agreement was not difficult for Shaaban and his radical fighters, as their enemy is the same as Arafat's: Syria. The fundamentalists in Tripoli are connected with and related to the Muslim Brotherhood in Hamah, and many of them lost family members and friends in the Hamah massacre. In the surroundings of Tripoli the Syrians have been the target of the heaviest fighting since their invasion of Lebanon.

I also met Sheikh Shaaban in embattled Tripoli. He made no secret of the fact that his concern ultimately is with an Islamic revolution, claiming that his movement will overcome the narrow borders between the Sunna and the Shia, making possible the liberation from Zionism and imperialism. Shaaban said: "The Palestinian question also can be solved only by the participation of the *umma*, for here, too, we again see the battle between Islam and heresy. All Muslims, not merely the PLO, must participate in the Palestinian question. For a long time I have told Yasser Arafat that the proclamation of the Islamic revolution would make more sense than all this political maneuvering."

Quite rightly the remains of Arafat's embattled PLO rely on international aid, which was worked out at the last moment, leading to a second evacuation of the fighters from the torn country of Lebanon. Sheikh Shaaban and his Islamic commandos remained behind to continue their tactic of needling the Syrian occupation forces. During a visit in Arafat's new training center in North Yemen, I was able to confirm a few weeks later that supporters of Shaaban were already receiving instructions there in the use of modern weapons. Yasser Arafat is grateful for that.

There is to be no breather for Lebanon. In February 1984 it was at the absolute brink of disaster as a consequence of President Amin Gemayel's short-sighted policy. His administration, from the outset weak and restricted in its ability to act, had retained its course of confrontation with the increasingly self-confident Islamic forces until it had finally become too late. Negotiations in Geneva had failed, and last-minute concessions—participation in the power by all national forces—were no longer able to put a stop to the development. The Shiite militia, Amal, and the forces of the pro-Syrian Druse were deployed against the government and seized West Beirut in a surprise attack. President Gemayel sat in the bunker of his governmental headquarters and despairingly appealed for American and Israeli relief. His cabinet had deserted him, and half of the approximately 37,000 troops of the government had also gone over to the enemy, taking with them all their equipment. Almost exactly five years after the Iranian revolution, Khomeini's supporters had now also reached Beirut.

In February 1984 the city was again divided, as at the time of the first Lebanese civil war. The actual power of the state was embodied in an unequal twosome, Walid Jumblatt and Nabih Berri. The thirty-six-year-old Jumblatt is the leader of the 200,000-strong Lebanese Druse. The dialogue between Jumblatt and the colorless Amin Gemayel has broken off. The Druse leader, hearty and wearing a mustache, publicly wishes nothing but death for the president of his wracked country.

The moderate lawyer Nabih Berri, age forty-five and leader of the strong Shiite militia, expressed his aversion toward the administration more politely: "The president is looking for a new cabinet, and I am looking for a new president." Berri invited the Christians to a dialogue, and during the days of the worst destruction in West Beirut even managed to win the support of the uncompromising Khomeini admirers. Following the military victory by the opposition, there now began for Lebanon months of partial anarchy. Discussions in Lausanne by parties involved in the civil war resulted in nothing but greater confusion. Only one thing was clearly shown: The old country of Lebanon was dead. As a consequence, the Christian idea of an oasis of European character was also dead. The predominance of the Maronites has been broken, and once again the Islamic forces have gained territory. The small country's slow death continues.

13

Brother Colonel

THE MOST SCINTILLATING CHARACTER of the Islamic world is a chic colonel who considers himself a prophet and redeemer: Muammar el-Qaddafi. Of no other head of state is it so often assumed that he might possibly be crazy. No other leader of a mere three million subjects keeps the world in such suspense. Libya's "Brother Colonel" is mentioned in the gossip columns of the gutter press and on the covers of news magazines ("The most dangerous man in the world," according to the German magazine *Bunte*). He enjoys the publicity and makes himself scarce at the right moment. Most of the Islamic underground movements, which for the most part are strict, want to have nothing to do with Muammar el-Qaddafi, since they regard him as a terrorist and false interpreter of the true teaching of the Prophet. The governments of the Near East and North Africa have a similar attitude and, with the exception of the anti-Israeli Arabic Rejection Front (founded by Syria, Libya, Iraq, Algeria, the PLO, and South Yemen), keep him at a good distance. Any interpretation of the phenomenon Muammar el-Qaddafi must remain a mere attempt.

Qaddafi characteristically considers himself part of the world-wide resurgence of Islam:

Libya is the unique example of a comprehensive revolution offered to all mankind for the purpose of liberating the human being, whom the Koran calls God's deputy on earth, from all material and spiritual obstacles involving his will. Islam is nothing other than the humanistic revolution: absolute belief in people's innate good powers and capabilities, which enable them to overcome the effects of injustice and aggression that have held them back and which enable them to take the path of progress. Consequently the revolution of the people in the Libyan Jamahiriya is part of the worldwide Islamic movement which, following bleak centuries, is fighting for its fitting place in the world of today.

In the beginning, Brother Colonel fought for his place. He was born in 1942 in a tent made of camel skin, the only child of a Bedouin family from Sirte. His father was Mohammed Abd el-Salam Ben Hamed Ben Mohammed. Qaddafi was permitted to attend school, and from an early age he used this privileged position to organize student demonstrations against the ruler of Libya at that time, Sanussi-Emir Idris I. Qadaffi started his illegal political activity in 1962, while studying history at the university in Benghasi, and he continued this in 1964, when he began attending the military academy there. He surrounded himself with discontented students and founded the Organization of Free Officers. The king was still able to quell the opposition by his strict pan-Arab policy and by supporting the frontline states in the Palestinian conflict.

But he had neglected to take into consideration the young pioneer officer Muammar el-Qaddafi, who on September 1, 1969, abruptly declared Idris deposed while the king was vacationing in Turkey. The Revolutionary Commando Council assumed power in order to get rid of all Western influences. The entire coup took place under the code name Al Kuds ("Jerusalem"), which was intended to show the commitment the fomentors of this anti-colonialist revolution felt toward the Islamic world's intention of reconquering Jerusalem. Qaddafi, promoted from captain to colonel, denied the Americans the use of their Wheelus Air Base and expelled the last 25,000 Italian settlers, leftovers from the era of occupation. He reintroduced Arabic as the only language to be used in the country and Islam as the basis for all Libyan actions.

Despite these measures, Qaddafi was not a fundamentalist in quest of the roots of Islam. He wanted, rather, to follow in the footsteps of his revered model Gamal Abdel Nasser, whose shoes are still too big for him. His emulation remained confined to externals. The Libyan state radio tirelessly spouted forth Nasserist appeals for Arab unity, and the twenty-eight-year-old venerator in Tripoli repeated the statements in his own words. He wanted to achieve both socialism and Islam and, inexperienced in the ways of the world, placed his emphasis on the great "Arab nation." Muammar el-Qaddafi forbade alcohol, public pleasures, prostitution, even miniskirts; he closed Christian churches, declared the Koran to be the obligatory lesson for all the people in his country, and daily condemned the inveterate corruption in the Arab world. In terms of foreign policy, Qaddafi heated things up for the oil customers and, starting in 1964, drastically increased prices. Through these measures, he was able, within a decade, to make his extremely backward desert country into a kind of welfare state.

Brother Colonel soon made it clear to all Libyans that he would not tolerate any conception of Islam but his own. He condemned all other conceptions as heresy. In the early period of upheavals in his domestic policy, he filled the prisons not only with the secular opposition (for example, his cohorts in the coup), but also with the religious elite. The Muslim Brotherhood was a favorite target. Concerning this organization, Qaddafi commented: "I do not believe that the Muslim Brotherhood represents a Muslim philosophy in the true sense of the word, since it is against socialism, against Arab unity, against Arab nationalism. If they preach Islamic unification, then they cannot be against Arab unity." Qaddafi maintained that the Muslim Brotherhood, as well as the members of Sheikh el-Nabhanis' Islamic Liberation Party, were agents of the West in the pay of the CIA. Moreover, it was a question of foreign organizations from Egypt and Jordan, so their existence in Libya was cut off. The fundamentalists have still not made a comeback in the strictly governed military state.

Indigenous teachings fared no better in the hands of the self-appointed eccentric expert on Islam. The mystical sect of the Sanussiyya, which had made an important contribution to the liberation struggle against the colonial rulers, also had to cease all activity. The victims of this era, including Hassan Ahmed al-Kurdi (who can serve as a typical example), are still in detention. His sufferings began in 1972, when Qaddafi forbade all political parties. The colonel's thesis runs as follows: "The political party is the contemporary dictator. It is the modern dictatorial instrument for governing. The political party constitutes domination of a part over the whole. Since the party is not individual, it exerts a pretended democracy by the creation of parliaments and committees as well as by its members' propaganda."

Hence the Islamic Liberation Party (Hisbul Tahrir al-Islam) came under the ax. Hassan Ahmed al-Kurdi, who had studied in Benghasi and was working for a Libyan oil company, was arrested, along with 160 other people, and accused of being head of this religious organization and of striving to establish an Islamic state in Libya. Kurdi and others have been in the main prison in Tripoli since April 1973. Only in February 1977 did they come up for a secret trial by a "people's court." Kurdi was sentenced to fifteen years imprisonment. Several days later the Revolutionary Commando Council, under dictator Qaddafi, changed the sentence to imprisonment for life.

Hassan Ahmed al-Kurdi, born in 1941 in Rahaibat, 135 miles south of Tripoli, now suffers from a severe stomach ailment, which was probably caused by torture. In Libya torture involves being beaten with leather strips, being forced to walk on sharp stones, being beaten on the soles of the feet with a stick, being subjected to electric shocks, and being kept in darkness. Isolation chambers are also among the devices of the country of the so-called Islamic revolutionary Muammar al-Qaddafi.

In 1974 the self-appointed sanitizer with the Kalashnikov, the benefactor of Bokassa and Idi Amin, was "sent" by the Revolutionary Council to meditate in the desert. Upon his return he announced that he would devote himself only to organizational and ideological questions. The eccentric head of state arrived at his religiously oriented viewpoint during the period of incessant, intensive thinking about Allah in the hot, clear desert air. He formulated the so-called "third universal theory" in *The Green Book*, which is intended to accompany the "green revolution." Anyone who knows Qaddafi fairly well is aware that he has a drive toward the color green and is enchanted by anything having that hue.

Qaddafi's *Green Book* is modeled on the Mao bible. It thrives on the logic of the person in a state of nature, whose thinking constantly runs up against the narrow limits of his homeland. There it is stated: "Since we are confronted by a communistic and a capitalistic system, we are trying to discover a third system that would be differentiated from the one as well as from the other." Qaddafi concludes from this situation: "While capitalism places no kind of restraints on the individual and hence has transformed society into a circus, communism's claim of finding a solution to economic problems by the total and final suppression of private ownership ultimately turns people into sheep." Libya's leader maintains that the human being finds true happiness only in the "precepts of the Islamic religion." His prognosis: "The governments will vanish, the police will vanish, the regular armies, capitalism, salaries, wages, trade, profit, and interest charges—all that will vanish, and the people will be free." That is how simple it is.

Qaddafi's consciousness of his mission, which is primarily directed toward the backward peoples of Africa, was really displayed for the first time in 1977. From February 28 to March 2, the People's Congress, which is generally regarded with mistrust by the Libyans, met in the Sebha Oasis of southern Libya. Cuba's Fidel Castro was among those present. On this occasion all existing political institutions were eliminated and were replaced by new institutions; at the same time Qaddafi proclaimed the Socialist People's Libyan Arab Jamahiriya, a kind of Islamic republic governed by commissars. In a "declaration about the power of the people," it is stated that the "direct power of the people" will be the future "basis of the political system." Since the word "republic" has gotten a bad name as a result of its use by dictators, in Libya it is to be replaced in the future by the concept of "public." Qaddafi, praised by conformist supporters as a "great revolutionary theoretician, commander, and teacher," placed Islamic-revolutionary committees in all factories, government offices, schools, and universities, making them the basis for a surveillance system that extends even to the local warden. Until early in 1980, everyone was responsible for everything, and yet no one was competent. In terms of efficiency, this was not different from Egypt, which allegedly is organized and which in the West is always considered a good example of an Arab state.

Muammar al-Qaddafi encountered rejection whenever he tried to assist with his *Green Book*. Once an international Islamic commission even journeyed to Tripoli. The host hoped to garner rich blessings for his intellectual creation from the Muslim scholars. After days of discussions and studies, the green opus flunked the test; it was dismissed with the comment that it failed to address the topic. The author, presented with a collection of corrections consisting of twenty points, flew into a rage. The substance of the criticism was that he had deviated far from the route of the well-guided Muslim and was stranded in no-man's land, that Islam was compatible neither with Qaddafi's nationalistic nor with his socialistic ideas. The participants at the conference could in any case speak of their good fortune in escaping unscathed from Qaddafi's realm. In utter quiet and without farewell, they were taken to their plane at the airport. The final communiqué from the commission vanished in a desk drawer.

The small Libyan, with his high heels, his photogenic mop of curly hair, his delicate hands and beautiful eyes, was cross; he preferred in the future to preach his own homemade brand of Islam. Allah is great and Muammar al-Qaddafi is his prophet. He would like to create a large Arab realm that comprises all of North Africa and, if possible, also dominates the Near East. "The life in the desert gave me the fighting spirit," says the most famous son of the Berber tribe of the Kathathfa. The quick wealth from oil provided him with the means, and the forever calculating Russians provided him with the largest weapons arsenal in North Africa. There is nothing that Qaddafi's military machine lacks. Specialists from numerous Eastern bloc countries, including East Germany, keep the death-delivering instruments of Qaddafi's megalomania in working order. A moderately well-trained army of 60,000 men plays with a hodgepodge that comes from a variety of suppliers, in both the West and the East, willing to sell to Libya.

Not infrequently the generous son of the desert passes on entire shiploads and planeloads of weapons to needy underdeveloped countries, which use them for killing each other—as intended by the donor. Muammar ("The Architect") al-Qaddafi supports all guerrilla groups that trustingly approach him. Allegedly his most important investment was in being one of the major arms suppliers for Yasser Arafat's PLO and arming them well. During the Israeli invasion into Lebanon, the quantity of matériel found there would have been enough to equip the army of a medium-size nation. Many small arms and grenades were still packed in cartons marked as tractor batteries and replacement parts for machinery. When Qaddafi noticed that, despite all the weapons he had provided his beloved PLO brothers, they were unable to stand up to the Israeli invasion forces, he commended suicide to them and withdrew into meditation.

Like Khomeini, the world's favorite scoundrel has far more harmed than helped the reputation of Islam. The barriers between the Muslims and the Western world have been increased by him. The self-appointed missionary has become a negative figure par excellence. No one any longer takes him seriously when he wants to ally Libya with some more or less distant nation, or when he condemns all Arab leaders as incompetent and then immediately wants to sit down with them at a summit conference that he himself calls. Faced with his failure to elicit a serious response to such ideas, in the fall of 1982 he felt compelled to found his own International Islamic Council and an Organization of the Islamic World. Both appealed for the liberation of the holy shrines in Mecca, Medina, and Jerusalem.

Whenever a terrorist attack cannot be precisely explained, Muammar al-Qaddafi and his alleged tool, Carlos, come to mind. Qaddafi's country is generally considered the "sanctuary of international terrorism." The fact is that he dispatches killer commandos who basically aim at his own opposition. In 1980 he announced to his opponents that, if they themselves did not accept the challenge, they "would be liquidated wherever they were."

This promise Qaddafi kept. On April 11, 1980, the journalist Mohammed Mustafa Ramadam was shot while leaving a London mosque. On April 25, the lawyer Mahmud Nafa died in the entrance to his house. In Rome the businessman Mohammed Salem Rtemi was shot by Libyans. Only four weeks later was his corpse found in the trunk of his car. On April 19, 1980, three Libyans shot Abdul Jilal Aref, a textile wholesaler, in the Cafe de Paris on the Via Veneto. On May 10, Aballah Mohammed el-Kasmi, a Libyan who had fallen from favor, was shot twice in the head in the Hotel Torino in Rome by a fellow countryman. The former Libyan diplomat Omran Mehdawi died from four shots received while walking on a street in Bonn. Qaddafi is even reputed to have made President Ronald Reagan the target of a death squad. Although unable to prove the allegation, for this disclosure Reagan earned the sympathy of Americans, who were not favorably disposed toward Qaddafi following Libya's affair with Billy Carter.

Numerous attacks have already been made against Muammar

al-Qaddafi—the latest attempted coup in May 1984—who merely seems to be the beloved of his people. Each time he has escaped with injuries not even worth mentioning; occasionally he even resorts to using a double. Nonetheless, Qaddafi's situation is tense—not least because of the economic crisis produced by his chaotic system. Qaddafi resides with his wife and children in a villa surrounded by barbed wire within the heavily guarded Aziza barracks of Tripoli; he is fighting for his life. In January 1982 the man who dreams of a confederation of Arabs had difficulty in putting down a widespread uprising allegedly organized by Mohammed al-Mogarief's National Liberation Front. In order to do so, he required the helpful intervention of Russian, East German, and Syrian troops. There are ongoing preparations for new attacks. Brother Muammar al-Qaddafi will not die in bed.

14

Islam Versus Socialism—a Revolutionary Becomes Pious

Tunisia Fights the Fundamentalists

HABIB BOURGUIBA, an enlightened despot and republican monarch, has been governing Tunisia, the smallest nation of the Maghreb, since July 1957. (According to the opposition, his motto is: "A genius of the stature of Bourguiba is not to be found every day . . . I am a coincidence of history.") Constitutionally, he is head of the nation and the government, commander-in-chief of the armed forces, and also chairman of the ruling Socialist Dustur Party (PSD), but he delegates many of his offices to others. For a quarter of a century he has managed to choke off any opposition, whether from the communist or the Islamic direction. Primarily it is the unions that Bourguiba keeps an eye on; when they dared to make any demands, many union leaders were imprisoned, and for a long time. January 27, 1980 was the start of the greatest threat to the system, besides widespread food riots in January 1984; a Libyan-controlled commando unit took over the southern

Tunisian city of Gafsa and for three days defended it against the government troops, but the attempt to topple Bourguiba failed.

That changes nothing, however, in the inner weaknesses of the Bourguiba era, which is now coming to an end. Bourguiba, sick and in his late seventies, continues to serve merely as the indifferent figure in his power system. In reality, his underlings and his wife, the resolute First Lady Wassila Bourguiba, have taken over the leadership, but they can no longer eliminate such factors as the uncertain economic situation, heavy migration from rural areas to the cities, poverty, high indebtedness, and repression by the state—all of which are important in the emerging Islamic fundamentalism. An undeclared war against the regime has already begun. Just how insecure the Bourguiba clan has become is reflected in a historic address given by the elderly head of state at a special meeting of his Socialist Dustur Party in April 1981. In that speech he consented to the founding of additional political parties, but would not give his approval to any Islamic party. The first parliamentary elections since the country gained independence from France on March 20, 1956, were scheduled for November 1981, and were again manipulated in favor of Bourguiba.

Islam in Tunisia has to date been of a liberal, Western orientation. Habib Bourguiba broke more radically than any other Arab leader with the traditions of his faith. He forbade the wearing of the veil (Decree 108) and polygamy, introduced the equality of women, and declared that Ramadan, the month of fasting, was the private concern of the individual. Bourguiba legalized the marriage of a Muslim woman with a non-Muslim, which provided the fundamentalists with a plan that gradually took hold in the entire country. In mosques and mainly at the Saituna University in Tunis, cells were formed by the Muslim Brotherhood and Khomeini admirers, who are known in Tunisia as "integritists." Their position in regard to Habib Bourguiba became steadily clearer: "Anyone who does not believe in the revelation of the Koran is a nonbeliever. The Prophet said that the princes should rule, but he also said that if they deviate from the path of Islam, they should be killed."

The writings of Hassan al-Banna, Sayed Qutb, and Mohammed Iqbal have already been printed in quantities as high as 15,000. Newspapers and fliers are circulated, and dealers sell tape cassettes of speeches by the radical Cairo clergyman Sheikh Abdel Hamid Kishk and by such local prayer leaders as Hassan Ghodbani. Since the big economic crisis of 1969, the movement has gained a foothold. Sheikh Mohammed Salah Neifer heads the Organization for the Rescue and Dissemination of Islam, whose followers include many students and teachers. Although he is the historical figure of the integrity movement, the practitioner is Abdelfateh Moro. Sheikh Moro, a former lawyer with good connections to Saudi Arabia, has long been instrumental in establishing ties between the universities and the mosques, and has always maintained good contact with the people in the interior of the country.

The most important leader of the fundamentalists, however, is Sheikh Rashid al-Ganoushi, a man in his forties who is a member of the Muslim Brotherhood and a professor of theology. He heads the Islamic Trend Movement (ITM), which was banned by Habib Bourguiba on July 18, 1981. Sheikh al-Ganoushi and 105 other members—including Moro, who was his deputy at that time— were imprisoned. The legal proceedings ended with a harsh sentence: a ten-year imprisonment for Rashid al-Ganoushi and ten other leaders. (Sheikh Moro was placed under house arrest in late 1983.) Tunisia's Minister of the Interior Driss Guiga stated that "the Islamic zealots wanted to stage a coup." Guiga announced officially that the integritists had admitted that a secret organization, founded in 1979 (following Khomeini's coming to power), directed terrorist acts against the living monument Bourguiba and his government. The minister stated that the group had connections abroad.

In the meantime the remaining leadership of the Islamic movement—those still at large—has completely gone underground. Their spokesmen demand a sacred state; toward this goal, they proclaim armed struggle and carry out their agitation among the 6.5 million Muslims of the country, 5 million of whom follow the strictly orthodox Malikite ritual. Muslim women wear their veils in protest against the hated government. Fighting between fundamentalist and Western-oriented students at Tunisian universities always ends with massive police intervention and the closing of the institution in question. Acts of revenge are a regular occurrence. Fliers proclaim that "Islam is the basic element of Tunisia in the future. Only Islam is capable of providing answers to all questions."

Foreign visitors repeatedly have their attention called to the brutality of the Bourguiba regime and to the torture and miserable conditions in the prisons. The integritists emphasize the inflation, the country's diminishing purchasing power, and the luxurious lifestyle of a small minority. They cite the Koran and the *sunna* as their sole impetus, and of course angrily reject contacts among the youth with the troublemaker Qaddafi. Shortly before his arrest, Rashid al-Ganoushi preached in the Sidi Yussef Mosque in the kasbah of Tunis: "The example of Iran is for the purpose of testing us. The time of the awakening has come. . . . If the revolutions from the right and the left have not succeeded, it is because man has not made his own revolution. Let us start it in the name of Allah. Only of Allah are we afraid." Tunisia's revolutionary Islam is in the offing.

Ahmed Ben Bella: A Living Myth

Since the signal from Tehran in 1979, stirrings have also occurred in Tunisia's neighbor Algeria, which for decades has been socialist in character. Following unrest that was attributed to activities of the fundamentalists, President Shadli Benjedid had the unity party, the National Liberation Front (FLN), purged not only of leftist dissenters but also of Islamic forces. In an appeal he demanded that Algeria not be permitted to become an "ideological testing ground," stating also that Islam is the religion of social justice and equality of opportunity, and that anyone wishing to realize these goals should join the FLN. His warnings were evidently prompted by clashes between religious squads and Algerian security forces in the oasis city of Laghuat, situated on the northern edge of the Sahara, 155 miles from Algiers. There the extremely religious group allegedly drove the official imam from the mosque. The leader of the Islamic rebels preached that people should turn toward a simple life, enticed the schoolchildren out of the state schools, and opposed the practice that women go to work.

That may have been a marginal manifestaiton, or perhaps the tip of the iceberg. In any case, in the states of the Maghreb west of Qaddafi's Libya, there is increasing discontent among the integritists about the secularization and Westernization of their society. Houari Boumedienne, the leader of Algeria from 1965 to 1978, saw to it that the *ulema* would not become a danger to him in the political sector. As early as 1967, he prohibited Islamic organizations and had their most important representatives arrested. The Friday prayers were written in the Ministry for Religious Affairs, and the Koran schools were closed. Boumedienne's successor, Shadli Benjedid, has pursued a more conciliatory policy toward Islam. Nonetheless, it seems doubtful whether such measures suffice, for the integritists are no longer content with freedom of worship. They are demanding an Islamic state, which means that they are demanding power.

On their side is a man who has mythic stature in all of North Africa and in the entire Muslim world despite the fact that he was imprisoned for fifteen years and subjected to strict house arrest: Ahmed Ben Bella (whose followers weepily and lovingly call him B.B.). Ahmed Ben Bella comes from Marnia, in the old department of Oran, where he was born in 1919 to a trader of Moroccan descent. He was in the French army during World War II and immediately afterwards joined the Algerian liberation movement. The later National Liberation Front (FLN) grew out of a secret paramilitary organization named O.S., which was headed by Ben Bella. Ahmed Ben Bella was part of the historic committee, the FLN's "Nine Brothers," that triggered the uprising against the French occupation on November 1, 1954. He was the organizer and chief of staff of the liberation army. When the French finally captured him in 1956, they imprisoned him for almost six years.

After independence was declared in 1962, the martyr and hero of the people rose to become the first prime minister of his country. That was a mere formality, though. Together with his old comrades, he promoted the introduction of socialism into Algeria. Starting in 1963, he did so as president of the country. Islam as the basis of alliance during the war of liberation receded into the background. Ahmed Ben Bella was received with all honors and accorded great distinction in Moscow. In July 1953 he eliminated unpopular critics from the country's leadership class, but was himself overthrown by Colonel Houari Boumedienne on June 19, 1965. There was never a public trial against him, because Ben Bella was too popular and famous as a leader of the Third World. Later it was merely said that he had a tendency toward making himself into a cult figure, that he got rich from Algeria's budget, and that his Algerian socialism led to mismanagement and corruption.

Ben Bella had to spend the next fifteen years alone with his books and studies, completely shut off from the world. Only occasionally was he permitted a visitor, but in 1971 he was allowed to marry Zohra Sellami, a journalist almost thirty years younger than he. They adopted two orphaned children.

Boumedienne refused to be influenced by Tito, Qaddafi, or Castro to give Ahmed Ben Bella his freedom. Only after the president's death was Ben Bella's "living burial," as he himself called it, ended, on July 4, 1979. The world confirmed that the vanished Ben Bella had kept himself fit and had not lost his almost youthful smile and dynamic manner. After a pilgrimage to Mecca in September 1981, Ben Bella did not return to Algiers, because his increasing criticism of the new president had again brought him into danger.

Ahmed Ben Bella went with his wife into exile in Paris and Geneva, where, from fear of an attempt on his life, they live in extremely secluded circumstances. In Ben Bella's first interview, it turned out that while under house arrest he had developed into an Islamic revolutionary and had become a strict fundamentalist. And although he does not admit it, he has turned toward the Muslim Brotherhood; in September 1981, he was given an important assignment as director of the London-based International Islamic Commission for Human Rights at the Islamic Council for Europe. In this capacity he observes and responds to violations of human rights in the Middle East.

But as a converted politician from the great reorientation phase of the Islamic world, he also fulfills an important function as a display figure. For the brilliant, extremely impressive man, the Iranian revolution represents a turning point in the history of his civilization. Certainly it suffers from childhood diseases, but a first step must be made. "Not everything is positive in a revolution," he explains to me. "I am against spilling blood. . . . But a lot of blood will flow before this matter is concluded. It is impossible to make a revolution without having blood flow." Passionately and with resolute persuasiveness, Ahmed Ben Bella announces the forthcoming conquest by Islamic civilization.

I asked him in Paris whether he too holds the widespread view that Iran constitutes a danger to many of its neighbors. His answer: "No, I do not believe that the possible danger constitutes the main problem. Iran today provides many Muslims with answers to a series of questions. It is not the military but the cultural aspect that constitutes a threat for the systems of government on the Gulf. If you want to speak of danger, then you must define it ideologically."

"Si Ahmed," as he is known to his people, is sitting in exile as in a waiting room; with obvious composure, he glances toward Algeria. Anyone who has tasted power as intensely as he wants to have it again. When he speaks of an uprooted society whose tie of solidarity is not yet broken, of the return to a great civilization, and of the true religion, he also thinks of Algeria—and he again feels himself indispensable. Ahmed Ben Bella knows that the Algeria of his era no longer exists. He has also long been aware that the days of the *zaim* (clan chiefs) and martyrs are passé, at least for the majority of contemporary Algerian youth, who regard the generation from the war of liberation as alien. With an astonishing ability for concealing his own errors during the presidency, the still-youthful hero contemplates the Algerian society that meanwhile has become so diverse.

Ben Bella—who has said, "I am no longer a socialist and do not even know what it means"—commented on contemporary Algeria in an interview for the French magazine *Jeune Afrique:*

We are living in a situation that is comparable to Iran before the fall of the Shah. The people will decide (after my return) whether my truth or that of the others is better. By free elections for all groupings, for all directions. . . . To die? That is one of the risks, especially if one knows the nature of those who rule Algeria today. But I have chosen exile in order to be able to speak. I am a militant, not a pensioner. If I would not restrain myself, I would be a corpse.

Just how militant Ben Bella is today he showed most recently in his obituary for the assassins of Sadat: "Allah may show them His mercy and have pity on them. Their blood was unjustly spilled on this earth. Will that ever be forgiven?"

A King Between the Jet Set and the Koran

The wave of the resurgence of Islam does not stop at the western corner of the fragmented Islamic realm. And it is here, between the jet set and the Koran, that King Hassan II, a descendant of the Prophet Mohammed, reigns. The ruler is considered clever, moderate, and friendly toward the U.S. Since taking over the throne in February 1961, publicity has always been favorable. The unrest among the students and the unemployed of Casablanca was crushed by the military in 1965, and internationally was no longer taken seriously. The king's repressive measures against all kinds of opposition and the unsolved social problems of Morocco continue, even today, to be concealed by the cloak of monarchy. The food riots of January 1984 were an exceptional event. Now, however, the fundamentalists are coming, and they are incapable of having anything to do with royal dynasties since their doctrine only approves caliphs. Islam is already undisputedly predominant in Marrakesh, Casablanca, Rabat, Tangiers, and Fez. The flat country perseveres in medieval structures and, unlike Tunisia and Algeria, there were never any Westernized or socialist models. Only the elite of the three countries is oriented toward the pleasantries of the West and mistrustfully observes any form of change.

Conditions in Morocco are ideal for the Muslim Brotherhood, and for years it has registered a strong increase in membership. One of the organization's leaders is Sheikh Abdessalam Yassine, who holds the position of inspector of the educational system. He was already so bold as to write his king a letter, requesting that he show greater respect toward the faith of the fathers. Members of the Muslim Brotherhood of Morocco are mainly entrenched in the universities and hold academic positions. Many of them have already been condemned, but they have never had to remain in prison for long. The government does not quite know how to deal with them, for they preach of the earth and of Islam—and that has won them eighty percent of the Moroccan population, without necessitating the emergence of a Khomeini. Although King Hassan's integritists live far from the Near East, their ties to the underground movements in the Arab motherland are close. Three of them, including Abdelkarim Moti, founder of the Society of Young Muslims, even participated in the occupation of the Grand Mosque in Mecca. After the murder of the socialist Omar Benjelloun was ascribed to him, he fled to Saudi Arabia in December 1975, but his disciples remain in Morocco, waiting for their hour.

15

Next Year in Khartoum

THE HOT SUDAN is the largest country of Africa, yet it is one of the least developed. As President Jaafar Mohammed al-Numeiri is apt to say, it already belongs entirely to international sponsors. Nonetheless, or perhaps because of that, out of strategic considerations the West fosters relations with the Sudan, for next door in Ethiopia are the Russians. Qaddafi, too, can best be observed from the two countries on the Nile: Egypt and Sudan. For years, insiders said that if Sadat fell, then Numeiri would not be sitting in his old colonial palace along the great river much longer. He is still there, however—but that has more to do with the Muslim Brotherhood. The organization is so strong in the Sudan that it could take over the government any day. But what would it gain from a totally bankrupt state? Therefore the fundamentalists continue to feign weakness while waiting for the propitious moment, one for which they themselves will have created the precondition —namely, that the damages done by Numeiri be repaired immediately. In other words, they are waiting for the presuppositions of the Islamic state they are striving for. And that can be next year in Khartoum, or it can be later.

The history of the Islamic movements in the Sudan can basically be traced to the Mahdiya, which was Mohammed Ahmed's country. The Anglo-Egyptian rule lasted until 1955. The Sudan was in fact a British colony, although *pro forma* the khedive in Cairo appointed the English governor-general. In the northern part of the country, which traditionally is Arab in orientation, there are two rival Islamic sects—the Khatmiyyah under the leadership of al-Mirghani and the neo-Mahdists under Abd al-Rahman. The old Mahdists were in the pro-British Ummah Party, founded in 1945. When the Muslim Brotherhood was again banned in Egypt after Hassan al-Banna had died, many of the members of the organization moved away, some to the Sudan. Here they promptly recognized the necessity of building up an organization against the growing communist influence. Years later, however, the strongest Marxist-Leninist party on the African continent came into being in the Sudan. Initially two Brotherhoods were formed: one was conceived as a defensive organization against the danger emanating from Moscow, and the other as a supplement to the Egyptian parent organization. Neither one of the organizations produced important or charismatic leaders, for their membership consisted mainly of students until 1955.

An Anglo-Egyptian agreement of 1953 made provisions for granting Sudan independence within three years. The youngest son of the Mahdi, Abd ar-Rahman al-Mahdi, at that time the leader of the religious Ansar sect, also had a hand in the agreement, since he had good connections with the British. After his death, the grandson inherited the title, followed by the greatgrandson Sadeq, who is still the leader of the Ansars. Shortly before independence, unrest among the black Christians in the south developed into a civil war, and on November 17, 1958, a group from the military under the command of General Ibrahim Abboud, a member of the Khatmiyyah, assumed power. At this time a young captain by the name of Numeiri was kept under guard for nineteen months on suspicion of anti-government activity.

The Muslim Brotherhood was still weak and functioned only as a lobby for an Islamic constitution. Its present leadership was still studying at the universities; in 1964 the situation was different. The military dictator Abboud was overthrown, mainly by students who belonged to the Muslim Brotherhood. During a general strike they tested their strength once again. The civilian transitional government was unable to accomplish its most important task of ending the fighting in the south, so the traditional parties allied themselves with the newly formed Islamic Charter Front (the Muslim Brotherhood under another name) and forced new elections. The new leadership of the country struck brutally at the separatist Anyanya movement in the south at a time that coincided with the Mahdi great-grandson's nine-month tenure as prime minister. Meanwhile the Muslim Brotherhood had established a network that included subdivisions for women, youth, and laborers. In 1969 the parliamentary system collapsed. Corruption and an acute economic crisis did the rest.

It was time for a new strong man: Jaafar Mohammed al-Numeiri, who was brought to power in a bloodless coup by a group of "free officers." He became major general, commander-in-chief of the armed forces, and chairman of the Revolutionary Command Council. Sadeq al-Mahdi was arrested and expelled to Egypt. On the Nile island of Aba and in Omdurman, the fundamentalist forces placed themselves under the leadership of his uncle, Imam al-Mahdi. Gun-fighting that resembled civil war broke out. Numeiri summarily had the rebels bombarded, and hundreds were killed. The Muslim Brotherhood went underground and was heard from only occasionally in the form of oppositional ideas. In the fall of 1970, Numeiri got rid of the leading Sudanese communists who had assisted him to power.

In July 1971 he survived a takeover attempt by leftist officers through the help of loyal supporters from the military, who freed him from prison within seventy-two hours. Numeiri now eliminated the communists. All those he could get a hand on, he executed, including the entire leadership of the party, and thus weakening the position of the Soviet technicians and military advisors in the country. In 1972 Jaafar al-Numeiri ended the seventeen-year civil war in the south by granting the three provinces extensive autonomy. He switched to a Cairo course, abandoning Qaddafi. The vengeful Libyan did not forget that, and his response came in 1976. In July of that year approximately 2,000 well-trained followers of Sadeq al-Mahdi, the leader of the Ummah Party and of the Ansar, and members of the Muslim Brotherhood entered the Sudan from Libya and tried to take power. They were armed with automatic weapons, and the fighting with the regular army lasted for days. Ultimately the army got the upper hand, and Numeiri took revenge by having all the surviving attackers executed. In the wake of this "sanitizing" operation, he expelled the ninety remaining Soviet advisors from the country in May 1977.

Numeiri noticed that he stood alone in fighting lost causes, so he introduced national reconciliation. His first step was to let Hassan al-Turabi out of jail. The sharp-witted Hassan al-Turabi, head of the Muslim Brotherhood and brother-in-law of Sadeq al-Mahdi, is today the real strong man in the Sudan, and no one gets around him.

Born in 1932, al-Turabi lived in various parts of the Sudan, since his father was a judge and frequently changed his residence. Al-Turabi studied law in Khartoum and, starting in 1950, belonged to various Islamic movements. Since Khartoum did not have an independent university, Hassan al-Turabi went to London in 1955 and completed his degree in 1957. He worked in the Sudan for a brief period as a teacher at the university, and then went to Paris to obtain his doctorate in law at the Sorbonne. In 1964 al-Turabi arrived back in Khartoum at just the right moment to participate in the revolt against General Abboud. He entered public life and became leader of the Islamic Charter Front. After Numeiri's coup, he traded his office in the party for a prison cell, where he remained until 1977.

He then worked as a lawyer until Numeiri asked him to join a cabinet designed to neutralize all the opposition. Members of the Muslim Brotherhood were given two key positions: Hassan al-Turabi became minister of justice and chief public prosecutor; Ahmed Abdel Rahman Mohammed was appointed minister of the interior. Since that time, together, they have been able to ensure that members of the Muslim Brotherhood are spared the extremely disagreeable Sudanese prisons. Numeiri promised amnesty to the Mahdi, who then returned to the Sudan. Together with Hassan al-Turabi, he was even taken into the politburo of the Sudanese Socialist Union (SSU). By these measures, Numeiri believed he had assured his survival. He expressly professed his belief in Allah and established a Commission for the Incorporation of Islam in the constitution and in the justice administration. The result was the creation of new mistrust among the southern Sudanese and content among the Muslim Brotherhood. President

Numeiri later even wrote two books about his conception of Islam, which, by his own admission, even Hassan al-Turabi, meanwhile become national security adviser to the President, has not read.

The Sudanese, who are all sitting in the same boat, have been trying to put the leaky ship of state on a new course, an attempt that fails repeatedly. Never before has the economic condition of the country been so bad. It is so bad that Western technology, Saudi Arabian petrodollars (in an exchange against the increasing resurgence of Islam), and American weapons systems can no longer help it. The state is confronted with bankruptcy and suffers from every conceivable problem of a developing country. The galloping inflation rate was posted at sixty percent in 1980. Basic foodstuffs, although rationed, are mostly not to be had at all—a situation that early in January 1982 led to the most severe riots against the government to date. Triggered by price increases initiated by the government, the turmoil lasted four days before the police were able to regain control. Gasoline had become thirty percent more expensive; sugar was sixty percent higher. Numeiri fired most of his ministers, replaced them by new officials (members of the Muslim Brotherhood remained), and sent twenty-two high officers into retirement following the outbreak of rioting. These measures were merely external signs intended to pacify the people. The catastrophic economic and development policies, as well as the alarming balance of payment problem, remain. In addition, the Sudanese are burdened with a half-million refugees from wars in neighboring Ethiopia (mostly from Eritrea), Uganda, Zaire, and Chad. The refugees live in squalid camps in the eastern and southern parts of the country.

Numeiri is desperately trying to get control of things. In September 1983, he was in danger of being overrun by the Islamic movement. But Numeiri noticed the danger in time, and from that moment gave himself out to be more devout than the fundamentalists. He repeatedly had immense supplies of alcohol dumped into the Nile and ordered that English penal law be replaced by the Islamic *sharia*. Since the fall of 1983, a Sudanese who drinks alcohol can expect beatings, adulterors face being stoned, and thieves amputation of one hand. When Sadeq al-Mahdi condemned these innovations as too radical and as a diversionary tactic for the country's economic catastrophe, he fell from grace with the president.

In March 1984 Numeiri's foreign policy adviser Hassan al-Turabi stated that a new tax law and a civil code with an Islamic basis would be in effect. He also announced the introduction of a new constitution, likewise based on Islam. Precisely two months later, Numeiri dissolved the administration that had been formed only a short time earlier and, in keeping with the Islamic tradition, installed a sixty-four man presidential council to watch over governmental matters in the manner of an advisory board.

In a presidential decree, Numeiri pointed out that in the future he could now govern more in keeping with Islam. In the fifteenth year of Numeiri's rule, that marked an unprecedented highpoint in the resurgence of Islam in the Sudan. The next step could be the founding of an Islamic republic of the Sudan, which would doubtlessly usher in Hassan al-Turabi.

He and his supporters, the only force worth mentioning in the country, are waiting for this moment, in which case military conflict with the turbulent Christian south is preprogrammed. But that possibility is a minor factor for the Turabi faction at present. The blacks in the south do not want to live under a radical Islamic system. They have already let that be known, pointing to the anti-Christian measures taken to date by former Minister of Justice Hassan al-Turabi, which, among other things, included a ban on the traditional processions for the celebration of Christmas in 1980. They would prefer to resume the underground war against the central administration than submit to an Islamic system, as the leaders of the southern provinces have already advised Khartoum. The fuse to the Sudanese powder keg is once again glowing.

In a discussion lasting almost two hours I asked Hassan al-Turabi about the goals of the Muslim Brotherhood in the Sudan and about the background details of the muddled situation in his country:

"You are the leader of an organization that does not officially exist. How should I understand that?"

"That is for the purpose of complying with the formalities of the law. In the Sudan we are not at present officially permitted, but we are tolerated. After all, we are a social and a sociological movement."

"Are there differences between the Sudanese Muslim Brotherhood and the fundamentalists of other Muslim countries?"

"We began first with the elite of the state and only later included the people. Elsewhere the organization starts within the masses and only later then spreads into the universities. We have no sheikh or imam or *murshid* [Supreme Guide] within our leadership. We have only an advisory body to which one must be elected. We have no single charismatic leader."

"How closely are you connected with the mosques of the country?"
"Not very much at all. We work in mosques, but also in schools, universities, and factories. We are present in clubs, football associations, artists' organizations. What is involved is a very comprehensive movement to which, in contrast to the rest of the Arab world, many more women than is usually the case belong. That is the general Sudanese way of connecting Islam with everyday practice. The Sudanese are very tolerant and objective."

"How did you agree with the power-hungry Numeiri in such a way that he too adopted this Sudanese virtue?"
"We work as a supplement to his own policy, and from the beginning left no doubt about the matter that we are not now striving for power. In contrast, the other nationalistic movements were unable to come to any agreement with him, because they wanted many privileges from him. But Numeiri also knows that we are the only group, the only political power in this country that can cause him a lot of trouble. I am speaking of demonstrations, strikes, and everything else that can be done. In the instance of an attack on us, we would also resort to weapons. But we do not want to overthrow the regime, since at the moment there is no alternative to it. What advantage is there to us if we assist the country into chaos?"

"If that is the case, what do you want?"
"A kind of Islamic society, an open society. At present we are setting up Islamic banks everywhere. We are creating Islamic centers and showing what Islamic music and Islamic sports are. We are a movement that wants to achieve social change. That should occur freely and openly. Numeiri is in power and he will also still be in power tomorrow. We have enough time in the long run to get everything under control—the Islamic society in every area of life."

"In doing so, do you want to draw on the model of an existing system —for example, Iran?"

"In Iran they are destroying themselves. Religious energy is breathtaking. If it is liberated without having a constructive program, it is capable of destroying everything, including us."

"When will your Islamic state come about? In twenty years?"
"Much sooner, I believe."
In ten years? In one year?
That is certainly possible. Insha. Allah. If God wills it.

16

Islam Across Africa

"PLEAD THE CAUSE OF YOUR LORD with wisdom and beautiful exhortation, and dispute with them in the best manner. Truly your Lord knows best who has abandoned his cause, and He knows best those who are well-guided."

"Do not follow the infidels, but contend against them with the Koran with all your energy."

"You—the Jews and the Christians—should therefore not argue among yourselves in this matter; rather, summon them to your Lord. Truly you follow the correct leadership. If they nonetheless quarrel with you, then state: 'God knows best what you are doing. God will judge on the day of resurrection about what you were in disagreement with.' "

In three different *suras* the Koran deals with the transmission of the faith and proselytizing among non-Muslims. This is a realm that has completely vanished from the perspective of the Westerners following the conflicts in Iran, Afghanistan, and Lebanon. In Africa, however, the issue is mainly the thrust of Islam and the ambition of the entire religion.

Khartoum in April: even at 10:00 A.M. the air is shimmering; the mercury in the thermometer reaches the 120-degree mark. A taxi takes me out of the city, past the airport, through scorched landscape that has been transformed into a steppe. Suddenly, after perhaps a little over four miles, a *fata morgana*—the Islamic African Center. To the right, beside the street, is a row of buildings, including a brand-new mosque with a silvery shining cupola, its minaret in earth-colored brown with a white spire. Most of the other hues are stippled with gray and brown. Here plants really grow, and there is also a green lawn that is sprinkled constantly. The walls are erected precisely. A social center resembling any one might find in Europe—astonishing in Khartoum, where even in entrances to ministers' offices it is possible to look through cracks in the walls. When the host explains to me that seven Islamic countries, including three extremely wealthy nations on the Gulf, spent $54 million for this advertisement for the living faith, everything becomes clear to me.

In the Sudan a monument was erected to the missionary efforts of Islam. Under the direction of a dynamic, Western-trained intellectual, Dr. Al Tayeb Zeyn-Al-Abideen, himself a member of the Muslim Brotherhood, the Islamic Center is intended to show how earnestly the doctrine of the Prophet functions in the era of the resurgence of the faith. Construction on the extensive installation, which includes a school plus a boarding school, sports facility, administrative offices, and a mosque, was begun in 1977, and was completed in 1983. In the first level of training, 300 young Africans from forty countries—from Mauritius to Liberia, from the Sudan to Botswana—receive a broad general education, which includes basic subjects such as mathematics and languages as well as instruction in crafts. "Our education is intended to be followed by attendance at a university," explains Mohammed el-Arabi, the acting director and head of administration. Most of the graduates can continue their studies in the Arab countries, in countries on the Gulf, or in Islamic centers in Europe.

The largest Islamic training center for the cadres of Africa provides instruction in the Arabic language (which in the Sudan, in any case, is a sign of the return to Islam) and the consciousness necessary for students to disseminate the faith in their home countries. During a tour through the clean spaces of the institute with its modern furnishings, Mohammed el-Arabi comments: "Anyone unable to achieve the desired levels simply receives technical training so he can be certain of a good job at home. Experts are always in demand on this continent. Our students receive food, clothing, free trips home, and twenty dollars in pocket money per month. They participate in much sport and spend summer vacations together in camp. Our kitchen has even discovered a satisfactory solution to the extremely varied tastes on this enormous Islamic continent." All the kings and leading politicians from the donor countries have already visited their prestigious creation. Selected teachers and missionaries travel to discussion forums in Nigeria, seminars in Nairobi and Accra. They minister to the plight of the Eritrean refugees. Before, the only center of this kind was in Burundi, one directed toward entire families.

The next link in the chain is in the center of Khartoum. And my next surprise is there, for I find myself sitting opposite a Sudanese with an American passport: Dr. Tigani Abu Guideiri, a man who was a fellow student of other important officials within the resurgence of Islam whom I met in other Islamic countries. The world of the fundamentalists is also small, and all of them are in contact with each other. General Secretary Tigani is head of Munazamat Al Dawa Al Islamiya, which translates to something like "Organization to Spread the Reputation of Islam." He is the person chiefly responsible for Islamic missionary activity in Africa, and since May 1979 has been establishing a network of propagators of the faith. He studied agriculture in Khartoum as well as at the University of Arizona in Tucson and the University of Wisconsin in Madison. Intermittently he concerned himself with the reproduction of sugarcane in the Sudan. In the U.S. in 1978, Dr. Tigani served as the president of the Muslim Students' Association and as the social scientist and general director of the Islamic Teaching Center in Indianapolis, Indiana.

Once back in the Sudan, the Westernized fundamentalist entered parliament and ultimately let himself be persuaded to accept the new assignment. In his words:

Together with forty-five people at present, we are building up the first systematic mission for Africa. In the future we will build Islamic centers with mosques, libraries, and schools everywhere and will offer our services in the realm of education. It is the duty of all Muslims to disseminate Islam and to conduct dialogues with persons of other faiths. If this effort is not accepted, then for all eventualities we will have done our duty. Force is not in our repertoire. In this manner we honor Allah. Our highest task is to make a contribution toward peace and understanding in the world.

Dr. Tigani Abu Guideiri's motto is: "Enjoy what is right, forbid what is wrong." He is part of the new generation of Muslims from the Third World who are returning to the roots of their faith and, in doing so, exploit the technological possibilities of the condemned modernity. Allah's PR man in Khartoum knows how he has to package his offering:

For us, capitalism and communism constitute the continuation of the colonial era and are therefore not acceptable. Our faith is not based on material desires; on the contrary, it leads to spiritual values. We should like to provide the human being with balance. That occurs pragmatically and scientifically. First we investigate all the religions in Africa and then decide how best we can address them. That take places personally and with books in four languages from our own printer.

In this way the missionaries' efforts are supplemented by the educators from the Islamic African Center. Both work hand in hand, even among the refugees from the bush wars. Dr. Tigani will not encounter any financial difficulties, since petrodollars flow generously for the dissemination of Islam. Even now Saudi Arabia's International Islamic Conference Organization (ICO) is in the process of financing a complete university in Uganda. The $60 million were paid by the Islamic Development Bank in Jiddah.

The shared history of the Arabs and Africans goes back a long time. Although for Mohammed, the enslavement of blacks was a matter of course, he tried to improve their situation, and numerous slaves and freedmen were in fact among his first disciples. One of them, Bilal, was appointed by Mohammed to be the first *muezzin* of Islam. The Prophet considered the freeing of slaves an act pleasing to God, and through Mohammed this act achieved the status of a repentance for various offenses. The freed black slaves were on the same level as their former masters. In the realm of the fine arts, they even overtook the Arabs after a period of time. During the era of the Abbasids, political competition was particularly great, and the Africans almost managed to conquer the realm of the caliph. At times black Africans ruled Egypt, Morocco, and southern Arabia. The Arab love poets even used the slogan "black is beautiful." The close cooperation was somewhat hampered by colonialism, but was never interrupted, and today even extends to the militant liberation movements in the southern part of the continent.

Since the faith is once again in the process of regaining its former strength, the spread of Islam can no longer be stopped. It is rapidly sweeping across the world. At the beginning of this century, only one-fifth of the blacks were receptive to Mohammed's revelation, whereas today their numbers amount to one-half of the entire population of 400 million. Within fifty years Islam has achieved more than in the previous millennium. Its propagandists support their missionary work with the thesis that Islam is an African religion and is suitable for people of that continent. In contrast, Christianity represents the faith of the colonial powers and is alien, European, arrogant, and elitist. And truly, for these people, Islam is more straightforward and therefore more accessible than Christianity. That starts even with the profession of faith, where concepts such as the trinity and incarnation are outside the Africans' cultural heritage. Islam has never questioned the customs and morals of native peoples, but instead has let them exist in relation to its own doctrine. The African customs of the extended family and polygamy were spared. From the Islamic point of view, faith points out a universal path through life on earth and also tolerates animistic ancestral cults and traditional sensuous festivities.

In the social sector, too, Islam has broadened the perspective of the African, which previously was strictly traditionalist. Whether from the Hausa, Banda, or Fulbe tribe, the African had typically entrusted his fate to spirits that dwelled in a fountain, a tree, or a river, and had regarded individual human life as a link within a long chain of being that extended back to the mysterious founder of his clan or tribe. And he had tried to make these spirits and his ancestors well disposed toward him. Through the Islamic faith, he now realized that his life was restricted to a brief period and that his actions on earth only acquired meaning by being directed toward the faith. From his Islamic teachers, he also learned that everything he had done in life would be examined after his death and that the only path on which he could save his soul and himself on the day of judgment was by the assumption of responsibility for this life.

Pater Artur Hand of the White Fathers, the order with the greatest amount of experience in the Christian mission in Africa, told me: "After independence from the colonial powers had been achieved, the situation in North Africa was almost idyllic. Christians and Muslims approached each other and worked together. Then the others said to themselves that they did not need us at all and rejected us." The Christians often had to experience that situation. With the increase in self-confidence, the Africans (like the Asians, too) turned away from the West, and in doing so turned away from the religion of the foreign "Khawaajaat" (the expression for whites in the Sudan).

In the process, such seeming liberators as Libya's Colonel Muammar al-Qaddafi cleverly set themselves up as friends of the poor and backward peoples—merely concealing, however, their own machinations for acquiring power that rival those of the colonialists. Qaddafi's oil money, for example, "purified" the bloodthirsty Emperor Bokassa I of Central Africa, although only in passing. Uganda's butcher Idi Amin lived as a pious Muslim for hard currency, and in return received asylum, first in Libya and later in Jiddah in Saudi Arabia, after his flight from his ruined kingdom. Gambia's ex-president Dauda Jawara, who converted to Christianity only in 1955, returned to the faith of his fathers. The head of the Mossi in Upper Volta, traditionally an anti-Islamic tribe, also switched, as did President Omar Bongo of Gabon.

The list could be greatly extended. At the prompting of their leaders, entire tribes repeatedly change their religion. Reverend John Maloe Ater, the representative of the Geneva World Council of Churches in Khartoum, expressed his sorrow about the uneven competition: "For centuries traders from the Arab states have been spreading Islam. They give money to the people, and we cannot compete with that. The churches of the West are not sufficiently well endowed financially." It is not merely a matter of cash. Thousands of new mosques, as well as Koran schools, have been built within recent decades. The Islamic Development Bank of the oil-rich countries does all the work. Many governments grant advances for the pilgramage to Mecca, and to some extent, too, the rich brothers from the Gulf make contributions. Often residents from many African cities are among the masses of people at the holy shrines of Islam. Within five years, no fewer than 200,000 Nigerians have traveled there.

The High Council of Societies for the Dissemination of Islam has its headquarters in Mecca, where many of the Muslim activities start. The African program of the World Muslim League is based in Dakar. The so-called Supreme Council for Islamic Affairs, which is closely connected with Azhar University in Cairo, also sends missionaries into the countries of the black continent. In some Islamic nations the Christian mission has already been forbidden. Books containing Christian theology are among the works banned in the United Arab Emirates. In 1911 Gottfried Simon was one of the most famous of the German Bethel missionaries during the heyday of colonialism, and what he predicted in his classic *Islam and Christianity in the Battle for the Conquest of the Animistic Heathen World* has now come to pass: "Islam is moving ineluctably forward in Africa. The missions have gained contact with it. The question of whether we should conduct missionary work among the Mohammedans has become superfluous in our era. We are the ones being attacked. The Mohammedan flood is already overflowing many dams. . . . Islam puts our property in question."

His contemporary colleagues, the representatives of the Christian churches that are steadily losing ground, no longer speak at all of their "property." In Pater Hand's opinion:

The resurgence of Islam is an understandable issue in the post-colonial era. We Christians have no right to deny that to the Muslims. Unfortunately the renaissance is not pointed forward but backward. There is a danger that Muslims will fall back on political and ideological ideas that no longer fit into our contemporary landscape. And besides, they are conveying an idealized image that never existed. We must consider new forms of dialogue and resume the discussions, especially in Senegal, in Nigeria, Niger, and Upper Volta, where we are in dire straits.

Father John, a front-line fighter in Khartoum, argues somewhat more angrily:

Here in the south of the country, as in all of Africa, we will lose if Europe does not notice the situation in sufficient time. It is like a plague. As soon as there are Muslims in a place, the faith spreads and repeatedly proves to us that we have not managed to establish our faith as a valuable tradition in people's consciousness. It is a pity that the West always concerns itself only with politics and economics. For a long time it has neglected its own religion. It has become rich in material goods and poor in religious blessings.

John Maloe Ater, a fifty-year-old black missionary who studied in Beirut, rebukes the Western governments for spending too much effort in courting the favor of the oil-rich countries and overlooking Africa in the process.

How does Father John regard the competition on his own ground, the Islamic African center of the Muslim Brotherhood?

It constitutes a danger for all of Christianity. In a short period of time the entire new generation of intellectuals will be educated here. These people will then follow the traders and missionaries with money. And they are backed up by an enormous power. We cannot survive this competition and cannot keep up with the speed of the Muslims—not unless we had a Christian Mahdi, a charismatic redeemer for all of Africa. But if that existed, it would probably also fail, because our own people in Rome go behind our backs. The more the experts of the Vatican study Islam, the more sympathetic they find it. That is true. As for the Muslim Brotherhood, it is now very important and very dangerous. Just tell me where we have a Christian brotherhood? You would have to look for that for a long time.

He should console himself with Pope John Paul II, who in May 1979 explained to North African bishops: "The public and communal nature of the witness demonstrated to God the Creator by the Muslim community is an exhortation to the Christians."

17

The Mahdi Has Arrived

THE FIRST RAYS of the morning sun pierce the horizon, showing Mount Arafat, the mountain of mercy, in a gentle, unreal light. The desert is alive, for people everywhere are getting up in order to pray to their God in the early morning. A new day is dawning on Mecca, the capital of the Islamic world. It is 5:20 A.M. on November 20, 1979, the first day of the Muslim year 1400. The voice of the imam of the Grand Mosque, Sheikh Mohammed Ibn Subayyal, sounds through all the loudspeakers in the 480,000 square feet of the holiest of all shrines of Islam, high above the 300,000 residents of the city of Mecca: "Allah is greater, Allah is greater."

Sheikh Subayyal ushers in the new century with the morning prayer. Hardly has he finished than he is grabbed by strong hands and thrown down. Three shots follow in rapid succession, and a Sunni clergyman lies in his own blood. Juhaiman Ibn Mohammed Utaili has shot him with a Kalashnikov AK-47. Within a second his bearded companion reaches for the imam's microphone, and his scream resounds from all the loudspeakers: "The Mahdi and his supporters are seeking protection and help in the holy mosque, because they are persecuted everywhere and have no other refuge."

The Mahdi, even though self-appointed, has arrived. The Mahdi is an enduring dream of the Muslims. The Mahdi, the last prophet sent by God, will complete the work of his predecessor Mohammed, lead the infidels along the route of salvation, and establish a just system in the world. "The one who is well guided by God, the one who stands under divine light" (in the translation from the Arabic) corresponds to the Judeo-Christian conception of the Messiah, or redeemer. At the end of time he is to restore the "kingdom of God on earth." The longing for such a savior becomes steadily greater, the worse the conditions of life. Political, social, and religious unrest have maintained a fertile ground within Islamic societies for a Mahdi figure. The most famous manifestation of Mahdi was Mohammed Ahmed Ibn Abdullah, who in 1881 declared himself the redeemer in the Sudan, destroyed the Egyptian army under Hicks Pasha in 1883, and conquered Khartoum in 1885.

Al-Imam-Al-Mahdi, his complete title, dates back to the vanished twelfth imam of the Shiites. As noted earlier, Mohammed Abdul Kasim, born in 872 in Baghdad, vanished without a trace when he was eight years old. About him there has developed a myth, to which the Shiites are receptive. It is said that he is in the Radwa mountains near Mecca, guarded by a lion and a panther, and will reappear only when the world comes to an end, when his task will be to prepare the last judgment. Equality, justice, and peace will rule in the future kingdom of the Mahdi.

In the course of history various men called themselves Mahdi, but none succeeded in converting the attribute into deed. One example was the first caliph of the Shiite Fatimid dynasty ruling in North Africa, Obaidallah el-Mahdi (909–933). The sects and tribes of North Africa were always gladly willing to accept a religious leader who called himself the Mahdi.

Supported by the simple people, the various redeemers revolted against the caliphs of early Islamic history and later against the Ottoman Empire. The title was also claimed by the legendary Mohammed al-Sanussi (1787–1859) from the West Algerian town of Wasita, who founded a movement of Islamic resurgence in the mid-nineteenth century and fought against Turkey and Italy.

The Iranian religious leader Ayatollah Ruhollah Khomeini is the only one to experience the honor of being "the imam," hence of being the redeemer and of actually being the Mahdi. Based on strict interpretation of the Shiite doctrine, the definition is also useable. Scarcely had this Mahdi assumed power in Tehran than another Mahdi, who up to that point was the last one, was preparing the big coup in Saudi Arabia.

The background history to the occupation of the Masjid Al-Haram, or Grand Mosque, of Mecca is still shrouded in mystery, but two factors stand out. One of these extends back for decades into the history of Saudi Arabia, which in a practical sense is still a young country. In 1901 Abdul Aziz Ibn Abdul Rahman Ibn Saud left Kuwait and with seventy camel-riders conquered the desert settlement of Riad, at the time an unimportant place, from which the Saudis had been banished in 1890. In 1913 the army, which had increased to 6,000 fighters, overran the city of Hofuf. Taif and Mecca capitulated voluntarily, followed by Medina in 1924.

The country that once had been divided into sheikhdoms and sultanates by tribal feuds and family wars was finally united, providing the basis for present-day Saudi Arabia. According to the British writer Robert Lacey, in his work about this still-mysterious oil-rich country, "The renaissance of Islam did not begin with Ayatollah Khomeini. It started eighty years ago in the Arab desert when Abdul Aziz took over the leadership of a religious order," for which the necessary doctrine had already been provided earlier in the century by Ibn Abdul Wahhab.

The Saudi order called themselves Ikhwan, and should not be confused with the Ikhwan Muslimun (Muslim Brotherhood) founded only at a later date. The Ikhwans believed strictly in Allah, the Koran, and the *sunna*, and also in their model Abdul Aziz, who waged his battles for the sake of the "pure Islam." They rode against their enemies with the shout, "The winds of paradise are blowing!" The Ikhwan kept a rein on their people much as ultra-orthodox rabbis on the holy Sabbath. During periods of holy war, laughter, not to mention music, was forbidden.

In their powerful desert kingdom, the Wahhabis established settlements in which agriculture was given priority; in this way the new nation became secure within a short period of time. The idyll was first blemished when Ibn Saud introduced the automobile and the wireless telegraph. The *ulema* were outraged, and most of the conservative Muslims expressed their displeasure.

Opposition to the House of Saud slowly increased. In the late 1920s there was again discontent when Ibn Saud let Iraq go unscathed after it had set up fortifications along the Saudi border and kept the Bedouins from their accustomed freedom of movement. These Iraqi acts were in contradiction to existing agreements.

For this reason, the Ikhwan wanted to get rid of the now-unpopular leader. In 1929 there was an uprising under the leadership of Sultan Ibn Bijad Ibn Humaid. Only after several open battles was Ibn Saud victorious, and he subsequently dissolved the Ikhwan militia and replaced it with a regular army. At that time the nation was still far removed from its present wealth, for the oil era began only on May 1, 1939.

When Juhaiman Ibn Mohammed Utaibi was born around 1940, in the small settlement of Sagir in the province of Quasim, the uprising and the defeat of Ibn Humaid were still fresh in everyone's memory. Juhaiman came from an Ikhwan village, so even during his childhood he heard of the great disgrace, and from his parents' house could see the ruins of Ibn Humaid's camp in Ghatghat.

As a small boy, his father dubbed him "the little grumbler," a nickname to which he also did honor as an adult. A profound feeling of belonging connected Juhaiman with the early Ikhwan. It is possible that he was a relative of Sultan Ibn Bijad Ibn Humaid. In later years he dressed as an Ikhwan and wore the traditional full beard. His orthodox attitude was also reflected, for example, in his protest against the introduction of television and photography into the country, as well as against the presence of foreigners. He considered all innovations to have been sent by the devil.

Modern "machinations" constitute the second factor, and for these Juhaiman blamed the House of Saud. Its newly rich representatives, mainly the majority of the 300 princes, were attracted by the worldly, highly industrialized life of Western consumer society and driven away from the real spirit of Mecca. They called themselves believing Wahhabis, within Saudi limits fulfilled their religious obligations, and indulged in the vices of Beirut and Cairo, London and Paris. As rulers, the House of Saud has had no rivals in leading a double life.

The disgusted Juhaiman always regarded that as the work of the devil. In his bitter attacks against the establishment, he did not even make an exception of the clerical ruling class. He reproached the *ulemas* for letting themselves be bought by the ruling house and even called them, the proclaimers of the new faith, corrupt.

In addition, there was Sheikh Abdul Asis Ibn Bas, the blind, extremely influential theologian who, in 1969, became the rector of the Islamic University of Medina. Abdul Asis Ibn Bas taught that the earth is flat, and through his radical ideas attracted many followers. His ideas attracted Juhaiman's attention; the young Saudi felt magnetized by the unusual clergyman. When the two met for the first time is no longer known. In any case, Juhaiman was a member of the Otaiba tribe, which grazes its camels on the broad expanse between Riad and Taif, and it was probably during the mid-'60s that he came to the Otaiba section of the national guard. Juhaiman was promoted to corporal but was dismissed from the national guard in Quasim. Later it was said that his discharge was dishonorable, but no proof of the allegation is available. Allegedly he studied law at the University of Medina starting in 1972.

Bas, who was also in Medina at this time, gave lectures in the mosque and was thus accessible to the public; in this way the reputedly illiterate Juhaiman was able to hear the revered sheikh. The atmosphere was charged with conflict. Sheikh Hamoud Ibn Saleh el-Uquail, the head clergyman at the mosque in Riad, later offered an explanation: "Through the presence of so many foreign students, there came into being an atmosphere that was advantageous for Islamic heretics." The high clergyman spoke of a group that turned against the prevailing doctrine and sought a way back to the old interpretation of the Koran and *sunna*. In the early '60s this group was on the way toward promoting the resurgence of Islam. The Saudi authorities, once aware of this trend, placed restrictions on the group and expelled the foreign students from the country. But the blow against the fundamentalists was of only short duration. After the death of King Faisal in 1975, the group rebounded.

To some extent was Bas helpful in the group's comeback: he demanded the return to the unadulterated traditions of the faith. But he simultaneously supported the Wahhabis and accepted the royal house (one reason in this was probably his wish to retain his teaching position). Through his amicable policy toward all sides, Ibn Bas lost the support of his most radical students, including Juhaiman, who did not acknowledge his gratitude to him for his two-year period of instruction. Juhaiman wrote that he and his friends had been impressed by Ibn Bas only at the beginning, but that Bas was now in the pay of the Saud family and was little better than their tool for selling the people short. In his words: "Ibn Bas may know his *sunna* well enough, but he now uses it as a support for corrupt rulers."

Juhaiman and his friends, ten students who can surely be called followers, set out for Quasim. Gradually their leader made a name for himself as he preached his radical-orthodox concept of Islam, for discontent among the tribespeople about the lifestyle of the ruling family was increasing. In 1976 the group of radicals surrounding Juhaiman went to Riad, the Saudi capital. Yusuf Bajunaid, a wealthy young man from a family of wholesalers in Jiddah who had joined the group, bought a house for Juhaiman. Later it turned out that it was Bajunaid who wrote the pamphlets, which were then signed by the quite uneducated Juhaiman. Certainly he financed the first of the group's statements, which was published by the Talia Press in Kuwait. Its title was: "The Rules of Loyalty and Obedience: Misguidance by Leaders." It was a fanatic attack against the clergy and the Saud family.

The group drew the conclusion that Muslim leaders who did not adhere literally to the Koran and the *sunna* did not deserve fidelity; on the contrary, they should be mercilessly persecuted. The Saud family was an example of rulers of this kind, as it was corrupt and avaricious and manipulated the laws in its favor. In addition, the Saud family associated with infidels and atheists.

Through this indictment, the state security service became aware of Juhaiman and his followers. The result was that he and ninety-eight other fanatics were put under lock and key in the summer of 1978. There was never a trial. Ibn Bas was summoned from Medina to interrogate the young men, but was unable to detect in their views any betrayal of Islam as practiced in Saudi Arabia. The publishers of the indictment were set free after six weeks, but admonished to cease the obscene attacks and political agitation.

The group surrounding Juhaiman, however, was not impressed by these restrictions and resolved to stage a coup that would completely change the political landscape of Saudi Arabia. In internal discussions there was talk of overthrowing the royal houses and all forces loyal to the state, even of an Islamic revolution. The political and religious climate became increasingly conservative during the course of 1979. Women were no longer permitted to travel alone or to work with men. The minister of the interior announced a binding dress code, and the hatred of foreigners became frightening. Experienced observers of the Saudi scene suspected that Juhaiman's religious organization would flourish brilliantly in this environment. Moreover, the organization had such influential mentors as the powerful Sheikh Saleh Ibn Lehedan. Nor could the effect of Khomeini's return to Tehran be overlooked. Fundamentalists in the entire Arab world saw a gleam of hope.

Juhaiman's power among the discontented grew. The closer the end of the Islamic century, the more intensively did Juhaiman's preparations progress for the planned seizure of power in the country. A Mahdi was to be proclaimed, a redeemer of the kind that can always be expected at the beginning of a new century. Juhaiman did not, however, claim this function for himself, but for his friend and prisonmate Mohammed Ibn Abdullah al-Qahtani. Qahtani was a former student of Islamic law at the University of Riad. Juhaiman later stated at the hearing: "I saw him, Qahtani, in a dream in mid-1979. Allah spoke to me and said I should proclaim Qahtani to be the future Mahdi who was come to free the world of all evil."

That prospect evidently pleased Qahtani, who drew steadily closer to his mentor and also married his sister. Then Qahtani himself started to dream. "Indeed," he confirmed, "Allah summoned me to be the well-guided one." The group tightened. Several of its members had studied theology; many were from the tribe of Otaiba—for example, Affas Ibn Muhaya, leader of the band of snipers and son of Ogab Ibn Muhaya, an Otaiba ringleader who was killed during the Ikhwan uprising. Quite a number were from other Arab countries such as Egypt, Kuwait, Yemen, and Pakistan. The Egyptians belonged to the Takfir wal Hejra, which at that time was being severely persecuted in their homeland. For them Saudi Arabia represented a new field of action.

Together, they drew up the plan for occupying the largest shrine of the Islamic world; the intent was to trigger a chain reaction in the entire country and subsequently proclaim their own Islamic state. The plan was to be carried out in Mecca during the New Year's celebration. The focus of Mecca is the Grand Mosque (Masjid Al-Haram) and the surrounding pilgrimage sites. In the middle of the Grand Mosque is the Kaaba, the main shrine of Islam: a large square building covered with black brocade. During the time of pilgrimage, as many as two million strangers are in the holy city.

That many were present in Mecca in November 1979. The largest contingent ever, at least in living memory, came from Iran. The Saudi authorities observed the revolutionary zeal of this group, for in the preceding months nothing but aggressive sounds had been heard from Tehran. Ayatollah Khomeini had announced the export of the Islamic revolution, and had also concretely demanded the oil sheikhdom of Bahrain as a rounding-off of Iranian national territory. According to an official statement by the Iranian leader, Bahrain exerted pressure on its Shiite citizens. Something had to happen. Only two years later things had come to such a pass.

While the Saudi security force directed its entire attention to the Iranian visitors, the Ikhwan, without being detected, were able to occupy the Grand Mosque. The preparations for the attack had begun weeks before. Some 300 supporters smuggled the weapons into the house of worship in seven carloads of dates and water, in coffins, and under long white garments. The use of coffins escaped attention, because in Mecca many deceased are brought to the mosque once more before burial so prayers can be said for them. After Qahtani and Juhaiman had announced the seizure of the mosque, they demanded that the worshippers present in the mosque join them, which triggered a discussion about the justification of the self-appointed Mahdi. Not only words were exchanged, however: fighting broke out within the mosque when the guards of the holy shrine opposed the invaders.

The outrage about the desecration of the Grand Mosque was enormous. From 50,000 throats came a scream of despair and fury. Sheikh Mohammed Ibn Subayyal, the imam, took off the robe that made him recognizable to everyone and ran to a public telephone to call for help. King Khalid was awakened in his palace in Riad with the bad news before 7:00 A.M. For him it was a shock, since one of the king's most pressing tasks is to protect the holiest of all shrines from any hostile act. Later it became known that on this day King Khalid had been deterred only by ill health from participating in the New Year's prayers. The attackers had evidently counted on his presence.

The first information from the mosque, which meanwhile had been sealed off, intimated a widespread conspiracy. It seemed as if the rebels expected other uprisings and perhaps even foreign assistance. The possibility of Khomeini's influence was logically perceived from the outset. King Khalid then ordered that all telephone and telex connections with the outside world be cut off. Not even Crown Prince Fahd, who was in Tunis for a meeting of the Arab League, was able to find out about the situation in his country.

The paucity of news from Saudi Arabia caused great excitement in the West. In the beginning, Western ambassadors reported that a military coup was involved. In Tunis, Fahd spoke of an "internal matter" and calmly continued the meeting, creating the impression that the government had the situation firmly under control. The Grand Sheikh at Azhar University in Cairo, Abdel Rahman Bissar, appealed to the entire Islamic world to defend the shrines in Mecca against the "sinful aggression" of the heavily armed apostates.

In Tehran, Ayatollah Khomeini resorted to the radio microphone and in his way defined the guilty ones, stating that it was not far-fetched to assume that "this act was carried out by criminal U.S. imperialism and international Zionism." Afterwards the largest anti-American demonstration since the overthrow of the Shah took place in Tehran. Already, at this point in time, in the hands of the revolutionary guards, the U.S. embassy in Islamabad was attacked and burned down by the roused masses. An attack on the U.S. embassy in Tripoli was also a direct consequence of the seizure of the mosque.

While the Saudi army and the national guard surrounded the mosque complex, there were wild conjectures about the identity of the people who had occupied it and taken hostages. In Beirut it was known that the main participants were Shiites.

The Egyptian and Kuwaiti news agencies attributed the incident to Charidshites (the name means "newcomers" or "outsiders"), one of the oldest religious-political sects of Islam. They murdered the son-in-law and cousin of the Prophet Mohammed, Ali Ibn Abu Talib. In the Koran these early fundamentalists are called the "truly pious ones who have left their homeland for the purpose of dedicating themselves solely to the service of Allah." Their most important goal was to combat any secular weakening of the true teaching and of the Islamic society; to this end, any infraction of Islamic rules was, without exception, punished by death.

The suspicion of journalists was in principle correct, for although those that occupied the mosque were not Charidshites, they were their descendants in the modern era.

The fundamentalists had barricaded themselves in, and from the minarets and merlons of the mosque shot at anything that moved in the neighboring streets. Their aim was excellent. The occupiers of the mosque swiftly realized that they were up against a strong opponent. The Saudi security forces learned from pilgrims who had just escaped the mosque that it was occupied by 500 at the most. Their weapons consisted of Soviet AK-47 automatic rifles, pistols, and 22-caliber weapons.

Later it became known that most of their weapons and ammunition came from arsenals of the army and national guard. Many also came from the black market. Juhaiman and his people had acquired weapons on the Bedouin market that were intended for use in the Lebanese civil war. The flourishing trade in arms smuggling in Saudi Arabia could not be halted because of the impossibly long border. Minister of the Interior Prince Naif Ibn Abdul-Aziz later admitted that during the year 1979 alone approximately 2,700 weapons, 481 machine guns, and 7,358 pistols had been seized. The true quantity of smuggled weapons can of course not be known.

By the second day of the occupation of the mosque there were 1,000 corpses in the enormous interior court of the Haram. Some had been shot, but most had been trampled to death by the panicked crowd. The rebels meanwhile consolidated their bastion, using cement that they had brought along for this purpose. They persuaded 6,000 pilgrims to seek cover in part of the more-than-one-thousand-year-old vaulted cellar, consisting of 270 rooms for which there are no cartographic records. With one blow they thereby gained 6,000 hostages who could be liberated only at great sacrifice.

In Riad a bomb hit the king's palace and exploded. Soon afterwards the mosque in Taif was attacked in a manner similar to that in Mecca, and in Tobruk gun-fighting broke out between Islamic fundamentalists and the army. Saudi Arabia's princes recalled the fate of their friend, the Shah of Iran, and became anxious.

On the first day alone, fifty government soliders were killed when, shouting "Allah is greater!", they tried to storm the Haram. An airlift between Saudi military airports and Mecca was already in full sway. Heavy Hercules C-130 planes transported soldiers, police, and national guard troops with large quantities of arms. Six hundred members of the elite security forces arrived in the afternoon.

On the second day of the occupation, the first storming of all entrances to the mosque started punctually at 11:30 A.M. The result was a large bloodbath. With their long-range weapons, the rebels holed up in the natural fortress hit everything that moved in front of the strong walls of the Haram. When the fighting subsided, the ochre-colored courtyard of the mosque was covered with corpses. The penetrating, unmistakable stench of death enveloped the shrine.

The king was both angry and concerned. He commanded a new attack against the apostates. The order was carried out the following day at 10:00 A.M. Assisted by twelve M-113 tanks and five helicopters, 3,000 soldiers attacked. The second grenade hit one of the tanks, causing it to catch fire and burn. Two other targeted vehicles exploded. Eyewitnesses reported that the personnel manning the vehicles were on fire as they leaped from the tanks and collapsed in the interior courtyard of the mosque. One of the five helicopters was also hit by a salvo and crashed. A spire of one of the minarets exploded. Black clouds of smoke hung over the holy mosque, and the stench of corpses became unbearable.

The Saudis were in a tricky situation. The Koran states that the holiest of all shrines can be desecrated even by having an animal killed in the mosque. It is forbidden to pick flowers on the premises. Moreover, all this was happening in the first month of the Muslim year, Muharram, when traditionally killing is forbidden. What, then, was the attitude of the fighting soldiers to be?

The military commanders could free themselves from this dilemma by receiving permission to act from the highest religious decision-making body, so on the first day of the occupation King Khalid summoned the *ulema*. He explained the situation to them and said that, as they themselves knew, it was almost impossible to issue the command to storm the mosque. What should be done in this emergency? The result of this meeting was a *fatwa* based on the Koran verse 2:192—"Do not fight them within the precincts of the holy shrines [of Mecca] unless they [the infidels] attack you there; if they fight you [there], put them to the sword. Thus shall the unbelievers be rewarded."

The approval for the attack was immediately conveyed to

Prince Sultan, the minister of defense, who had set up his head-quarters in the Hotel Subra in the vicinity of the mosque. But the command stated that it was necessary to proceed with care and that the building should be spared to the greatest extent possible. A small, two-week war against the group occupying the mosque began.

For a long time Juhaiman, Qahtani, and their followers were in the more advantageous position. They had entrenched them-selves with their hostages deep within the mosque and were protected by its thick walls. The Mahdi repeatedly drubbed into his followers and the captured pilgrims the idea that there must be an end to the weakening of the Islamic nation of Saudi Arabia. So-called modernization was changing the religious character of the population and destroying the traditional values. The pro-gram the West preached widened the gap between man and God; it was the work of the *shaitan,* the devil. The Mahdi demanded the elimination of television and music broadcasts on the radio, the banning of all women from public workplaces, the disbanding of all football teams, and the expulsion of all non-believing for-eigners. In the Mahdi's view, only by a rehabilitation in this world could one become ready for paradise. In saying that, the self-appointed Mahdi drew on Khomeini's words: "Paradise is not of this world."

The Saudi royal house once again looked over its shoulder and made contact with France. King Khalid despairingly described the situation to President Valery Giscard d'Estaing. The conflict could not be solved with conventional means, and the royal house needed the help of highly qualified anti-terrorist special-ists. Giscard d'Estaing promised support.

The attack arm of the French gendarmerie, called the Group d'Intervention de la Gendarmerie Nationale (GIGN) was en-trusted with the delicate task. On November 23, Captain Barril and two noncommissioned officers flew to Saudi Arabia in the special Mystère 20 belonging to the French air force.

The French were briefed in detail. One obstacle proved to be the ban against any non-Muslim entering the city of Mecca, but for this, too, an exception was finally made for Captain Barril. The emergency situation left no other choice. After detailed dis-cussions, Barril proposed the following tactic against the forces occupying the mosque: "For me, the most important thing is that most of the rebels are in the vaulted cellar, so at the moment they

The leader of the Lebanese Shiites, Musa Sadr, vanished in Libya.

Rabab Sadr Charafeddine, the sister of Imam Musa Sadr, in Beirut.

PLO leader Arafat with the author.
(Photo © Hans-Peter Kruse, Munich)

Libya's head of state Colonel Muammar al-Qaddafi is considered
the most dangerous and unpredictable representative of the
militant resurgence of Islam. *(Photo © Hans-Peter Kruse, Munich)*

Ahmed Ben Bella, former president of Algeria (second from right), at an Islamic symposium in Paris.

The followers of the oppositionist Sadeq al-Mahdi are recruited from Ansar sects in all parts of Africa.

Presidential adviser Hassan al-Turabi leads the Sudanese Muslim Brotherhood.

Dr. Tigani Abu Guideiri introduced the new growth of Islam in Africa.

A historic flight: Khomeini returning to Tehran from exile on
February 1, 1979.

Golbuddin Hekmatyar, the leader of the strongest Afghan underground organization, Hizb-e Islami.

President Zia ul-Haq, Pakistan's Islamic military dictator.

are in fact protected there. But it is also the only place where they can best be reached by nerve gas."

By November 25, tension in the royal kingdom had increased. In several places, friends of Juhaiman called for rebellion against the House of Saud. Meanwhile the Grand Mosque was encircled by 600 men from the national guard, 2,500 members of the army, and 125 parachutists.

As disclosed in a French report released two years later, Barril met with the Saudi commanders and obtained approval for his plan. In contrast to the Saudis, he even had maps of the fourteen-hundred-year-old vaults. Barril explained: "The cellars are laid out as large halls that are connected with one another by small passageways. At issue here is doubtlessly the oldest part, where there are a series of small spaces. The rebels have occupied the entire vaulted cellar, which must be approximately 72,000 square feet. But they have also occupied the minarets and the only ground-level story of the structure, so they must be forced to retreat into the cellar."

Barril ordered from Paris three tons of CB gas, thirty sprayers, 110 pounds of plastic explosive, fuses, and 200 special gas masks. Meanwhile the mosque complex was without electricity, but that did not affect the resistance of the besiegers. They continued to fire on anything in the immediate vicinity that moved. One victim was the chauffeur of Mecca's Gouverneur Fawwaz: hardly had his boss arrived at the front for the purposes of offering help than the chauffeur was hit by a bullet in the head.

An additional complicating factor was that the various Saudi troops had never before worked together, making for a problem in coordination. For example, the proud Bedouins from the tribes of Otaiba and Qahtan did not want to serve under the supreme command of the officers just arrived from the capital. In addition, a planned helicopter attack on the interior of the mosque had to be abandoned, since only at night would its surprise effect have made sense. And besides, the Saudi air force lacked experience in this maneuver.

Then their luck slowly changed. After suffering severe losses in isolated skirmishes, the government troops were able to take shelter in the upper passageways and drive the rebels from two towers. The Ikhwans, shielded behind mattresses and prayer mats, were slowly driven into the main building. Another three days were needed to reconquer the ground-level part of the mosque. Soldiers wearing bulletproof vests moved forward in clouds of tear gas, but it was impossible to gain control of the main building of the mosque. A more broad-scale operation would have posed too great a danger of losing the lives of all the hostages.

Once the Ikhwan had been routed from the interior courtyard, it was hastily cleaned up so a quick prayer ceremony could be shown on television. This measure evidently failed, however, to convince all of King Khalid's subjects; in the eastern part of the country the first Shiite villages were already in flames. The government troops had to put down the uprising: 60 dead and 300 wounded. In any case, on this day the Shiites were restless, for it was the tenth day of the month of Muharram, on which traditionally memorial ceremonies, climaxing in self-flagellation, occur. The fact that this year, for the first time in fifty years, there were violent attacks on banks, stores, and police stations, had to do, not least of all, with the newly awakened self-confidence of the Shiites and the inspiration provided by the Ayatollah Khomeini.

On December 1, at 8:41 P.M., the Caravelle carrying the chemical warfare materials and the protective masks arrived from France. The following day members of the special command squads instructed sixty selected Saudi soldiers and thirty officers in their use. On December 4, at 7:00 A.M., everything was set. Coundown for the last round in the liberation began. The signal for attack came at 10:00 A.M., with the call, "In the name of Allah, forward!" Firing heavily, the opponents answered with the slogan, "*Amr Allah*" ("Under God's command"). Whenever one of them was killed, his face was burned with pages from the Koran so he could not be identified later. This task fell to the women and children of the group occupying the mosque.

At around 10:30 A.M., the elite troops forced open the first of the twenty-two entrances to the subterranean vaults, a heavy nail-studded wooden door covered with paintings that were centuries old. In groups of threes they slowly groped through the dark passages and cellar. One door after the other was wrecked with plastic explosive. Noise, explosions, shots occurred repeatedly, although the strong, thick walls muted every sound. Only when the Ikhwan had been driven into a corner did the vigorous resistance cease. They had set up nests of machine guns at the entrances to the cellar, and from there they fired wildly in the direction of the attackers. But the attackers held back and used the containers of gas. By 11:30 they had released one and a half tons of gas through open doors and five cellar windows.

The the Ikhwan's resistance ceased. Fifty members of the group who had occupied the mosque were captured, but most were dead—suffocated or killed by explosives. Most of the hostages were among the masses of the dead in the mosque's cellars. There were thousands of dead. At 4:00 P.M. there was absolute quiet. The special units had sprayed two tons of gas. Approximately forty-five soldiers were dead, and on the ground surrounding the mosque there lay approximately a hundred soldiers. Thick clouds of poisonous gas ascended from the holy mosque.

Later the number of the dead Ikhwan was announced by the Saudi government to be 117. Among them was also the Mahdi, whose corpse was made available for photographing as proof that he was not a divine leader.

Breathing heavily and with tearing eyes, Juhaiman and his last followers staggered into the daylight, where they were immediately placed in chains. But that did not stop them from continuing to thrash about wildly and to appeal to Allah for protection against the faithless Saudis. The Saudi television cameras captured the scene. Juhaiman raged and cast crazed glances at the cameras. Dirty and with his long beard in a matted condition, he gave the impression of a wild animal.

There was still a ban on news about events around the mosque. When pressed by reporters for a commentary, Prince Salman Abdul-Aziz merely stated, *"El-hamdu-lillah, el-hamdu-lillah"* ("God be praised"). And there was nothing more. Only gradually did some of the background details become known. In a typically Saudi manner, Minister of Information Mohammed Abdul Jamami once explained that with Allah's help the situation had been taken care of and that the security forces had proceeded "with circumspection, wisdom, and caution." Minister of the Interior Prince Naif denied that a foreign government had had a hand in the matter. After his statement, Saudi television showed pictures of approximately 100 prisoners for fifteen minutes. They were sitting in the hallway of a prison, looking into the lens apathetically or anxiously. In keeping with the official dictates, they were called "mutinous gangsters" and terrorists.

King Khalid was the first to pray in the Grand Mosque. Only two days after the fighting had ceased, the usual numbers of pilgrims and Saudis streamed through the portals of the shrine.

Congratulatory telegrams arrived at the king's palace from all the Islamic countries, as well as from some Western nations. They were published in their entirety, and then the curtain fell on the event.

Nonetheless, there was still no peace in the House of Saud. The most severe threat to date to the ruling dynasty continued in the form of riots on the eastern coast. The Shiites, traditionally disadvantaged in Saudi Arabia, demanded more rights, including a more just distribution of the oil wealth—an obvious wish, since as many as forty percent of the Aramco workers in the Saudi oil fields were members of the discontented Shiite minority.

But two other groups came forward with an aggressive intonation against the "tyranny" of Riad: the so-called Saudi Arabian Liberation Front, with headquarters in Tehran, and the Organization of the Unity of the People of the Arab Peninsula, with headquarters in Beirut. The spokesman of the Saudis in exile in Beirut, Nasir as-Said, was abducted soon thereafter. The Saudi Baathists in Iraq consider it a certainty that this abduction was the work of the Saudi secret service.

The state security service also took drastic measures in the country of holy sites. In contradiction to assertions made in the first account, according to which the weapons used by the group occupying the mosque came from South Yemen and not from the black market or from Saudi military groups, the Saudi armed forces were thoroughly purged. Six high officers, including the commander of the army and police, lost their posts. Just how far the purge of lower-ranking officers went is difficult to ascertain.

After the conclusion of an extensive investigation, sixty-three male members of the group that occupied the mosque were taken to eight Saudi Arabian cities on January 8, 1980. "Kill those whose names are contained in this announcement," King Khalid had demanded in a letter to the Ministry of the Interior, "in order to be pleasing to Allah, to defend the holy consecration of the Kaaba and its worshippers, and to free the Muslims of their anxiety." On the morning of January 9, the sixty-three rebels were taken to the main squares of the cities and publicly beheaded—fifteen in Mecca, ten in Riad, seven each in Medina, Haman, Bereide, and Abha, as well as five each in Hail and Tabuk. According to information provided by the official Saudi press agency, of the sixty-three executed, forty-one were from Saudi Arabia, ten from Egypt, six from South Yemen, three from Kuwait, and one each from North Yemen, the Sudan, and Iraq. A great number of the mosque-occupiers who had served as lookouts and had acquired weapons were sentenced to prison. Women who had assisted by providing food and water were given two-year prison sentences, during which time they should receive religious training. Several young people were put into reform schools. Thirty-eight people were allegedly let go.

The Ministry of Religion ordered all mosques to condemn the rebels in their prayers on the Friday following the execution date. In fact, the Ministry of Religion was ever more extravagant in its comparisons for the purpose of concealing the true character of the Islamic revolt against the self-appointed guardians of Islam. One of the official theses was that Juhaiman and his people could best be compared with the Jim Jones cult and the mass suicide in Guyana—in other words, at issue was an incident that could have happened anywhere.

On January 17, 1980, thousands of roused Shiites again participated in demonstrations in Quatif, the capital of the eastern region. Saudi troops surrounded the city and put down all signs of opposition. A deceptive quiet set in that endures to the present.

18

A House Built on Sand

INSHA ALLAH (if God wills it), anyone who has overcome the sight of absolutely endless yellow desolation below while flying aboard a Saudi plane to Jiddah or Riad will soon be on firm ground again, according to the voice over the loudspeaker. Once landed and inside the futuristic glass and concrete structures of the super-rich, one is greeted by a new formula, *"Bismillah ar-Rahman ar-Rahin"* ("In the name of Allah, the Compassionate; the Merciful"). That is the beginning, middle, and end of everything in Saudi Arabia, a country that, for the foreigner, is inaccessible and difficult to comprehend. Everything is in the name of Allah —the Koran starts with it; so do newspapers and menus. The phrase is on the entrance to houses, and it is used in presenting test pictures on television. There is nothing that is not associated with the name of Allah. Prince Muhammad Ibn Faisal, one of 3,000 of his regal sort, says: "Here Islam penetrates everything in a manner and way that is hardly comprehensible to someone who has grown up in the West." That may be true, since there is nothing similar to it in the rest of the world.

Here Allah's flag is displayed in the same green allegedly used in the Prophet's coat. Printed in white letters on the flag is: "There is no God but Allah, and Mohammed is His prophet." "*Hamdullilah*," roughly translated as "thanks be to God," is what the taxidrivers say when they have found the right address. The answer to a question starts with "it is written," and "everything is His doing" serves as the universal comment for any situation. Mysterious, unfathomable Saudi Arabia, living according to its own norms and laws, and yet far removed from the completeness of the pure theocracy. Ibn Saud's country is now the leading nation of the Arab world, simultaneously the financier and angel of peace, mysteriously shut off and yet reveling in the luxury of the West. The Saudis live in the Middle Ages, and yet pay tribute to the modern era whenever it is useful.

But religion is never omitted from consideration. If it were a matter of frequency of religious ceremonies or number of prayers, paradise should belong exclusively to the Saudis, much as they now rent Western luxury hotels and purchase the most beautiful residential sections of London. For "Allah promised the faithful, both men and women, gardens laced by brooks and fine dwellings in the garden of Eden where they should remain eternally." Anyone familiar with the miserable landscape of Saudi Arabia knows why the Prophet Mohammed could at any time rouse his followers to good conduct and faith with such descriptions. Even today the absolute majority is on this path toward salvation, but many subjects of the pragmatic boss, King Fahd, require coercion by the police force of religion—in other words, by the *ulema*, who cooperate closely with the state and constitute its most important instrument. They see to it that people heed the calls to prayer by the *muezzin*, which occur five times daily, that all businesses are close for a half-hour during these intervals, and that traffic comes to a standstill. Utterly in contrast to Islamic doctrine, these guardians of morality, clad in their white *galabias*, spy on the private lives of the subjects and control the eagerness of the faithful. Anyone who leaves a bad impression is immediately prescribed graduated religious instruction in a group, and sometimes a sound thrashing too. Islam is Saudi Arabia's conception of the state, and the precise fulfillment of all its precepts is the citizen's first duty.

The entire country is still living in the puritanical spiritual realm of Ibn Abdul Wahhab. Newspapers provide updates on stock exchange rates, several sports reports, a glance at that part of the

Islamic world friendly to Saudi Arabia, and many endlessly long articles about the life and words of the Prophet. Preachers are given priority on the state-run television programs, and in second place are various religious broadcasts. The middle classes, numbering approximately 750,000, feel the pressure of these measures, but to a large extent they circumvent the system by a kind of double life. "A person cannot pray all day long," they say, inserting into a video recorder a film showing belly-dancing or brute sex, which was smuggled into the country with great difficulty. (All films for sale in the country are cleaned up by the Committee for the Promotion of Virtue and Prevention of Sin, often cutting down viewing time from ninety to twenty minutes.) Behind the high walls of their villas, the Saudis celebrate, drinking whiskey and wearing paper-thin, skimpy bikinis, all of which officially are deadly sins. The chaste world that is forced on them fosters the Saudis' unimpeded zest for life. As soon as they set foot on free ground, whether it is a nightclub in Damascus featuring beauties from Thailand or the belly-dance show by Azzia Sherif in the Cairo Hilton Belvedere Club, everything everywhere is more dissolute than in their homeland. It is no coincidence that it is precisely the privileged princes who have the reputation of being lady-killers; the sophisticated King Fahd is also reputed to have studied this world and its goodies very carefully during his years of storm and stress in France.

Discipline and order prevail in the hermetic kingdom, achieved by an extremely high living standard and by high social expenditures for all. Before 1960 there was no school for girls in the wealthy country of Saudi Arabia. King Faisal Ibn Abdul Aziz Ibn Saud was the first ruler to dare to break this taboo. (A supporter of the Palestinian leader Yasser Arafat, King Faisal was shot in 1975 by an allegedly mentally deranged nephew, Faisal Ibn Musaed Ibn Abdul Aziz.) The first female pupils had to be fetched from their homes and brought to school by the police. In compliance with the warning in the Koran, in order to avoid awakening lust in a male stranger, even today no woman is permitted to go unveiled into the street. The only exception usually made is for foreign women. Women are strictly forbidden to sit behind the wheel of an automobile or to travel alone in the country. Although they may now become teachers, doctors, nurses, or social workers, working in offices is still not one of their options. Seventy-five percent of the population of the country is still illiterate, but ninety percent of the children now attend school. There is no coeducation. Because of a lack of female university professors, female university students are provided instruction by male teachers via television. Although women have already been successful in their struggle to gain admission to institutions of higher learning and now comprise one-third of the student body, they are rarely permitted to go unveiled in Saudi Arabia.

Saudi Arabia has a population of slightly over seven million, many of whom are nomads whose everyday life and view of the world has not changed since the days of the Prophet. The Saudis have a shortage of workers and are therefore desperately dependent on foreign labor. Without guest workers, nothing would function anymore in the enormous desert country. The well-known German publicist Hans Ulrich Kempski offered his observations on the labor market after a trip to Allah's own country:

Every second resident of the capital is a foreigner. Everything, but everything, involving physical labor is done by guest workers. Consequently there are enough jobs for approximately one-and-a-half million Yemenites, 100,000 workers from South Asian countries, and another 100,000 from the Near East. There are approximately 100,000 from America and Europe, of whom approximately 12,000 come from Germany. Most of the Germans are construction experts, while America supplies doctors, pilots, construction workers, and advisors. Egyptians, Jordanians, and Palestinians serve mainly as teachers. India provides mostly secretaries, bank employees, salesmen. The Pakistanis are predominant as waiters, servants, messengers, and elevator operators. Upper- and middle-level management positions in businesses and hotels are mostly held by Lebanese. And the army of those who really have to labor is recruited mainly from Thailand, the Philippines, and South Korea. Because of their discipline, the Koreans provide the elite among the craftsmen.

From this view, one should not be astonished by Lord Kimberley's complaint, made years ago, to the effect that Arabia's inhabitants "do not let themselves be drawn into work."

Many of the workers are in the monopoly that produces black gold, for the Saudis are sitting on the largest supply of fluid energy under the earth. A single well produces 4,400 barrels, or approximately 2.24 million gallons, per day. The average daily production level of 10 million barrels only involves the use of fifteen of the fifty-one Saudi oil fields. In itself, the twenty-four-mile Ghawar field contains more oil than all drilling sites on the

North American continent. With this treasure entrusted to the people by Allah, the inhabitants of the miserable peninsula are steadily becoming more and more wealthy. The price of oil is eighteen times higher than before the oil crisis. In 1981 the Saudis earned approximately $130 billion, which amounts to somewhat more than $350 million per day—an inconceivable amount, which surely can no longer be grasped by the recipients and which of course promotes corruption and extensive cronyism among the elite.

The better things fare with the Saudis, the more they feel themselves menaced. Surrounded by resentful neighbors, by such discontented Muslims as the 400,000-strong Shiite (who are even more orthodox than the Saudis themselves); subjected to pressure (the occupation of the mosque was a warning from Allah); and made insecure by communism; they take flight in financing all and everything. No less than 126 Islamic organizations receive financial donations from the guardian of holy sites. To a significant extent, the aggressive PLO was sponsored by Riad for the purpose of keeping both it and the leftist South Yemenites at a distance. The Saudis no longer even keep a record of what all their checks are supporting. The Soviet's Syrian friend Assad, who leveled the mosques of Hamah, is kept afloat by them, and recently support has been resumed for Egypt, which under Sadat was unpopular with the Saudis. The bankrupt Sudan is spared its bill for oil, and the Islamic state of Pakistan also receives assistance. The only ones disliked by King Fahd and his advisory council are the Israelis and the competing Qaddafi. The Zionists are repugnant to the Saudis, because they are considered the occupiers of holy Islamic ground and because they do not want to let go of the shrines.

The relationship with Qaddafi could never fare well, since this competitor in the area of oil production and propagation of Islam in Africa once toppled a monarchy—the monarchy of Idris. Moreover, Qaddafi has criticized the strong American influence in Saudi Arabia. He characterizes the Saudis as impious and calls for divesting them of their role as protectors of the holy sites, and preferably of all their power. King Khalid was so outraged by the suggestion that he once called the young revolutionary an "incarnation of the devil." And coming from the restrained, almost shy Saudi, that was a malicious retort.

Militarily the Saudis feared Iran, its aggressive neighbor on the Gulf. Finally, in the summer of 1982, the royal house appealed for holy war against Imam Khomeini and his fanatic supporters. King Khalid and his associates considered it the peak of hypocrisy when Ariel Sharon, Israel's impulsive minister of defense, admitted having supplied Iran with weapons for use in the war on the Gulf. A Saudi commentator formulated their extreme displeasure: "All the veils covering the faces and beards of the *ayatollahs* from Tehran have fallen since its alliance with Israel." Muslims everywhere now had the duty of rising up against this people who were more dangerous for Islam than the enemies of the faith.

Khomeini immediately fired back with a broadside, warning the conservative states on the other side of the Gulf against incurring his enmity. "If you do not return today to the lap of Islam, it will be too late to do so tomorrow," is the message he had his son Ahmed read at the Friday prayer service at Tehran University. Khomeini—the destabilizing factor who otherwise perceived "the cause for the suffering and problems of the Muslims as well as governments of Islamic countries in the inconsistencies and conflicts of these countries among one another"—was once again completely in his element. In addition, he proved how flexible Islam is, once the issue concerns political justification.

The greater the unrest in the Islamic world and the more the patriarchal domination of the Saud family is attacked by forbidden opposition within the country—of which the Sunni fundamentalists are an example—the more clearly it is shown that the Saudi royal house is built only on sand. An increasing number of Saudis are socially uprooted by the severe collision between a medieval, archaic society and modern industrial development. The comparison with Iran under the Shah has often been made, and during the riots in 1979 against the royal house the princes even asked themselves whether the Americans would give sanctuary to 5,000 shahs—by which they meant themselves. The Western-oriented desert kingdom is now highly armed, and it has purchased weapons suitable for use within its own borders. The country's troops number 76,500, including the national guard. Present here as in other sectors, guest workers drill the soldiers and to some extent serve in the armed forces. The troops are in effect the fire brigade, prepared for all eventualities, although there is still the possibility of a coup coming from their ranks. Or as Vice-Minister for Planning Faisal Beshir expresses it in local parlance: "The Prophet taught us not to let our camel stand freely in the desert, simply trusting in Allah, but first to hitch the camel and then to trust Allah."

19

The Revenge of the Old Man: Mullahcracy in Iran

THE ROCKY FOOTHILLS of the Elbur Mountains—a craggy, brown massif that starts on the outskirts of the city of Tehran, with its population of four million—come closer and closer. Leading to this northern part of the Iranian metropolis is one of the newly designated streets, named after the Pasdaran, a particularly fanatic paramilitary troop whose members are faithful "guardians of the revolution." Immediately after passing Shah Reza Pahlevi's formerly magnificent winter palace, called Niavaran, the road veers off to the left. We are in Jamaran, an elegant suburb still inhabited by many representatives of the wealthy aristocracy, those who did not succeed in escaping to the West or were not imprisoned by the *mullahs*. Foreign heads of corporations and diplomats have taken over some of the villas, but some of the residents lived in this pleasant setting even before the revolution.

We now turn off to the right into Yaser Street. High walls to the left and right keep out all uninvited guests, and television cameras guard the peace of the privileged residents. A few hundred feet farther down the road is where Iran's security zone number one begins. We have reached the outer border of an extremely intricate tangle of streets and roads, in the middle of which lives an elderly man, born in 1900, who changed the world. Imam Haj Sayid Aga Ruhollah Mussavi al-Khomeini is referred to by the newspapers loyal to the government as the "leader of the revolution and founder of the Islamic Republic of Iran."

All traffic in Pasdaran is stopped at the first checkpoint by battle-clad sentries in a shelter complete with firing slits. Only residents, guests of the "government section," and official vehicles are permitted to pass, and then only after showing official documents and opening the trunk, hood, glove compartment, and all containers inside the car. All vehicles are throughly searched by these sentries equipped with short-range automatic pistols. Every empty space is carefully inspected.

After checking with headquarters by telephone, permission is given to proceed along the Pasdaran. The street leads up toward the mountain. A few hundred feet farther, we turn slightly to the right, pass another post of guards of the revolution, and after approximately 1,500 feet reach a high iron-barred gate guarded by numerous armed sentries. The gate is on wheels and can be easily moved. But not everyone is permitted to travel this last stretch of approximately 450 feet in a vehicle. We are stopped and told to wait along the side of the road. Behind us an Alfa Romeo with two *mullahs* in the back is allowed to pass, escorted by two motorcycles, each with a passenger. The drivers of these heavy cycles are wearing leather, which is not customary in this country, and their passengers carry machine pistols. They pass through the gate to the street.

We arrive at a small square bordered by buildings with high walls. It is teeming with civilian secret service people, bodyguards in jeans (with large-caliber revolvers stuck into their waistbands), and guards of the revolution wearing green army parkas. Among them are a few visitors looking for the route through this labyrinth to the center of the Iranian power. The correct route is pointed out to them by one of the sentries at the hut, which bears one of the imam's slogans: "We must be victorious in war, because the nation is on our side."

The guards at this checkpoint are still more exacting. They immediately want to place all our possessions in storage, something we are able to prevent in this instance. The route left leads straight into the camp of the Pasdaran. By passing straight through a broad iron gate and continuing beside a high exterior wall, we come 600 feet closer to our goal. To the right of the road are newly constructed houses, in which the most faithful of the faithful are permitted to reside. Through the trees and bushes one can occasionally glimpse Tehran down in the valley.

Immediately thereafter is another Pasdaran checkpoint. The guards of the revolution have protected the nearby house of the imam with a green gate. This hurdle we overcome only with the help of the quickly summoned secretary to Khomeini, Hojjat al-Islam Tavasuli, a tall theologian with a full gray beard and alert eyes. *Hojjat al-Islam* (meaning "authority on Islam") is a high Shiite title, just below the rank of *ayatollah* ("symbol of God" or "mirror of God"). Anyone who has received Tavasuli's theological approval is permitted to freely interpret the Koran, its precepts concerning the faith, and the sources for the law. He automatically becomes a "renewer of the religion" (*mujtahid*), and in the eyes of the devout Shiites acquires an unearthly power.

At the behest of Khomeini's son-in-law, Vice-Minister of Religion Mahmud Burodjerdi, a man is summoned to accompany me. The high clergyman now directs my companion and me into the innermost circle of the far-flung security zone surrounding Imam Khomeini. While I am still studying an inscription on the left wall praising Islam and the Iranian system as the rescuers of the oppressed of this earth, I am requested to enter an open space. There I am subjected to a thorough search of my person. They spread out all my possessions—sunglasses and comb, purse, ballpoint pen, tape recorder, and camera—on a small table and then stuff them into a plastic bag, which is then closed with a rubber band, labeled, and placed on a shelf.

Under the mistrustful glances of the Pasdaran troops as they toy with the triggers of their machine pistols, we walk up the last 150 feet of the hill. To the right, in a dead-end street, stands the brand new car of a doctor making an emergency call. The car's plates indicate it is from Fuerth in Bavaria. To the left is the portal of Khomeini's own Hussein-i Jamaran Mosque, which has become famous in all of Iran. Inside the mosque it is cool and quiet, more quiet even than its almost completely silent surroundings. The space is covered with thick carpets. In a gallery resembling a catwalk are three permanently installed television cameras, placed on top of high pedestals and covered in plastic. Also in the gallery are an easy chair with a gray-blue cover and a microphone; it is from this second-story vantage point that the imam receives and speaks to groups. The door behind the gallery leads directly to his house. From this setting Khomeini's speeches are broadcast to Iranian living rooms fourteen times daily.

The wood-paneled ceiling forms a striking contrast to the mosque's walls, which have not been plastered for years. On the wall opposite the entrance is the only decoration, a painting showing fists dripping with blood, which protrude from the ground, and above a dove in the twilight, radiated by a yellow sun. In Persian (Farsi) is written: "Each day is Ashura, each place is Kerbela," a kind of personal motto of the vengeful owner of the house. In the sixty-first Muslim year on the day of Ashura, the tenth day in the month of Muharram, the Prophet's grandson Hussein, whom the Shiites regard as the lawful heir of Mohammed, was killed at Kerbela, in the vicinity of the Euphrates, at the behest of Caliph Jazid. On the anniversary of this event, the Shiites commemorate the highpoint of the month and mourning, and are particularly easily irritated, as shown by the riots and excesses of recent Iranian history.

We leave the mosque and turn left to the next iron gate, where it is written in English: "With Allah's help, victory is near." Another search of our persons takes place, and only then are we permitted into the small courtyard bordered by the revolutionary leader's ochre house. The modest one-story building is surrounded by high walls. On the flat roof is a terrace, shut off from view. Tavasuli guides us through a small door into the innermost courtyard. Within moments we are standing in front of the elderly imam, who is on a slightly higher level.

Ruhollah Mussavi Khomeini is sitting in a garden chair on a kind of veranda. On his lap is a simple yellow blanket with large checks. He is wearing a long, white garment resembling a *galabia* and a black prayer cap called a *shabkolah* on his almost bald head. His abundant full beard is snow-white, hie entire appearance carefully groomed. Imam Khomeini is physically larger than he appears in photos. He has strikingly large ears and large, very soft hands. His eyes, emphasized by bushy brows and set deep into their sockets, are lively and alert. The imam is quietly dignified, a wise old man receiving his students.

Khomeini speaks with a voice lacking heights and depths. His words are scarcely audible. He impresses one as being in fragile health, even suffering. The years of power in Tehran have taken their toll. When he returned to his homeland on February 1, 1979, after an almost fifteen-year exile, he asked Allah for two more years for the purpose of putting his model of an Islamic state into practice. Allah granted him much more. Often declared dead, Khomeini lives in the manner to which he has become accustomed for the last forty years—spartanly, piously, and with great zest for action.

It is precisely his penchant for discipline that has enabled him to carry out one of the great revolutions of the century. The fact that Khomeini must sustain the commitment of his followers after such a short period of time by increasingly audacious war maneuvers suggests the danger of attrition threatening his regime.

Khomeini comes from a country that during the entire modern era has been a playground for the superpowers—first, England and Russia; in more recent history, the United States. During the era of colonialism the issue was of course not only political gain but also enormous economic interests. During the 1860s, the colonial powers were after Persia's raw materials. Nasir ed-Din Shah accommodated them, even granting the tobacco monopoly to an Englishman in 1890. The first mass protest movement was formed by the Shiite clergy, the modernists, the liberals, and the middle classes of the big cities. The Shah was forced to retract his decision.

At this time a wandering clergyman by the name of Sayid Mustafa Mussavi returned from India. The later *ayatollah* was always active on behalf of the poor and demanded social reforms of the Persian feudal lords. He became famous throughout the country through protests against granting the tobacco monopoly. He stood by the side of the leader of the demonstrations, Ayatollah Mirsa el-Schirasi. The family lived in the small city of Khomein, north of Isfahan, where the last of six children, Ruhollah Mussavi Hendi, was born on May 17, 1900.

The strengthening of the Iranian clergy broke new ground in 1905. The Shah was forced in 1906 to establish a first Persian parliament and to accept a constitution. Sayid Mustafa Mussavi was already dead—the victim of a political assassination in 1903. But the movement had achieved its goals. The new constitution provided that in the future every legal decree of consequence would have to be examined and approved by the Islamic constitutional counsel for its compliance with the Koran.

The young government was not capable of surviving, however, since the superpowers intervened ever more directly, ultimately dividing up the country among themselves in 1907. Oil was first discovered in Iran in 1908 and, starting in 1914, was in the hands of the Anglo-Iranian Oil Company. The needed raw material was siphoned off to Europe, which was rich and waging war, while the Persians were starving. With the economy of the country exhausted, the strivings for independence of individual provinces increased.

All these events were experienced by the young Ruhollah Mussavi Hendi as he was reared by his mother and his Aunt Sahiba. In 1914 or 1915 the young man was sent to the nearest large city, Isfahan, to study theology. From 1920 to 1921 he continued his studies, primarily literature, with the famous Shiite scholar Abd al-Karim Hairi Yazdi in Arak. Later, he followed his teacher to the holy city of Ghom, the center of the faith and Persia's most important pilgrimage destination, ninety-three miles south of Tehran. Anyone approaching it sees from afar the golden cupola of the Fatima Mosque, built in memory of Reza, the eighth imam. Such famous Shiite schools of theology as Feizieh have given the city the reputation for being the country's center of theology. From Ghom comes the younger generation that fills all the important positions within the clergy, and Ghom is the source of impulses that reach the entire Shiite world.

In 1921 the colonial power Great Britain appointed as minister of war the highest Cossack officer, Reza Khan—bringing to an end the Kadshar dynasty that had ruled up to that time. Reza Khan took drastic measures and brought about a reunification of the torn country. After the retirement of the weak Ahmad Shah, he took over the government in 1925 and, against the will of the conservative clergy, founded the new Pahlevi dynasty. From that time on, he strove for a secular republic modeled on that of his famous contemporary Mustafa Kemal (Ataturk). Conflict with the *ulemas* was foreordained.

The student Ruhollah Mussavi Hendi was at this time attending the Darushafa School in Ghom. Already, following the death of his mentor Ayatollah Haeris, he had become an authority on Islamic law, and he had also brilliantly distinguished himself in the fields of astronomy, philosophy, and mysticism. In addition, he had become *ijtihad* (a theologian entitled to teach). In the wake of a strengthened national consciousness, he had to make his name sound Iranian, so he simply called himself Khomeini after his place of birth. In the official German biography published by the Tehran Islamic Ministry of Leadership, it is stated:

From his earliest days Imam Khomeini has had the goal of becoming an independent person, someone whose behavior is beyond reproach. Among all the groups in Ghom he was famous for his virtues. He places particular value on the practice of religious rituals and the observance of Islamic principles. He is an early riser even though he frequently stays up until midnight in order to pray and speak with God. He has dispensed with carnal desires, practices strict asceticism, and maintains strict discipline in everything.

Khomeini became a respected teacher and the author of some thirty theological treatises written mainly in Arabic, the language of the holy book. In 1928 he married Batoul, the daughter of the Shiite theologian Aga Mirza Mohammed Saqafi; he has remained monogamous all his life. The five children from this marriage are his sons Ahmed and Mustafa (the latter murdered by the Shah's secret service SAVAK while he was in exile in Iraq), and his daughters Farideh, Seddigheh, and Fahimeh. Farideh is married to the Ghom businessman Mohammed Hussein Arabi, and Fahimeh, to Vice-Minister Mahmud Burodscherdi. Seddigheh is the widow of Ayatollah Shahab Eshragi, who died of a heart attack. (Although these biographical details are not published in Iran, they are for the most part known.)

Shah Reza, the new ruler of Persia, wanted to create a model Western-style country from the deteriorated feudal nation. Supported by his army and a rapidly assembled bureaucracy, he started out by concentrating on the city of Tehran and building up productive industry. There followed numerous new laws, conceived to be the foundation of a secular state—in other words, a system with strict separation of politics and religion. These measures included the introduction of Western dress for men and the elimination of the veil. Such acts were clearly directed against the strong Shiite clergy, whose influence was altogether to be diminished.

Neither Shah Reza nor his son Mohammed Reza, who already at that time had a significantly weaker position, noticed that their fanatic belief in progress and desire to lead the hopelessly under-developed country from the Middle Ages into the twentieth century within the shortest possible period of time destroyed the people's social institutions. Inevitably the impoverished rural population and the people from the slums of southern Tehran flocked to the *ayatollahs* in droves.

During the 1930s, Ruhollah Mussavi Khomeini was one of the many high clergymen who carried out their official duties in Ghom, observing with increasing embitterment what the Shah was doing in Tehran. Khomeini was the ideal Shiite clergyman, since he expressly and emphatically concerned himself with social problems. In his lectures he dealt forcefully with the situation of the simple believers—profoundly, as his former students now remark.

In the late '30s the Shah adopted an anti-British policy that led to an increase in German influence. After the attack by Hitler on the Soviet Union in 1941, England and Russia again invaded Iran and summarily deposed the Shah in August. They had achieved their goal of protecting the exposed southern flank of the Soviets.

Khomeini, already an opponent of the Shah, used these events as the provocation for writing his first nontheological book. Published in 1941, his *Kasf ol-Assraar* (*The Revelation of Mysteries*) is a passionate indictment of the persecution of Muslims by the Shah, the systematic destruction of the Islamic civilization, and the increasing dependence on foreign powers. In Khomeini's words:

Religion is the only thing that is capable of keeping mankind from deception and crime. Unfortunately those people at the helm of the Iranian state have an erroneous faith or none at all. These demagogues speak with passion about the protection of the country's interests, but in reality their glance is directed solely toward their own fortune. If a candidate for a seat in parliament throws about so much money for the purpose of purchasing votes, the reason is that he expects to make more if elected. After several months in office, a minister whom we assume to be poor can amass great wealth. Are such persons really serving their country wholeheartedly?

The old Shah had gone into exile in South Africa, and his successor, the twenty-two-year-old Mohammed Reza, found himself in a precarious situation. The foreign occupiers of the country accepted him only as a helper in the realization of their goals. The future of the monarchy was at stake. A constitutional system, complete with a cabinet of ministers and political parties, maintained order even though the discontented provinces of Azerbaijan and Kurdistan wanted independence. The *ulema* in Ghom did not yet have at their disposal the powerful system of the *mullahs* now ruling the country. Beginning in 1945, at the helm of the *ulema* was the moderate, peace-loving Ayatollah Sayid Aga Hussein Borudjerdi. The high clergyman was recognized and revered by a vast number of believers. His position was uncontested up to the time of his death in 1961 at age eighty-four.

The radical wing of the clergy, however, was pressing for change in the constellation of power. An especially active representative of this faction was Khomeini, whose sharp attacks against the errors in the economic, political, and cultural spheres and against the foreign exploiters found strong support among his angry young followers. Khomeini's first motto for the masses was: "Resistance against tyranny is the first duty of a Muslim." The declaration of war had been made. If the Grand Ayatollah Borudjerdi had not decisively intervened for a separation of state and religion, his discontented brothers in the faith would have attracted attention during the '50s.

The nationalists were victorious in the 1950 elections. On April 30, 1951, their leader Dr. Mohammed Mossadegh was elected prime minister of Iran by a large majority in the parliament. Pressure from the discontented people left him no choice but to keep his campaign promise of nationalizing the largely British-controlled oil industry one day after the election. In a press conference on June 21, 1951, Mossadegh stated:

An end must be made of these unbearable conditions in our country. We perceive that the way to overcoming them is the creation of sufficient capital to be used for the people and for raising the standard of living. There is a choice of two possibilities for the creation of capital: on the one hand, foreign loans; on the other hand, the state's own income, which in our country derives mainly from oil. But years of negotiations with foreign powers concerning the lawfulness of our claim to ownership, which we have made to the oil industry and which no power on earth can deny us, have not yet led to any result. With the aid of oil income, we could cover all of our expenditures and combat poverty, disease, and backwardness among our people. In addition, there is the very important factor that, with the elimination of the power of English society, corruption and intrigues will be eliminated through which influence is exerted on our country's domestic issues. If this patronizing situation has ceased, Persia will have achieved its economic and political independence.

The British government planned an invasion of Persia and the occupation of the oil-rich island of Abadan, but that remained only a threat. Cruising along the coastline was the largest concentration of British strike forces since World War II, but it was not used. To this day there is no clear explanation of whether the danger of Russian intervention deterred the British from further acts or whether the Americans intervened. London appealed to various international organizations to act as an arbitrator. When that brought no success, England regarded an international oil boycott a suitable means for combatting the situation. A rigorous economic blockade was imposed on Iran. The London government published a warning that any purchaser of Iranian oil would be subject to legal prosecution.

When that also failed to achieve much, this colonial power directed its efforts against Mossadegh and his administration. Legally they were unable to overthrow him, since at least ninety-five percent of the population enthusiastically backed their prime minister. Instead, they painted a picture of the danger of massive communist intervention, and that in turn caused the new American administration headed by Eisenhower and Dulles, which had entered office in January 1953, to take notice. But the Americans continued to pursue a solution through negotiations while the British prophesied the growth of the communistic Tudeh Party, which had been founded after the war. Political unrest during these months seemed to confirm their thesis. The position of the young, inexperienced Shah became increasingly shaky. On January 24, 1953, Mohammed Reza Pahlevi declared his willingless to leave the country for the time being. However, Abol Ghassem Kashani, a moderate *ayatollah* and head of parliament, approached him and on Feburary 28 roused the masses against Mossadegh. At that time Ruhollah Khomeini had no say in matters. Compared with the great religious leader Abol Ghassem Kashani, he was an unimportant figure. Moreover, the mood of the people was still in support of the Shah.

Peace and order were temporarily restored. Beneath the surface, though, things continued to seethe. The Shah wanted to have Mossadegh removed from office, since the prime minister had effectively curtailed his authority and had restored to the people land holdings unlawfully seized by his father. Still another, more far-reaching land reform was to take place—one that caused the wealthy people in the country to turn against Mossadegh. Ayatollah Abol Ghassem Kashani was on their side, which was characteristic of the Shiite clergy at that time.

On August 6, 1953, U.S. President Dwight D. Eisenhower explained at a press conference: "The increase in communist influence in Asia provides reason for fear and will not remain without serious consequences for the United States." He stressed particularly that its expansion in Iran must be opposed. On August 15, there was a failed coup against Mossadegh. Instigated by the Shah, the coup was to have been carried out by his bodyguards. As a result of the defeat, the Shah and the Empress left the country, flying to Rome via Baghdad.

Subsequently the U.S. Central Intelligence Agency intervened. The uprising against Mossadegh took its course. It was an uprising instigated by the Iranian *mullahs* and financed by approximately $5.4 million. On the morning of August 19, a street mob, armed with cudgels and knives, marched from southern Tehran toward the center of the city. Their battle cry was: "Down with Mossadegh." The Shah's guards did the rest and arrested the leading politicians. On August 22, the Pahlewis returned to the country. Mossadegh was tried by a military court and sentenced to three years arrest. August 19 immediately became known as the "day of the nation." That is how the Shah wanted it. In his view, what had occurred was "a liberation from foreign powers that came within a hair of eliminating our independence."

Mohammed Reza Pahlevi was now obligated to the Americans, and he was often given the chance to perform services for the new colonial power. In the ensuing years he first once, and then for all, crushed all suggestion of opposition. The parliament no longer played any role. In 1954 the Shah signed a new oil agreement, which led to a significant economic upswing, and during the '60s he introduced a number of social and economic reforms, the so-called White Revolution, involving a system of land reform accompanied by planned improvements in the educational system. This act by the Shah was sold to the Western world by the mass media as the long-withheld, final liberation of the enslaved Iranian people.

In reality the so-called land reform benefited primarily the landowners. The peasants received only ten percent of the arable land, for which they had to pay high rates, which without exception brought them closer to ruin. The dependence of the peasant on the landowner remained, and the large landowners profited greatly.

Haj Sayid Aga Hussein Mohammed Borudjerdi died in 1961.

No official successor was named for the Grand Ayatollah (a title that came into being only in 1920). Later, Khomeini became the first to call himself *Ayatollah al-Uzma,* and since that time also carries the title of a "source of imitation" that is associated with this honor. He must share the title, however, with five other high Shiite *ayatollahs,* including his greatest rival, Haj Sayid Kasem Shariat-Madari. In order to distinguish himself from clergymen of the same rank, at the highpoint of his power he had himself called imam, which constitutes a step away from the hierarchy toward a messianic status, for the title is closely associated with the mystical return of the vanished twelfth imam.

In 1963 the political power of the Ayatollah Kashani and Behbahani had vanished. Ayatollah Khomeini's hour was coming closer. The Koran confirms in *sura* 7:36 that "A space of time is fixed for every nation; when their hour is come, not for one moment shall they hold back, nor can they go before it." The particularly conservative clergyman organized an open revolt against the Shah and his White Revolution. Mohammed Reza Pahlevi was also accused of wanting to divide up the land holdings of religious organizations and, in addition, of unjustifiably introducing the right of women to vote. The slogans of the agitators were not far from proclaiming: "Fight the enemies of Islam."

Ayatollah Khomeini took over the leadership of the revolt. From the outset, he strove for the model of Mohammed's Islamic theocracy in Medina. "All power comes from God," he proclaimed, calling it the basis of Iran in the future. The idea of the transformation of the monarchy into an Islamic republic had long ago gripped Khomeini. A few years previously Ayatollah Nehini from Isfahan had inspired him with detailed descriptions of this thesis. Khomeini spoke at that time and repeatedly at a later period of the Prophet's last era in Medina, and as a partisan of Shiat Ali recognized only Ali, the fourth caliph, and his five-year reign. It is from this position that Khomeini derives his contention that Islam has not yet been given a chance. Given Ali's brief tenure in power, the people of God had had only a slight foretaste of the era of justice. From this perspective, Khomeini can vary his vision greatly; he does not have to base his position on historical models.

The highpoint of the 1963 uprising came on June 4, the anniversary of the death of the Shiite martyr Hussein. Khomeini had a manifesto containing ten points read in the mosques, demanding the return to constitutional government and calling the Shah the "Jazid of our era." Khomeini and other high dignitaries were arrested that same day. Demonstrations in Tehran and Ghom were the answer of the masses who, roused by the shout, "Either death or Khomeini," marched through the streets by the thousands. Nine thousand people allegedly died in the bloody fighting with the government troops.

Khomeini was at first put in the Qasr Prison in Tehran, and later in the barracks of Ishrat Abad. When the situation on the streets became steadily more explosive, the Shah sent the head of his secret service, Nematollah Nassiri, to Khomeini, offering him his freedom under the condition that he move from Ghom into the distant town of Mashad. The *ayatollah* remained unimpressed: "The doctrine is older than regal power, and my paths are not the same as yours."

When Khomeini did not comply, the Shah, not knowing what to do released him from prison. The Shiite leader was triumphant, and immediately after arriving in Ghom gave his next heretical speech in the Azam Mosque:

You call us reactionary. Certain foreign newspapers are handsomely bribed to write that we are against all reforms and are attempting to lead Iran back to the Middle Ages. The *mullahs* are against the repression from which the people here are suffering. We want them to maintain the country's independence. We want them not to be submissive servants of others. We do not want them to beg for more help. Do such ideals belong to the past? We are not against civilization, and Islam is also not against civilization. You, the government, have abused all rights, both human and divine rights. The radio and television programs grate on our nerves. The press poisons the minds of our youth. You have called in military experts from Israel. You are sending Iranian students to Israel. We are against all those things. We have nothing against freedom for women, but we do not want any decked-out dolls, who serve the lustful purposes of men, to pose as women. Your educational system benefits foreigners.

In late 1963 Khomeini complained of an alleged deception in the parliamentary elections and was placed by the Shah under house arrest—in Imaran, in the north of Tehran. In mid-1964 the Majlis (the Iranian lower house of parliament) passed a law granting extra-territorial rights to American citizens in Iran, exempting them in the future from Iranian laws. That made the Shiite leader so angry that he recalled the old laws of capitulation from the era of the colonial powers: "Why should Iranian courts be cheated of making rulings? Why is our sovereignty no longer of value—only because of a $200 million loan for which we pay $100 million in interest? Why are we selling this country for a starving wage?"

The Shah finally blew his top. He set in motion the "special action against Khomeini." Around 4:00 A.M. on November 4, 1964, a general and a division of the military police kept a watch out for Khomeini on his way to the mosque. They grabbed him, dragged him into a military truck, and quickly drove him to Tehran's Mehrabad Airport. Only when they had put him in a plane was he informed of the destination of his involuntary trip: Turkey. Fifteen years and three months were to pass before Khomeini again set foot on Iranian soil.

In the clergyman's homeland, numerous religious leaders were arrested. Many of them, like Khomeini's son Mustafa, were expelled. It had been agreed that Khomeini would be kept in Bursa in the old capital of the Ottomans, a region that was purely Sunni. There he passed his days in isolation, wrote books, meditated, and prepared the grand revenge on the Shah and all his friends. No person in Western Anatolia took notice of Khomeini, now age sixty-four, who was living in a two-story house on Bursa's Acemler Caddesi (Persian street). In Iran, too, his name was increasingly banned from public discussion. Anyone who spoke of Khomeini landed in SAVAK's torture chambers; at this time a few Shiite clergymen vanished forever.

Khomeini contacted the worldwide network that he had already set up in Ghom. He maintained contacts with his faithful followers in many Western countries and also kept himself informed about the events in Iran. Only after a period of eleven months was he able to exercise his will and change the place of his exile to Najef in Iraq. In October 1965 he arrived in the holy city of the Shiites, the site of the grave of the Caliph Ali. Here Khomeini felt more at ease than in any other place outside his homeland, for Najef is an important center for news from the Shiite world. From there Khomeini could keep reins on the Iranian clergy. Starting with the first speech in the Sheikh Ansari Mosque, Khomeini's words were recorded week after week on tape cassettes and secretly taken to Iran, where they were eagerly snapped up. The later revolutionary leader liked to speak in public, write books, and study Islamic writings. Five years later he had already written six large works.

His words carried weight all over Iran, as was known to the government in Baghdad, which supported him during the long years of his exile. It was politically opportune to oppose the Shah. Only when the antagonistic neighbors had agreed on a unified tactic against the rebellious Kurds on both sides of the border did sad times come for the famous clergyman. Iraq's new strong man, Saddam Hussein, subjected him to house arrest and then in 1978 expelled him from the country. That angered Khomeini so much that it is possible to regard the war against Iraq as belated revenge by the elderly man.

Khomeini, however, had founded a revolutionary network made up of all kinds of opponents to the Shah. They surrounded him and, unnoticed by the Western public, prepared the day of his return. In Iran they managed day by day to get news from the leader:

In the name of the merciful and blessed God. Those who cultivate proper behavior and, in agreement with their religious duties, forbid neglect in the intention of supporting Islam and its holy principles and protect the Islamic people from the domination of foreign powers and for this reason are arrested and killed, causing their families to lose their main source of support, must be supported with firm belief by all, but without injuring their pride and self-confidence.

Time was running out for the Pahlewi regime. The Shah could no longer fully deceive himself with the statement: "I have 99.9 percent of the population behind me." Nevertheless, in some ways, the ruler remained convinced of the assertion; until the end of his life he did not comprehend that the Iranian people had risen up against a despotic, inhuman regime. He did not recognize or accept the fact that his rule had established new yardsticks for corruption in the realms of justice and administration, extending even into the imperial palace. He never wanted to admit that it is impossible to bring a people like the Iranians into the atomic era within a few years. That could not be accomplished by his subjects and was therefore rejected.

In addition, the Shah was not aware that the practices of his gigantic secret service system, SAVAK, which had been built up in the '50s, differed not at all from those of its Stalinist counterpart on the other side of the long northern border. In the mid-'60s approximately 60,000 agents are reputed to have been actively involved in SAVAK, and during the last months of the

Shah's rule the number may have been around 700,000. Opponents of the regime reported on the horrible torture methods used by SAVAK. Twenty thousand political prisoners were a matter of course in Iran during the Shah era.

When the Shah's family, together with illustrious guests from all over the world, celebrated the alleged 2,500-year existence of the Iranian monarchy in 1971, Khomeini, who was in exile, angrily observed:

The tyrannical regime believes that I am content with my life. Rather would I be dead and returned to God than to live now and have to see the suffering of these oppressed masses. I consider it my duty to protest. Repeatedly we were told that we should not interfere in matters of the state. We were banished from the battlefield against the regime. But the history of mankind shows that it was always the prophets and the religious figures who rose up against autocratic rulers.

But still another eight years were to pass before the Iranian revolution reached its finale. During these eight years, Khomeini tirelessly spun his threads. Inside Iran things remained relatively quiet for a long time. The 180,000 members of the Shiite clergy vacillated between maintaining the existing situation and overthrowing the Shah. Until the end of 1977, only verbal protests were forthcoming from them when they disagreed with measures taken by the government. Khomeini was the only one who, 250 miles away in Najef in Iraq, spread his hatred beyond the border at Shatt al-Arab. Ayatollah Shariat-Madari, a moderate clergyman and one of the most important religious leaders in Iran following Khomeini's expulsion, assessed the situation at that time: "The people are uprooted. Their only support is provided by religion, the mosque, and the *mullahs*. The people therefore mainly turn to us, because they feel that modernization and the development that is so highly praised brings no peace to the soul."

Shariat-Madari then alluded to the Shah's intention of making Iran one of the five leading economic powers by 1985. Mohammed Reza Pahlevi felt secure on his throne. He had at his disposal much oil, and he was certain of the friendship of the U.S. Iran was of as much value to the U.S. in the most explosive region of the earth as the bridgehead of Israel, in a more forward position. Between the years 1972 and 1977 alone, the regime in Tehran purchased $18 billion of American weapons. The suppliers even sent items that had not yet been used in the U.S.

army. The Shah's appetite for armaments was endless; for them, one-third of the income from oil was spent in the United States. That also covered payment for the 50,000 American military advisors working in Iran. In addition, the Shah bought interests in large multinational industrial corporations such as Krupp in the Federal Republic of Germany.

As the royal family became ever more elegant and powerful, their environment became steadily more corrupt. The leading class in Iran consisted of the nobility, the secret service SAVAK, the leadership level in the army, and the rich business people. At the expense of the population, which was steadily becoming poorer, they financed a life resembling that of *A Thousand and One Nights* and filled up their numbered bank accounts in Switzerland. The bazaar dealers, traditionally a powerful class among the simple people, suffered greatly. The Tehran bazaar had always been oriented toward tradition and religion. Under the domination of Shah Reza Pahlevi, the dealers lived with the latent anxiety that they would be squeezed out by the Shah and big business. In 1978, for example, a plan was put forward to build an eight-lane highway through the bazaar, which would have been the death of this retail trade. Powerful favorites of the Shah would have liked to get their hands on the lucrative import of wares. As early as the 1950s, the rulers had taken away the grain-trading monopoly from the bazaar dealers. Because the Shah family was increasingly involved in the economic destruction of the bazaar, the bazaar dealers were driven into the arms of the *mullahs* from an early date. They financed Khomeini's revolution to a large extent and supervised a conspiratorial trade in the necessary weapons.

The revolution started in the mosque. There the masses, whose lives were continually made more difficult by rent hikes and price rises in the necessities of life, regularly listened to the cassette recordings coming in from Najef across the border. Khomeini provided instruction in his typical messages: "The oppressed people are forced to accept the monarchical system, a corrupt system that is rejected and condemned by Islam. The regime wants to destroy the Koran. The Iranians are condemned to shout approval to a blood-sucking ruler. The Shah speaks of constitutionalism and of constitutional law while himself doing everything to eliminate it."

An instance of death ushered in the last phase of the gigantically staged Iranian revolution. On October 23, 1977, Khomeini's son died in a mysterious manner in Najef. Mustafa had been an authority in the area of theological and canonical law. Everything pointed to his having been murdered with a poisoned weapon by SAVAK agents. Khomeini subsequently stated that this death was the signal for the explosion in Iran. The large funeral in Najef and memorial ceremonies all over Iran set the stage for the new confrontation with the Shah. Overnight the name Khomeini, whose utterance had for so long been forbidden, became the symbol of the approaching liberation. The first strikes and demonstrations were held.

On January 7, 1978, religious unrest in Ghom resulted in approximately twenty deaths and injuries. In the Shiite tradition, members of the family of the deceased mourn again forty days later, and this was the case with the family and followers of Khomeini. Once again the military intervened, leaving nine dead and 120 wounded on February 18, in Tabris, the second-largest city in Iran. On March 30, there was rioting in twelve cities, including Tehran, Isfahan, and Mashad. For the entire forty days the people protested and set in motion the pattern of force and counterforce. Khomeini saw that time was on his side. He tended the fires of the revolution—among other things, he issued an open letter to the Iranians and challenged the military to liberate the country.

On August 11, the shocked Shah declared martial law in Isfahan. This measure had been preceded by bloody riots, resulting in at least thirteen deaths. In the week following, the Rex movie house of Abadan was set afire by unknown arsonists. The exits were blocked, and more than 370 persons died in the flames. Word quickly spread that SAVAK agents had committed the act in order to attribute it to the opposition. Khomeini stated that quite precisely: "The Shah and his henchmen let hundreds of people burn to death."

On September 7, there was a general strike. In the largest demonstration to date against the ruler of Iran, who called himself "light of the Aryans," 100,000 subjects marched through the streets of the capital. Martial law was extended to Tehran and eleven other cities, but that did not deter anyone on the following day, the so-called Black Friday, when the people staged a challenge to the announcement on the Jaleh Plaza. The military shot into the crowd, in which there were many women and children, reportedly resulting in approximately 3,000 deaths.

The Shah once again attempted to provide leadership. He had

already determined that the deeply religious Sharif Emami was
to be the new prime minister. The new appointee tried to put the
mullahs in a forgiving mood; to this end, the Islamic calendar was
again introduced and the gambling casinos told to close. The
Ministry for Women's Concerns, extremely unpopular with the
fundamentalists, ended its work. Radio and television to some
extent tailored their program to the wishes of the *mullahs*. The
Shah ordered an investigation into the business enterprises of his
extensive family. Emissaries hastened to the "old man" in Najef,
begging him to come home again, telling him that everything was
forgiven and forgotten. But Khomeini, in a triumphant mood,
remained tough as always: "As long as the Shah is in Iran, I will
not return."

Additional concessions by the Shah regime—such as measures
against censorship and the secret police, as well as the freeing of
political prisoners—could no longer pacify the radical *mullahs*.
They knew that they would be victorious, and they—which is to
say, chiefly Khomeini—demanded the head of the hated ruler.
The preparatory work by the *ayatollah*—"We are creating a generation of the faithful who some day will destroy the throne of
the tyrant"—was already bearing fruit. Khomeini incited the
masses: "Blood will ultimately be victorious over swords." On
cassettes, he commanded the soldiers: "Leave your barracks, you
are dishonoring yourselves."

The fall of the monarchy could no longer be stopped. But most
Iranians were unable to imagine that the Shah could really be
deposed. On October 31, 37,000 oil workers, the new industrial
proletariat of the country, stopped work. On November 5, Tehran was engulfed in violence and destruction. The underprivileged of the southern suburbs looted and set property afire. The
West finally started to watch the events in Iran carefully and
reported that not all the people, it seemed, loved the fairytale
king, Mohammed Reza Pahlevi. The London BBC detected an
"inferno of destruction and a hell of hatred."

Ayatollah Ruhollah Khomeini now became a media personality
for the average Western consumer. In fact, he had been living in
the Paris suburb of Neauphle-le-Château since October 6, 1978.
Iraq's Saddam Hussein ended the revolutionary leader's asylum
following intervention by the Shah. As Saddam Hussein told a
press conference: "We respect religious leaders, and we support
their effort to teach the people, but we do not permit priests to

replace politicians. By the same token, politicians are not permitted to replace priests." In making this statement, he incurred the wrath of the vengeful Iranian.

On December 2, large demonstrations took place at the beginning of Muharram, the month of mourning. Approximately seventy deaths allegedly resulted. Ten days later was the start of the heaviest riots, to which the Shah's regime could respond only with slogans. The highest Shiite holiday, the commemoration of Ashura, united all believers in hatred of the Shah. A resolution proclaimed: "Imam Khomeini is our leader, and his activities thrive on the inspiration of the people. . . . We demand that the Muslim people of Iran be entrusted with the freedom to decide about its own future. We demand the establishment of the primacy of Islamic law."

Meanwhile in Paris a meditating Khomeini could be seen sitting under an apple tree or praying with numerous followers in a blue tent made to serve as a mosque. He provided many explanations and saw to it that there was an Oriental spectacle that dominated the headlines everywhere. Only now was the West beginning to learn of the implacable opponent of the Shah. But the West still had difficulty comprehending why, in the name of Allah, thousands and thousands of people in faraway Iran deliberately walked into the machine-gun fire of the Shah's army for a tired old man without charisma, who was 2,800 miles away in Paris.

On the last two days of 1978, there was again a general strike and demonstrations in all Iranian cities. Hundreds were killed in Mashad. The seventy-four-year-old Ayatollah Mahmud Taleghani, Khomeini's general chief-of-staff in Tehran, supervised the organization of attacks against the Pahlevi regime. On January 16, 1979, the Shah-inshah-i-Iran Aryamehr, King of Kings, sun of the Aryans, and Empress Fara Diba left Iran for a "vacation." The ruler of thirty-six million people was a broken man. As he would later recall, "I had lost my people and did not notice it. I had rushed the direction of the future without feeling that my people remained behind and that the people did not at all want to participate."

When the news of the Shah's departure became known, journalists asked his antagonist in Neauphle-le-Château what he felt upon his victory. Khomeini, without emotion, answered briefly: "Allah is greater." He then added: "That is merely the prelude to our victory." The Americans, who had let their favorite protégé fall, did not yet know how they should categorize the first Islamic revolution in current times.

In Tehran the masses had assumed power. Prime Minister Shahpur Bakhtiar, who had not yet taken office under the Shah, was compelled to observe the goings-on helplessly. The shout, "*Khoda* [God], Koran, Khomeini," became steadily louder. "For God, Shah, and fatherland" was suddenly no longer a wise motto. Khomeini characterized Bakhtiar's administration as illegal and successfully challenged the members of the council of the regency to resign. Bahktiar gambled on gaining time, but, on February 1, 1979, he had to reopen the airports, which had been closed two weeks previously. He was no longer able to impede the return of the elderly saint with the bushy white beard and the thick black eyebrows.

A skeptical Western world noted the takeoff of the white Air France jumbo jet for Iran on February 1, 1979, at 1:15 A.M. It was a special flight, not posted anywhere. The *Deutsche Zeitung* observed: "At an elevation of 35,000 feet, the pious elderly man is flying back into the Middle Ages almost as fast as the echo." At 9:39 A.M. the next day, he stepped on Iranian ground with his closest staff of co-workers. "*Aga Amad* [the master] has arrived," spread from mouth to mouth. A triumphant reception greeted Khomeini, whose first act was to visit the cemetery of heroes, Behescht e-Zahara, 126 miles south of Tehran.

With a placid expression, he raged against the Shah and his deputy Bakhtiar in his address there. Then he appealed to the armed forces to accept the victory of the *mullahs:* "We are going through an era of troubles. We have sacrificed blood, the blood of our youth. We have involved our honor and in the process have accepted the arrest and torture of our priests. All that we now want is your independence, Mr. General. Do you not wish to be independent? Mr. Major, do you not want to be independent? Do you really want to remain lackeys forever?"

Prime Minister Bakhtiar resigned and was able to escape abroad. On February 5, Khomeini appointed Mehdi Bazargan as the new prime minister. Bazargan, for years a professor at Tehran University, had previously been a civilian ally in the struggle. Weapons from the supplies of the fragmented army were distributed to the faithful people. Then, on February 10, shooting and riots began in Tehran. When they ended on February 12, Khomeini's followers had won. Police stations, barracks, and prisons were in their hands, as well as the ministries and the parliament. At the time, 11,000 prisoners were in the prisons.

Troops loyal to the Shah laid down their weapons. Leading officers of the old regime came before courts of summary jurisdiction and were executed immediately after sentencing. Within the first weeks after Khomeini came to power, it became apparent that the route back to normality was by no means so simple. The opposition front against the "king of kings," which had previously seemed so unified, was now split. A number of more secularly oriented groups—for instance, the leftist Mujahideen-e-Khalq, which had begun its guerrilla war against the Shah as long ago as 1971—were not prepared to exchange a monarchical dictatorship for a religious dictatorship. They supported the idea of a republic with an Islamic basis, one which would have councils for the people and for the workers, one employing co-determination models. In consequence, they attracted the fury of the revolutionary leader, who in the course of his acts to restore peace in the country also appealed for battle against the "godless Mujahideen-e-Khalq." An enduring underground battle between the rule by the *mullahs* and the leftist guerrillas still shatters the labile Islamic republic.

The decision about the form of state came about in a vote by the people on March 30, 1979. On that occasion differences came to light between the uncompromising Khomeini, who for health reasons had withdrawn for a half-year to Ghom, and his antagonist Shariat-Madari. Khomeini, however, got his way, and on April 2, 1979, the Islamic Republic of Iran was proclaimed. In June and July there was extensive nationalization of banks and insurance companies, and of industry as well.

A new constitution establishing the leading role of the Islamic clergy was approved in December 1979 by ninety-eight percent of the people (i.e., twenty-two million voters). Khomeini himself, in accordance with the Shiite imamate, was granted a special role as *Velayat-e-Fakih* (authority over practicing clergymen scholars), and gained comprehensive power as the final authority in all political and religious questions. He was even mentioned by name in the constitution.

Shariat-Madari again expressed his mistrust in the 151 principles of the first constitution of the Islamic Republic. Article Five is the most important of all in this legal document. It states:

Within the Islamic Republic of Iran, in the absence of the missing twelfth imam—may God will that he return as soon as possible—the assignment of leadership (imamate) and the authority of leadership (*velayat-e-amr*) in matters of the Islamic community is entrusted to the just, God-fearing, brave legal scholar who is informed about the needs of the era and who is recognized and confirmed as the leader by the majority of the population.

In the event that no Islamic legal scholar achieves such a majority, the leadership council of Islamic legal scholars takes over in accordance with Principle 107.

In Principles 107 to 110, the sharing of force provided by the constitution is again suspended, for the supreme religious leader chooses the "Council of Guards," a body of three to five high clergymen who are above the parliament and the government. They examine all laws and, if necessary, can block them by their veto. The leader appoints the highest judge, in effect putting himself in charge of the entire judiciary; he also appoints the commander-in-chief of the armed forces, the chiefs of staff, as well as the commanders of all troop divisions. Moreover, he must approve the president of the nation, who is elected by the people. If he rejects him, then the president is not considered elected. He can also dismiss the head of state overnight "on the basis of considerations of the interests of the nation" if he does not like his manner of conduct.

The absolute ruler of the Islamic theocracy later provided an example of how seriously he took these paragraphs. In January 1980, the former Minister of Finance and Economics Abolhassan Bani Sadr, a more socialistically oriented theoretician, was elected president by a three-fourths majority. In February Khomeini approved the appointment of the president to head the secret revolutionary council, which was still ruling at that time, and in addition appointed him commander-in-chief of the armed forces. But Bani Sadr was still more, namely "the first and only head of state in the world who simultaneously was also leader of the opposition," as the German weekly *Die Zeit* explained. That meant that Abolhassan Bani Sadr steered a course against the exclusively theocratic direction and was ultimately devoured by the revolution.

After his first year in office, Bani Sadr increasingly warned of the wiles of the *mullahs*, of the danger of economic collapse within Iran (which was extremely unstable), and of goals that were possibly too high in the war on the Gulf, which had been in progress since September 1980. He observed the countless executions of domestic political opponents and alleged enemies of all persuasions—allegedly 15,000 from the time of Khomeini's return until autumn of 1982—and feared a lapse into the horrible despotism of the Shah. Bani Sadr commented to *Die Zeit:* "With all my might and within the framework of my possibilities, I am trying to thwart the dictatorship." He did not succeed. When he became too critical of the strong fundamentalist forces concentrated in Ayatollah Beheshti's Islamic Republican Party, his newspaper *Ayendegan* was banned. Beheshti, next to Khomeini the second most powerful man in Iran, announced Bani Sadr's replacement by a triumvirate. The incited masses demonstrated against their own president. In the summer of 1981, Bani Sadr had to go underground when Khomeini gradually divested him of his offices. In July he fled to his exile in Paris in a hijacked army plane flown by a friend who was a colonel in the air force.

From his new place of refuge, Auvers-sur-Oise, where he functions as a member of the newly founded National Council of Opposition, Bani Sadr states: "This Khomeini is today no longer the same person he once was. . . . Our historical error consisted in the fact that we choked him off from every criticism and censored ourselves. We behaved like a woman who has fallen in love and gives herself up without reservation to her lover. Only because we did not act did Khomeini become so strong." A belated, too belated bit of self-criticism.

The last remains of the political middle vanished from Iran with Bani Sadr's departure. In April 1982, the elderly and moderate Ayatollah Shariat-Madari was accused by a religious court in the holy city of Ghom of involvement in a planned attempt to overthrow Imam Khomeini. The highest Shiite body, the Circle of Religious Science, divested him of the title "Source of the Shiite Faith." His numerous followers were declared "betrayers of Islam and of the Islamic revolution." The former Iranian Foreign Minister Sadegh Ghotbzadeh was similarly denounced. He was put into prison, and the eighty-two-year-old Shariat-Madari was placed under house arrest. The bloodthirsty Judge Sadegh Khalkhali allegedly personally controlled his every movement, which meant that the last serious opponent of the imam was rendered harmless within the Iranian borders.

In the summer of 1982, Ghotbzadeh and twenty-four others,

less well known outside of Iran, were hauled into court as conspirators. Sadegh Ghotbzadeh admitted that he wanted to overthrow the Iranian government. Jamaran might be bombarded, but the final decision had not yet been made. Ghotbzadeh did, however, want to avoid the death of Imam Khomeini. He was concerned only with a new leadership for the state, of which he would have wanted to be a part only temporarily. Ayatollah Shariat-Madari and his role as spiritual leader in the projected coup were mentioned only tangentially during the court proceedings; he was subjected to a special trial by Iran's highest judicial authority. In any case, it was revealed that Shariat-Madari, Khomeini's most important competitor, was supposed to become the imam of the new government.

In the grounds for the judgment it was stated that, to realize his plan, Sadegh Ghotbzadeh had made contacts with such "reactionary regimes" in the Near East as Saudi Arabia as well as with numerous Western countries, including the U.S. He admitted to accepting money from authorized persons from those places and distributing it to his associates. Ghotbzadeh's argument, that he did not wish to tamper with the Islamic character of Iran but merely wanted to establish the "true republic," was rejected in the judgment as an "approximate excuse." The Islamic revolutionary Sadegh Ghotbzadeh was shot by a firing squad in the dawn of September 16, 1982. Other conspirators were later hanged.

During the years following the revolution, the imam's environment became increasingly lonely. The armed opposition of the estimated 100,000 members of the Mujahideen-e-Khalq and several other splinter groups increasingly decimated the ranks of Khomeini's closest co-workers. On May 1, 1979, Ayatollah Morteza Motahhari, one of the most important theoreticians of the Islamic revolution, was murdered after a meeting of the revolutionary council of fighters belonging to the organization called Forqan. On June 28, 1981, a bomb in the headquarters of the governing Islamic Republican Party mangled its chairman and the highest judge in the country, Ayatollah Mohammed Beheshti, and seventy-two of his supporters. After the removal of Bani Sadr, the fifty-two-year-old Beheshti belonged to the triumvirate that conducted the business of the president of the country. The Khomeini deputy from Isfahan had been head of the Hamburg Mosque from 1965 to 1969. He was extremely well educated, well groomed, and irrepressibly energetic. His death came as an incredible shock to the mullahcracy. The regime spilled still more blood when the chief ideologist of the Islamic Republican Party, Hassan Ajjat, was shot by two motorcyclists on August 3, 1981. Minister of Defense Mustafa Chamran died in the Gulf War. Another bomb exploded on August 30, 1981, at a meeting of the National Defense Council to which, in addition to Imam Khomeini, the ten most powerful men of the state belong. Among the high-ranking victims were the new president of the country, Ali Rajai, and Prime Minister Mohammed Javad Bahonar. Ultimately the only remaining member of the old leadership was the president of the parliament, Akbar Hashemi Rafsandjani. Today he goes into public only under the strictest security and also has any place in which he is staying heavily guarded.

In the meantime Khomeini himself cannot count on the certainty that the house is guarded (meaning the regime) and that the domination by the religious people will remain stable for the foreseeable future, since it is based on the majority of the Iranians. Ayatollah Husseinali Montazeri, born in 1922, has been the strong man in Ghom since Khomeini's departure from there and is backed by most of the brothers in the faith. Montazeri, who pursues a policy only a few nuances more liberal than that of Khomeini, was particularly much in evidence during the 444-day martyrdom of the hostages in the U.S. embassy in Tehran while it was under the control of the Pasdaran. It was Montazeri who was the fire-brand against Jimmy Carter, the "big Satan."

Montazeri, a student of Ayatollah Borudjerdi and Imam Khomeini, was educated in Ghom and played an important role in the uprising of 1963. His biography is similar to that of most religious leaders of Iran. He was repeatedly jailed and tortured by the Shah's secret service. Several times the Tehran government ordered him to change his residence so he would be far away from the turmoil of the people. Since his convincing manner always influenced people in his surroundings in favor of fundamentalism, he was required to move frequently.

Ayatollah Montazeri spent most of the '70s behind bars. In 1978 he and the highly respected Ayatollah Taleghani were set free. He went to Paris to be with Khomeini and subsequently remained close by the revolutionary leader. After the victory of the *mullahs*, he became leader of the Friday prayers in Tehran, and was finally appointed director of the important theological center in Ghom. He has also carried out numerous special assignments.

On December 10, 1982, the council of experts called the Khobregan, a kind of ancillary parliament made up of religious dignitaries, was elected for the first time. Its sixty-nine members are entrusted with the task of making certain that actions taken by the government and the parliament are in compliance with Islamic law and of deciding on Khomeini's successor following his death. It is of course possible that the question may arise as to whether the imam should have any successor at all. During the last week of July 1983, the council was given a handwritten document of approximately thirty pages by Khomeini's son Ahmed. The assembled delegates observed how the Iranian leader's will was bound with ribbons in the Iranian colors of green, white, and red and sealed with wax.

The last will of Khomeini can be opened and made known only after his death. Confronted with the thought that even the imam could die, sobbing was heard among the ranks of the bearded *mullahs*. Apart from Khomeini himself, no one knows whether the name of Montazeri is mentioned in the will or whether the written document recommends instead a collective leadership. In any case, the group surrounding Montazeri and Rafsandjani seems at present to have the best prospects of directing the fate of Iran after the death of the eighty-four-year-old revolutionary from Ghom.

Although it seems inconceivable, I found more pictures of Montazeri in Jamaran, where Imam Khomeini lives, than of the elderly revolutionary himself. Normally, though, pictures of Khomeini are everywhere in the country. When the talk turns to the leading man from Ghom, Khomeini's expression reveals the trace of a smile and seems pleased. He is on Montazeri's side and seems to believe the ideals of his revolution are best represented by him.

The audience in Jamaran is over when he extends his hand and with an almost kindly glance assures me: "I will pray for you!"

20

Khomeini: Questions and Answers

BECAUSE IMAM KHOMEINI decided not to grant any personal inter-
views with foreign publicists after the one with the Italian journalist Oriana Fallaci in the summer of 1979, our discussion could
take place only in an indirect manner. His confidant Dr. Sadegh
Tabatabai made himself available as an intermediary. There was
no possibility for me to ask additional questions. The unusual
dialogue is presented here in a somewhat abbreviated form:

*"Imam Khomeini, how do you regard the future of the Islamic world?
Do you consider a reunification of the Sunnis and Shiites possible in the
foreseeable future?"*

"The Shiites and Sunnis of the Islamic world have more things
in common than they have differences. There is an astonishing
range of sociopolitical, economic, cultural, geopolitical, and other
factors that give them a shared fate. The population of the Islamic
world should require their politicians and statesmen come to an
agreement soon about this matter. But as for what concerns the

various schools of law, based on the various interpretations of the theological sources, it is more the task of the theologians and scholars to concern themselves with the questions and to seek an agreement. Since both groups live in accordance with the teaching of the Koran and want to be in the service of God and of mankind, an agreement is certainly possible. It is the task of politicians to try to see to the elimination of the discrepancy between Sunnis and Shiites, which only serves the imperialists and does not serve the Islamic cause.

"Our first goal is to combat the non-Islamic forces and the superpowers that try to keep Shiites and Sunnis apart, to oppress them and exploit them separately. Supported by their populations, statesmen are capable of finding guidelines against the superpowers in the West and in the East."

"Has there ever been an attempt to have those responsible for the situation meet?"

"Unfortunately very little has happened so far on a legal basis. Isolated attempts were made, but never resulted in the desired result."

"What do you anticipate for the future of Iran? Will the slogan, 'Neither East nor West,' continue to be in effect?"

"This motto of our Islamic republic does not mean that we should keep ourselves completely isolated from the West and the East. It means that we have before our eyes our own guidelines and value systems and are building on them independently of what the East or the West thinks of this value system. The Prophet said: 'Seek knowledge even if it is in China!' At his time there was certainly no academy of Islamic theology in China, so the Prophet could have said that Muslims should go there for the purpose of teaching Islamic law! By that, he meant the quest for knowledge. In our view, which is based on the Islamic value system, there should be guidelines independent of East and West. As for technology and science, we are free for progress. We want to introduce the technology that we consider necessary for the fulfillment of our needs."

"Sheikh Azhar told me in an interview that he did not consider Iran an Islamic system. From him and similar sources, I have heard that the world should not evaluate Islam based on the events in Iran and on

terrorism, oppression, and executions. What do you think of these judg-
ments?"

"That is more a political attitude and not at all a religious attitude. Besides, that also does not surprise us. It does not sound
any different from what foreign powers say against Iran. Islam is
not a religion of revenge and violence. Many people do not see
what our opponents, the counterrevolutionaries, have done in
Iran. They do not see how bombs are placed in schools and buses.
Recently children and pregnant women were killed in such an
incident. But if we protect ourselves against such terrorist groups,
then all manner of political propaganda against Iran is unleashed,
and there is again talk of mass oppression and mass arrests.
Everyone has the freedom to express himself politically in Iran as
long as it does not lead to violence. The entire imperialist world,
whether in the East or in the West, sees its interests jeopardized
by the existence of the Islamic Republic of Iran. An independent
Iran on the route of progress interferes with the military interests
as well as the economic and political interests of the Americans
in the entire region.

"The Soviet Union also pursues cultural interests, for during
the '60s it was always said that anyone fighting against oppression and for justice, anywhere in the world, should use Marxist
ideology, because it is the only ideology of revolution against
capitalism. It was said that everything else was purely idealistic
and that ultimately religion was the opiate of society. But if
'opium' carries out a revolution, it is of course against the interests of Marxistic ideas and theories.

"As for our future in Iran, I believe that we are moving along
our route and should not be interfered with by the outside world.
If that is granted us, then Iran, using almost exclusively its own
energies, will be in a position to build a future and make a connection to modern and progressive technology. No one can expect, after the briefest period of time, that all organizations, the
entire structure of the state, and the new religious institutions
based on the value systems of the Islamic revolution to work
together harmoniously, without any friction. That attitude would
be too idealistic. We have proved that within a short time we
have achieved much that is positive and that conditions are now
much better for people with low incomes. Despite the ongoing
war, no one has to go hungry.

"Just look at the statistics on schools and hospitals, the system

for supplying electricity, road construction, and energy supply
since the revolution, and compare them with those of the last
fifty years."

*"How is the war between Iraq and Iran supposed to continue? How is
it going to end?"*

"We want it to stop immediately. We of course attach certain
conditions to that. The aggressor started the war. That should
not set a precedent. It must be punished. Our expenses must be
covered. Generally speaking, we cannot let that go unpunished.
Damage has been done, and we know that this regime in Iraq is
not based on the people but, on the contrary, is an opponent of
the Iraqi population. The present regime must reimburse our expenses, which—roughly calculated—are around $150 billion. If
you go today to Khusistan, you will not see any walls higher than
three feet. Everything has been leveled to the ground. The same
thing applies to many cities in the Western part of our country."

*"Until now [August 1982] has there been any official offer of peace
from Baghdad?"*

"Not up to now, at least not in the form and amount demanded
by us. Once the Saudis offered $25 billion, but we are no beggars.
The one who committed the deed, the crime, must be punished.
We also know why we make our demand of the system and not
of the population, which itself suffers from it. If there were a
military takeover in Iraq today, we would not come to terms with
it. We would only renounce our demand if we had to deal with a
government that, like Iran, came to power on the basis of the
population. In that instance, the state of war would in any case
automatically be over."

*"Is this situation not also connected with the preceding liberation of
the holy sites of Najef, Kerbela, and Al Quds?"*

"Naturally, that is all one single complex. We regard the existence of Israel in the Near East as a cancer that cannot be cured
by medication but must be operated on with a surgical knife.
Israel is an illegitimate child of the imperialist powers, an American settlement. The liberation of Najef and Kerbela is not independent from the liberation of Iraq from the present regime. But
that must primarily be accomplished by the Iraqi population. We
will help them in the process. Consciously or unconsciously, that
is often wrongly understood. Certainly we wanted to export the

Iranian revolution. But by that we did not mean that in various countries we want to try to put a group to our liking in power, the way the superpowers and imperialists do. We are solely concerned with presenting Iran as an example and pointing out the routes of liberation, but in the process the people of the respective countries should make the decisions. They should orient themselves by how the Iranians were prepared to sacrifice themselves for their religion and to accept martyrdom in the bargain. First it is necessary to combat the ruling system, and then to build up a new Islamic system. That is what we hope for in the entire Islamic world, because religion is the strongest force. If all Muslims unite with its help, they will become an enormous political power that will mainly achieve independence!"

"I have been told that it is precisely this attitude that produces conflicts with the neighboring countries in the Gulf region. How do you see these relations?"

"The principles of our foreign policy are not unknown: anyone who recognizes and accepts basic rights, anyone who recognizes our territory and our Iranian system and does not attack us will also be accepted by us and will not be attacked. Iran has no territorial interest in the nations on the Gulf. Not an inch of our neighbors' ground interests us."

"Then what about what happened in Bahrain in December 1981?"

"We issued a denial that we had anything to do with it. It is utter nonsense that the Iranian government sent groups for the purpose of causing or starting a revolution or a coup there. That is absurd. That is not how we envision the export of our revolution."

"Under what conditions would Iran make use of petroleum as a weapon?"

"That I cannot say. I want only to mention this much, that our own petroleum was once used as a weapon against us. That was in 1953. Why should we not some day do what the Americans did to us? In general, though, we do not go into detail about that."

"How do you see the role of women in Islamic society? Has anything in your attitude and in their situation changed since the revolution?"

"In contrast to the antagonistic slogans, in general I am unable to find any difference between men and women in Islamic society. Concerning vocational training and occupation, study, or activity outside the home, I see no restriction for women. You yourself have surely seen that our women have more rights and tasks today than in the past era. In addition to their strong socio-political involvement, they even receive military police training. They are also permitted to be elected."

"One more thing: is the chador *still an object of contention?"*

"The *chador* is a non-Islamic, ancient Iranian custom. In contrast to the practice of covering one's head, there are no rules for wearing it. And that, too, should by no means debase the woman; on the contrary, it should work to her advantage."

"What is your attitude toward contraceptive devices and the birth-control pill?"

"In general that is not permitted unless the mother's life is in danger. But that can only be judged by an expert."

"What about science and culture? Are there restrictions in these fields that derive from Islamic law?"

"There is no restriction on science and culture in present-day Iran. Without any reservations, the door is open for the progress of science in all branches and directions. Everything that occurs in the service of mankind is fostered without any restrictions. That also applies to art. Radioactivity, for example, is a splendid tool when it is a matter of producing energy, combatting disease, and curing people. But if it is used for making bombs, then that is the worst thing there is."

"Does Iran reject nuclear weapons?"

"We are not thinking about producing anything inhuman. But let us remain in the realm of science and culture. At all levels our efforts are 'Ebadeh,' which is how a prayer or a pilgrimage is evaluated. The Prophet said: 'An hour of reflection is worth more than sixty years of prayer.' "

"It is always said that Iran oppresses its political and religious minorities. Is that true?"

"Our constitution recognizes the Jewish and Christian minority and the ancient Persian sect of Zarathustra. In keeping with the constitution, religious minorities have a free hand in the practice of their religious duties and commands. The political groupings are permitted to assert their interests at any time, but only at the political level. If they resort to action and, for example, want to change the system by the use of force, then they are fought by us, regardless of their religion or race. Anyone who fights against the interests of the Islamic world and against Islamic principles must be opposed."

21

And Tomorrow the Entire Islamic World

IT IS A FRIDAY MORNING in Tehran, a national holiday. For hours the streets around the university have been blocked off by the police. No car that could hold a bomb or an assassin can get through, and only authorized armed persons are permitted near the center of learning. From the south of Tehran and villages from the surroundings, dozens of special buses have been bringing in masses of people. Many also arrive by public buses and taxis. Children and young people march in step for the last 300 feet. Their destination is the Friday prayer service, the largest and most important in the entire Islamic Republic of Iran.

The Friday prayer takes place once a week in place of the noon prayer, and Muslims consider it their duty to participate in this religious service. Since ancient times, those who lead the Friday prayer—the caliphs, imams, and sheiks—use this opportunity to be able to speak to a majority of their subjects. In a long prayer (*khutba*), the high dignitaries (*hatib*)—holding a staff or a weapon —discuss war and peace, social questions, and perspectives on the future. The Friday prayer has always fulfilled the purpose of informing the faithful about secular matters, as well as praising God. It is precisely in the Friday prayer service that the character of Islam and the combination of faith and politics fostered by it becomes clear.

In a revolutionary society such as that in Iran it is a matter of course that the Friday preacher agitate the masses. In Tehran the event, in which 100,000 people participate, starts with someone who animates the crowd by providing slogans that are then repeated by the masses, who rhythmically beat with their fists on their chests while shouting: "Down with America! Down with Saddam! To hell with him! Long live Khomeini! He is our leader! *Allah-u-Akhbar! Allah-u-Akhbar!*"

That lasts approximately twenty minutes. I am able to observe the increasing agitation of the men within the first fifty rows, which are protected from the sun. This communal experience causes them to fall into a kind of trance. Many hold up Khomeini posters showing front-page newspaper headlines celebrating the Iranian advance into Iraq. In the first rows in front of a stage that is used as a pulpit, there are many young men in wheelchairs or on stretchers—the wounded from the war now in progress. Almost the entire cabinet of Prime Minister Hussein Musavi and a series of high-ranking guests from friendly states are in places reserved for guests of honor. All are sitting on the ground on the university playing field.

Parliamentary President Hojjat al-Islam Akbar Hashemi Rafsandjani's entourage arrives. He is riding in a bulletproof Mercedes limousine with tinted windows. Four strong bodyguards with high-caliber revolvers leap out of his limousine and the following car and accompany the last survivor of the first post-revolutionary generation of Iranian politicians to the stage. Other guards of Rafsandjani in clerical garb—*galabia*, turban, and *aba* (the black robe of the *mullah*)—spread out to strategically favorable positions. These days it is dangerous to hold an important office in Iran—another sign of how little established the Khomeini regime is. The idea of the Islamic Republic itself is stable and entrenched among the faithful masses, but its propagandists rarely die in bed. For this reason, the politicians leading the country tend to be younger than their predecessors. Imam Khomeini has only managed thus far to survive the system built up by him by never appearing in public and by living completely closed off from the world.

The scene is framed by banners. On one, for example, is written: "You Palestinians, be sure that neither West nor East will help you." Another reads: "We have arrived in Iraq not for the purpose of occupying the country but of liberating it." Beside it is written: "Our feelings are for Allah, and we are fighting only for Allah. This war is between Islam and the devil. That is a religious command. All Muslims must fight against the devil." Hojjat al-Islam Rafsandjani also hammers that in: "When we fight, we fight only for peace." And yet he speaks with extreme aggression, interrupted by shouts, "Allah is great." In Iran that means agreement. "We are so close to Basra," he continues, "that any day now we could fight with 10,000 grenades, but we do not want to do that. . . . Egypt and Jordan are supporting Iraq. We have only Allah. You states on the Gulf, if you help Iraq, you too will die. When we have conquered Iraq, the same thing is going to happen to Israel. That will be our bridge. . . . First there must be free elections in Iraq without any intervention by the East or the West." In the first row a middle-aged man enthusiastically nods in agreement: it is Sayid Bagher al-Hakim, the son of the deceased Iraqi Shiite leader Ayatollah Muhsin al-Hakim. The Khomeini regime has chosen him to rule Iraq as an Islamic republic after it is freed of Saddam Hussein.

Parliamentary President Rafsandjani ends his one-and-a-half hour speech, which he delivered in the Persian language, with a shortened version in Arabic, since the broadcast is transmitted live by Iranian television to the Gulf states. Through my translator, I learn that Rafsandjani demanded revolt against the governments in the Emirates that betrayed Islam, and that he also engaged in a polemic against the Saudis. With clenched fists, men and women alternate in shouts of "Allah-u-Akhbar."

In a "message to the noble and oppressed Iraqi people and to the peoples of other Islamic countries, particularly the sheikhdoms in the region," Imam Ruhollah Mussavi Khomeini asserts:

You and we have heard that in the war between Islam and the concealment of truth, many sheikhdoms along the Gulf and several Islamic countries have decided in favor of the concealment of truth and will provide military and propaganda assistance to the corrupt and criminal Baath government [of Iraq]. It is regrettable and astonishing that people who call themselves Muslim and want to be leaders of Islamic countries act against Islam and the holy Koran. I am warning them to stay away from the opposition against Islam and from taking sides in favor of concealing the truth. They should fulfill their human and Islamic duty and not play with fate. . . . I am warning the Islamic countries not to oppose Islam.

A clear statement by the revolutionary leader, one of many that has justly caused anxiety among the neighbors to the west and south. The signs are increasing that Iran wants to use fire and the sword to propagate within the entire region the Islam that it considers true: tomorrow the entire Islamic world is to be subjugated by the radical Khomeini regime.

The Gulf war with the hated neighbor on the other side of the Shatt el-Arab would be merely the beginning. Khomeini has proclaimed that the long-term goal is the reconquest of Jerusalem:

No Muslim can remain indifferent if Islam and its holy sites are threatened by invasion. And at a time when Israel is massacring innocent, homeless Muslims, the rulers in the region have only uttered empty words and conciliatory statements. And it is even more tragic that they seek protection from the threat by Israel in the arms of the U.S.A., as if in the flight from a snake they would seek refuge with a dragon. As earlier stated by the Islamic Republic of Iran, it can do nothing but first conquer Iraq and bring about the end of Baath rule. If Iran's demands are fulfilled, then more than at present it will help the Arab governments in their war against Israel and welcome the opportunity to fight as a powerful Muslim nation with other countries in the region against Israel.

The causes of this murderous war go back a long way. For generations the Iraqis and the Persians have disputed territorial rights to the Shatt el-Arab. In 1848 the border was shifted to the east side by the Ottoman Empire. Consequently, the Persians were forced to travel through Arab territory when using this waterway. Shah Reza Pahlevi was the first ruler to change this situation. In 1975 he forced Iraq's Saddam Hussein to recognize the middle of the waterway as the boundary, and in return Iran ceased delivering weapons to the rebellious Kurds in northern Iraq.

Saddam Hussein was feeling in a very strong position in the fall of 1980 when Iran appeared to be weak as a result of being embroiled in revolutionary discord, so he abrogated the treaty and put his troops on the march. Baghdad demanded not only the entire Shatt el-Arab but also former Arab territories such as the Iranian petroleum supply area of Khusistan (Arabistan). Even at this point in time the attacker's first expectation was not ful-

filled. Saddam Hussein's troops soon came to a halt. The petroleum workers of Khusistan felt no solidarity with the Iraqis and
instead supported the *ayatollahs* of Tehran. Saddam Hussein
achieved precisely the opposite of the effect he had intended: he
stabilized the Khomeini regime. A wave of patriotism gripped the
country. While the armed forces were tied up at the front lines,
Khomeini was gradually able to eliminate internal opposition. At
the same time, the Iranian economy recovered. The flow of oil
filled the treasury, annually providing funds of approximately 12
million dollars for the war.

The Gulf war began on September 22, 1980. In a surprise attack
the Iraqis occupied 4,126 square miles of Iranian territory. But in
late December the offensive was slowed down. The first counterattack by the Iranians, which occurred in January 1981, was a
failure. In contrast, the counteroffensive in March was all the
more successful. With three large offensives between November
1981 and May 1982, the Iranians almost completely forced their
opponents back from the border, and subsequently there was a
stalemate. The antagonists piled up huge earth parapets and dug
trenches. The comparison with the lengthy trench warfare between 1914 and 1918 is compelling.

The Iranians constructed broad roads that end along the 744-
mile front. Signs at regular intervals show that Kerbala, the Iraqi
shrine of the Shiites, is "not much farther." The *mullahs* provided
the slogan, "The road to Jerusalem is via Baghdad." With legions
of volunteers, including boys and elderly men, they have repeatedly been trying to go this route since mid-1982. In February and
in April 1983 Iran conducted major offensives in the region of Al
Amarah. At the end of July 1983, the next wave occurred in Meh-
ran, which is southwest of Kermanshah, and another in October
along the northern section. In February and March 1984, the Iranians attacked in five zones of the front simultaneously. All these
offensive operations were accompanied by a great number of Iranian casualties and never resulted in a real breakthrough. It is
said that lightly armed commandos were the only ones that managed to get in the vicinity of the strategically important Baghdad-
Basra highway. It would probably be decisive for the war if the
Persians were to succeed in cutting off this lifeline.

In the fourth year and after approximately a half million deaths
as well as six hundred thousand wounded, the Gulf war escalated
in a surprising manner. Iraqi units that were cornered used poi-

sonous gas to stop the fanatical Khomeini supporters. When after months there was proof that this proscribed way of waging war had been used, the leadership of the army conceded the truth of the accusation. Major General Mahed Abel El Rashid, commander in chief of the Iraqi southern sector, stated that he "justified any means to destroy the vermin."

The regime of Saddam Hussein, heavily in debt as a result of the war, also resorted to naval war in the spring of 1984. To impede the export of petroleum from Iran and to provoke Tehran, Iraqi fighter planes attacked a large number of tankers and freighters approaching the Iranian oil terminal on Kharg Island and the port of Bushir at the northern end of the Persian Gulf. President Saddam Hussein stated that in the future Iraq will also "attack any oil tanker in the war zone." Kharg Island, the source of petroleum, is situated in the war zone, which is determined by Baghdad. Iraq, frustrated by the months-old blockade of its own oil exports, managed within a short period of time to decimate Iranian exports by 55 percent.

In a public announcement Iran's President of Parliament Hashemi Rafsandjani threatened, "Either the Persian Gulf is secure for everyone or for no one." Twelve hours later Iran contributed to the general insecurity. Missiles fired from one of its F-4 fighter planes landed in tank number two of the Saudi Arabian supertanker *Yanbu Pride*. And that was not all. Iran, too, now conducted intensified naval warfare and attacked tankers of the Arab Gulf states. Tehran repeatedly threatened that if there were an Iraqi air attack against Kharg Island, the twenty-eight-mile-wide Strait of Hormuz at the foot of the Persian Gulf would be closed, interrupting international shipping.

Internationalization of the Gulf conflict seemed to be in the making. Behind the scenes, the U.S.A. and the Soviet Union agreed for the time being to maintain neutrality. President Reagan sent anti-aircraft missiles to Saudi Arabia. Insurance rates for tankers increased, and the price for petroleum also got out of balance. Japan, the main customer for petroleum from the Persian Gulf, stopped its tankers from sailing.

The Gulf war had become the most dangerous source of conflict in the world. In early June 1984, one of the most important American experts on the situation in the Middle East, Professor Zalmay Khalilzad of Columbia University in New York City, assured me, "The Iranians will not consent to any compromises and also will not seek any peace negotiation, as repeatedly proposed by the Iraqis. No one will be able to stop them as long as Khomeini is alive. Iran cannot lose the war, whereas Iraq can. Neither the Soviet Union nor the U.S.A. nor the Arab world wants to see Iran win, because that would have an incredible effect. It would destabilize the entire region. I believe that Khomeini's next holy crusade would not be Israel, as the propaganda from Tehran constantly attempts to make us believe, but would be the Gulf. The Saudis were even willing to pay as much as thirty billion dollars if Iran would end the war. If Iran were to conquer Iraq, even a doubling of this offer would no longer help them."

While the battle against the West is conducted on the offensive and with much propaganda, "five columns" are marching into the extremely sensitive Gulf nations and inciting the Shiites there. They have already attempted once to come to power through a coup in a country on the other side of the Persian Gulf: in Bahrain in December 1981. Further details about the coup are treated as hot coals; what happened is veiled in secrecy in the entire region of the Gulf, ostensibly to protect against imitators.

Bahrain, a former British colony, is an archipelago of thirty-three islands, twenty-five miles from the Saudi Arabian coast. The population of Bahrain is 400,000, half of whom are poor Shiites, the other half the ruling Sunnis—which leads to tensions. Only the influential Persian minority of approximately 7,000 has managed to carve out a key position within the structure of the state. The Shiites in Bahrain are extremely devout and interpret the Koran much more narrowly than the ruling Sunnis. In the small sheikhdom, religious legitimization is in the opposition.

At present the Khalifa family holds power; traditionally it has maintained good relations with Saudi Arabia, which is extremely orthodox. The emir is Isa Ibn Sulman Al Khalifa; his son, the crown prince, is minister of defense. Almost half of the cabinet is related to the emir. Although during the 1970s there were merely demands made on the ruling family for increasing democratization, the situation changed drastically in 1979. The successful Iranian revolution was a source of fascination among simple believers across the Gulf. The Bahrainis were receptive and started to organize. The first test of strength with the government took place in August 1979, when approximately 1,500 Shiites demonstrated in the old bazaar of the capital city of Manama. In response, a Shiite sheikh was expelled from the country in October. Since that time there have repeatedly been smaller acts of protest and opposition by the state until Ayatollah Husseinali Montazeri and Ayatollah Sadegh Ruhani in Tehran summarily pronounced the emir of Bahrain to be corrupt and declared the country "the fourteenth province of Iran." While the fighters in the newly founded People's Liberation Movement for the Gulf trained in camps in northwestern Iran, South Yemen, and Libya, the discontented Bahrainis gathered new strength with Iranian help. Finally in December 1981, at the time of the turmoil in Poland and the annexation of the Golan Heights by the Israelis, they attacked without being noticed in the rest of the world. The first reference to the coup in Bahrain appeared on December 16, in the local newspaper *Akhbar al-Chalidsh*. The talk was of fifty-three arrested, mostly Bahrainis who reputedly attempted to take over the government offices and seize the ministers. From governmental sources it leaked out that the conspirators had been trained and armed in Iran by an organization called the Islamic Front for the Liberation of Bahrain.

For months that was the only official statement. Only on May 3 did Prime Minister Sheikh Khalifa Ibn Sulman Al Khalifa of Bahrain consent to be interviewed by Jonathan Wallace, the publisher of the London-based *Middle East Economic Digest*:

We uncovered this plot, which was supported by a foreign power and organized by other countries. We are very happy about having been able to catch the subversives in time. They could not have been dangerous to us, but since we are not accustomed to such things we had to react forcefully this time. But that is not to say that nothing serious for Bahrain was at issue in this incident. For this reason, we could not permit it to continue or to reoccur. We believe that, with the help of neighboring countries, we have gained better information about the events in this region and that we also were able to find out who is sowing discontent in our countries.

Who do you think is behind the discontent?
We have said enough about the country behind these people, because from the beginning we knew that there were training camps in the neighboring country. They were established for the purpose of spreading discontent in the countries on the Gulf. This intention has already been put into action not only in Bahrain but in all the nations on the Gulf.

What are the consequences of this incident? Are there now better security measures?
Yes, we have strengthened our security. But when you look around here, you will notice that Bahrain has the fewest security measures of

any country in the Gulf region. Naturally what happened in December shocked everyone, because no one expected it. People still do not understand how close the island was to a catastrophe. For this reason, security was strengthened, and we will continue to improve it, because we are still at the beginning.

Only Western intelligence services and experts on questions of security in the Gulf were granted insight into the events of December 1981. According to these sources, a group of approximately 130 extremely well-armed men, under the leadership of the Iranian Hojjat al-Islam Hadi Modarresi, attempted to occupy key positions of Manama—ministries, radio and television stations, the emir's palace. Tht failed only because a short time before information about the planned Iranian attack had been provided by the secret service. A conspirator who was arrested in the United Arab Emirates stated that Tehran had delivered the necessary travel documents, plane tickets, and money. At the head of the guerrillas was a Khomeini representative who had been expelled from Bahrain.

In any case, seventy-three men were arrested, including forty-five Bahrainis and twelve Saudis. The majority of the survivors of the strong counterattack by Bahraini troops and their British ex-colonialist officers escaped by boat across the Persian Gulf to Iran. Saudi Minister of the Interior Prince Naif Ibn Abd el-Aziz, a very well-informed man, stated: "The act of sabotage was hatched by the Iranian government and was directed against Saudi Arabia." A surprisingly clear and unusual statement in diplomatic circles, particularly in the Arab world. That must have stirred up the displeasure of the Saudis, who are famous for their secret diplomacy. There was also immediately an offer from Riad to the emir of Bahrain to send troops. Prince Naif personally flew to the east coast to meet with his colleague Sheikh Mohammed Ibn-Khalifa. At this meeting he promised extensive aid. After signing an agreement to that effect, Prince Naif told reporters: "The security agreement made today will regulate relations between the ministers of the interior and the security authorities of Bahrain and Saudi Arabia." Prince Naif also expressed the hope that the other Gulf states would participate in the agreement.

A few days later a discussion was started about the founding of a rapid deployment force based on the American model. Everywhere in the region politicians indicated that it was advisable to work more closely with the superpower Saudi Arabia. Only by these measures would it be possible to keep Iranian aggression from breaking apart, piece by piece, the front made up of the neighboring countries. The investigations and the trial against the captured conspirators lasted for months. Among Near East experts in London there was even at times talk to the effect that 1,000 had been arrested, but that was decisively denied by Bahrain's Prime Minister Sheikh Khalifa Ibn Sulman Al Khalifa. He seemed to be satisfied, however: "We also know everything about the ones who escaped. We have their names and know where they are staying."

The emissaries of the Iranian revolution were locked up in Bahrain's most secure prison, on the eastern side of the main island, in a village by the name of Jau; it was there that the trial by the supreme court took place. Ultimately only two of the conspirators were accused of being agents of a foreign power. From all appearances, these were the contact men to Tehran. The proceedings progressed slowly, however, because on the first day of the trial the defense requested a two-week delay to become more familiar with the details. On April 5, the defense requested doctors who would be able to estimate the ages of the accused. In many countries of the Third World it is not yet customary to have births registered, and any guerrilla under eighteen could not be brought before court. The Bahrain opposition advised, however, that the task of the team of doctors should be to determine whether the prisoners had been tortured. The supreme court rejected the request, and the government confirmed that none of the accused was under twenty years of age.

Ahmed Ben Bella, chairman of the International Islamic Commission for Human Rights, tried, through a letter to the emir of Bahrain, to exert influence on the decision of the court. Ben Bella complained about the absolute secrecy of the proceedings, considering it dangerous that under an existing law it was possible to pronounce a collective death sentence, and maintaining that a trial conducted behind closed doors could not be considered legal by public opinion. Ben Bella demanded more rights for the defendants and requested permission to send an international commission of Muslim attorneys to Bahrain.

This attempt had little effect, so the trial continued without observers. On May 23, 1982, the sentence was pronounced. An announcement by the news agency of the Gulf states stated that three of the accused had been sentenced to arrest for life;

the other seventy had to spend seven to fifteen years in prison. The verdict for all of them mentioned "preparation of a coup." The grounds of the court's opinion were never published.

In connection with the trial, the death of five of seventy-three of the accused became known. Unconfirmed reports spoke of death resulting from severe injuries caused by torture by the secret police. The government of Bahrain reputedly stated that there was a separate trial against these five men. They had been condemned to death and were then executed. That, too, is an unconfirmed report. *Crescent International*, the news magazine of the Islamic movement, subsequently threatened in a lead article: "Those in power should keep in mind that their present manner of 'justice' can be regarded tomorrow as a 'crime,' and there will be no escape from the mills of divine justice. The trial in Bahrain is more for the purpose of assuring the future of the government there than of taking into consideration the fate of the seventy-three accused of conspiracy. Rulers all over the world should keep in mind that those who fear Allah have no fear of death!"

The Iranian reproaches against Bahrain are identical with the accusations of all fundamentalists against those nations in the region having a modern structure. Bahrain has replaced Beirut as the banking center of the Middle East because of the civil war that has been raging in Lebanon since the mid-1970s. The fifty-eight banks located offshore—in which the Saudis are heavily involved—show a balance of $45 billion. Since the destruction of the Iranian Abadan, Bahrain's refinery is the largest in both the Near and the Middle East. There are movie houses and discothèques, and 100,000 foreign experts have been in key positions there, providing important services, since the 1973 oil boom. In terms of liberalization and Westernization, that is more than strict Islamic movements can bear.

Once the Muslim Brotherhood has its bases and sources of money among the wealthy people in the East—in other words, in Saudi Arabia and its neighbors (especially Kuwait)—the organization takes heed of realities and issues only guarded reproaches about the oil sheikhs' addiction to show and loose living. The situation is different, though, for the old imam from Ghom, who need not display any caution and who everywhere finds broad support among the underprivileged. Khomeini and his supporters are giving a new interpretation to their victory

over Shah Mohammed Reza Pahlevi, who was considered undefeatable by the whole world; they see it as their just claim to
spiritual and political domination in the entire Muslim world. For
this reason, the further course of the war started by the Iraqi
attack on Shatt el-Arab is increasingly becoming a proxy war in
defense of the entire Arab world, which feels threatened by Khomeini. Iraq is supposed to divert the danger forthcoming from
Iran from the other countries.

The first step taken against the threat posed by Tehran was
made on May 25, 1981, in Abu Dhabi, when the president of the
United Arab Emirates, Sheikh Zayed Ibn Sultan al-Nayhan,
opened the first summit meeting of the six conservative Arab Gulf
states, which was to lead to the founding of the Gulf Council of
Cooperation. The lords of immeasurable oil deposits and finances
sat down together at the round table and complained about the
unpredictable Khomeini. In addition, they were uneasy about
the Soviet invasion of Afghanistan. After detailed discussions,
the rulers of the Gulf countries decided to create a council for
cooperation (no bloc and no alliance) in political, economic, military, and cultural affairs. To pacify the radical Arabs, it was expressly agreed that this new union was merely "one more step
toward Arab unity" and toward independence from Western
powers.

King Khalid of Saudi Arabia, Emir Jaber al Ahmad of Kuwait,
Sheikh Khalifa Ibn Hamad of Qatay, Emir Isa Ibn Sulman of Bahrain, Sultan Qabus Ibn Said of Oman, and Emir Zayed Ibn Sultan
of the United Arab Emirates, participated in the meeting. They
were clad in their traditional garments—Sheikh Qabus in a colorful turban, King Khalid and the emirs of the Gulf states in white
dish-dasha head-coverings, held in place by the black *agal*, and
floor-length white garments with a brown and gold-braided border. A typical Arab contrast was that with their heavy gold wristwatches, gold chains, and rings with precious stones, they wore
simple leather sandals.

As already agreed in February 1981, at the Islamic summit conference in the Saudi Arabian city of Taif, the six heads of state
placed their signatures on a charter that provides for a "high
council," the highest body of the Gulf region, to which all prime
ministers belong. Under it is the council of the six foreign ministers, to which a minister who is an expert can be called in if
needed. The former Kuwaiti ambassador to the United Nations,

Abdullah Jaqub Bishara, was appointed general secretary of the Council of Cooperation, which had been set up in Riad.

"The baby has just been born, it just does not have any teeth yet," Bishara announced right after his appointment. Probably true, for although the 100,000 soldiers of the armies consolidated in the Council of Cooperation are equipped with the most modern equipment, their fighting strength is questionable. Key positions within the six armies are still held by Jordanian and Pakistani pilots, British officers, Indians, and Jordanians. Only in late January 1982 were the defense ministers of the six threatened nations far along enough to agree in Jiddah about common defense measures against enemies from without. There was talk of a joint air defense, collective weapons purchases, and joint efforts in weapons production. The defense budget of the six Gulf states at that time was $30.6 million. Spokesmen then opposed "the Iranian attempts at undermining the security of Bahrain."

Meanwhile the Iranians across the Gulf perked up their ears. It was clear that the Arab neighbors could only feel themselves acutely threatened. At the Friday prayer services President Ali Khamenei warned the neighbors on the Gulf that were in the process of arming themselves against continuing "to disturb the quiet in the region," stating that Iran was far and away the strongest power and would not tolerate having any other Gulf country take over the role of policeman. Secretary General Bishara fired back: "We neither are nor wish to be in the position of playing the role of policeman on the Gulf. The stability of the Gulf region cannot be achieved without the cooperation of all nations on the Gulf, including Iran and Iraq. Even if we wanted to, we are not so presumptuous as to take over the Shah's role as policeman on the Gulf. The Shah lost, because this task was too great for him."

The ideological tiff continued in newspaper articles and broadcasts. After the Gulf Council on Cooperation had become necessary because of the Iraq-Iran war, all attention was on events in Tehran. People realized that the Iranians repeatedly helped their Shiite brothers on the Arab peninsula in creating unrest, that they agitated among the oil workers in the eastern part of Saudi Arabia, as well as among the faithful in Mecca and Medina. Saudi soldiers frequently had to use their clubs against Iranian pilgrims. In recent years Persian pilgrims were stopped at the border of Saudi Arabia because they had brought with them large quantities of propaganda material in support of the Islamic revolution.

Since Imam Khomeini came to power, the people of the Gulf states have again had to become accustomed to a stricter Islamic lifestyle. In Dubai the *zakat,* or alms tax, was reintroduced by law. Kuwait promised a reform of textbooks and the introduction of Islamic law. Alcohol is now also extensively banned. But that is not enough for Khomeini. Immediately after his return to Iran, he renewed the territorial demand previously made by the Shah for the oil sheikhdoms of Bahrain and Qatar. Khomeini's original tone: "The despotic governments will learn a lesson from the Iranian revolution." His designated successor, Ayatollah Montazeri, formulated the famous and notorious statement: "Iran will export its revolution to all Islamic countries."

Khomeini created unrest in what was previously a functional coexistence between Sunnis and Shiites in Arab countries. Everywhere he appointed Shiite clergy to be his "personal deputies" without recognition by their host countries. One of them, Hojjat al-Islam Hadshi Sayid Abbas from Kuwait, was arrested after giving rabble-rousing speeches in a mosque and expelled from the country with seventeen of his followers. In this country with the highest per capita income in the world, the Shiite minority constitutes thirty percent of the population (in other words, 400,000); 25,000 of them are Iranian. The Gulf war heightened domestic political tensions, since the Shiites were on Iran's side, while the Sunnis and the leadership of the country supported Baghdad.

During the Gulf war the Iranians several times used bombers to attack petroleum facilities in the vicinity of the northern border-crossing of al-Abdali, the checkpoint for traffic to Iraq. At the beginning of the war, a large part of Iraq's imports was in fact destroyed not in the Iraqi harbor of Basra but in Kuwait. Tehran warned the Gulf states several times that any support of Iran's opponent in war would be answered by force of weapons, and he kept his word. The Kuwait daily newspaper *Al Anba* answered sharply: "The fate of the Shah should be a lesson, but not for us. In our stable homeland there are no butchers, no hangmen, and no torture chambers. We do not slit open anyone's stomach, we do not cut off the heads of our prisoners, and we do not slaughter any children. We hope that the fate of the Shah will be a lesson to those who, as the result of his fall, perhaps inherited his regal mentality but not his throne and his awards."

The extremely sensitive reminder arrived in Kuwait on December 12, 1983. At 12:30 A.M. local time a truck loaded with explo-

sives broke through the barriers at a side entrance of the
American embassy in Kuwait. The suicide terrorist exploded his
heavy cargo, causing the collapse and burning of a part of the
building. The wave of pressure also damaged neighboring houses
and the Hilton Hotel opposite the embassy. Additional car-
bombs, this time guided by remote control, went off a short while
later at the French embassy, at the control tower of the new
international airport, in one of the housing compounds inhabited
by American military advisers, at the oil refinery in the suburb of
Shuweiba, and at the Ministry of Irrigation.

A total of seven persons were killed and eighty-four wounded.
Material damage was significant. As usual, Iran denied having
any part in the attacks, and Radio Iran stated that the attempt to
credit Iran for the deed was part of a large-scale plot against the
Islamic revolution by the U.S.A. and its henchmen. At the same
time, however, further attacks by Muslim terrorists against American and Israeli facilities in the Near East were expected. Iran's
ambassador to the UN, Khorassani, stated that the U.S.A. and
Israel had bombarded civilian targets in Lebanon and must therefore anticipate "an additional punishment by the Lebanese Mohammedans and further revenge for the attacks against Lebanese
civilians." Both the U.S.A. and Iraq announced reprisals against
the perpetrators, who in all probability received their orders from
Tehran. The Kuwaiti security agency reacted swiftly and effectively. Fingerprints of the kamikaze driver were identified as
those of the twenty-five-year-old Raad Meftel Adshil from Iraq.
The police, assisted by a CIA unit that arrived immediately after
the series of bomb attacks, investigated everyone associated with
him. The Israeli secret service Mossad is reputed to have provided important clues.

Precisely two months later, twenty-two suspects were brought
to court, and an additional three suspects were tried in absentia.
According to the indictment, all were members of Bagher al-Hakim's underground organization Al Dawa ("The Call"), an Iraqi
group based in Iran. Most of them had come to Kuwait from Iran
after having smuggled their ammunition and a sizeable arsenal of
weapons across the Gulf by boat. All of the accused were Shiite
fundamentalists with the exception of the Lebanese Maronite and
explosives expert Elias Fuad Saad, who had been signed on as a
mercenary for this enterprise. In late March six of the accused
were condemned to death, seven were given lifetime sentences,

and seven were sentenced to prison for five to ten years. Five of the alleged perpetrators were let go.

Islamic Holy War, an organization that cooperates closely with the members of Al Dawa and even trains some of their suicide fighters in the same Iranian camps, promised bloody revenge on the Kuwaiti government. For a long time, however, in the entire Gulf region measures have been taken against sneak attacks. Following the most recent wave of bombings, the ruling Sunnis keep a more suspicious eye than ever on their Shiite minorities.

The increasing sympathies of the residents in the Gulf for the revolutionaries in Tehran has led to much reorientation of opinion in the Arab world. Old quarrels are put aside, and the new foe is jointly scrutinized. Since the coup attempt on Bahrain, the Jordanians and Egyptians have backed Iraq. Saudi Arabia had long been supporting Saddam Hussein with large sums of money. For the moderate countries, the specter of a unified fighting alliance between Shiites, Syrian Alawites, and Libya's Qaddafi has been making the rounds. Immediately after Sadat's death, therefore, there was a reconciliation between Jordan's King Hussein, Oman's Sultan Qabus, and the condemned Egypt now represented by Hosni Mubarak. After the death of King Khalid, Egypt and Saudi Arabia again drew closer together. As a Western diplomat in the Near East described the situation in the summer of 1982: "The Saudis are sitting there as if lamed, giving money to all sides and hoping that their hangmen can be bought. One of their greatest fears is the victory of Iran over Iraq. That would produce the conviction among simple Muslims that Allah had helped. And they will think that if we trust in Allah and return to the old values, then we will gain."

Khomeini is sending Iranian scholars to the universities in the Gulf region to invite students to Iran for further indoctrination. Students are permitted to visit Tehran without having their passports stamped as conspirators; there they are treated to festive hospitality and taken to cadre centers. An office of the government sees that contact is maintained after their return home. Children who are armed only with keys intended to open the doors of paradise are sent by Khomeini into Iraqi gunfire. In the name of Allah, Khomeini is out to conquer and destroy.

After the reconquest of the Iranian harbor city of Khorramshar, so decisive for the war, he reminded the Gulf neighbors: "You know today that our victorious government and nation speaks from a position of strength."

Khomeini also constitutes an extreme threat to the other oil countries through his aggressive oil price policy: Iran circumvents the prices established by the Organization of Petroleum Exporting Countries (OPEC) and sells what it can produce.

Against that, not even written protests by the foreign minister of the Gulf Council on Cooperation are of any help. After the Bahrain affair, they turned "against all terroristic activities of Iran that are directed toward influencing peace and stability as well as the expansion of confusion and chaos" in the region. "Each attack on one of the Gulf states would be considered as an attack on all its neighbors," it is stated in the joint declaration. One thing is certain: Imam Khomeini, who is repeatedly declared to be dead, will still be good for many surprises and will use guns and the Koran to export his revolution. Just as the devil fears holy water, the oil princes already have valid reasons for fearing Khomeini's attempts at expansion. And they would rather see the replacement of the dangerous mullahcracy in Tehran today than tomorrow, but there, too, only Allah can be of help to them.

On July 28, 1982, the lead article in the Tehran newspaper *Kayhan* stated:

The Islamic revolution and Imam Khomeini constitute a hope for the Islamic world, a hope for rescue and liberation from the satanic powers and their devilish agents who represent the illegal interests of the superpowers. All responsible officials in Iran who are concerned with the international relations of the Islamic revolution must assist the devoted Muslims and friends of Iran. Reports reaching us from many Islamic countries speak of strong pressures exerted by Muslims on their governments to be informed about Iran and the Islamic revolution.

And according to Principle 154 of the Constitution of the Islamic Republic of Iran:

The Islamic Republic of Iran regards the happiness of people in the entire human community as its ideal and recognizes independence, freedom, and the rule of law and of justice as a right of every person in the world. Although it refrains from any intervention into the internal matters of other nations, it supports the just battle of the oppressed against the oppressors all over the world.

22

Death to the Shurawi!

The continent of Asia is a living body.
The heart within this body is the people of Afghanistan.
The destruction of Afghanistan means the destruction of Asia.
Only as long as the heart can beat freely
Does the body remain free.

—MOHAMMED IQBAL

THE AMIR HAD ESCAPED a bombing plot only a few days before I met him. A messenger had entered the Fakir Abad from Peshawar, the capital of Pakistan's northwest border province, in order to deliver a small package containing a copy of the Koran. The amir was expected in this region, where he has his headquarters. Scouts had reported that the pages of the holy book had been torn out and fitted with an explosive, so the amir's people swung into action and detonated the lethal present. The fate of the person who delivered this dangerous surprise is unknown, but the amir asserted that he was in a Pakistani prison.

In a monotonous voice, one too soft for his imposing presence, my discussion partner indicates what is unavoidable: "That is what I have to live with. They have often tried to kill me by such means, and I am still living. Allah is with me."

"But aren't you afraid?" I ask.

"No," the Amir responds still more softly, "I only fear God, the Most Blessed, the Merciful One."

The amir is Golbuddin Hekmatyar, a man who rarely sleeps in the same bed for more than a few nights. He is considered one of the Soviet Union's most dangerous enemies, and his death would surely be greeted in the Kremlin with great relief. But, according to his own assertion, he is the leader of 110,000 freedom fighters (possibly as many as 170,000), and he knows how to protect himself. He lives in the border town of Peshawar, which is where we meet, long after the sun has gone down behind the repelling, bleak rocks of the mountains dividing Pakistan and Afghanistan. Security is extremely tight.

A tall, disciplined man with extremely sensitive, melancholy eyes sits opposite me. The ascetic is wearing the comfortable white garment of the Pashtoons and a warm gray jacket, for the nights in the mountains on the Afghanistan border are extremely cold. Hekmatyar's fine white face is framed by a thick, black full beard and the usual cap made of karakul lambskin. Born in 1948 and trained as an engineer, Hekmatyar answers my questions alternately in English and Pashtu. His smart right-hand man, Haji Mangal Hussian, serves as interpreter.

I start my interview by commenting: "In the Western countries we get an inadequate picture of Afghanistan, where a secret war is being waged that militarily is hardly comprehensible. It has already cost many millions of people their lives or has driven them from their homeland. This war is being waged by an unyielding, proud people against an invincible occupation power. How do you characterize your own people?"

"Our Afghan people believe in God," Hekmatyar replies. "The people know that their faith is capable of giving them much courage. The Afghans are a very dignified people, who can tolerate difficulties and endure oppression. They are unable to bear barbarism by foreigners or by their fellow countrymen."

"It is not only for nationalistic reasons that your people are fighting for their homeland," I comment. "In the name of Allah they are also waging a holy war against nonbelievers. Which is the more important factor?"

"Islam is a far-reaching religion that is practical for all areas of life," Hekmatyar explains. "It is closely related to our tradition and determines all our actions. Actually Islam is our tradition. We are guided by Islam, which determines our entire manner of action."

That was the picture when the wild area of Afghanistan be-

longed to the eastern Islamic kingdom. This remote, mountainous country is the connecting link between Persia and India. Until
the eighteenth century, it was the plaything of its neighbors and
a passageway in which foreigners never tarried for long. The
Durrani dynasty was the first to succeed in founding a national
state. Ahmad Shah Abdali (also called Durrani), an Afghan general under the Persian Shah Nadir, made himself independent
and started to unite the country's numerous tribes. In 1747 an
independent kingdom came into being, but the Afghans had not
anticipated the resistance of the colonial powers.

In 1837 to 1838 the British attacked from the east and from the
west, and the Afghan King Dost Mohammed found himself compelled to appeal to the Russians for help. These neighbors were
just in the process of annexing the Asian lands north of the Oxus
River, now called the Amu Darya (the present border) and expanding toward the warm sea in the south. The British acted
quickly, occupied Kabul with an expeditionary corps, and deposed Dost Mohammed. Since most of the tribes did not accept
Shah Shuja, who was appointed by England, an uprising against
the foreigners occurred in 1841. Immediately the British fought
back mercilessly, rehabilitated Dost Mohammed, and put him
back on the throne. When the Russians threatened Afghanistan
with increasing intensity, the British finally bought their political
ascendancy with money.

Only in the third war, in which the Afghan King Amanullah
announced that he wanted "to liberate India from the English,"
did the ruler regain independence for his country. He introduced
many reforms and created a state in the modern sense of the
word. Instead of a princedom determined by tribal rivalry, Afghanistan was now a commonwealth with ministries, foreign del-
egations, and its own army. In 1921 Amanullah made a treaty
with the newly founded Soviet Union, one that provided more
advantages with its neighbor to the north than with the British.
The Russians immediately exploited this situation by temporarily
occupying Afghan territory in 1925.

The conservative Muslims were not really pleased with Amanullah Shah. His attempt to foster the equality of women was
expressed by banning the veil. His economic innovations were
also rejected by the *ulema* and led in 1929 to his overthrow. A
bloody civil war ensued, which was finally ended by General
Mohammed Nadir, a relative of Amanullah. When he was mur-

dered in 1933, he was succeeded by his son Zahir Shah, who managed to remain on the throne until 1973. While he was away on a visit to Europe, his cousin, Prime Minister Mohammed Daoud, seized power and declared Afghanistan a republic.

Soviet influence increased steadily. Through generous financial aid, however, Pakistan and Iran led Mohammed Daoud to do an about-face. In the long run, though, leftist groups loyal to Moscow were unable to accept that, and discontent within the opposition increased. Daoud had in the meantime become a psychopath who impeded progress, and he fought back vigorously by having leftists sympathetic to Moscow arrested and murdered. In doing so, Mohammed Daoud overlooked the fact that the majority of the officer corps had been trained in the Soviet Union and effectively indoctrinated with communist ideas.

Daoud did not survive the coup by the leftist military in 1978. A revolutionary council came into being which appointed as head of state the leader of the formerly banned Democratic People's Party, Nur Mohammed Taraki. A friend of the Kremlin and an author, Taraki was merely thrust into the position. Real power was in the hands of Foreign Minister Hafizullah Amin, who later also held the office of prime minister. Taraki represented Moscow's interests in Afghanistan, had great numbers of Soviet military advisors brought into the country, and persecuted all political opponents with merciless cruelty. His policy roused the opposition of the influential Islamic clergy and the mountain tribesmen sympathetic to them. The government had few sympathizers outside the capital of Kabul.

Meanwhile the Islamic movement kept itself in readiness to have a say in the future development of Afghanistan and to accelerate the creation of an Islamic state. The revolutionary mood in neighboring Iran further strengthened the desires of the *ulema* for a theocracy. Until the 1940s, the Sunnis had played only a minor role as an effective organization. Several spokesmen acquired practice in defensive tactics, but only in the 1950s did the strength of the radical fundamentalists increase. This development was triggered by the acts of the strong Muslim Brotherhood in Egypt and by its affiliated organization in Pakistan, the Jamaat-e Islami.

Since this time, there have been close connections between the Muslim Brotherhood and Abul Ala Maududi's organization of discontented students in Kabul. During the '50s, Professor Ghulam Mohammed Niazi returned from studying Islamic literature at Azhar University in Cairo. Having become a member of the Muslim Brotherhood while in Egypt, Niazi brought to Kabul the ideas of Hassan al-Banna and Sayed Qutb—ideas unwelcome to governments in Islamic countries. Niazi started out by building up an organization based on the model provided by the Muslim Brotherhood. Through diligence, he managed to become the rector of the university. His followers held the view that he should devote himself entirely to teaching, so he resigned and appointed Ustaz Burhanuddin Rabbani, a professor of theology, as his successor.

Others in this puzzling, fantastic country attribute the origin of the Islamic fundamentalists to another Niazi—to Ustaz Abdul Rahim Niazi, who earned his degree in theology at the University of Afghanistan. According to plausible information given me, this Niazi invited seventy-five friends, mostly students, to the Polytechnic Institute and founded an organization named Muslim Youth. This same Niazi was poisoned in 1970 by the regime in Kabul and died in a hospital in New Delhi. The response to the return of his corpse to Kabul was mass demonstrations against the government of Zahir Shah. The Muslim Youth attracted many followers, and in that same year won the elections for the student council at the University of Kabul, thereby establishing the basis for the later Islamic Party (Hizb-e Islami). Their history is closely associated with the life of Golbuddin Hekmatyar.

Afghanistan's "Arafat," so to speak, was born in Wartaz Hazrat-Imam-Saheb. Hekmatyar relates:

It was a small mining village at the foot of the Hindu Kush in the province of Kunduz, eighteen miles from the Russian border. It consisted merely of a few yellow brick houses, like those in use here since time immemorial. Anyone who owned a herd of sheep in this arid landscape was considered a rich man. In those days, too, we kept a gun in the house, and it hung right above my father's bed. But at that time no one would have thought of using this weapon for anything but hunting.

After his graduation from secondary school in the provincial city of Kunduz, Hekmatyar began his preliminary studies in engineering in 1968 and was accepted by the technical faculty at the University of Kabul a year later. He stuck it out until the fourth semester, when the King's secret police arrested him as a notorious rabble-rouser and imprisoned him for eighteen months. Hekmatyar was always a leading member of the student government; with him as their leader, the Islamic students achieved a seventy percent majority in the student elections of 1973. Once again he was immediately put in prison, but this time only for a short period.

Documentation on the *mujahideen* of Afghanistan describes the early '60s and '70s as follows:

Since there was not yet any revolutionary organization capable of defending the Islamic faith, the role was taken over by many groups of youth, whose model was a Western or Eastern lifestyle, depending on their sympathies toward capitalism or communism. In contrast to other movements, however, the Islamic movement had assumed the task of liberating the Afghan people from the yoke of despotism and eliminating domination by either superpower.

Slowly the movement began to arm itself and to provide forceful opposition to the government, which even under Daoud's leadership was considered communist. Both sides exceeded each other in brutality. Daoud's secret police were increasingly concerned with the fundamentalists. Many were tortured in death in prison; others remained behind bars for years without being tried. Even holding meetings of more than five people was subject to punishment, so the Afghan division of the Muslim Brotherhood organized small, well-armed groups that suddenly popped up, attacked, and then vanished again into the underground.

Hekmatyar explained to me:

At that time, under the Daoud regime, there was only a single Islamic movement, our Hizb-e Islami. All other organizations had allied themselves with the government and had become very quiet; for this reason, our membership increased greatly. Many of our people were imprisoned, murdered, or became martyrs in the heavy fighting. The simple people recognized that only Hizb-e Islami was capable of getting rid of the criminal Daoud regime. Our *jihad* started with empty hands and the traditional old weapons of the *mujahideen*. Things were to develop in a way no one had expected.

After an attempted uprising in May 1974, Hekmatyar had to go underground. Wanted circulars by the thousands were posted in the country. The engineer was given refuge everywhere and protected from his persecutors. While he was in hiding, the whole country did everything to continue to build up the structure of Hizb-e Islami. Although the state authorities were unsuccessful in finding Hekmatyar, they arrested twenty-four other leading members of the Islamic movement. In the summer of 1976 they were condemned to death by a military court on grounds of "creating unrest and stirring up the people." The hangman only got three of them; the others were pardoned, but were later killed in their cells.

Hekmatyar went to the province of Paktia in the area bordering Pakistan and stayed there for some time. In 1975 he became leader of the armed resistance against the central government in Kabul. Along with Maulawi Habiburrahman, he took over responsibility for the military training of the freedom fighters in the remote, mountainous sections of eastern Afghanistan. The first battles took place in August 1975 in the provinces of Kunar, Jalalabad, Laghman, and Panjshir, where the capital remained in the hands of the *mujahideen* for a week. The government in Kabul, not yet accustomed to such strong resistance, suffered severe losses.

The discontent of the population provided a favorable base for the rebels. During the 1960s, living conditions in Afghanistan had worsened considerably. According to statements by the opposition, one-half million people were starving. Many emigrated to neighboring countries or sold their children to spare them death by starvation. Anyone familiar with the Oriental social system and the traditional attitude toward the family knows the significance of such a step. Under Daoud, prices and unemployment continued to rise, which could only be pleasing to Moscow, since the increasing dependence of the Afghans accelerated their takeover of the country.

Starting in 1975, the Islamic groups expanded the structure of their underground. From the outset, membership in Jamaat-e Islami and Hizb-e Islami was restricted, which let the followers of the two leaders, Golbuddin Hekmatyar and Ustaz Burhanuddin Rabbani, become a new religious elite. As with the Muslim Brotherhood, the restricted acceptance of members is an imperative for conspiratorial fighting. The members of Hizb-e Islami are divided into four categories: the first group is called "organ," followed by "members," "promoters," and "sympathizers." The first two levels elect the members of the internal leadership body and the general assembly. Only the first category elects the amir, the highest leader. The organization is democratically structured, with executive committees, counseling bodies, and a secretary general. The same applies to the twenty-eight provinces, which are divided into 216 districts. For basic decisions the amir calls on the counseling committees, whose chairmen he himself appoints. Each guerrilla group has an amir, his deputy (the *mawayn*), and a military "commander."

But even today the two most important Islamic groups, particularly the Hizb-e Islami, pursue a course strictly guided by that of the Muslim Brotherhood of Egypt. In the basic programs it is stated that the rise of the Afghanistan group is due to a turning away from the true Islam and could be suspended only by the creation of the caliphate. The Jamaat-e Islami voices the same idea in its manifesto: "Our beloved Afghanistan is and will remain an Islamic country forever. The realization of Islam in this country is our highest goal and our holy duty. We will fight for that until victory. We will oppose every attempt to destroy the Islamic character of our country."

The basic position of Hizb-e Islami is: "When the sun of Islam illuminated all social, cultural, educational, moral, and ethnic aspects of human existence, its radiation also penetrated our homeland Afghanistan and awakened in us the sense for justice and the right to conditions worthy of human beings." Particularly "in times of tyranny and barbarism, in the darkness of exploitation and of colonialism," Islam is the only route to justice.

The Hizb-e Islami is also committed to combatting socialism, atheism, a one-sided materialistic attitude, corruption, and every form of immorality. But only with reluctance do the representatives of the Islamic party, particularly Hekmatyar, express the details of the religious state they are striving for. If pressed, the only answer they ever give is: "Islam is our model. If you read the Koran carefully, then you know the future form of our Islamic state. All that is very clear for us Muslims and need not be explained in detail."

In response to my question, "Would you want to adopt the Iranian model?" Hekmatyar said; "Our brothers in Iran are trying to live Islam, but the situation in that country cannot be compared to ours. There are certain differences."

The differences between the two societal models are probably slight, since the revolutionary regime of Iran supported the Afghan resistance from the beginning. In the headquarters of the *mujahideen*, I saw numerous Khomeini posters and placards with statements of the imam. In turn I saw posters of Rabbani and Hekmatyar, particularly the latter, in the streets of Tehran. One-and-a-half million people from Afghanistan have fled to Iran. The majority of them are working there, and a small number live in refugee camps. With the support of the Iranian government, many of the Afghan men are given training and sent back to the guerrilla war. These measures of assistance have been played down in Iran, dampening the love for the Islamic brothers in Afghanistan and sometimes reducing revolutionary zeal to mere lip service.

It is difficult to find out why Golbuddin Hakmatyar resigned in 1976. He justifies this step by pointing to the legal obstacles that were in the way of his leadership. Qazi Mohammed Amin, the former secretary general, became his successor, but he was not able to override tribal rivalries, which are particularly extreme in Afghanistan. In 1978, attempts were made to unite all Muslim groups into one fighting unit under joint leadership. That was not possible with Qazi Mohammed Amin as leader, though, since his capacities were still contested by many of the group's allies; all he could do was resign. The members of Hizb-e Islami again elected Golbuddin Hekmatyar their amir in December 1978; Amin remained second in command.

In the meantime the wheel of Afghan history has ineluctably continued to turn. Mohammed Daoud was overthrown on a Thursday afternoon, April 27, 1978. Hours later Radio Kabul announced: "For the first time in the history of Afghanistan, the last remains of monarchy, tyranny, despotism, and the power of the old dynasty of the tyrant Nadir Shah has ended. Power is in the hands of the revolutionary council of the armed forces." Three days later the Democratic Republic of Afghanistan was proclaimed. For the first time the name of the new strong man was heard internationally: Nur Mohammed Taraki. He called his deed "true revolution."

The list of ministers, published on May 1, 1978, showed Taraki as prime minister and Hafizullah Amin as his deputy and foreign minister. Another deputy of the prime minister was Babrak Karmal. Together with the army, they had carried out the coup—at the behest of the Russians. Daoud was not to the Kremlin's liking because in the last year of his administration he had been strikingly friendly toward Islam. There was no danger of such an attitude among the new group in power, however. Taraki immediately set about realizing his conception of a secular state. A radical program of land reform caused the peasants to revolt against the government. The group loyal to Moscow also started to revamp the educational system and to make provisions for girls to attend school. Such a reform went against the grain of the tribal leaders, and they withheld their approval. In their eyes, instruction by male teachers for the daughters of the tribe is more than immorality—it is a sin against God and incompatible with the teachings of the Koran.

Mohammed Daoud's National Revolutionary Party, merely a pseudo-democratic display, was totally dispensed with and replaced by Taraki's Democratic People's Party. Founded in late 1964, it had been an unimportant factor until the coup of 1978; it had also split into two factions: Parcham and Khalq. Taraki and Amin governed Khalq, while Karmal and his companion Dr. Anahita Ratibzad ruled Parcham. It was only their agreement on joint Moscow-oriented goals that created the basis for the coup.

The first ten months of the new administration passed relatively quietly, as Hekmatyar, Rabbani, and the other religious leaders first had to adjust to the new situation. The regime received no support from the country's population, but it was also no longer the target of attack. The party in power had its hands full with fighting within the ranks. The Khalq clan managed to exclude the Parcham people, while within his own group Amin tested the revolt against Taraki. In the border section near Pakistan, traditional unrest increased among the Baluchi and the Pashtoons. The Iranian revolution caused relations between the two neighboring countries to deteriorate into an attack. In addition, Iran expelled Afghan migrant laborers by the hundreds of thousands—another blow for the lagging economy of Afghanistan.

At this point in time, activity among the Muslim rebels increased. Operating from their Pakistani camps, the *mujahideen* attacked in the border provinces of Kunar and Paktia. On February 14, the test of strength escalated when the religious fighters kidnapped the American ambassador in Kabul, Adolf Dubs. The Afghan police fought back brutally, resulting in the death of the diplomat and his four kidnappers. The first attacks made against Soviet military advisors aggravated the situation. By this time the number of Soviet troops in the country had increased. There were now more Russians in Afghanistan than there were Americans in Iran before Khomeini's seizure of power.

In March 1979 ongoing resistance was directed against the Shurawi, the "unbelieving devil," as the Russians in Afghanistan are called by the *mujahideen*. In the Afghan city of Herat, mobs of troops and the roused population attacked the Russians, reputedly resulting in the death of more than 100 people. Days later the government troops managed to reconquer Herat. Approximately five hundred to one thousand people were killed. There was fighting in the provincial capital of Jalalabad, halfway between Kabul and the Khyber Pass, and in August 1979 there was unrest in Kabul. Once again the Russians had to expect trouble with their Afghan leadership. Amin governed only by resorting to mass murder. One of his brothers alone had thousands of political prisoners executed without trial. An entire people was full of hatred toward the rule of no more than 3,000 communists. Babrak Karmal and his supporters resigned from the government in the summer of 1979 and went into exile, allegedly to Prague. In August the military leader of the coup, Colonel Abdul Qader, was put into prison, ostensibly because of his opposition to Amin, who let no one who might eventually be dangerous to him go unscathed.

Because of the "Wild West" climate in the rough southeast, the Kremlin banked on Taraki, whose immediate neighbor in the lower house of parliament was a certain Vasily Safrontshuk, the man in charge of Soviet policy in Afghanistan. Officially Safrontshuk functioned as advisor to the Soviet embassy, but in reality, as is so often the case in Soviet diplomacy, his authority exceeded that of Ambassador Alexander Puzanov. He made certain that by late summer of 1979 there were 5,000 Soviet instructors in the Afghan administration. The Soviet armed forces took over Bagram, the air force base north of Kabul, and their officers were in command, down to the company level. Months previously the order had been issued that every Afghan military plane have a Soviet pilot on board. The Afghan army of 80,000 no longer seemed sufficiently trustworthy to the Russians.

The Soviets themselves took a hand in combatting the Muslim rebels. In the summer of 1979, they first destroyed the harvest, which resulted in attracting to the amirs still more young men capable of fighting. Holy war was proclaimed throughout the country, and at times the provinces of Kunar and Paktia were completely conquered. Only the large cities remained in the hands of the government. An increasing number of soldiers and members of the administration went underground. Entire brigades (each consisting of 1,000 men), with all their equipment, including tanks, switched sides. The fighting increased in brutality—on principle, neither side took prisoners.

The civilian population, women and children, in particular suffered from the ruthlessness of the Soviets. Entire villages were eliminated. *Mujahideen* reports of the most terrible acts of cruelty claim that in one village, near Dagar, the government troops and their Soviet bosses called out all the men, killed them, and chopped them to pieces. In the village of Kerala, near Chagha Serai in the province of Kunar, all male residents were reportedly lined up after having been told they were to hear an important announcement. Suddenly the Russian troops opened fire with their machine guns, killing all of them. In February 1980 the communists allegedly invited people in the province of Laghman to a meeting. All 650 guests were arrested on the spot, locked up, and later buried alive. The *mujahideen* relate that after they reconquered the region, they found the walled-in corpses.

Taraki and Amin repeatedly asserted that they were not enemies of Islam. They maintained that the enemies of the revolution were "brothers of the devil" rather than Muslim brothers. Taraki even led the concluding prayer of Ramadan, the month of fasting. Yet on both Mohammed's birthday and August 11, 1979, he announced to the council of *ulema* (Ulama Jirgah) that it was permitted to kill enemies of the revolution—that is, members of the Muslim Brotherhood. "Obey Allah, the Prophet, and your ruler," is how spiritual help for the simple people is expressed in the extremely flexible Koran. In the most solemn tones, bribed dignitaries praised the regime's accomplishments. No one asked why everything had suddenly acquired socialist designations—five-year plan, collective, working class.

A typical speech by Amin contains the following passages:

There is a new thesis concerning the epoch-making theory about the working class. Through the heroic battle of the party of the working class, it was possible for the revolution of the working class to come into being from the feudal society. . . . Since the working class plays the leading role in overthrowing the capitalist regime in the capitalist industrialized countries, provided the working class has class consciousness and works as a party in the awareness of the epoch-making theory about the working class, our great leader discovered that there are other forces within the developing countries capable of overthrowing the feudal administration that controls everything.

Astonishing words in one of the most traditional Islamic countries.

In early September, Taraki took part in the meeting of the nonaligned nations in Havana. On his return trip, he stopped off in Moscow to visit Leonid Brezhnev, the Soviet head of state and party chairman. Allegedly Taraki also saw Babrak Karmal and his Parchamis there. Taraki assumed the task of getting rid of Amin, who had also become unpopular for the Russians. After his return to Kabul, he summoned Amin to the presidential palace, where an exchange of shots occurred, accompanied by explosions. Taraki is said to have been fatally wounded in the incident. In any case, on September 16, the government announced his "resignation due to health reasons," and on October 9, Radio Kabul announced his death "due to his illness." As an eyewitness described the incident: "A dispute between Taraki and Amin occurred because of Amin's dismissal of three leading members of the military. Amin called the president an old incompetent who should finally resign. Asadullah, the head of the secret service, then forbade Amin to speak. At a sign given by Amin, the bodyguard Taroon suddenly drew his pistol and shot at Taraki. When Asadullah subsequently shot at Amin, Taroon threw himself in front of his mentor. Twenty shots were later found in his corpse."

Radio Tehran issued its rebuke in a commentary of September 22: "Things will continue to seethe in Afghanistan until the victory of the just. This oath was sworn in mountains and valleys by thousands of Afghan fighters, who are marching forward from all parts of the country against the bastion of atheism in Kabul. . . . In the end, the throne of Hafizullah Amin will yield to the will of the people just as Taraki and his friends had to yield."

The Soviets seemed surprised when they heard of the latest development in Kabul. They immediately recalled Ambassador Pusanov and replaced him with Fikriyat Tabejew, a member of the Central Committee of the Communist Party of the Soviet Union and secretary of the Autonomous Republic of the Tartars since 1960. Pusanov was evidently punished for his lack of ability. Together with Safrontshuk, he is alleged to have been in the presidential palace at the time of the shooting, but failed to help

Taraki. Amin continued to rule without being contested, and for a while even took a liberal turn. At the same time, though, he made certain that anyone who might be a Taraki supporter landed in prison. The lethal chain of resistance, force, counterforce, bombarded settlements, massacred gatherings of people, and new arrests found no end. The most notorious dungeon in the country, Puli Charkhi in Kabul, was always crowded.

Then came the historic December of 1979. The guerrilla war was in its annual winter lull. Even in the summer the mountains are virtually inaccessible, and winter makes the conduct of war there impossible. The Western world stared in fascination at the first major challenge by an Islamic revolution: the seizure of hostages in the U.S. Embassy in Tehran. At the time the Muslims were still suffering from the shock of the occupation of the mosque in Mecca.

During December, the Russians mobilized fresh troops along the northern border of Afghanistan and flew several thousand soldiers to Kabul. These were pure combat units, and they landed expressly at the civilian airport of Kabul, not in Bagram. By the end of the invasion, 85,000 members of the Red Army, under the command of Marshal Sergei L. Sokolov, were reputedly in Afghanistan.

The airlift from the Asiatic Soviet republics (the Central Asian provinces) to Kabul started during the night of December 24 and continued throughout the next day. At ten-minute intervals, under the protection of fighter planes, 250 Ilyushin JL-76 and Antonov-An-22 transport planes landed, rolled to the northwest corner of the airport, in a flash unloaded troops and light tanks, and immediately took off again. By December 26, approximately 5,000 men from the 105th airborne regiment of Argona landed in Afghanistan. Most of these elite units were hidden away in Soviet construction projects, such as a factory for concrete prefabricated components in the vicinity of the airport. At the same time endless Russian military columns rolled from the border points of Termes and Kushka, along a Russian-built highway, into Kabul. During the actual coup, at the break of dawn on December 27, Amin was already a prisoner in his residence in Darulaman. At 5:00 P.M. an advance guard of the troops blew up the telephone headquarters on Pashtoonistan Square. Around 10:00 P.M. troops took over Radio Afghanistan, which was in the process of broadcasting a cheerful radio play. The only fighting involving troops loyal to Amin occurred in Darulaman. What precisely happened in Hafizullah Amin's residence remains a matter for speculation. Some Western observers believe the president and his family were killed in a missile attack.

Many experts blame the Afghan army, others the Soviets. The Russians do not respond to the question at all, stating that Amin wanted to make common cause with Hekmatyar. I asked Golbuddin Hekmatyar about his information concerning Hafizullah Amin's death. He replied: "Anyone who maintains that the Afghan army killed Hafizullah Amin is completely in the dark. After all, it is clear that the first Soviet unit attacked the presidential palace immediately after arriving. That can be proved by the bullet holes. During that night all military units of our country had to remain in their barracks."

Moscow's new man in Kabul arrived by plane from Tashkent around 2:00 A.M. He immediately went to Radio Afghanistan, where he met battle companions from his days in Parcham. Even before this, a pre-recorded speech had been broadcast by Radio Tashkent, in which the fifty-one-year-old Karmal announced the death of Amin, the "criminal and unmasked CIA agent," and thanked Moscow for its fraternal assistance.

Karmal then had pictures of the "martyr Taraki" hung up again. The official propaganda branded Hafizullah Amin as the "incarnation of Satan, a hangman, professional criminal and spy who, with the help of his filthy cohorts, Amin's treacherous clan, established a bloody regime and transformed our country into a large prison and slaughterhouse." Since Karmal had previously been on a good will tour, he pardoned 4,500 political prisoners. After all, it was necessary to create room in the prisons for the victims of Karmal's future regency.

Radio Kabul broadcast the following explanation by the revolutionary council on December 28:

The government of the Democratic Republic of Afghanistan, taking into consideration the advanced and spreading interventions and provocations of Afghanistan's external enemies, and with the goal of defending the achievements of the April revolution [1978], territorial integrity, national independence, and the maintenance of peace and security as well as the establishment of the Treaty of Friendship, Good Neighborliness, and Cooperation of December 5, 1978, turned to the USSR with the urgent request for swift political, moral, and economic assistance, including military aid, which the government of the Democratic Republic of Afghanistan had several times previously requested of the Soviet Union. The government of the Soviet Union granted Afghanistan's request.

On January 10, 1980, Babrak Karmal announced in Kabul:

In the name of Allah, the Merciful and the Compassionate, it is as clear as day that the Soviet Union is the most honest friend of all plagued peoples, including the Muslims in Afghanistan. Hafizullah Amin and his supporters worked with international imperialism and the local reactionaries. The last remains of Amin's conspiracy have been eliminated. In compliance with its principled and peaceful foreign policy, the Soviet Union will never interfere in a country's internal affairs. It has never done so. Moreover, Russia was always committed to supporting the Afghan people; never was it committed to support the bloodthirsty terrorist regime of Amin.

The first setback came at a staged presentation for the international press on January 11, 1980. Two dozen journalists were taken to the Puli Charkhi Prison, fifteen miles south of Kabul, to witness the freeing of what were allegedly the last 126 political prisoners. Suddenly, thousands of Afghans tried to storm the dungeon with stones and iron bars and pipes, overrunning the three-deep rows of Afghan soldiers. But inside the second courtyard there were Soviet soldiers and three tanks; the military staged a bloodbath. That is only one incident that became known. At this time, however, massive resistance against the Soviet Union took place throughout the country, resulting in the death of 6,000 members of the Red Army by mid-1980 and as many as 14,000 by the end of 1983.

In view of the high losses, Leonid Brezhnev spoke up, and on January 18, 1980, told the party newspaper *Pravda*:

Together with its accomplices, imperialism started what basically can be called an undeclared war against the revolutionary country of Afghanistan. So under the leadership of the Democratic People's Party, with Babrak Karmal at the helm, the people rose up against the Amin dictatorship and brought it to an end. The moment came when we could no longer avoid complying with the request of the friendly government of Afghanistan. Had we acted differently, it would have amounted to standing idly by and letting Afghanistan be torn to pieces by imperialism and allowing the aggressive forces to repeat there what they succeeded in doing, for example, in Chile. . . . Had we acted differently, it would have amounted to idly watching the center of a serious threat to the security of the Soviet nation come into being on our southern border. We are not after the possessions of others. It is the colonialists who are attracted by oil.

Kabul's bloody Friday made a mark. The *mujahideen* called for the first big test of strength with the new regime and its protectors. In a handwritten flier that had been distributed the previous day, the "Muslim Brothers of the City of Kabul" were commanded by the *mullahs* to commit civil disobedience and to close their businesses. The message read:

The brave citizens of Kabul declare holy war against nonbelievers and oppression by the Soviet aggressors, the implacable enemies of Islam. Every person has to die some day. Why then do we shy away from a praiseworthy death? We are summoned to defend our country and our women, and if we die in the battle against our enemies or kill them, we gain paradise for ourselves. If holy war should not be possible, we will fulfill our duty by holding demonstrations and strikes against the Soviets.

And that is what happened. With the piercing shout, *"Allah-u-Akhbar,"* the people marched through Kabul and gave vent to their displeasure with the occupation. The "flying fortresses," Soviet MI-24 battle helicopters, circled menacingly above the demonstrators' heads. MiG-21 jets and Suchoi-7 ground-attack fighter planes from Tashkent flew in mock attacks on Kabul. Only when the large crowd reached the center of town did the Russians open fire. They also shot in the sections of Demasang and Kharga, where the rebels were on the grounds of the barracks of the Afghan Seventh Infantry Division, allegedly resulting in 300 to 500 deaths and thousands of wounded. Since that day the Afghan people commemorate the anniversary of this massacre every year.

Babrak Karmal's regime had long been discredited internationally; it was not at all a matter of individual incidents or the fact that Karmal was by no means as bloodthirsty as his predecessor. It is true that for years he was liked and recognized. Under different circumstances, he would certainly have had the opportunity to be accepted by the Afghans, but as the foster child of the Soviets, Babrak Karmal's chance of political success was absolutely nil. It did not help to have Islamic references included in the constitution or to have the red flag of Socialism replaced by the green flag of the Prophet. In vain, too, was his letter to Kho-

meini, which started with the salutation, "Blessed Brother, su-
premely revered Imam Khomeini," and then went on to explain
that the Soviets were only temporarily in Afghanistan.

Babrak Karmal has no future. He is a tragic figure of history,
for he is completely beholden to a foreign power. In a discussion
with the German news magazine *Der Spiegel* (number 14, 1980),
Karmal described himself in glowing colors as "a man who loves
his fatherland; who has placed himself in the service of his people; who defends national independence, national sovereignty,
and territorial integrity; who is a declared enemy of old and new
colonialism; an opponent of imperialism, Zionism, racism, fas-
cism, and Apartheid; and a politician who works toward a happy
and democratic society."

That sounds as promising of success as is Karmal's information
about Kabul's black Friday unrealistic:

Those were not street battles, that was a limited bit of commotion that
corresponded precisely to the plan of the reactionary forces prior to
December 27. The foreign enemies slipped approximately 6,000 bandits,
murderers, and terrorists into our country. This commotion was mainly
staged by agents of the Israeli secret service who, as you know, had
close connections with the Shah's SAVAK. The provocateurs threw
hand grenades and shot at everything for thirty-five hours.

Babrak Karmal at least admitted that between April 1978 and
April 1980 some 1.5 million people had been killed in the name of
the government. According to the most recent estimates, the
same number of people have lost their lives *since* the easily irrita-
ble, European-trained technocrat took power. Almost three million Afghans fled across the border to Pakistan and are on the
verge of dying there in countless refugee ghettos. The U.N. High
Commissioner of Refugees and the International Red Cross are
not always able to help them. Hizb-e Islami and Jamaat-e Islami
of Pakistan, and three other moderate organizations which are
closely allied, also have only limited powers of assistance. They
provide medical treatment for the inmates of the refugee camps
from three of Jamaat-e Islami's hospitals.

In a discussion held in the old garrison city of Peshawar, along
the border, Mohammed Firdans Khan, the manager of the Afghan Surgical Hospital, told me about the plight of the refugees
and about his international supporters: "Our Egyptian brothers
helped us very much in setting up this hospital," he explained.
"Kemal Sananiry came here personally for the purpose of inform-

ing himself about everything. The only thing that distinguishes us from the Muslim Brotherhood is the method of propagating Islam, and this method is determined by external circumstances. We are trying to do it with elections. They are resorting to revolution. But both of us are seeking humanity, not communism and not capitalism."

The *mujahideen* of Peshawar have set up schools and workshops. In their social missions the pious fighters are in agreement about how to spend the money donated by the Islamic countries, as well as by the West. Nevertheless, it is extremely difficult to solve leadership questions among members from different tribes. Almost everyone wants to be the leader and have the last word.

No less than six groups based in Peshawar fought for dominance in the *jihad* against the Shurawi. There is Nabi Muhhamadi's Revolutionary Islamic Movement, a group of radical Islamic Pashtoons. Then there is the Liberation Front of Afghanistan, headed by the religious scholar Sibghatullah Mujaddidi. The second most important organization is the Islamic Society of the scholar Burhanuddin Rabbani, which fights mainly in northern Afghanistan and is strongly supported by the Gulf states. The only thing the Islamic Party of the *mullah* Yunus Khalis has in common with Hizb-e Islami, which is headed by Golbuddin Hekmatyar, is the name. Then comes the Federation of Islamic Unity, led by Ahmad Gilani, an orthodox Muslim who is also not opposed to the restoration of a royal dynasty. And finally there is the main branch of Hizb-e Islami, which was considered for a long time as the most powerful group under the *mujahideen.*

Initially the Afghan version of the Muslim Brotherhood accepted military development assistants into its ranks—members of the Syrian Muslim Brotherhood. Since the time of its founding, there have therefore been targeted attacks on governmental buildings and representatives of the regime. But sometimes fighters angrily fire on each other for days on end.

That was also the last impulse for having a group of some two dozen highly respected religious leaders of the Sunni world travel secretly to Peshawar. All indications are that the majority of them were members of the international body of experts of the Muslim Brotherhood. The delegation invited the heads of the Islamic *mujahideen* to a ten-day conference, likewise allegedly under the auspices of the Muslim Brotherhood. There it was decided that all leaders, including the moderates not present at the meeting, should without warning cancel membership in both of the still-existing alliances. The seven fundamentalist organizations complied with the pronouncement and issued almost identical letters to the leadership of their alliance: "If that leads to the unity of the struggle, we will adopt that measure."

The fifty-seven delegates entitled to a vote at the strictly secret conference agreed to disband all previously existing parties and to consolidate the entire membership, finances, and weapons in a new organization called Islamic Alliance of the Mujahideen of Afghanistan (Al Islami li Majahidi Afghanistan). As later reported by the Dubai-based newspaper *Al Eslah* ("The Improvement"), which is sympathetic to the Muslim Brotherhood, the conference saw to the formation of committees responsible for work in specific areas. With forty-eight of the fifty-seven votes cast, Hekmatyar's friend Ghulam Rasul Sayyaf won the election as chairman of the alliance for the next two years. Two days later Sayyaf invited all the important leaders of the fundamentalists to a dinner at which they took the following oath: "In the name of Allah, I swear I will follow you faithfully as long as you go on the path of Allah."

As an additional measure, the Islamists founded two important committees. One has the task of supervising the entire alliance, the other is responsible for the implementation of the decisions and for the finances. Since that time, the most important agreements are made at weekly conferences. When the secret agreements of Peshawar showed up in a manifesto entitled *Almisak*, I asked a spokesman of the Muslim Brotherhood why the leaders of the moderate alliance, likewise devout Muslims of three organizations, had not been included in order that the resistance in Pakistan could speak with one voice. His answer: "Anyone who does not want to cooperate with us can go his own way. We are not making any more compromises." The split between the radicals and those considered moderate by the West now seems unbridgeable, and the opposition will have to live with that.

Hekmatyar is still the most radical leader, even though now only second in command within the new alliance of fundamentalists. He would like to be Afghanistan's Khomeini, and he knows, despite the clear loss of popularity starting in the year 1982, that he is still backed by a strong organization. But if he seized power (far off in the future), his fate in Kabul would be much like that of his Iranian model. There would be a deep cleavage between the enlightened, Western-oriented population, whose numbers are relatively small, and the uncompromising fundamentalists, and this would lead to a double life in "liberated" Afghanistan. Since the fall of the Shah, it can be seen how strict and implacable Islamic forms of society are and how little consideration is given to deviating opinions. If it were to come to a seizure of power in Kabul, then the strategists of the Muslim Brotherhood would be in the forefront of command. So far, they have accepted the Afghan members both in terms of guerrilla strategy and ideology. The constitution of the *mujahideen* alliance stems from the pen of no less exalted persons than Syria's chief ideologist, Said Hawwa, and Cairo's Kemal Sananiry.

At the moment, however, both sides are preoccupied with the holy war against the nonbelievers and their Afghan "Russian lads" (in the words of Hekmatyar). It is a seemingly hopeless war, maintained at a great cost in human life—a proxy war between East and West. A governmental official in Islamabad told me in 1982 that Afghanistan belongs to Brezhnev by day and to Reagan by night. The Soviets are no longer able to withdraw easily from Afghanistan without losing face. According to their logic, they have to carry on the war because Afghanistan was on the verge of falling prey to the Iranian virus, from which as many as fifty to sixty million discontented Muslims in the Asiatic provinces of the Soviet Union could be infected. Access to the warm sea has so far not been achieved by their involvement in Afghanistan, since the Russians would first have to occupy another nation—for example, the unsettled Baluchi province of Pakistan.

The opposing side is also well supplied with weapons and money. In the process, it is clearing up the mess for the otherwise much maligned imperialists. The West just has them on the dole, hardly supplying anti-aircraft missiles (for example, captured Soviet Sam-7 equipment) that were so decisive in the Vietnam War. Ultimately the practical effect for both Zia ul-Haq, the nearby Pakistani military dictator, and the faraway Ronald Reagan is that the Russian bear is kept involved and blocked off in an unimportant country: Afghanistan. For the West, Afghanistan is a useful theater of war.

The *mujahideen* have an ideal position. They are invincible, since they know their terrain and come from the population. They attack, then hide for days in the mountains, and march for weeks to the next battle site. Then new, elaborately embellished battle statistics are published, which speak of countless dead enemies and much booty. The tribal elders again proclaim holy war. Village leaders attack Russian reconnaissance troops, and the *mullahs* then have trenches dug. The strong connection to Islam and the typically Afghan penchant for weapons and violence are what keep this unexplained, concealed war going in the Hindu-kush. As long ago as 1857, Friedrich Engels characterized the Afghans as a "brave, bold, independence-loving race." He continued: "For the Afghans, war is something exciting, a welcome change from the monotonous everyday life, and the unpredicta-bility of their acts makes them dangerous neighbors," as can be read in the collection called *Concerning Colonialism* issued by Prog-ress Publishers of Moscow.

"In the name of the Prophet, the people are ready. Angels sprinkled the fighters with holy water. The people are ready." These are the messages contained in the *mujahideen*'s tape-re-corded revolutionary songs that give them courage. The Russians have replaced their Asian soldiers and flown in equipment suit-able for the guerrilla war. Afghan's rulers, the "Soviet mari-onettes," have barricaded themselves in and rarely leave Kabul. Karmal repeatedly calls up older men into the armed forces in order to compensate for the high drop-out rate. Three-fourths of the 80,000-man force have gone underground. The Afghan econ-omy thrives only at the expense of the "praiseworthy Soviet Union" (the phrase used in an official reference). In the name of Allah, sixty tribal organizations are fighting for survival against starvation. In Moscow Brezhnev personally pinned the "son of freedom" order on Karmal's chest, referring to him as "a glowing and happy future." The news reports continue, fragments of a mosaic from the torn country of Afghanistan.

Golbuddin Hekmatyar says:

Sometimes I recall my country's joyful times and how we used to live. Every Friday on the outskirts of the villages there were daredevil Buz-kashi riding games, when hundreds of horsemen with their tanned, broad-boned faces competed eagerly to get an animal cadaver to a par-ticular place. Within seconds a tangle of horses and people gathered, dust flew, and whips cracked in the air. A forceful game of *tshapanduz*, well-trained men with the fighting spirit of our ancestors. I am con-vinced that our fighting spirit is a legacy of our mothers and forefathers. History has made us into a warring people, as is also now evident in the resistance against the Soviet occupation. We will never let our coun-try be taken away from us. Even today, no one can take it away from us. Not even Moscow. We would sooner die than lose our independence.

23

Allah and His General

I WAS IMPRESSED by the city of Islamabad on my first visit there. It seemed to me like Brasilia, only not so monumental. It is an entirely different world from the noisy, dirty humdrum life of Rawalpindi, fifteen miles away, or the medieval border citadel of Peshawar or the tropically damp Karachi with its teeming seven million residents. Islamabad's high plateau of Potohar, extending from the hills of Margalla to "Pindi," can be very hot, but mostly there is a friendly warm wind. In the winter, when the temperatures are near freezing, one notices the nearness of the Himalaya Mountains. The 24,000-foot Nanga Parbat is only 124 miles away.

Islamabad smells of roses and jasmine. Broad alleys lead through large parks and past embassies and government buildings. The military is much in evidence, especially in the section with the elegant white villas. Chauffeured Mercedes limousines are in evidence. Islamabad is green, cosmopolitan, expensive, Western—not at all the Pakistani world of poor people, only eighteen percent of whom are literate. Anyone who can afford to live in Islamabad is over age fifty-one, which is the average life expectancy of the 81 million Pakistanis.

Islamabad is the way Islam would like to be set up, and the tie of the name of the city to the religion is no coincidence. Islamabad was already a showplace, a jewel of the upward-striving Third World, at a time when the magnificent structures on the Persian Gulf were still under construction. Islamabad, a projection into the future that is precisely eighteen years old, is inhabited by 210,000 people. The focus of the city is revealed in figures from the second general conference of mayors of Islamic capitals held in April 1982: 17,000 houses for government officials have already been built, and 2,000 more are planned. A test-tube city decorated for display. In the urban center of an Islamic republic, the spiritual sector is of course one of the focal points. At the express wish of the president, the visitor is emphatically told that six new mosques will be constructed in the traditional style. The blueprints have been completed, according to the head of the Pakistani architectural organization, S. A. N. Gardezi, who proudly adds: "Then we will also be known as the city of mosques."

And no wonder, because the largest mosque in the world is now completed in Islamabad: the Faisal Mosque, named for the Saudi Arabian king who financed the entire endeavor before his assassination in 1975. In 1959 the decision was made to erect the building in the northern part of Islamabad while the city was still in the planning stage. The 120-foot-high structure stands beside the mammoth Shahrah-i-Islamabad highway and from a great distance can be recognized as the future emblem. The architectural competition for the Faisal Mosque and an associated religious university, which was restricted to Muslims, was held in 1969. In 1975 construction began on the prayer house with its pyramidal tent roof and four gigantic, 200-foot-high minarets. The building can hold 74,000 worshippers. Originally the date set for the dedication of the mosque was June 1985, but the regime wants it completed sooner.

Even today one sees an indestructible illusion written on the numerous banners on Faisal Avenue: "Long live Islamic unity and solidarity"—a dream that will not be fulfilled even with the completion of the large national mosque. Indeed, it was precisely this thought that was the impetus for the founding of such a state as Pakistan, a state in which the wishful thinking of idealists could never keep pace with raw reality.

Before its separation from India in the year 1947, the country had never been independent. Generals crossed the famous Khyber Pass and the Bolan Pass and passed through Pakistan to conquer the Indian subcontinent. The Europeans were the first to find the approach by sea more agreeable. When Alexander the Great came upon the tracks of the Persians, through what is now Pakistan, he found a civilization that was already 3,500 years old. The Islamic conquest started 700 years later, around 1030 A.D., and was followed by the Mongols, who founded the Mongolian Empire, which was ended by the British in the middle of the nineteenth century. The creation of the British-Indian kingdom was accompanied by pain, and in 1906, in Dacca, quite a self-confident Muslim League was founded, whose chief ideologist demanded independence for northwest India—in other words, Pakistan. But years of intensive fighting between the Congress Party of the Hindus and the Muslim League were to pass before Mohammed Ali Jinnah, an arch-pragmatist heading the Muslim League, finally led the "country of the pure" to independence.

In order to judge contemporary Pakistan, it is necessary to know the man whose influence a visitor encounters at every turn. His picture hangs in old frames above fireplaces everywhere, in administrative offices, hotel lobbies and bookstores, in grocery stores, and at the airport. Quotes by him, accompanied by a photograph, are constantly blended into television programs. The photograph shows Mohammed Ali Jinnah as a thin, beardless, elderly white-haired man who looks skeptical. He wears a Western suit with tie and an elegant pocket handkerchief and the familiar karakul cap. He was a tactician and a thinker, peaceable and conciliatory.

Freedom fighter Jinnah, the son of a businessman, was born in Karachi in 1876. After graduating from Sind Madrasah, a religious school, he traveled to England in 1892 to study law at Lincoln's Inn. When he was accredited as a lawyer ten years later, he was the youngest Indian Muslim entitled to practice. After years of successfully pursuing his profession, he entered politics via the Indian National Congress in 1906 and was elected three years later to the newly created Imperial Legislative Council. During his forty years of parliamentary activity, the slim Jinnah became the first Indian to succeed in fighting through the bill of a small Muslim minority.

The moderate Jinnah worked for an agreement between Hindus and Muslims. Gokhale, the first Hindu leader before Gandhi, once characterized him as follows: "He is cut from the best timber and is free of any prejudice concerning sects." By 1917 Jinnah was president of the All-India Muslim League and was also a leading member of the Congress Party. During the '20s, the influence of the extremists within the Congress Party increased, and Jinnah resigned. At a conference held in 1928, he predicted revolution and civil war if suppression of the Muslim minority did not cease. For security reasons he left the country in 1930 and lived for four years in England. His supporters called him back in 1934.

When he took over the leadership of the insecure community in 1936, he introduced a kind of Islamic resurgence—long before this idea came to dominate discussion—and he became one of the great Islamic leaders of this century. Primarily, the discouraged masses looked to him to formulate a clear political direction. Within three years Jinnah managed to unite the completely disorganized Muslims and provide a basis for their battle for independence. The actual campaign started in 1940 when 100 million Muslims were confronted by a threefold Hindu majority. Jinnah's opinion was clear: "Majorities tend to become oppressors and tyrants, and minorities always fear that their interests and rights will suffer and could be put at a disadvantage."

Jinnah's antagonist, Mahatma Gandhi, saw everything differently: "I find no historical parallel for the situation in which a group of converts and their descendants need to be a different nation from their forefathers. If India was a nation before the arrival of Islam, it must remain one." Jinnah did not give in: "We firmly maintain that we, Muslims and Hindus, are two nations— with our separate civilizations and cultures, languages and literature, art and architecture, names and values; with our legal systems and ethical norms, our customs, our history and tradition, our inclinations and ambitions. We simply have a different view of the world."

Using strong power of persuasion, Jinnah worked toward splitting the enormous country of India into a Hindu and a Muslim state. The world was horrified by bloody massacres that could not be stopped, even by the colonial power, Great Britain. The British finally had no other choice but to approve the division of the country, so two national congresses came into being in 1947: the Indian one headed by Jawaharlal Nehru and the Pakistani by Mohammed Jinnah. In his correct manner, Jinnah implemented strict standards for parliamentary procedures, which thus far have not been upheld by his latest successor, Zia ul-Haq. The founding of the secular state of Pakistan on August 14, 1947, initially as East Pakistan and West Pakistan, was followed by the worst kind of violence. The Muslim population of Pakistan gave vent to their enormous hatred of Hindus and Sikhs, murdered millions, and radically drove the Hindus, who were now a minority, from the country. In response, millions of Muslims were driven out of India.

During the last year of his life, Jinnah worked for his countrymen without taking his health into consideration. The death of *"Quaid-i-Azam"* ("the Great Leader") on September 11, 1948, came much too soon for his people. With his consistently conciliatory manner, it was precisely Jinnah who would have been able to prevent or at least lessen the postwar confusion in Pakistan. In 1948 (and again in 1965), the Pakistanis and Indians fought for the first time over the Kashmir province. In 1951 Liaquat Ali Khan, the first prime minister of the country, was the victim of an attack and died. While India had no shortage of leaders, in Pakistan there was only a small class of intellectuals and estate owners, who were already in conflict about the issue of a democracy based on the British model versus an Islamic state.

Despite its only average political leadership, Pakistan prospered, because the Americans considered it an ideal source of support. The Korean War provided the cotton industry with high profits and the country with viability. Although it was the leading political force in the country, the Muslim League suffered a severe setback in the first provincial elections following independence. When the country's status as part of the British Commonwealth was ended in 1956, a constitution strongly resembling the original model from the era of the British in India was drawn up. Governor General Iskender Mirza immediately proclaimed the Islamic Republic of Pakistan and himself became the temporary president. In 1958 he suspended the party system, and in October of that year General Ayub Khan, the commander-in-chief of the armed forces and minister of defense, seized power. Until 1971 the country was ruled by the military, first by Ayub Khan, then by Jahja Khan.

In the mid-1960s there was severe unrest, for progress had been so slow that the population had become aware of the social injustice and exploitation. Martial law had to serve as the instru-

ment for enforcing discipline. Religion was also a factor in the
mass demonstrations that occurred in 1968 and 1969 in the wake
of Ayub Khan's intention, against the will of the people, to create
a new interpretation of the faith with the help of a so-called Islamic Institute of Research. A progressive form of family planning
was to be part of the program. Ultimately Ayub Khan failed because of Muslim opposition.

In 1970 General Jahja Khan implemented the only free elections
held in Pakistan during the '70s. For the first time, the Democratic
People's Party of Zulfikar Ali Bhutto came into the limelight. As
a result of the elections, which were won in East Bengal by Sheikh
Mujib ur-Rahman and his separatist Awami League, a violent
dispute between the two parts of the country broke out, leading
to the war of secession. Decisive in the split of the country into
two parts, separated by a 1,000-mile region under sovereign jurisdiction, was a quarrel about language. In West Pakistan, Jinnah
had introduced the use of Urdu, which was rejected by countrymen beyond the subcontinent, who insisted on Bengali. Since
West Pakistan did not consider Bengali to be Islamic, there were
repeatedly violent clashes. In 1971 the West Pakistani army finally
had to suppress an uprising of the people in the East. The price
was high—two million deaths in nine months. The followers of
Mujib ur-Rahman, who was subsequently murdered, went underground. Operating from India, they fought for Bangladesh.
The Indians intervened, and West Pakistan attacked its neighbor.
The Indians occupied East Bengal, capturing 90,000 Pakistani soldiers. Soon thereafter Bangladesh declared its independence.

Jahja Khan resigned on December 20, 1971. The strongest opposition, Zulfikar Ali Bhutto, took over the administration. He
stimulated the economy and started a program of land reform.
Through a series of nationalizations, a slip to the left started,
which was halted by Bhutto. The financial influence of the conservative Gulf states led to a strengthening of Islam. Bhutto lost
ground to the religious opposition, but was once again able to
recover when, at the 1974 Islamic Summit Conference in Lahore,
he effected a reconciliation with Bangladesh and as a consequence became the leader of the Muslim camp in the Third
World. But Bhutto had to give in to the demands of the strict
fundamentalists; on the basis of a parliamentary vote, he declared the followers of the Ahmadiya movement within Islam, a
peace-loving sect involved in missionary activity, a non-Muslim

minority. In other words, the group was excommunicated. A comparable example of persecution is Imam Khomeini's treatment of the Bahai minority in Iran.

I asked a high-level representative of the banned Jamaat-e Islami of Pakistan, which is an affiliate of the Muslim Brotherhood, about the background details of the elimination of Pakistan's Ahmadiya movement. Khurram Murad, who now directs the Islamic Foundation based in Leicester, England, replied: "Mirza Gulam Ahmad, an Indian, declared himself a prophet. But in accordance with our basic doctrine, Mohammed, peace be with him, was the last of all prophets, and after him there can never be another. If Ahmad had been a real prophet, then we would not be Muslims, for we would not believe in a true prophet. If he was a false prophet, his followers would not be permitted to be Muslims. We were not able to live as parts of the same body."

Despite various weaknesses, Bhutto proved to the most serious and popular politician since Jinnah. His position, however, was considered a thorn in the side by both the Russians and the Americans. Elections, scheduled for 1977, were to provide the prime minister with support for a constitutional change to a presidential dictatorship. Bhutto had long been vulnerable, and he had had numerous opponents, including influential *mullahs*, imprisoned. Bhutto manipulated the elections so as to achieve a seventy percent majority. His rivals in the Pakistan National Alliance contested the results. After months of riots, the military again seized power in July 1977. Bhutto was imprisoned, hauled into court on the accusation of incitement to murder his political opponent, Ahmed Raza Kasuri, and was sentenced to death. Despite vigorous international protest, in April 1979 the new president, Zia ul-Haq, ordered the execution of his predecessor. The result was the loss of much sympathy for Pakistan.

The general entered office with the ambition of establishing a genuine Islamic state, as expected by his supporters and the sympathetically inclined Muslim fundamentalists. For this reason, the fall of Zulfikar Ali Bhutto was a manifestation of the resurgence of Islam, even though the country already had a constitution that strongly reflected the influence of Islam. Bhutto's regime clearly had secular traits, and the extremely devout representatives of the middle class and the Islamic intellectuals always attacked his lax attitude; in their opinion, it reflected corrupt influences from Europe and the U.S., to the detriment of Pakistan. They vehe-

mently condemned a luxurious lifestyle, sexual excesses, criminality, corruption, and the liberation of women.

So General Mohammed Zia ul-Haq, called "the smiling cobra"
by the people, came to power. I heard him give a speech in
Islamabad and found that, his martial appearance notwithstand-
ing, he enjoys speaking to his people at length in a warm, gentle
voice. In contrast to the persuasiveness of his voice, the gaze of
the former cavalry officer is ice-cold and penetrating. Since seiz-
ing power, Zia ul-Haq has not given a single address that omits
reference to Islam as the legitimization of his action. He speaks
casually of democracy and human rights, stating for example:
"We will always be on the side of the free world and will actively
support freedom and the protection of the individual from a reg-
imented society." In saying that, however, he is not thinking of
a contemporary Pakistan.

Zia ul-Haq is a typical product of the British colonial army,
cynical and obsessed with power like many other despots within
the Commonwealth. Born in 1924, Zia fought during World War
II in Burma, Malaya, and Indonesia. His ascent in the newly
founded Pakistan army started in 1947. He was trained in the
U.S. in the early '60s. In 1965 he participated in the war against
India. Five years later, as a military advisor to Jordan's King Hussein, he assisted in the resounding defeat of the Palestinian freedom fighters in Amman, and still wears the two highest
Jordanian awards in memory of this period in his life. Nonetheless, in his address to Islamic mayors in April 1982, he stated:
"Let us include in our prayers the wish that in our lifetime
the all-powerful God will give our Palestinian brothers their
freedom."

After the war against India in 1971, Zia ul-Haq rose to the rank
of major general and division commander. In 1975 he was promoted to lieutenant general, and in 1976 Bhutto appointed him
chief of staff of the army, although officers with greater seniority
had a greater claim to the post. One year later Zia ul-Haq expressed his gratitude by overthrowing his mentor.

With the assistance of Jamaat-e Islami, which had continued its
activities under many other names, and financed by large sums
of money from the Saudis, he initiated an arbitrary resurgence of
Islam within all areas of life. In February 1979 Zia ul-Haq changed
the constitution by granting the supreme court the power to declare permanently invalid any law that was allegedly not Islamic.

So-called *shariat* senates were created that alone were capable of clarifying whether or not a law was God-given. At the only national university in Islamabad a faculty with an emphasis on Islamic law came into being.

Zia ul-Haq personally explained to the public what he meant by the "new" law. He proclaimed draconian punishments for infidelity and illicit sexual practices—even for false accusations of these two offenses—as well as for infractions of the strict ban on alcohol. Since 1979, murderers in Pakistan are publicly hanged, and the right hands of thieves are cut off by law. For those who abduct or molest children, Zia's prescription is: "I will put the fear of God in them." Because he stole sixty dollars, a young Pakistani burglar was sentenced by an Islamic court to amputation of his hand. That is how the Koran wants it: "And as for the man who steals and the woman who steals, cut off their hand as revenge for their sin. For Allah is powerful and wise." In the presence of 200,000 onlookers, three child-murderers were beheaded on the marketplace of Lahore.

"Islam is a progressive religion that teaches us to be kind and just," comments Zia ul-Haq in his well-meaning manner. "Cutting off people's hands and whippings serve the well-being of mankind. A light tap on the ankles will do you good." For taking a sip of alcohol a faithless Muslim gets eighty lashes. A non-Muslim foreigner caught drinking alcohol outside his embassy, residence, or hotel room is subject to thirty lashes and three years imprisonment.

Zia ul-Haq has also introduced the traditional Muslim alms tax, which amounts to an additional two-and-a-half percent assessment on all savings or shareholder deposits and ten percent on income from agriculture. Under Zia ul-Haq, censorship has been extended to all areas of life from textbooks to television programs. Dancing and music are forbidden, allegedly because they violate religious feelings.

Despite all this, the resurgence of Islam fostered by Zia has thus far failed all along the line. The general never formulated a conception of his Islamic state. Apart from Islamic law, Islamic economic doctrine, and pious sayings in front of large audiences, he has not offered any idea of how the faith might be implemented politically. For this reason, the fundamentalists are as displeased with him as Bhutto's supporters are, particularly Bhutto's widow and daughter, who now lead the banned opposition.

General Zia ul-Haq does not know how to translate his Islamic ideas into action by means of a suitable popular system, so under his rule the old, corrupt bureaucracy remains firmly in the saddle.

The mouthpieces of the fundamentalists publicly rebuke him for his failure. In June 1982 the London-based magazine *Arabia* analyzed the situation as follows: "Unlike the practice in Iran, the mosque never became transformed into an institution for public administration. The life of the simple people in Pakistan was not affected by General Zia's measures to foster the resurgence of Islam. By no means do things look much different from the way they were under his oppressive predecessors."

Just one year earlier the biweekly newspaper of the fundamentalists, *Crescent International*, came to a still more drastic judgment about the leader of the Islamic Republic:

Pakistan now needs something it never had: a truly dynamic and revolutionary Islamic movement. The spirit of democracy that cast its spell on the thinking of Jamaat-e Islami for a decade must now be eliminated. It must become clear that democracy, even it if is "restored," can never be the vehicle of permanent change. . . . It must become clear that periodic revolts are no substitute for a dynamic Islamic revolution. The Pakistani Army will suffer the same fate as the Shah's Army in Iran. The army officers, the bureaucracy, the aristocracy, and the capitalists must all be rejected and eliminated in the streets of Pakistan. Until that happens, the Pakistanis will continue to die for a cause that is not worth their blood.

The "genuine" Islamic revolution dreamed of by still more conservative forces is not possible at present, because Zia ul-Haq has a firm hold on the country. In his personal synthesis of a goal, he vacillates between a constitutional state and Islam, and tries to avoid rubbing really influential groups the wrong way. Disappointment is increasing among intellectuals, who also consider themselves the embodiment of the state under the general, and they are waiting for further developments. If asked directly about the situation, most respond with evasive answers.

"Just how Islamic is the military state of Pakistan?," I asked Dr. Anis Ahmad, professor of comparative religion in Islamabad and an expert on the resurgence of Islam. His response: "I feel a discrepancy between what is said and what is done. Perhaps there are practical reasons for that, but I do not notice much carrying out of what is said. We are somewhere at the beginning, but I cannot say that serious progress has been made."

General Zia ul-Haq is depending on his military power and the war in Afghanistan. Scoffers in Islamabad assert that when the pious Muslim bows five times daily toward Mecca, he thanks Allah each time for the blessing of having permitted the Russians to invade the heartland of Asia on the Hindu Kush. As long as the undeclared war in the neighboring country occupies the Russian superpower, Zia ul-Haq is of great value to the Americans as the last bulwark. Despite the fact that under his rule Islamic fundamentalists were not deterred from leveling the U.S. embassy in Islamabad, the Americans maintain contact with him and, along with the Saudis, keep Allah's general afloat. In return, Zia ul-Haq supports the Afghan rebels to the extent permitted by his interests. As Western analysts state, there is yet another reason he would consider a rapid end to the war extremely disagreeable: because then the Soviet Army might suddenly be at *his* door, since Pakistan is situated on a warm sea.

In such a situation, the "Islamic bomb" (through whose existence the clever Zia ul-Haq repeatedly makes the West insecure) would be of no help to him. According to unconfirmed reports that regularly pop up, supplies from the Pakistani nuclear reactor in Karachi have been made available for the construction of "three small bombs per year." The London *New Scientist Magazine* reported in July 1981 that in the vicinity of Rawalpini, Pakistan had supposedly built a secret nuclear fuel–reprocessing plant for the production of ten to twenty kilograms of plutonium. According to the report, the first tests were to take place in the People's Republic of China, with which Pakistan maintains friendly relations. The first discussions between Islamabad and Peking had been initiated during the visit of Prime Minister Zao Zhang the previous month.

Reflecting on American indicators that Pakistan was constructing an "Islamic bomb," the International Atomic Energy Agency (IAEA) in Vienna was very restrained in its comments. A spokesman of the organization stated that the heavy-water reactor is significantly more difficult to monitor than a light-water reactor using only enriched uranium. Pakistan also has its own natural uranium and is itself producing rods for this type of reactor.

Bhutto even called this mysterious explosive device "Islamic," because allegedly the Islamic states of Libya, Niger (as the supplier of the raw material), Saudi Arabia, and Iraq were involved in Pakistan's project. (This is conceivable since the technological prerequisites are present.) Moreover, the Islamic side has said that it is necessary to offset Israel's nuclear activities and take revenge for the destruction of the Iraqi nuclear plant at Osirak by the Israeli air force on June 7, 1981. In support of this position, the Koran is quoted: "And if you want to take revenge, then do so to the same extent that evil was done to you."

Bhutto's family is also out for revenge, and with free elections the chances are good that Pakistan's People's Party, which still has the support of the majority of the people, will regain its honor. Zia ul-Haq knows that and has ensured that his junta forestalled free elections. The highest administrator of martial law always has a new answer ready when blocking the promised use of the ballot box. In response to the question of when he will again permit political activities in Pakistan, Zia answered in 1982 that it was first necessary to create stable relations, on which he had been working for the last four and a half years. He is determined to consolidate "healthy reason" in the political landscape before allowing political activities again.

In terms of foreign policy, Pakistan is isolated. Many international contacts are still maintained only because of the Afghanistan question. In terms of domestic policy, the opposition is stirring and waiting for its hour. The "federal council," described by Zia ul-Haq as a parliamentary alternative, is generally regarded as a mere farce. The increasing guerrilla activity in the country is partly supported by the Al Zulfikar organization, operating under the auspices of Bhutto's sons Murtaza and Shahnawaz. "The state terrorist Zia leaves us no other choice than to strive violently toward overthrowing the military junta in order to restore democracy in Pakistan," Murtaza Bhutto tells Olaf Ihlau, a correspondent of the *Süddeutsche Zeitung*. Zia has already tried several times to set a trap for the sons of his deceased enemy, but that attempt has failed, as had his plan to infiltrate the guerrilla troops with an agent loyal to the regime. In the summer of 1981, a secret commando of Pakistanis armed with automatic pistols stormed what was believed to be Al Zulfikar's headquarters in Kabul. The result was allegedly ten people dead, none of them Bhutto supporters. In 1983 Bhutto's sons left Afghanistan.

At the Islamabad airport I made the acquaintance of a prosperous businessman from Karachi, who openly admitted his sympathies for the party of the deceased Bhutto. In his view, Zia ul-Haq was not a good person, but unfortunately Pakistan had no alternative at the moment, and besides, no one had yet been able to surpass his carefully doled-out Islamic trick. With a deep sigh, the businessman said: "We are a nation that has experienced only tragedies since 1947. I have seen so much blood and senseless suffering. We are a disappointed people, but a people always ready for new foolishness." Gesturing toward the people at the airport, he added: "Look at this waiting room. There are many educated people sitting here, yet with certainty sixty percent of them are radicals and fanatics, which is an average among our people. That is what will determine the future. May Allah have pity on us."

24

Marx, Mao, and Mohammed

The Soviet Union—the Tide Is Rising

THE SOVIET UNION is the fifth-largest Muslim nation in the world, surpassed only by Indonesia, Pakistan, India, and Bangladesh. Approximately 50 to 60 million Muslims live within the Soviet Union's Asian provinces of Turkmenistan, Azerbaijan, Tadzikistan, Uzbekistan, and Kazakhstan, and by the year 2000 the number will probably be 100 million. At the present birthrate of Soviet Asians (1.5 million per year), they may then have almost caught up with the Russians, whose population is decreasing. The Soviet Muslims are inflexible and self-confident. The powers in the Kremlin have not effectively coped with the *mullahs* for the last half-century; today they merely keep them quiet. Actually the projected increase in the Asian population of the Soviet Union will probably soon be inaccurate, because the revolutionary religious influences from the areas of the traditionally friendly tribes in Iran and Afghanistan are threatening to get the upper hand.

After a trip through the Soviet Union's Asian territories, the well-known German journalist Dr. Peter Scholl-Latour noted: "It would be an error to believe that the Ayatollah Khomeini's message in neighboring Iran or even the bloody events in Afghanistan will remain without consequence in Soviet Central Asia. . . . In Buchara I heard the guarded comment that Khomeini's influence was considerable."

On guided tours visitors are permitted to view the picturesque mosques in Buchara, Samarkand, Tashkent, and Baku, including the mosque of Tamerlane, the Mongol who once plundered half the world. In Chiwa there is even a completely preserved medieval city. Travelers see old Koran schools, called *medresen*, minarets, and fortresses with dark dungeon cells, and everywhere are the lively *souks* and colorful dress so highly praised by the Intourist travel guides. Only rarely, however, does the ever-present state permit people on religious tours to encounter such dignitaries as the imam of Samarkand, Mustafa Kulmelikow. He is one of 1,500 imams tolerated and possibly even controlled by the atheist authorities. Islam is at best unwillingly permitted; its leading figure is the seventy-five-year-old Ziautdin Babakhanow, the Grand Mufti of Central Asia. Both his and Kulmelikow's statements have long been subject to control by the Soviet authorities; their complaints are about nuclear rearmament in Europe, coupled with accusations that the U.S. is supporting counterrevolutionary influences in Afghanistan.

There *are* underground forces, but if one encounters them at all, it is only beyond the long southern border. Heavily laden with Islamic writings for their brothers, they cross the Amu Darya River at night from the Afghanistan side. (At the official selling price a copy of the Koran would cost a full year's wage.) From groups of Afghan *mujahideen*, I heard that this kind of cooperation with relatives and friends on the Soviet side of the border has already led to armed attacks on Russian installations, but it was naturally impossible to obtain confirmation of this in Moscow. A guerrilla leader told me: "We are carrying the war into the country of the Shurawi."

Not much is needed to set off the powder keg in the southeast of the "laudable Soviet Union" (a party propaganda phrase), for the strong minority considers Allah far stronger than their monitors equipped with party handbooks and official status. The Muslims have already succeeded in fighting for greater religious

freedom than other groups. Several dozen pilgrims are permitted
to go to Mecca annually, several mosques are open, and meetings
in teashops are not immediately broken up by the police. But that
is simply the result of the standstill agreement between the show-
piece *ulema* and Moscow. As soon as Islam, now confined to the
back rooms, opens the way and the aggressive fundamentalists
revolt, the Kremlin will have a new Poland on its hands, this time
within its own borders. And it will be a situation that cannot be
dealt with by European measures and means. The Shiite Muslims
of Baku congratulated Khomeini on his seizure of power, and the
elderly revolutionary leader would like to return the compliment.
For Khomeini and the Central Asian world of Islam, the fall of
the Shah was merely a beginning. In Samarkand, I learned, there
had been a nocturnal incident in which a message was painted
on the walls of houses: "Our Shah's name is Leonid."

India's Underdogs Are Getting Self-Confident

The history of Islam in India is closely connected with the ongoing fighting between Hindus and Muslims. When the Muslim
state of Pakistan split off, millions of people killed each other in
gruesome massacres. Since that time the minority of 70 to 80
million followers of the Prophet Mohammed within India's total
population of 680 million has not resumed a peaceful existence.
Street battles and attacks have become an everyday occurrence.
Since 1947, there have reputedly been more than 20,000 skirmishes in India, making the community of Muslims more cohesive than ever. Islam is now more consciously experienced, and
its political strength is better organized than that of its opponents.

Only a few Muslims have thus far achieved high positions in
India, and their representation in parliament and economic life is
meager. Now the underdogs want to revolt. The Jamaat-e Islami,
which is affiliated with the Pakistani party by the same name,
experienced an increase of several hundred members following
independence, and as many as 100,000 Muslims gathered at the
annual meeting in 1980 in Haidarabad. When Indira Gandhi governed what is allegedly the largest democracy in the world by the
use of martial law, the Jamaat-e Islami was banned and 200 of its
leaders put behind bars, where many of them died. The result
was an unexpected increase in the organization's membership.
Moreover, contacts increased between the Islamic spokesmen

and the representatives of other branches of the opposition, who were also persecuted and imprisoned by Indira Gandhi. A broadly based countermovement that will certainly be heard from is beginning to emerge in India. The only thing the Muslims still lack is a detailed political plan tailored to the needs of the masses —that is what the apologists of Islam want to provide as soon as possible. The government is to be presented with an alternative plan for the solution of the country's immense social and economic problems, restoring to the minority the rights now denied them.

The numerous sects of Islam are zealously engaged in missionary work. As a result, just within eight months in 1981, 32,000 Indians, mostly from the ranks of the oppressed pariahs, converted to Mohammed's faith. As in many non-Arab countries of the Third World, in India there are strong Sufi orders and *tarikas* —in other words, mystical groups. I spoke with the Muslim official Shabbir Potia from Bombay, in western India. He is a member of the Dawoodi Bohra sect, whose one million followers live mostly in India and Pakistan, as well as on the east coast of Africa and in small groups all over the world. Their leader is Svedna Mohammed Burhanuddin from Sanaa in North Yemen. The Dawoodi Bohras are orthodox Muslims who believe in the existence of twenty-one imams (because they believe the vanished twelfth imam has already reappeared); they consider themselves Shiites. According to Shabbir Potia, "The Shiites are the fundamentalists in India. The Sunnis are quiet, while the Shiites are attempting to make the whole society more Islamic. That is increasing, particularly since the coup in Tehran."

The Shiite Muslims in India have discarded the *sari* and returned to the *chador*. The mosques are again filled, and the congregations are becoming more radical. Shabbir Potia told me: "Especially in such centers of Islam as Lucknow and Aligarh, there is constantly fighting between Muslims and Hindus. I myself saw how the Shiite masses streamed into the streets and threw a barrage of stones at the Hindus on Muharram, the holiday commemorating Imam Hussein. They fight and kill each other in groups. I do not think that is going to lead to the solution of our problems. What we need in general is a strong leader who will govern all Muslims and lead us to new strength."

Unrest Spreads to the Islands

Against the background of the ancient, highly developed directions of faith within Hinduism and Buddhism and a long colonial history, centuries were needed before the population of Indonesia converted to Islam. Today 147 million people in the island world in the Indian and Pacific Oceans between Asia and Australia profess belief in the Koran and the *sunna*. Altogether they consist of 360 different peoples, which does not exactly facilitate the striving for a purely Islamic state. The old plan for a theocracy was repeatedly postponed for two reasons. In the first place, differences between the conservative, orthodox *ulemas* and radical reformers kept them from taking the same route. In addition, the class of small landowners—the so-called Abangan, whose Islamic faith includes various nature deities—blocked a purely Muslim order.

Islam was always a strong anti-colonialist force on the islands of Bali and Java between Sumatra and Timor. Such thinkers as Jamal ad-Din al-Afghani and Mohammed Abduh influenced the self-confident Indonesians, but did not result in the emergence of a cohesive plan. Powerful political movements such as the Sarakat Islam (Islamic League), founded in 1911, emerged only to disintegrate again. After independence had been achieved, the nationalistic direction represented by the Third World leader Ahmed Sukarno was the victor. Daoud Beureuah, leader of the Aheh movement, lamented: "We worked for so many years for an Islamic state, but now we are obliged to recognize more clearly every day that our Indonesian leaders took the wrong route and wanted to push us, too, into the purely nationalistic direction. President Sukarno told us he feared that the people who would not like an Islamic state would turn away from him. Very well, then we will be the ones to secede!" Several underground movements joined together and declared their independence as a participating state. The full force of Sukarno's army was needed to defeat the movement. Muhammad Natsir's rebellious Masjumi Party, until that time the strongest political force of the Islamists, was banned.

Indonesia was fragmented, and conflicts emerged between the increasingly influential communists and the army. In this situation, the Islamic forces tended to side with the army. The disputes, with members of the Muslim youth organization the most important factor, ended with massacres in which a half-million people died. When the communists were beaten, the army was under the control of the Muslims. Sukarno had to resign. General Suharto became his successor, first serving as prime minister in 1966 and becoming president of the country the following year. During his term in office, he repeatedly loosened the screws on the spokesmen of the Islamic state just a little, only to tighten them up again. He never left any doubt about the fact that under no circumstances would he approve a theocracy. But today the fragmented opposition, finally united by the resurgence of Islam, is growing.

Farther east in the Malay island world are the Philippines. In the extreme south, in western Mindanao, Palwan, and the Sulu Islands are the Moros, a small minority of radical Muslims. As far back as the thirteenth century, their ancestors were converted to the teaching of the Prophet by Arab and Indian traders. Then came priests and members of the Sufi orders. Slowly the faith spread, and in the sixteenth century it clashed with the explorer Ferdinand Magellan's Spanish colonizers. In honor of the Spanish King Philip II, the islands were renamed and taken over. The Muslim sultanates in the south defended themselves against the foreign invaders up into the nineteenth century, and only after 300 years did the Spanish manage to subdue the Moros.

In 1898 the Americans took over the legacy of the Iberian colonial rulers. Christian missionaries arrived, and so did experts interested in the rich natural resources. The Moros, always on the defensive, were never able to regain their former strength. Through the settlement policy of the government in Manila, they were registered statistically as a minority, so even after the Philippines gained independence (in 1946) their own Islamic state was out of the question. Therefore in May 1968 Datu Udtog Matalam founded the Muslim Independence Movement, later called the Mindanao Independence Movement. The fighting between Christians and Muslims became steadily more brutal. After President Ferdinand Marcos proclaimed martial law in 1972, the National Liberation Front of the Moros was formed. The war involved all the islands in the south, and with help from Libyan and Saudi petrodollars the guerrilla movement was armed and has been successful to date in opposing the equally well-equipped government troops.

Since 1979 there have been two autonomous Muslim regional

governments in Sulu and Mindanao, which Marcos was compelled to recognize as a result of international negotiations (e.g.,
the Tripoli Agreement of 1976). But even after 60,000 deaths, the
guerrilla war continues, although within a smaller area. The
Christians oppose the new administrative model, and in the absence of a clear military victory the government troops continue
to operate in Moroland.

The liberation movement under the leadership of the head ideologist Nur Misuari, a former student leader from Manila now
living mostly in the Middle East, wants to stop fighting only after
the Marcos clan has stepped down. The prospects for that, however, are not very good, so the southern provinces survive without any trust in the central administration. Significantly, Romulo
"Mohsin" Espaldon, the minister of religion, was formerly commander of the Philippine army against the Moros, and is hoping
for total independence from Manila without any occupation
forces from the central government. On a visit to Saudi Arabia,
the rebel leader Nur Misuari stated: "The government in Manila
wants to destroy the cultural identity of seven million Muslims in
the south, for which purpose it uses all kinds of weapons and
instruments of death, including chemical warfare. Employing the
means used by the Americans in Vietnam, sixty percent of the
Philippine army is fighting us. Our battle against the extermina-
tion of an entire people continues. *Allah u-Akhbar!*"

Resurgence of Islam behind the Bamboo Curtain

In the wake of the resurgence of Islam, even behind the bam-
boo curtain there is an increasing Muslim minority, probably 115
million. Very little is known in the West about Muslims of the
People's Republic of China. Despite the fragmentary news, it is
known that the Muslims have more freedom since the ousting of
the anti-religious Gang of Four under Mao's widow Jian Quing.
During the Cultural Revolution, they were persecuted, mistreated, and robbed by the Red Guard. The state's ideology characterizes any form of religious practice as a mental illness, so the
mosques were closed—a situation that was exploited by the Russians in its propaganda war against the Chinese. In radio broadcasts they pointed out the "marvelously free" life of Muslims
within the Asian provinces of the Soviet realm. Even today Moscow broadcasts selections from the newspaper *Yeni Hayat* (*New*

Life) in the Uighur language for the purpose of stirring up trouble. Moscow's hypocrisy in doing so is not immediately apparent to the listeners, as the broadcast seems more like a friendly message to the related tribes of the Uighur, Tartars, Kasakhs, and Turkmen beyond the border.

Ethnic and religious groups now have greater freedom since Deng Xao Ping came to power in the People's Republic. Professional observers of the scene believe that the purpose of the greater liberality is to steal the Russian's ideological thunder. Mosques have been reopened, and Muslims have been rehabilitated both within and outside the Communist Party. After thirty years of hesitation, the government in Peking even promises to issue a Chinese edition of the Koran. Once again Muslims are permitted to bury their dead instead of cremating them, as was the rule during the Mao era. The Russians observe the relaxation of Chinese customs with mistrust and call it an attempt to improve the Chinese position in the Near East and South Asia. The descendants of the Mongolians in the province of Xinjiang, where most of the Muslims live, have trust in the fact that the Chinese central administration does not want any unnecessary trouble in its sensitive area along the border with the Soviet Union. In addition, the presence in this area of valuable raw materials—oil, for example—and China's most important nuclear installations gives them hope of tolerance and of the possibility of gradually spreading the faith.

25

Islam Enters the West

Two DECADES AGO the German Near East expert and authority on Islam, K. L. Kaster, made a prognosis about the future of Islam in Europe: "The Muslim can be proud of being part of a religious community of worldwide importance whose apostolic zeal is evident in many places. But it does not escape the notice of the thoughtful Muslim that, despite the propagandistic zeal and missionary thrust, the effectiveness of Islam is restricted. During the last half-century in Europe, to an increasing extent it is diminishing." Kaster admitted that there are some guest workers and also a few converts, but he considered that of no further consequence. In his book *Islam Without a Veil*, he comes to the conclusion: "There is no evidence of a resurgence of Islam in Europe."

He, like others, made a grave mistake. With somewhat less presumption on the part of the West, it would have been possible even then to realize what Sheikh Said Belal told me in his home town of Nablus in the summer of 1982: "The body of Islam is here with us; its spirit, though, has long been in Europe." The spirit had often taken refuge to avoid the suffering of the body. In 1964 an official census in West Germany showed 100,000 Muslims; in mid-1969, a quarter of a million. Then the big wave of immigration started, mainly consisting of Turks. Precisely twelve years later the Federal Office of Statistics in Wiesbaden reported 1.54 million Turks. In 1982 the number of Muslims living in West Germany was slightly less than 2 million, 1,200 of German ancestry. The actual figure is probably larger, though, since the Federal Office of Statistics does not count spouses who convert to Islam.

Islam is therefore the third-strongest religion in West Germany. Nonetheless, it is not recognized as an entity by public law, which would mean equating it with the large Christian churches and the Jewish congregations. But that is by no means the only problem of Muslims in Germany. Among themselves they are split and in conflict; as guest workers, they are no longer liked by the Germans, who are fed up and suffering from their anxiety concerning the future; as a political grouping, they are subject to observation by the country's security service and by the police, and in the German political environment are often branded as radicals and terrorists.

Muslims in 700 congregations have a corresponding number of prayer houses, most of which face Mecca in courtyard sheds and abandoned factories. Only in Berlin, Aachen, Hamburg, and Munich are separate mosques available, with their tall, thin minarets. The Islamic Center in Munich-Freimann is a typical example. The mosque building commission, comprised mainly of Arab students and members of the Muslim Brotherhood, met for the first time in 1960. Because of a feared detriment to the Upper Bavarian image of the city, the religious structure was only permitted outside the city gates in the vicinity of the turnoff to a huge, stinking rubbish heap and a group of small garden plots. A Turkish architect was commissioned for the structure, and the cornerstone was laid in 1967. By completion of the attractive Munich mosque in 1973, its cost had risen to over $8 million. The huge financial gap of slightly over $4 million was covered by Libya's Muammar al-Qaddafi, and the salary of the director is now paid by the Saudis, who like to compete with Qaddafi.

The political head of the Muslim Brotherhood of Syria, Adnan Sadeddin, made the following comment about the organization's intentions in Europe: "The members of the Muslim Brotherhood, or in general the Muslims in Europe, are either there to study or to work and learn about development. In Europe they have two goals: not to lose their identity and to make the society in which they live familiar with their religion." The Muslim Brotherhood is strongly represented in Germany, particularly in the Islamic Centers of Munich and of Aachen (Bilal Mosque). It cooperates at all levels with other Islamic organizations, but strictly rejects spectacular activities in the host country. Its underground work is concentrated on the enemy states in the Near East, mainly Syria. Assad's killer squad, arrested on March 1, 1982 in Stuttgart, was by no means on the wrong track. The Muslim Brotherhood operates in an absolutely conspiratorial manner within a relatively secure environment, such as that along the Rhine, Isar, and Elbe. Its members are involved everywhere, although they never admit it publicly. Anyone who is not directly involved with them will never gain insight into their affairs, and any evidence of too much curiosity in the Islamic Centers dependably encounters barriers.

Whereas Arabs are in the majority in Munich and Aachen, Turks control the Islamic Center in Cologne, which is also the site of the Association of Islamic Cultural Centers, otherwise known as the Suleymanli movement. Dating from Sheikh Suleyman Hilmi Tunahan (1888–1959), the Suleymanli movement has branches in 130 German cities. Even during the era of Ataturk, its goal was the maintenance of religious values. It is a Sunni-Hanifiti movement and is in effect a kind of people's church.

Another organization of the Turks is the Nurjuluk movement, which resembles an order and functions in a conspiratorial manner. Also located in Cologne, it is involved in the twenty-eight Koran schools in West Germany and West Berlin. The Nurjuluk actively opposed Kemal-style absolutism and was severely persecuted in Turkey until the reinstatement of the multiple-party system. It conducts a kind of missionary activity and deals particularly with the problems of Muslim pupils and students.

Another organization on the scene is the Gray Wolves (MHP), which is headed by Alparslan Turk, a Hitler admirer, and is more oriented toward nationalism and the radical right than toward Islam. In addition, there is the National Order Party of Necmettin Erbakan, which was disbanded in Turkey but has 200 local branches in Germany, where it is know as Milli Görüsh (National Standpoint).

Following Imam Khomeini's victory in Iran, the strength of the

Islamic forces among the Turks increased noticeably, and a growing influence of the Koran schools, the *hodshas*, and the *mullahs*
was noted in German businesses and schools. Many of these
schools acquired the reputation of being ideological hotbeds.
Turkish teacher organizations, to varying degrees, regretted that
hodshas lacking pedagogical and religious training hammered
suras into children by resorting to the cane. These organizations
also maintained that the children were taught to hate everything
foreign and that the scholastic achievements of the young Turkish
pupils would suffer from the disproportionate strain, as they
were required in their meager free time to learn the 114 *suras* of
the Koran in what for them was a foreign language. Juergen
Miksch, head of the parish council in Frankfurt, expresses concern that "in West Germany, Islam is developing into a restor-
ative, reactionary, and nationalistic movement that will
consequently end in a ghetto." The Chairman of the Islamic Center in Cologne, Necdet Demirguelle, responded to that accusation
in 1979: "Our Koran schools impart to the children the idea that
they must contribute to shaping this society and must live peace-
ably with one another. They should not forget that their parents
came here to earn a living and that the friendship between Turkey
and Germany is based on a long tradition." That changes nothing
in the fact that the politically oriented Islam uses the so-called
Turkish "idealist organizations" and the cultural centers as a cov-
erup. The response of the German public to date has consistently
been a lack of understanding and rejection, and hatred of foreigners is increasing.

While the politically oriented Turks conceal themselves, at the
mosque in Hamburg there is open discussion about Imam Khomeini. The Islamic Center in Hamburg is the spiritual center of
the Shiites in Central Europe (approximately 24,000) and the Sunnis in northern Germany. Ayatollah Mohammed Beheshti, until
his death in 1981 the best prospective candidate among the successors to Khomeini, was director of this center from 1962 until
1970. Muslims in Germany, as in all of Europe, have to contend
with many problems: uprootedness, the feeling of being exposed
to social injustice and exploitation, concealed or open discrimi-
nation, legal insecurity, concern about jobs and residence permits. Since Islam is a structure of religious traditions, social
orders, and political ties involving the person's whole life, the
Muslims do not have an easy time. Fatima Heeren, a German

Muslim from the Islamic Center in Munich, described to me a typical problem: "Many girls are subjected to pressure because they wear scarves on their heads in Germany. Many teachers forbid it; saleswomen lose their jobs. My son is now in the army and tells me that I must understand the impossibility of his praying five times a day. I believe that in Germany Islam is going to fail because of the Octoberfest and beer gardens. It simply cannot be expected that Germans will convert by the hundreds of thousands."

Because of cultural limitations, the guest workers will always have to live in a "miniature Turkey," anonymous and misunderstood in an alien, highly industrialized world. Even in the future, German Muslims will remain exotic people in quest of understanding.

This situation can be found not only in West Germany but also in other countries of the West. There are 5.5 million Muslims living in Europe. Their increasing activities are evident in the growing number of mosques and Islamic centers. Prayer houses are being erected, mostly financed by Saudi funds. For the 50,000 Austrian Muslims, a stately mosque was built in 1979 on Vienna's Hubertusdamm, right next to United Nations City. In the Islamic city of Granada, in Spain's Andalusia, a rapidly growing Muslim community is increasingly heard from, and Spanish converts are extremely welcome. The wish to retrieve El Andalus, which was lost in 1492, endures and is not confined to the radical fundamentalists.

The largest Islamic congregation, consisting of more than 2 million faithful, is in France. The splendid mosque in Paris, completed as long ago as 1926, is considered the center of the faith for the entire European continent, and is therefore in competition with the large mosque in Regent's Park in London. There are 300 mosques and 1.3 million Muslims in the British Isles. In contrast to the North Africans in France, the Muslims in England mostly come from the former Commonwealth countries of the Indian subcontinent, West Africa, and Malaysia. There are approximately 4,000 Muslim organizations in England. In London and Paris can be found the most important international organizations, the editorial offices of Islamic newspapers and magazines, and even an Islamic press agency. Fathi Osman, a member of the Muslim Brotherhood and chief editor of an attractive, Saudi-and Yemenite-owned magazine, *Arabia* (with a circulation of 50,000), confided to me in his London office: "Based here, we concern ourselves with the Islamic world, because we can say what we please. No one censors us. Of course, there are also technical reasons for that." (The *Islamic Defense Magazine* and the *Islamic Medical Magazine* are published in the same house.)

The Islamic Council for Europe, the umbrella organization of Muslim organizations and centers founded in 1973, is located in London. It is headed by the energetic Salem Azzam, a former Saudi ambassador. During a personal interview in London, he expressed his concerns: "I believe that there are many rulers in the Islamic world who are not real Muslims. Something has to happen, since none of us wants this situation. The masses in the Muslim world are not content with it, and they will show the governments their true power." First, however, the governments will deliberate on Grosvenor Crescent how they can best equip their armies. The Institute for Defense Technology, directed by Mukarram Ali, the Pakistani group captain, analyzes the military situation in the Islamic world and serves in a consulting capacity for various organizations, including the Islamic Council. Despite activities that are recognized, the council has not yet succeeded in convincing the majority of Muslims in Europe. Its most active supporters are the Islamic student organizations and Muslims from Arab countries, as well as Africa and Asia. The Turks, however, are not among them, preferring to trust their own organizations.

But the Yugoslavs remain faithful to the umbrella organization. The communist country has more Muslims than any European nation: fifteen percent of the 22 million inhabitants bow toward Mecca. Within Bosnia alone, there are 1.5 million Muslims, or forty percent of the population. Within the last decade, Islam in Bosnia has experienced an unexpected renaissance. Although the government in Belgrade has thus far displayed tolerance and permitted various ties to the Arab world, in the long run the state is expected to adopt a stricter policy, for the mutli-ethnic nation is not particularly secure.

In the United States the fundamentalists have also strengthened their position. Various organizations function under the auspices of the Muslim Student Association (MSA), founded in 1963, and offer various services—they hold conferences and meetings, sponsor youth camps, distribute a variety of publications, and provide aid for all needy Muslims. The social network, particularly of the Muslim students, is constantly expanding. The Muslim Student Association, with headquarters in Plainfield, Indiana, wants to convey the true faith together with the opportunity of academic training. Its members come from all realms of the Islamic world, including a relatively small number of converted Americans and Canadians. They also have ties to the radical Black Muslims, the movement created in 1930 in the slums of large American cities. Differences between the fundamentalists and blacks are present, however, because the Black Muslims, unlike the orthodox Muslims, consider the founder of their organization, Elijah Muhammad, a prophet. When Elijah Muhammad died on February 25, 1975, he was succeeded by his son Wallace Deen Muhammad.

The Black Muslims were an important factor in the racial unrest of the sixties. But in the meantime their influence, like that of all radical orgnizations of the blacks, has diminished. The Dar-ul-Islam Movement, an additional example for the influence of the Koran in the U.S.A., was founded in 1962. The organization, based on the West Coast, is still in existence at the universities and participates in student demonstrations. It follows the militant line of Malcolm X, but is not particularly cooperative with other organizations or with Muslims who have recently arrived in the country. According to all appearances, the Dar-ul-Islam Movement wants to be more exclusive than the popular Islamic student organizations. All the less do their members notice how isolated they actually are. Like all Western countries, the United States is not really fertile terrain for such a strict all-encompassing faith as Islam. In December 1983 the usually well-informed Islamic news magazine *Crescent International,* which is published in Toronto, investigated the true situation of the Muslims in North America. The author of this study, Muhammad Abdullah of Los Angeles, reached the following conclusions: "The real obstacle in the path of unity among the (Afro-American) Muslims is their failure to examine their past and deal realistically with themselves as a people whose past has been so dehumanized that it has generated a sense of self-hatred among them. Even after embracing Islam, these characteristics have retarded their understanding of the true essence of Islam." Abdullah in particular laments the fact that the American Muslims have no splendid martyrs to be used as models and that there are no outstanding religious leaders in North America.

What is urgently needed is a kind of parliament of Muslims that could provide direction to the Islamic movement in North America, making it possible to spread the faith "in the cities full of sex, drugs, and alcohol," to really organize the adherents, and to spare no exertion (*jihad*) for the glory of Allah. "All these are essential for our survival as Muslims, because they have been ordained for us by Allah in the Koran. There must be an Allah-fearing Islamic vanguard to rise up in this country of oppression. Allah says in the Koran: 'Let there become of you a nation that shall speak for righteousness, enjoin justice, and forbid evil. Such men shall surely triumph.' " (3:104).

The Islamic Center of Washington reported three million U.S. Muslims in March 1980. The figure has meanwhile allegedly reached four million. Two hundred Muslims participated at the first conference of the Islamic Movement of American Muslims in Charlotte, North Carolina, held on June 5, 1982. Iranian, Afghan, and Turkish delegates were kept out by the police. The observers were nonetheless unable to curtail an aggressive mood, as the general topic was "Islam in the U.S.A." and "The Islamic Struggle," and a memorial service was held in honor of the slain black Islamic leader Malcolm X (also known as Al-Hajj Malik Shahbaz). In front of the building where the meeting was held hung a large banner which read: "We support Imam Khomeini, the great leader of the Islamic world revolution against international oppressors and exploiters." In the U.S. that can be considered an expression of great courage.

26

Islamism and Nationalism

MOHAMMED HASSANEIN HEIKAL, born in 1923, the intellectual spokesman of the Arab world, is its best-informed journalist, the publicist with the most extensive connections, the author with the greatest courage. In his opinion, there is one only large Arab nation, and he has repeatedly challenged his people "to talk less and think more." He himself follows his own advice. In 1957 the former reporter, war correspondent, and editor of several Arab newspapers managed to become chief editor of the Cairo daily *Al Ahram*. From this perspective he observed, analyzed, and fostered the policy of his friend Gamal Abdel Nasser, a living monument. He also functioned as personal advisor to Nasser and shared state secrets with him. In 1970 the Western-oriented Heikal became minister of information for a brief period of time. During the first years of President Anwar el-Sadat's term in office, he was an advisor, temporarily represented Egypt as foreign minister and as minister of information, and finally he kept the position of chief editor and publisher of *Al Ahram*.

[336]

Following differences of opinion concerning Egyptian policy, President Sadat fired him in 1974. Heikal, an unshakable Nasserist, became Sadat's most sharp-tongued critic. What the Muslim Brotherhood attacked from a religious perspective, he attacked from the position of a nationalist. Sadat, removed from reality, even put Heikal into prison when he lashed out against the opposition in 1981. In his last interview, Sadat accused Heikal of having used the religious unrest in the country for his political purposes. After seventy-five days and the death of the "pharaoh," the dynamic Heikal returned to freedom. I met him in Cairo. Here are excerpts from our discussion:

"Mr. Heikal, you wrote a book about Imam Khomeini called The Return of the Ayatollah.*"*
"I did not write a book about Khomeini, I wrote a book about the Iranian revolution. Imam Khomeini is merely the most important, or one of the most important, figures in the book."

"Do you believe that he realized the dream of humanity?"
"I do not believe so. I think what he has in mind is more the realization of his own dream, the Islamic Republic of Iran."

"The Western world considers that a very brutal system."
"From the outset, I hesitate to regard what the West likes as a generally valid rule. Europe and the West are important, but they do not embody our entire world. That is one consideration. The other is that I will not discuss good and evil. You forget your history. How would you have lived at the time of the French Revolution? Imagine that the media, particularly television, witnessed that event. If the mass executions during Robespierre's time had been shown in every living room, wouldn't that have looked bad? What you see in Iran—with all its turmoil, with all its agony—is a human drama. But I am telling you that during an operation you cannot stop at the sight of blood and say you do not like what you see. Let us wait until the operation is over. I see many negative things in Iran—much I do not like. But I do not grant myself the right of making a judgment in the middle of the whole process. In addition, I must again ask you: what was the difference between the terror of the French Revolution and the terror of the preceding monarch? That can be known only at the end."

"In your opinion, what will the end be?"
"We are now witnessing a deeply rooted historical process. A clear picture cannot yet be seen."

"What kind of future do you consider probable for Iran?"
"What came after the feudal system in Europe?"

"Democracy. Do you really expect that for Iran?"
"There is no other alternative, no other fate. Many years ago you Germans got your Hitler. He was worse than all the *ayatollahs*. Neither under the Kaiser nor under Hitler were you in a position to stop world war. Within a quarter of a century, you repeated everything. Permit me to be candid with you. After all, you accepted democracy only as the result of a defeat. You Europeans had 400 years to achieve everything you now possess. Only after such a long period of time did national states and a certain kind of harmony come into being. In modern times, everything happens more quickly, but we can say it is just as arduous and just as bloody—hopefully less bloody."

"You have studied Arab nationalism. You have observed the unsuccessful attempts of the communists to achieve power in the Arab countries. Now the Islamic movements are in the process of doing the same thing."
"I think you are making an invalid comparison. In this part of the world, Islam is not only a religion but a way of life. The secular idea, in which I believe, and all processes of modernization must take into consideration the legacy of Islam and its origin. No one can separate Islam from the life of the Muslim countries. For that, Islam is too deeply rooted. I differentiate between Westernization and modernization. Under the Shah you saw what Westernization means. Modernization works only if you recognize who you are and what you want to achieve. Islam is a very important component in our thinking. If we speak about our language, about the laws, about the importance of belonging to a state, then we more or less speak about Islam or about a product of Islam. For genuine modernization, a great historical compromise between religion and nationalism is necessary."

"According to what I have seen, nationalism, communism, and Westernization have failed in the Islamic nations. Is this why people have returned to their roots?"

"That is not true. You arrive at a particular point in history and assume that the historical process has already ended, and you then make a judgment about that. I think differently, however. Arab nationalism suffered a shock in 1967 and again in 1977. This fragmented Arab world that you now see is not the end of the story. Europe also will never again be totally united. The people of this region first want to establish national states. It is not true that Arab nationalism has failed, it is merely in a crisis."

"You know the fate of the Baath Party and its split. Considered historically, that is surely the last political party of Arab nationalism."

"Once again that is not true. Certainly the Baath Party belongs to a different period. But when you look around in Egypt now, you will notice a genuine feeling of community, which will bring us back into the Arab world. Even if it emerges from the ground only as a little plant, it is there. Perhaps the people of the Baath Party, or even Nasser, failed in their attempts. But I believe that what is happening at present is more important than what they did. For what I now see emerging is the importance of an Arab identity and an Arab obligation. I see the longing for a charismatic leader who will restore Arab honor."

"The Islamic movements are nonetheless a reality, and they cannot be dismissed. How do you judge their future?"

"I believe you are right in referring to the Islamic flood as a factor. What we now perceive is the sign of a crisis. It is the result of disappointed hopes. You know that there was a time when everyone had great hopes and believed that, with reasonable planning, weapons, and money, everything would function. We then had to confirm that our mission and the challenge of the West required more than we were able to give and more than we were able to understand. The symptoms of defeat increased during the crisis. The people needed pacification. For this reason, I believe that the resurgence of Islam is a symptom of a malaise in which people must live. They want to withdraw from the unknown to a terrain they are familiar with, a terrain where they can be secure, a terrain within their own borders."

"So we again come back to the fact that, in your view, such movements are merely a transitory solution, a kind of drug that employs the idea of the divine. Your goal is a secular, nationalistic state. What should it be like?"

"Like any secular state in Europe. We even want to have political parties such as the Christian Democratic Party. But I also believe that there are certain values in religion we should not ignore. One of the errors of secular revolutions in the Arab world was that the religious components were always ignored. The revolutionaries always thought they should best avoid the question of religion. People are more strongly touched and more strongly led by Islam than by anything else. We must find a secular state into which we build Islamic values. I do not consider myself a fanatic or a sheikh, but I believe that there is more in Islam than in any other religion. If you read the Koran—I hope you do read it—then you will discover the incredible emphasis on the spirit."

Glossary

Allah: "the God." According to tradition, in pre-Islamic Mecca, Allah was worshipped along with various other deities. Only through Mohammed and his tradition did merely one God remain. The Koran assigns ninety-nine attributes to him—the Omnipotent, the Merciful, the Creator of the world. Arab storytellers say that only the camel knows Allah's one-hundredth name, hence its haughty expression.

ayatollah: "symbol of God," the highest theological title among the Shiites. The office can be passed from father to son. According to the Shiite concept, an *ayatollah* is himself the bearer of divine light, his authority inviolable, his knowledge infinite. Since 1920 there has been an *Ayatollah al-Uzma*, a Grand Ayatollah, who corresponds to the Sunni Grand Sheikh who heads Azhar University in Cairo. At present the Iman Ruhollah Mussavi Khomeini holds the title. In Iran there are approximately 1,200 *ayatollahs.*

Bismillah, or *Bismillah ar-Rahman ar-Rahim:* "In the name of Allah, the Compassionate, the Merciful," which is the beginning of every *sura* in the Koran with the exception of the ninth. In everyday usage, it is a magic formula.

caliph: the Prophet's successor in the political leadership of the people. The caliphate was abolished in 1924 by Ataturk.

dar al-Harb: "house of War"; according to Islamic international law, countries not yet under the domination of Islam.

dar al-Islam: "house of Islam," the part of the world completely controlled by Islam.

fatiha: "the opening," the introductory *sura* of the Koran, comparable to the Christian use of "Our Father." The text reads: "In the name of Allah, the Compassionate, the Merciful. Praise be to Allah, Lord of the

Creation, the Compassionate, the Merciful, King of Judgment Day! You alone we worship, and to You alone we pray for help. Guide us to the straight path, the path of those whom You have favored, not of those who have incurred Your wrath, nor of those who have gone astray."

fatwa: a directive or decree by a high religious authority, a legal opinion.

fundamentalists: the radical direction within the resurgence of Islam. The fundamentalists reject the separation of politics and religion and exclusively advocate an Islamic state.

hadith: the oral or written tradition of the words and deeds of the Prophet and his closest associates.

haj: the pilgrimage to Mecca.

haram: "the sacred, the forbidden." Basically what is meant by the term is the area of the holy cities of Mecca and Medina, but the concept is also used for the most important shrines of Islam. Derived from it is *harem,* the women's quarters in the palaces of Oriental potentates.

hijira: the Prophet Mohammed's immigration from Mecca to Medina in September 622 A.D., which is also the beginning of the Islamic era.

hodsha: village clergyman and teacher of religion. In Turkey, it is an honorary title for any teacher.

imam: a leader, defined in various ways. (1) Among the Sunnis and Shiites, it is a synonym for caliph, the Prophet's successor in the *ummah,* the people of God. (2) The Shiites, however, recognize only the fourth imam (Ali), not the first three. Among the Shiites there were eleven other imams, each of whom was in opposition to the caliphs of the Sunnis. The twelfth imam vanished without a trace in 873 A.D. His return is expected for the end of all time. In their revolutionary enthusiasm, the Iranians declared Khomeini an imam. (3) In legal literature the imam is regarded as the leader of the army (also the prayer leader in the mosque) and is identical with the sultan or the caliph. (4) There are four Sunni schools of law (*madhab*) and one Shiite school of law (twelfth *shia*). Their founders have the title of imam. The correct plural of imam: a'imma.

Islam: "submission or consecration" (to the wills of Allah).

jihad: "a struggle." It does not necessarily involve a warlike act. *Jihad* also means an inner struggle (religious, social, and moral). It is meant as any effort to spread the faith, including one's own religious improvement.

kefija: scarf used as traditional head-covering in the Near East (Palestinians).

Koran: "lesson or recitation," the holy book of Islam that was disclosed to the Prophet Mohammed by the angel Gabriel.

muezzin: a Muslim crier of daily prayers in the mosque.

mufti: a legal scholar who provides an opinion on the basis of the

Islamic legal order, or *sharia*. Also the highest Islamic dignitary of a country.

mujahideen: religious fighters, originally the designation for fighters in the *jihad*, in the morally motivated struggle against the enemies of Islam, against the devil, and against personal egotism, and in support of the Islamic order of the world. Various nationalistic guerrilla movements, such as those in Iran, call themselves *mujahideen*. In Afghanistan there are 70,000 to 170,000 *mujahideen*. (The singular is *mujahed*.)

mullah: a simple Islamic Shiite clergyman and interpreter of the Koran who lacks theological training. In Iran there are reputedly 180,000 *mullahs*.

Muslim: an adherent of Islam, a "believer who has entered into the status of salvation."

pan-Arabism: the nationalistic movement for unity on the basis of the shared language, culture, and religion. It strives for the unification of the Arab world into a nation. Since 1945, its institutional framework is provided by the Arab League (with headquarters in Tunis), to which twenty countries and the PLO belong at present.

pan-Islamism: the countermovement to the colonialism of the previous century that strives for the union of all Islamic peoples under one caliph. During the 1920s, the nationalistic movements gained the upper hand. Only with the resurgence of Islam and the founding of the first Islamic nations did pan-Islamism again acquire intensity.

Ramadan: the ninth month of the Islamic lunar year. Mohammed experienced his first revelation in Ramadan. Fasting during Ramadan is one of the basic tenets of Islam. The holy month also requires other forms of abstinence (from cigarettes and sexual relations) between dawn and sundown.

SAVAK: the feared Iranian secret service during the era of the Shah. The name comes from *Sazman-e Ettela'at va Amnigat-Keshwar* (Organization for News and Security of the Country). Under Khomeini, the secret service has been renamed State Organization for National Documents.

secularists: a group that propagates the resurgence of Islam. The secularists, however, do not insist on an Islamic state.

shahid: martyr. Anyone who dies in the holy war or in the execution of a deed useful to Islam enters paradise as a *shahid*.

sharia: the Islamic law. It allegedly assures the earthly as well as the heavenly well-being of the faithful. The dispensation of justice based on the Koran and the *sunna* was completed in the ninth and tenth centuries.

sheikh: "old man." The Oriental reveres age and respects hierarchy. A sheikh can be a scholar, but can also be the head of a Dervish cloister, and hence an Islamic mystic. Purely religious leaders, as in the Muslim Brotherhood, also carry the title.

Shiites: followers of Ali (Shiat Ali), approximately one-tenth of all Muslims. They live mainly in Iran and Iraq.

Sufi: an Islamic mystic, the same as dervish.

sunna: the tradition of the deeds and utterances of the Prophet Mohammed (*hadith*); following the Koran, the second source of faith for the Muslim. The Sunnis were named for the *sunna* as the main direction within Islam.

sura: one of the 114 chapters of the Koran. A *sura* consists of a varying number of verses.

ulema or *traditionalists:* Authorities on the faith. They perform official functions in the fields of politics, justice, and social welfare. The singular: *alim.*

ummah: "people," "community," the religious community of Islam.

zakat: tax for the poor, in practice the same as social welfare. The *zakat* is used to support poor Muslims.

Index

Index 349